D1557275

V&R Academic

Izaak J. de Hulster / Brent A. Strawn /
Ryan P. Bonfiglio (eds.)

Iconographic Exegesis of the Hebrew Bible/Old Testament

An Introduction to Its Method and Practice

Vandenhoeck & Ruprecht

With 303 Figures

Cover Image: "The vinters picking the grapes and pressing out the wine", west wall of the tomb of Nakht in Thebes, ca. 1400 BCE. Source: Norman de Garis Davies, *The tomb of Nakht at Thebes* (with plates in color by L. Crane), New York: Metropolitan Museum of Art, 1917, page 162, plate XXVI.

Bibliographic information published by the Deutsche Nationalbibliothek
The Deutsche Nationalbibliothek lists this publication in the Deutsche Nationalbibliografie; detailed bibliographic data available online: http://dnb.d-nb.de.

ISBN 978-3-525-53460-1

You can find alternative editions of this book and additional material on our Website: www.v-r.de

Typesetting by SchwabScantechnik, Göttingen
Printed and bound by Memminger MedienCentrum Druckerei und Verlags-AG, Fraunhoferstraße 19, 87700 Memmingen

Printed on aging-resistant paper.

To Othmar Keel

Table of Contents

Preface

The present book is the first of its kind, but certainly not the last word on the subject. It is intended as a textbook that introduces students to iconographic exegesis, by which we mean the use of visual materials (iconography) in textual analysis of the Hebrew Bible/Old Testament. The study of ancient Near Eastern art is as old as the first discoveries of artifactual remains from the ancient Near East. It traces back, then, to Napoleon's *Description of Egypt,* if not earlier, even if these earlier "descriptions" were often neither professional nor systematic. The application of iconographic data to the study of the Bible, too, is not new. In the case of the Hebrew Bible/Old Testament, the breakthrough work was Othmar Keel's *The Symbolism of the Biblical World: Ancient Near Eastern Iconography and the Book of Psalms,* first published in German in 1972 and subsequently translated into English in 1978 and into many other languages since that time (hereafter *SBW*). Keel's book and his continued labors in iconography inaugurated an approach, a school of thought – the Fribourg School – that grew over the course of time, developing its method and extending its reach. Iconographic approaches are now several, involving datasets, specific ideas, and applications not originally present in Keel's pioneering work, even though it remains seminal. And iconographic approaches are now practiced far beyond Switzerland: in Germany, France, and especially in South Africa and the United States.

This is not the place to discuss all of this research, or track the trends and developments in the work of Keel and the Fribourg School, let alone iconographic approaches more generally. Instead, the present volume is designed as a *textbook,* and this means that it is (1) intended as an introduction, and (2) designed especially with students in mind. As an introduction for students, this book obviously cannot cover every aspect of iconographic exegesis, and certainly not in great detail or equal depth. And so, while each of the editors has written on the theory, method, and practice of iconography when it comes to biblical exegesis – and the same is true for each of the contributors (see the cumulative bibliography) – we have endeavored to make each chapter understandable and accessible for students new to the field. Toward this end, we have incorporated several design elements that should maximize the utility of the book either in classroom contexts or for independent study. So, for example:

– The essays are organized around the tripartite structure of the Hebrew Bible: Torah (law), Nebiʾim (prophets), and Ketubim (writings). This structure is designed to show readers that iconographic approaches are widely applicable across the entire canon. There is also one essay on the book of Judith (chapter 18), showing that iconographic approaches need not be limited solely to the Hebrew canon. Of course, even essays that occur within one of the three parts often have recourse to other texts in other parts of the Bible.

–   Each chapter includes an assignment/exercise section that specifies a task for students to undertake. These assignments/exercises are designed to reinforce the main pedagogical lessons of the chapter by asking the student to practice a similar approach on their own. In many cases, it will be helpful for the student to have access to a corpus of pictures such as that contained in *ANEP, ABAT, CSAPI,* or *CSAJ,* or have the online database at Fribourg (www.bible-orient-museum.ch/bodo/) open.[1] In some cases, the images in the particular chapter, or elsewhere in this volume, will suffice. At still other times, recourse to *SBW* or *GGG* or some of the more comprehensive volumes in the OBO series will do the job.

–   At the end of each essay a short bibliography is provided for further reading. These bibliographies have been kept to a bare minimum and contain only the most important items for the chapter's discussion. They include the items that would be the first things to read to find out more information about the topic covered in that chapter, and they will also prove helpful for many of the assignments/exercises. These chapter bibliographies have been collected together, along with a great deal of additional secondary literature cited throughout the volume, in the cumulative bibliography found at the end of the book.

–   Several of the essays make explicit reference to other, classic methods in biblical exegesis such as textual criticism, form criticism, literary analysis, and so forth. Such references show how iconography, too, fits with the other aspects of the exegetical task, and how at times it complements, if not supplements, the other methods. These intra-disciplinary references also show how even classic exegetical methods can benefit from recourse to iconography. Finally, the relating of iconography to other exegetical techniques is intended to highlight the title of this textbook – namely, that it is about iconographical *exegesis,* not iconography as such per se or unto itself. The study of iconography for its own sake is certainly a worthy use of the visual evidence, but here the task is always and everywhere the use of such data for a better understanding of the Old Testament and ancient Israel.

–   Given its nature as a textbook, the contributions give more pronounced attention to method and practice than might otherwise be the case. The essays make arguments, to be sure, but they are also designed to be transparent about how such arguments can be (and are) made. The hope is that each chapter not only provides the reader with insight into a particular topic or exegetical question but that it also lays out an exegetical approach that the reader can apply to other topics and questions.

These are just some of the features that we hope will make this volume a helpful and useful resource to those new to iconography as well as to those seasoned in the arts of exegesis.

---

1   For more on these volumes and the others mentioned below, see the Introduction.

A few additional notes are in order. First, several of the chapters depend on earlier research published by their respective authors; these works are cited in the chapter bibliographies and sometimes throughout the chapter itself. More information – niceties of the argument or more fulsome discussion of some of the trickier parts of the interpretation – may be found by interested readers in those earlier publications. Second, translations are usually based on NRSV, unless otherwise noted, but versification, when it differs from English translations, typically follows the Hebrew text (MT). Third, dates are BCE, unless otherwise noted. Fourth, we have attempted to place the images in close proximity to the text that describes them (in a few cases, that has meant reduplicating an image). Most readers find this practice more helpful than having all of the images collected at the end of a chapter or the end of a book. While convenient, this format often does not allow proper indication of the relative size of the images in question, so readers should keep this important point in mind. The captions accompanying the images usually mention media (image carrier), date, provenance, and the source of the image. A description is sometimes added, but the images are often described more fully in the main text, when that is pertinent. Based on the media, one can get a rough sense of the size of the object. For a number of reasons, the print version of the textbook contains only line drawings and a few black and white photographs; the electronic version has several color images.

Last but not least, it remains to thank several individuals who were helpful at many times and in various ways. For research assistance, we thank Aubrey Buster, Reed Carlson, T. Collin Cornell, Mathis Kreitzscheck, Justin Walker, Justin Pannkuk, and Sandor Fejevary. For financial assistance, we thank Dean Jan Love of the Candler Shool of Theology, the Humboldt Project on monotheism, and the Louisville Institute. For his insight on copyright issues, we are grateful for our discussions with Prof. Dr. A. Wiebe, L. L. M. (Georg-August University, Göttingen). We also thank our various contributors for their good work and good humor, and especially Joel M. LeMon for crucial advice and help along the way. The idea for the textbook was born in the Society of Biblical Literature's "Ancient Near Eastern Iconography and the Bible" section and all of the contributors to the volume are members of that section if not also on its steering committee. We are grateful for the collegiality of these excellent scholars and friends.

We reserve our most heartfelt thanks for Jörg Persch, Moritz Reissing, Elke Liebig, and the entire staff of Vandenhoeck & Ruprecht for their patience through the course of several lengthy delays and for their excellent work in bringing the volume to completion. Given its relationship with the Fribourg series Orbis Biblicus et Orientalis (OBO), Vandenhoeck & Ruprecht has long been associated with iconographic studies. It is a true delight, then, to have this textbook published by this prestigious house.

Izaak J. de Hulster
Brent A. Strawn
Ryan P. Bonfiglio

Abbreviations

ABAT	*Altorientalische Bilder zum Alten Testament.* Edited by Hugo Gressmann. 2d ed. Berlin: de Gruyter, 1927.
ABD	*Anchor Bile Dictionary.* Edited by David Noel Freedman. 6 vols. New York: Doubleday, 1992.
AEL	*Ancient Egyptian Literature.* M. Lichtheim. 3 vols. Berkeley, University of California Press, 1971–1980.
AJA	*American Journal of Archaeology*
ANEP	*The Ancient Near East in Pictures Relating to the Old Testament.* Edited by James B. Pritchard. 2d ed. with supplement. Princeton: Princeton University Press, 1969.
ANETS	Ancient Near East Texts and Studies
AOAT	Alter Orient und Altes Testament
ATANT	Abhandlungen zur Theologie des Alten und Neuen Testaments
BA	Biblical Archaeologist
BDB	*A Hebrew and English Lexicon of the Old Testament.* Edited by F. Brown, S. R. Driver, and C. A. Briggs. Oxford: Oxford University Press, 1907.
BHK	*Biblia Hebraica* (16th ed.; 1973)
BHS	*Biblia Hebraica Stuttgartensia* (1983)
BZAW	Beihefte zur Zeitschrift für die alttestamentliche Wissenschaft
CBET	Contributions to Biblical Exegesis and Theology
CBQ	*Catholic Biblical Quarterly*
CEB	Common English Bible
CHANE	Culture and History of the Ancient Near East
ConBOT	Coniectanea biblica: Old Testament
COS	*The Context of Scripture.* Edited by William W. Hallo and K. Lawson Younger, Jr. 3 vols. Leiden: Brill, 1997–2002.
CSAJ	Jürg Eggler and Othmar Keel, *Corpus der Siegel-Amulette aus Jordanien: vom Neolithikum bis zur Perserzeit.* OBO.SA 25. Fribourg: Academic Press; Göttingen: Vandenhoeck & Ruprecht, 2006.
CSAPI	Othmar Keel, *Corpus der Stempelsiegel-Amulette aus Palästina/Israel. Von den Anfängen bis zur Perserzeit. Einleitung.* OBO.SA 10. Freiburg: Universitätsverlag; Göttingen: Vandenhoeck & Ruprecht, 1995.
CSAPI 1	Othmar Keel, *Corpus der Stempelsiegel-Amulette aus Palästina/Israel: von den Anfängen bis zur Perserzeit: Katalog Band I: Von Tell Abu Farağ*

	bis ʿAtlit. OBO.SA 13. Freiburg: Universitätsverlag; Göttingen: Vandenhoeck & Ruprecht, 1997.
CSAPI 2	Othmar Keel, *Corpus der Stempelsiegel-Amulette aus Palästina/Israel. Von den Anfängen bis zur Perserzeit. Katalog Band II: Von Bahan bis Tel Eton. Mit Beiträgen von Daphna Ben-Tor, Baruch Brandl und Robert Wenning.* OBO.SA 29. Fribourg: Academic Press; Göttingen: Vandenhoeck & Ruprecht, 2010.
CSAPI 3	Othmar Keel, *Corpus der Stempelsiegel-Amulette aus Palästina/Israel. Von den Anfängen bis zur Perserzeit. Katalog Band III: Von Tell el-Farʿa bis Tel el-Fir.* OBO.SA 31. Fribourg: Academic Press; Göttingen: Vandenhoeck & Ruprecht, 2010.
CSAPI 4	Othmar Keel, *Corpus der Stempelsiegel-Amulette aus Palästina/Israel. Von den Anfängen bis zur Perserzeit. Katalog Band IV: Von Tel Gamma bis Chirbet Husche.* OBO.SA 33. Fribourg: Academic Press; Göttingen: Vandenhoeck & Ruprecht, 2013.
DDD	*Dictionary of Deities and Demons in the Bible.* Edited by Karel van der Toorn, Bob Becking, and P. W. van der Horst. 2d ed. Leiden: Brill, 1999.
EA	*El-Amarna Tablets. According to the Edition of J. A. Knudtzon. Die el-Amarna-Tafeln.* Leipzig, 1908–1915. Reprint, Aalen, 1964. Continued in A. F. Rainey, *El-Amarna Tablets, 359–379.* 2d revised ed. Kevelaer, 1978.
EBR	*Encyclopedia of the Bible and its Reception*
FAT	Forschungen zum Alten Testament
FOTL	Forms of the Old Testament Literature
FRLANT	Forschungen zur Religion und Literatur des Alten und Neuen Testaments
GGG	Othmar Keel and Christoph Uehlinger, *Gods, Goddesses, and Images of God in Ancient Israel.* Minneapolis: Fortress Press, 1998. German original: 1992. 1998[4].
HALOT	*The Hebrew and Aramaic Lexicon of the Old Testament.* Koehler, L., W. Baumgartner, and J. J. Stamm. Translated and edited under the supervision of M. E. J. Richardson. 4 vols. Leiden: Brill, 1994–1999.
Herm	Hermeneia
HSM	Harvard Semitic Monographs
IEJ	*Israel Exploration Journal*
IPIAO 1	Silvia Schroer and Othmar Keel, *Die Ikonographie Palästinas/Israels und der Alte Orient. Eine Religionsgeschichte in Bildern. Band 1: Vom ausgehenden Mesolithikum bis zum Frühbronzezeit.* Fribourg: Academic Press, 2005.
IPIAO 2	Silvia Schroer, *Die Ikonographie Palästinas/Israels und der Alte Orient. Eine Religionsgeschichte in Bildern. Band 2: Die Mittelbronzezeit.* Fribourg: Academic Press, 2008.
IPIAO 3	Silvia Schroer, *Die Ikonographie Palästinas/Israels und der Alte Orient.*

	Eine Religionsgeschichte in Bildern. Band 3: Die Spätbronzezeit. Fribourg: Academic Press, 2010.
IPIAO 4	Silvia Schroer, *Die Ikonographie Palästinas/Israels und der Alte Orient. Eine Religionsgeschichte in Bildern. Band 4: Die Eisenzeit bis zum Ende der persischen Herrschaft.* 2 vols. Fribourg: Academic Press, forthcoming.
JBL	*Journal of Biblical Literature*
JLCRS	Jordan Lectures in Comparative Religion Series
JNSL	*Journal of Northwest Semitic Languages*
JR	*Journal of Religion*
JSOT	*Journal for the Study of the Old Testament*
JSOTSup	Journal for the Study of the Old Testament: Supplement Series
JTI	*Journal of Theological Interpretation*
KAI	*Kanaanäische und Aramäische Inschriften.* Edited by Herbert Donner and Wolfgang Röllig. 3d ed. Wiesbaden: Harrassowitz, 2002.
KJV	King James Version
KTU	*Die keilalphabetischen Texte aus Ugarit, Ras Ibn Hani und anderen Orten/The Cuneiform Alphabetic Texts from Ugarit, Ras Ibn Hani and Other Places.* 3rd, enlarged ed. Manfried Dietrich, Oswald Loretz, and Joaquín Sanmartín. AOAT 360/1. Münster: Ugarit-Verlag, 2013.
LHBOTS	Library of Hebrew Bible/Old Testament Studies
LIMC	*Lexicon Iconographicum Mythologiae Classicae.* Edited by Nikolaos Yalouris. 8 vols. Zürich: Artemis-Verlag, 1981–1997.
LXX	The Septuagint (Greek translation of the Hebrew Bible)
MANE	Monographs on the Ancient Near East
MT	Masoretic Text (Hebrew Bible)
NASB	New American Standard Bible
NEAEHL	*The New Encyclopedia of Archaeological Excavations in the Holy Land.* Edited by Ephraim Stern. 5 vols. Jerusalem: Israel Exploration Society, 1993–2008.
NIDOTTE	*New International Dictionary of Old Testament Theology and Exegesis.* Edited by Willem A. VanGemeren. 5 vols. Grand Rapids: Zondervan.
NIV	New International Version
NJPSV (Tanakh)	New Jewish Publication Society Version
NRSV	New Revised Standard Version
NTOA	Novum Testamentum et Orbis Antiquus
OBO	Orbis Biblicus et Orientalis
OBO.SA	Orbis Biblicus et Orientalis. Series Archaeologica.
OIP	Oriental Institute Publications
OLA	Orientalia Lovaniensia Analecta
OTL	Old Testament Library
OTS	Old Testament Studies
PdÄ	Probleme der Ägyptologie

PTMS	Pittsburgh Theological Monographs Series
RBS	Resources for Biblical Study
REA	*Revue des etudes anciennes*
RIMA	The Royal Inscriptions of Mesopotamia, Assyrian Periods
SBL	Society of Biblical Literature
SBLRBS	Society of Biblical Literature Resources for Biblical Study
SBLWAW	Society of Biblical Literature Writings from the Ancient World
SBW	Othmar Keel, *The Symbolism of the Biblical World. Ancient Near Eastern Iconography and the Book of Psalms.* Reprint ed. Winona Lake: Eisenbrauns, 1997 (1978). German original: 1972.
SemeiaSt	Semeia Studies
SHCANE	Studies in the History and Culture of the Ancient Near East
SJOT	*Scandinavian Journal of the Old Testament*
TUAT	*Texte aus der Umwelt des Alten Testaments.* Edited by Otto Kaiser. Gütersloh: Gütersloher Verlagshaus, 1984–.
UF	*Ugarit-Forschungen*
VT	*Vetus Testamentum*
VTSup	Supplements to Vetus Testamentum
WOO	Wiener Offene Orientalistik
WUNT	Wissenschaftliche Untersuchungen zum Neuen Testament
ZAW	*Zeitschrift für die alttestamentliche Wissenschaft*
ZBK	Zürcher Bibelkommentare
ZDPV	*Zeitschrift des deutschen Palästina-Vereins*
ZTK	*Zeitschrift für Theologie und Kirche*

Introduction
Iconographic Exegesis: Method and Practice

Izaak J. de Hulster, Brent A. Strawn, and Ryan P. Bonfiglio

1. The Rise of Iconographic Exegesis

The basis of most exegetical methods is that the Hebrew Bible/Old Testament[1] can be read as a text and in light of other texts. After all, the Hebrew Bible itself is a book – or, better, a collection of books – and as a result it is possible to ask textual and "bookish" questions about the nature of its contents. In fact, a variety of exegetical methods address issues regarding the Old Testament's development: the compositional pieces of a text, for example, including its redactional layers, textual variants, editorial history, genre, literary devices, intertextual allusions, and so on. The study of aspects like these (and others) might be termed an "internal" or text-immanent kind of approach to the Old Testament. But it is also possible to approach the Hebrew Bible from an "external" or comparative perspective in which aspects of its language and literature are examined in light of the vast library of written materials that have been recovered from the ancient Near Eastern world. This kind of approach is also text-centered, but rightly recognizes that the texts of Israel's neighbors – whether in the form of epic poems, legal collections, royal treaties, and the like – afford modern interpreters extraordinary access to the historical, cultural, and literary background of the Old Testament.

Whether "internal" to the Hebrew Bible, or "externally" aware of cognate literature, both of the exegetical approaches described above (each of which is replete with subareas having different aims and interests) are, in the end, decidedly "logo-centric" – concerned primarily, if not exclusively, with texts, writing, and literature. It is no exaggeration to say that, when it comes to interpreting the Old Testament, most exegetical approaches tacitly assume that words and texts are the proper, if not the only, object of study. As a result, it is not surprising that the vast majority of textbooks on biblical exegesis do not contain a single image, even if they grant significant importance to historical approaches to the Bible that include, among many other things, attention to archaeology and artifactual remains. Even in the rare cases in which a picture of a coin, a seal, a monument, or a piece of pottery is present in an exegetical handbook – if it is not included for "illustrative purposes" only – the point is usually

---

1   The terms "Old Testament" and "Hebrew Bible" are found throughout the present book, depending on the author's preference. We use the terms synonymously in this chapter, with full realization that they are not exactly identical.

to highlight the presence of an *inscription* on the object in question, with the material and artistic aspects of the object left undiscussed if not completely ignored. Exegesis, as traditionally pursued, has tended to be a rather art-*less* affair.

The present volume is also concerned with the task of biblical exegesis but charts a very different course. While the goal remains a better grasp of the meaning and background of the biblical text, the approach employed in this textbook relies heavily on artistic remains. Each of the essays gathered here represents what might be called *iconographic exegesis*, which can be defined as *an interpretive approach that explains aspects of the Hebrew Bible with the help of ancient Near Eastern visual remains.* This method was pioneered by Othmar Keel of the University of Fribourg (Switzerland) in the early 1970s. His breakthrough work, *Die Welt der altorientalischen Bildsymbolik und das Alte Testament: Am Beispiel der Psalmen* (1972; ET: *The Symbolism of the Biblical World: Ancient Near Eastern Iconography and the Book of Psalms* [1978; repr. 1997; hereinafter: *SBW*]), represented the first systematic attempt to compare the "conceptual world" of an Old Testament book with ancient Near Eastern art reflecting the same or similar notions. Since that time, a network of Keel's students and colleagues (known as the "Fribourg School") along with a subsequent generation of scholars throughout Europe, Israel, South Africa, and North America have further refined the theory, methods, and practices of iconographic exegesis.[2] The present textbook should be situated amidst the growing interest among biblical scholars to explore the relationship between the visual and the verbal, the *ikon* and the *logos,* when it comes to understanding the historical and cultural background of the Hebrew Bible and the meaning of its specific texts.

2.   Using Images to Study Texts

While ranging widely across various biblical texts and ancient Near Eastern iconography, the essays in this volume are united by their use of the latter to study the former. Given the dominance of text-only approaches in the exegesis of the Hebrew Bible, some justification is required for this attention to artistic data. Several reasons may be noted.

First, when it comes to comparative approaches to biblical interpretation there is often more iconographic material to work with than textual data. Archaeological discoveries from the past two centuries have shown that visual artifacts generally outnumber written remains in the material culture of ancient Near Eastern civiliza-

---

2   To be sure, other work – some of it prior to Keel's initial monograph or otherwise outside the Fribourg School proper – is also important and in some instances even foundational. See, e.g., the volumes by James B. Pritchard (*ANEP*); Hugo Gressmann (*ABAT*); and Martin Metzger (1985) – the first two for their collections of ancient Near Eastern art, the last for his study of the throne of God.

tions. Finding an abundance of images in the archaeological record is probably to be expected when the region is ancient Mesopotamia, Egypt, or Persia. What is striking, however, is that the same is true of Syria-Palestine. Texts were no doubt important in ancient Israel, but images seem to have been produced and distributed in far greater quantities and so were more likely to have been encountered in everyday life than inscriptions. Thus, whatever one may conclude about the scope and meaning of the ban on certain types of images in the Ten Commandments (see Exod 20:4–6; Deut 5:8–10), it remains the case that the Hebrew Bible was written and read in a culture that had its fair share of images (Schroer 1987). Unfortunately, until relatively recently – indeed, only after the work of Keel and those he inspired – these iconographic data have gone largely untapped as a comparative resource in the interpretation of the Old Testament.

Beyond their relative abundance, images matter in biblical exegesis for a *second* reason: namely, their function. Cultural theorists and art historians emphasize that images, no less than texts, are a constitutive component of any given culture's symbol system. Rather than serving as mere decorations, images – whether ancient, medieval, or modern – are capable of conveying crucial information between senders and receivers. This was perhaps especially the case in the ancient world, where textual literacy rates were likely to be extremely low. In such contexts, images constitute a type of communication or "language" in their own right. Indeed, in the form of coins, seals, and other types of "miniature" or "minor art," some images might have been the ancient equivalent of modern mass media. Due to the large volume of their production and small size, these types of image-carriers were capable of disseminating ideas across vast territories and throughout diverse segments of society. Still further, as communicative media, images no less than texts can be described as cultural repositories, containing information about society, religion, politics, economics, and so forth. As such, they reflect the thoughts of human agents (e. g., the artists and/or people who commissioned or purchased the images) and were designed to be understood – even "read" – by their respective audiences. In this way, and exactly as textual remains, ancient Near Eastern iconography provides a window into the cultural, social, religious, and political world that lies behind the Hebrew Bible. Insofar as both image and text shed light on the ancient world, a dynamic of relationships between the two can be established (see § 3). And so it is that some essays in the present textbook begin with exegetical questions that are rooted in a textual crux of some sort, while others take a literary image or imagistic theme as their starting point, with still others beginning with the artistic data proper.

A *third* justification for using images to study texts pertains to the various ways these media forms are linked. At least three types might be discussed (see Schroer 1987): (1) some biblical texts describe visual artifacts, as in the description of a Chaldean wall relief in Ezek 23:14 or the two pillars of bronze in 1 Kgs 7:15–22. (2) Other biblical texts reflect a less direct, but no less apparent awareness of specific images and the broader visual culture of their day. So, for example, the descriptions of the seraphim in Isaiah 6 or the four living creatures on Yhwh's throne in Ezekiel 1 appear to have been influenced by similar images commonly known in the ancient Near Eastern world. (3) Finally, certain types of figurative expressions in the Old Testament evoke a mental picture in the reader/listener. These expressions and their accompanying mental pictures can be pursued in the plastic arts. So, for example, light metaphors in the Psalter paint a "verbal image" of God as a solar deity whose radiance dawns upon the righteous and whose wings provide refuge for the afflicted.

In each of these cases (and others might be added), examining iconographic remains can help interpreters visualize what a biblical text describes or better understand the symbolic world from which the Bible and its descriptions emerge. In these ways (and so far to this point), iconographic exegesis is clearly an historical approach to interpretation, perhaps best understood as a subset within historical-critical methodology writ large (see Oeming 2006:49–54; Gertz, Berlejung, Schmid, and Witte 2012:52–57). In most – but not all (see below) – applications of iconographic exegesis, interpreters study how ancient images influenced the production of the Old Testament texts or are otherwise germane to understanding these texts.

Though not entirely unrelated, this line of inquiry should be distinguished from what is often referred to as "reception history." The latter is also often interested in relationships between images and texts but typically from a point *subsequent* to initial composition and/or audience reception. Hence, much of reception history is primarily concerned with how (later) art can function as a means, instance, or example of biblical interpretation (see, e. g., Terrien 1996; Exum and Nutu 2007; Harvey 2013). In other words, text-image studies within reception history tend to investigate how the Bible has been interpreted through (much) later works of art; iconographic exegesis, on the other hand, examines how the biblical authors appropriated, adapted, and/or were influenced by *then-contemporary* or *pre-existing* visual motifs. Of course, this, too, could be seen as a kind of reception history, just not reception history of the Bible (into, say, Renaissance art). Instead, it would represent a much earlier stage: the way *the biblical texts themselves* have received preexisting information (ideas, images, themes, and so on) previously known in and through ancient iconography.

In sum, there are numerous reasons recommending the use of images in the study of texts, but, even with this important point granted, there is still much to be said. Indeed, careful reflection on the nature of the image-text relationship is necessary since iconographical exegesis depends precisely on it.

3. The Image-Text Relationship

There is no single or easy way to describe the various sorts of interactions that occur between any given image and a text. Readers will note that the essays in this textbook use different terminology and/or emphasize different aspects of what it means for an image and text to be "related." Even so, and while a variety of approaches can fall under the general rubric of iconographic exegesis, it is still possible to identify three general aspects of the image-text relationship, each of which addresses a distinct set of interpretive questions. These can be conveniently summarized with three "C's" (see further Bonfiglio 2014):

1. image-text *congruence:* Which images and texts can be thought of as being related, and to what extent do they share similar (or manifest different) themes, motifs, and/or subject matter?
2. image-text *correlation:* At what level are images and texts related, and how have scholars understood both the type and direction of interaction that occur between these two media?
3. image-text *contiguity:* To what extent does the presence of historical lines of influence and/or mechanisms of contact determine whether a given image and text are thought to be related, and what are the implications for comparative methodologies?

Each of these three aspects is discussed below, after which a very short example is offered by way of explication (§ 3.4).

3.1. Image-Text Congruence

Perhaps the most common way of describing the image-text relationship is in terms of similarity or *congruence.* In this perspective, to say that a given image and text are related is to assert that they reflect similar themes, motifs, or subject matter. The presence of some degree of congruence is often taken as a necessary (though perhaps not sufficient) condition for comparing certain sets of visual and verbal data. Yet adjudicating whether an image and text are congruent is perennially "open to interpretation" and, occasionally, subject to considerable debate. As a result, researchers can and often do disagree, not only about which images and texts are thought to be related but also about exactly how congruent such materials are (or need to be) with one another.

Prior to the work of Othmar Keel, scholars interested in relating ancient Near Eastern art to the biblical texts tended to operate with a rather low threshold for what constituted congruence. Images and texts were often compared on the basis of very general similarities, and in most cases the precise nature of this similarity was left implicit. This approach is especially evident in catalogues of ancient Near Eastern art, such as Hugo Gressmann's *Altorientalische Texte und Bilder zum Alten Testament* (*ABAT*: 1927 [1909]) and James B. Pritchard's *The Ancient Near East in Pictures Relating to the Old Testament* (*ANEP*: 1969 [1954]). These volumes tend to compare only small portions or fragments of images and texts, thus leaving unexplored the nature of the relationship between the larger artistic and literary compositions in which this material is found (for the perils of such fragmentation, see Keel 1992b).

A more helpful and sophisticated approach to image-text congruence has emerged in recent years, as is evident in Joel M. LeMon's monograph, *Yahweh's Winged Form in the Psalms: Exploring Congruent Iconography and Texts* (2010). Rather than juxta-posing isolated images and texts on the basis of general points of similarity, LeMon demonstrates the need to establish wider patterns of congruence between ever-larger constellations of literary imagery and iconographic motifs. This procedure not only helps to clarify which images and texts are related but it can also help to explain the extent of the congruence present.

3.2. Image-Text Correlation

Second and closely related, iconographic exegesis can speak of the image-text rela-tionship in terms of *correlation* – at what level are images and texts related? In its most basic form, the question of image-text correlation seeks to clarify the presence of image-text congruence. In other words, correlation explores what sort of interaction or level of dependence (if any) must exist between visual and verbal media in order to account for the fact that certain ancient Near Eastern images seem to represent in artistic form themes or motifs that are also evident in the Hebrew Bible.

Prior to the publication of Keel's *SBW*, it was sometimes presumed that a thematic similarity between an ancient Near Eastern image and a biblical text was the result of one form of media being directly dependent on, or genetically related to, the other. In this view, either the Old Testament was understood as interacting with ancient art in some mechanistic fashion or ancient art was thought of as "illustrating" the bib-lical text much like a drawing in a "picture Bible." While neither of these models is completely implausible, they are not the only, nor the best, ways of accounting for the manifold relationships that may exist between ancient Near Eastern iconography and the Hebrew Bible. It is equally possible, for example, and probably far more likely in most instances, that image-text congruence is the result of both media being depen-dent on a common underlying (mental) concept. In this understanding of image-text correlation, both texts and images can function as "dual reflexes" (Strawn 2007:114) of a same or similar preexisting notion. This means, further, that an image and a text could be related via a shared theme, motif, or idea that exists *independently* of any given form of media, at least one that is still extant. To put this in a slightly different way: some mental concepts are capable of being expressed in *both* visual and verbal modes. One can, as it were, "think in images" or "think in pictures" – which is to say, think *visually* (cf. Arnheim 1966, 1969, 1986, 2004) – and these thoughts can be manifested in word and text or in image and art.

Images thus provide "a way to share in the mental map of a culture" (de Hulster 2009a:21) including the cognitive processes that inform the production of figurative language. Thus, rather than suggesting that ancient Near Eastern art merely *illustrates* biblical texts, iconographic exegesis looks to the visual remains as a resource that *illu-minates* the Bible (its background and foreground) by helping contemporary readers "see through the eyes of the ancient Near East" (Keel 1997b:8). Said differently, ico-nography should not be understood simply as *informative* for the interpretation of the biblical text (though it is certainly that) but also as *formative,* which is to say *generative* in important ways for the hermeneutical endeavor, not simply "illustrative." To cite an example, numerous studies have shown how analyzing ancient Near Eastern iconography can help one better "visualize" the source domains and background knowledge that give rise to biblical metaphors. Since image and text can be correlated at a conceptual level, iconography may be used to provide a window into the world (or mind) behind a metaphor – and into its workings – and the same holds true for a host of other language-forms in the Old Testament. Numerous essays in the present volume demonstrate this kind of image-text correlation, especially the chapters that deal with divine metaphors.

3.3. Image-Text Contiguity

The third major aspect of the image-text relationship has to do with the question of *contiguity.* To put this matter in terms of the previous discussion, if image-text congruence identifies the existence of common motifs between visual and verbal artifacts and if image-text correlation seeks to explain the level and degree of interaction that produces such congruence, then image-text contiguity seeks to historicize those interactions through discernable lines of influence and/or plausible mechanisms of contact and interaction. At this point iconographic exegesis touches upon a broader question about the nature of comparative methods – namely, must two objects of study come from the same (or similar) geographical, chronological, or sociological contexts in order to be considered related?

The bulk of research in iconographic exegesis has tended to answer this question in the affirmative. Most studies have concentrated on intra-cultural comparisons in which the images and texts in question are historically contiguous with one another. Such an approach is on display in Othmar Keel and Christoph Uehlinger's invaluable volume, *Gods, Goddesses, and Images of God in Ancient Israel* (1998). In this and similar studies with explicitly historical interests, demonstrating image-text congruence is only the first part of a larger comparative story. In order to make the best case for image-text contiguity, it must be shown how the images under investigation came into contact with and/or had an influence on the biblical authors and/or their original readers/listeners. This work is typically accomplished by appealing to Syro-Palestinian art that predates or is contemporaneous with the corresponding texts in the Hebrew Bible. An emphasis on image-text contiguity may also lead to a special focus on the minor arts insofar as these materials were ideally suited for the preservation and diffusion of iconographic motifs across vast regions and time periods (see above). Whatever the case, when used in service of historical-critical interests, iconographic exegesis often seeks to establish plausible mechanisms of contact between certain images and texts. This is the burden of image-text contiguity.

However, comparative historical methods – whether these involve texts, images, or both – need not be limited to contiguous phenomena, especially if that contiguity is understood in the sense of direct, genetic relationships. Jonathan Z. Smith has noted that the process of comparison is a hermeneutical endeavor, "the result of mental operations undertaken by scholars in the interest of their intellectual goals" (2000:239; cf. Strawn 2009a). In other words, comparison is never a matter of genetics but of interpretation, and comparative methods that work with perceived similarities (or differences) that do not derive from direct, genetic dependence can be quite appropriate even if (and when) they serve different interpretive goals.

For instance, in his *Seeing the Psalms: A Theology of Metaphor* (2002), William P. Brown draws on a broad, intercultural network of ancient Near Eastern art as a type of evocative context through which his readers can more fully encounter the metaphorical theology of the Psalter. Though Brown's study is not uninterested in historical matters, his express purpose is not to demonstrate clear lines of contact between any given image and text. Rather, through a comparison of non-contiguous (or at least not *explicitly* contiguous) images and texts, Brown prompts readers to visualize the figurative language of the Psalter as a way to more fully appreciate its poetry and more fully engage its theological imagination. In other words, Brown is as much concerned with what images *do* for contemporary readers of the Psalms as he is with what images *did* for the Psalter's ancient authors (and audiences). While the more historical (comparative) concerns of image-text contiguity remain dominant within most studies devoted to iconographic exegesis, it is important to note that non-contiguous comparisons of ancient Near Eastern art and the Hebrew Bible constitute a viable way of talking about the image-text relationship (cf. Strawn 2009a, 2014).

The above typology reveals the need for biblical iconographers to be more explicit about which aspects of the image-text relationship they are addressing and how these decisions inform their methodological procedures. Doing so would not only entail a more consistent use of terminology but would also involve a more careful appraisal of how certain approaches relate (or fail to relate) to one another.

3.4. A Brief Example

The different ways of understanding the image-text relationship are on display throughout the present collection of essays, each of which serves as an example of iconographic exegesis and the various ways it can be practiced. Most of the chapters also offer explicit commentary on matters of method and practice when it comes to iconographical exegesis. Even so, in the interest of clarity – especially with respect to the three "C's," which are mutually enriching and overlap somewhat in actual practice – a brief example may be offered as a foretaste of the rest of the volume. It is taken from Isa 63:1–6 (see further de Hulster 2009a:144–68).

> [1] "Who is this that comes from Edom,
>   from Bozrah in garments stained crimson?
> Who is this so splendidly robed,

marching in his great might?"
"It is I, announcing vindication,
    mighty to save."
[2] "Why are your robes red,
    and your garments like theirs who tread the wine press?"
[3] "I have trodden the wine press alone,
    and from the peoples no one was with me;
I trod them in my anger
    and trampled them in my wrath;
their juice spattered on my garments,
    and stained all my robes.
[4] For the day of vengeance was in my heart,
    and the year for my redeeming work had come.
[5] I looked, but there was no helper;
    I stared, but there was no one to sustain me;
so my own arm brought me victory,
    and my wrath sustained me.
[6] I trampled down peoples in my anger,
    I crushed them in my wrath,
and I poured out their lifeblood on the earth."

If one were to approach this text from an iconographic perspective, one would first need to search for images dealing with grape-treading or, more broadly, grape-processing so as to establish *image-text congruence*. Some examples are found in **figs. 1–3**. With images like these available, the exegete can explore both similarities and differences between them and the text of Isaiah 63.

Fig. 1. Grape processing scene, wall relief on the East Wall of the tomb of Ptahhotep in Saqqara (Egypt), ca. 2400 BCE. Source: Davies 1900: Pl. XXI (detail)

Fig. 2. Grape harvest scene on a painted wall relief in the
tomb of Petosiris in Tuna el-Gebel (Egypt), 4th c. BCE.
Source: Lefebvre 1923: Pl. XII

Fig. 3. Tomb of Nakht, Thebes, ca. 1400 BCE. Source:
Davies 1917: 162 Pl. XXVI (detail)

Next, one might consider the issue of *image-text correlation*. It seems safe to assume
that the grape harvest and the processing of grapes was well known throughout the
Near East wherever grapes were grown. It follows that **figs. 1–3** are generally reflec-
tive of daily life. So far, then, Isa 63:1–6 and the images of grape processing can be
correlated as reflecting a commonly known occurrence in the ancient world such that
it is found in both texts and images.

Correlating the text and the images reveals differences along with the similarities, however. Indeed, the correlation reveals some surprises in the text of Isaiah that
only come to light when it is viewed alongside the images. So, for example, in Isaiah
63, Yʜwʜ works alone, unlike the groups of workers that are found in the images.
Also, unlike those workers who are almost-naked (and thus non-elite), Yʜwʜ wears a
(royal) robe. He is no average grape-treader, a point further underscored by observing

that the grape-treaders in the images often hold onto each other or hold something above their heads, whereas YHWH is assisted only by his own arm. Moreover, YHWH does not collect the precious juice but spills it out upon the earth. This is, then, no typical instance of grape-processing. Indeed, as the unit progresses, it becomes clear that YHWH does not tread on grapes, but on *humans* – a posture found in ancient Near Eastern images of war. In **fig. 4**, for example, Pharaoh Tutankhamun in the guise of a sphinx tramples his enemies.

Fig. 4. Side panel of Tutankhamun's sandal chest from his tomb, 14th c. BCE. Source: Tiradritti and de Luca 2000:213

The king in theriomorphic form trampling or standing upon his foes is a widely-attested motif, also known in the miniature art from ancient Syria-Palestine. **Figure 4** displays one side of Tutankhamun's sandal box. On the other sides he is shown trampling enemies in his chariot (**fig. 5**) and hunting lions (**fig. 6**). It is noteworthy that this particular motif – domination by treading or riding upon the enemy – is found on a chest containing King Tut's *footwear!* Indeed, the bottom of Tutankhamun's sandals contained images of his enemies so that when he wore his shoes, he was quite literally standing upon his foes.

Fig. 5. Painted wooden casket, Tomb of Tutankhamun (1358–1349). Source: *SBW*: Pl. XVII

Fig. 6. Painted wooden casket, Tomb of Tutankhamun (1358–1349). Source: *SBW*: Pl. XVI

Images like these clarify further what is already evident in the text of Isaiah 63 – namely, that in this context grape-treading is a *metaphor for war,* which recalls Yhwh's presentation as a warrior in Isa 59:15b–18 and elsewhere. The iconography also suggests that the textual imagery is somewhat mixed: first, the grape-treading is not of grapes but of people; second, the grape-treading is not an occasion of harvest but of violence and war. Still further, instead of describing what was likely to be a joyous time, the grape harvest in the scene of Isaiah 63 is beyond grim. But this latter point, too, is not unknown in the artistic record: punishment in the afterlife could be represented by grape processing, especially by means of the sack press (**figs. 7–8;** cf. **fig. 1,** right side). These images show that (divine) punishment and grape processing were, in fact, correlated and "imaged" long before Isaiah 63.

The respective dates of the images and the date of Isaiah 63 leads, finally, to the matter of *image-text contiguity.* In the present example, the specific date of Isaiah 63 is not of crucial importance vis-à-vis the date of the images because grape harvesting and processing enjoyed a long and rather stable existence throughout the ancient Near East. The traditions and methods in this area of agriculture changed little, as evidenced in the continuity of grape (wine) presses that have been recovered from archaeological excavations. So, in this particular case study, the issue of chronology is less important than the overall constellation of images and the wider contexts of both

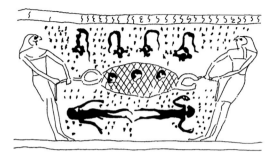

Fig. 7. Detail from the 18th c. BCE 'Book of Amduat' in the Papyrus Torino (catalogue number 1785; ca. 200 BCE), showing an afterlife punishment using a sack press for extracting blood from heads; above the net are torches that will be placed on the beheaded corpses. Source: Poo 1995:152 fig. 15

Fig. 8. Detail of a wall painting in the tomb of Imery in Giza, ca. 2400 BCE. Source: Zonhoven 1997:67, fig. 2 after a painting by Gaetano Rosellini (Italian expedition to Egypt, 1828–1829)

art and text. Precise historical dates are also less important when the comparison is phenomenological – concerning a notion or concept, especially one that was widely known and not limited to a particular period, region, or media. The example from Isaiah 63 is something of this sort, and so the issue of contiguity is not dependent on the identification of a mechanism of influence or transmission that would plausibly connect the art and/to the text, but is more akin to Brown's study on the Psalms, insofar as the image-text nexus has allowed us to appreciate the figurative language of Isaiah more fully and with greater color, depth, and detail.

In this example from Isaiah 63, the biblical text was the driving force or starting point. But iconographic exegesis need not proceed only in that fashion. One can begin with a biblical text and then search for thematically-related images, asking after their relationships, historical connections, and so forth, but other possible approaches exist as well. So, for example, a group of images might be selected based on their date and geographical provenance, can be studied as such, and then related to biblical texts from the same (or similar) horizon (e. g., Persian Period iconography vis-à-vis texts from the Old Testament that date to that period). Alternatively, a particular theme or metaphor or image or image-type could serve as the starting point for iconographic exegesis (see, e. g., Strawn 2005a). Once again, the chapters that follow illustrate these and other approaches, all in service to the main goal which is illuminating the biblical text by means of the study of ancient Near Eastern iconography (cf. de Hulster 2009b).

4. Working with Images

If iconography is as important as the preceding discussion suggests, the use of images in research is not simply recommended – it is required. This leads to some practical remarks with regard to how to work with artistic remains. In what follows, then, we offer brief orientations to the different types of images available (§ 4.1), to various sources for images (§ 4.2), to image analysis (§ 4.3), and to the presentation of images (§ 4.4), all of which we hope will be useful to newcomers to iconography as well as to seasoned researchers. We deem such comments necessary, in any event, because students of the Hebrew Bible are typically trained to work only with words and texts. The logo-centrism of the field means that many hours are spent (and more than a few tears shed) learning ancient languages and acquiring requisite philological and literary skills. Very few students receive any formal training when it comes to images. This situation is only starting to change as programs in Hebrew Bible start to incorporate courses in archaeology, art history, and visual culture alongside more traditional offerings. This latter kind of training is essential not only for developing a "good eye" (observational skills with careful attention to detail; Rose 2007) when working with artistic remains, but also for cultivating increased interest in iconographic exegesis as a mode of biblical interpretation.

What follows below is no substitute for a more formal and sustained treatment of the methods of image analysis and the nature of visual hermeneutics (see, e. g., Bonfiglio 2014; de Hulster 2009b; LeMon 2009; Brown and Feldman 2014). Instead, it is a brief and practical overview of how interpreters interested in iconographic exegesis might find, analyze, and present images in their research. What is said deductively here is on display in more inductive ways across the various chapters of the present textbook.

4.1. Types of Images

Ancient Near Eastern art can be categorized based on the size, medium (image carrier), and mode of manufacture of the artifact in question. The most important categories are introduced below (cf. Hartenstein 2005:175–77).

Amulets and Seals

Due to their miniature size (usually no more than 5–10 cm in height), amulets and seals are often termed "minor art." Amulets in the form of animals, deities, or symbols were worn or carried as a means of protecting a person from demons and other sources of danger or as a way of bestowing blessing, good fortune, or power on their carriers. The vast majority of amulets found in ancient Israel are Egyptian imports or are based on Egyptian prototypes.

Seals and seal impressions are by far the most common type of iconographic remains from the ancient Near East. The impressions were made when a cylinder seal was rolled in clay or a stamp seal was pressed into a malleable material such as wet clay (creating a bulla), wax, or even soft metal. Despite their diminutive size, seals and seal impressions often contain elaborate artistic designs, including depictions of worship scenes, animals, vegetation, geometric shapes, human figures, and divine symbols. The seals themselves were typically made out of stones, ivory, or metal. Like amulets, they were occasionally worn on the person (by means of a string threaded through a drilled hole) and were often thought to have an apotropaic function like amulets. Scarabs are a particular subcategory of seals in which the shape of the seal resembles an Egyptian scarab (dung beetle).

Ivories

Another type of minor art consists of carvings on small pieces of ivory from an animal tooth or a bone fragment. The best-known ivories stem from Mesopotamia (especially Nimrud) and Samaria and take the form of figurines or small reliefs. Because many ivories have been recovered from Samaria, they have assumed an important role in the study of the Old Testament (see, e. g., 1 Kgs 22:39). Common motifs on the ivories include the suckling cow, the woman at the window, the sun-child born from a lotus, or enemies being trampled.

Coins

First appearing in Asia Minor during the seventh century BCE, coins were used to help facilitate trade and pay soldiers. In addition to their economic value, coins often contained images on one or both of their sides. The series of coins minted by Darius the Great of Persia in the late-sixth and early-fifth centuries were the first to contain a likeness of a king. These and other coins reached Syria-Palestine through Mediterranean trade, though by the end of the fifth century, Judah (Yehud) had begun minting their own local varieties. The motifs found on these coins are primarily borrowed from Athens (the owl) and Asia Minor. Thus, not unlike seals, coins also functioned as a type of "mobile" mass media in the ancient world.

Statues and Figurines

This category of images consists of freestanding, three-dimensional representations of animals and/or divine or human figures, along with items like cult stands containing the same. A well-known example of this type of image is the Judean Pillar Figurines (JPF), which date to the late Iron Age. Standing approximately 15 cm in height, these figurines have a pillar-shaped body with prominent breasts (often supported by the arms); the meaning and significance of these figures is heavily debated (see Darby 2014; Darby and de Hulster fc). Another famous type of statuette is the terracotta "horse-and-rider" figurines. Larger statues are also attested. For instance, cult statues of ancient Near Eastern deities were fashioned from wood or stone and often overlaid with precious metals. Housed in temples, these images often had anthropomorphic features, though they could also take zoomorphic form, as might be the case with the bulls Jeroboam sets up in the sanctuaries of Dan and Bethel, if these are meant to represent YHWH (1 Kgs 12:28–29). Statues of deities were thought to manifest the presence and/or power of the deity that they represented. They were often stolen in the context of war or processed in and around temples during festivals or rituals.

Monumental Art

This category of ancient art includes large-scale reliefs and paintings on palace walls, exposed rock faces, and tomb façades. In some instances, entire architectural complexes could qualify as "monumental art" (see Russell 1991). Due to their large size, monumental images were able to display elaborate visual narratives, including depictions of battles, worship scenes, and royal processions. Well-known examples include the royal lion hunt scenes from the Neo-Assyrian palaces at Nimrud and Nineveh, the tribute procession scenes found on the north and east stairways of the Apadana at Persepolis, or the reliefs of Ramesses III at Medinet Habu. While wall reliefs were often made by carving on stone surfaces, colored paint was also applied in some instances – though faint traces are typically all that survive today. Also included in this category are the large stone monuments known as steles. Steles contain images but also frequently carry some form of inscription. The standing stones known in Hebrew as *massēbôt* might be considered in this category of monumental art, though these are often aniconic, lacking any visual representations.

The images found on monumental art often reflect a larger artistic program that was commissioned by and carried out under the supervision of the king and/or his royal officials. They were frequently intended for posterity. Given their public and propagandistic purposes, these images – while remaining valuable sources for ancient Near Eastern art (and history) – should not be taken as offering a straightforward "portrait" of past events or historical figures. Indeed, individualized depictions are quite rare and come rather late in ancient Near Eastern art, where the presentation is typically far more general, symbolic, idealized, and/or non-descript. Even so, monumental art, perhaps more than other categories, can contain highly symbolic and ideologically-charged depictions intended to display a specific political and/or religious message. These factors impinge on how they are best understood, interpreted, and utilized in iconographical exegesis.

4.2. Sources of Images

A vast collection of ancient Near Eastern art has been recovered from archaeological excavations over the past two centuries. More material comes to light every year and so publication is ongoing. Even so, several important repositories of images exist that can be of particular use in the task of iconographical exegesis. Two classic, though now somewhat dated volumes are Hugo Gressman's *ABAT* and James B. Pritchard's *ANEP*, both of which are primarily photographic collections. Keel's *SBW* includes numerous line drawings along with a few photographs organized by specific thematic categories and with special reference to the Psalms. Keel's multivolume *Corpus der Stempelsiegel-Amulette aus Palästina/Israel (CSAPI)* provides unprecedented access to the rich repertoire of minor art from the Levant; the volume focused on Transjordanian sites is by Jürg Eggler and Keel (*CSAJ*).[3] Two other important repositories of images useful for the study of the Old Testament are: Keel and Uehlinger's *Gods, Goddesses and Images of God in Ancient Israel (GGG)* and Silvia Schroer's multivolume series entitled *Die Ikonographie Palästinas/Israels und der Alte Orient: Eine Religionsgeschichte in Bildern (IPIAO)*.[4] While *GGG* offers an assessment of the history of Israelite religion based on iconographic data, *IPIAO* provides a chronological overview of artistic material from ancient Israel/Palestine with reference to the Hebrew Bible across a far more expansive timeframe.

It should be noted that not every object or image included in volumes like the ones mentioned above (or housed in museums for that matter, see below) come from controlled excavations. Many have been acquired on the antiquities market. Objects acquired in this way may be, and often are, ancient originals but the existence of forgeries is a well-known phenomenon and always a possibility for those objects and images whose exact archaeological find spots are unknown. Keel, among others, has argued that unprovenanced materials should be included in iconographic exegesis, since, to leave all unprovenanced materials aside would be to greatly limit the data at hand. We agree with Keel even as we also agree with him that unprovenanced objects should be treated very carefully and perhaps completely separate from those objects whose provenance is known (cf. Strawn 2005a).

In addition to published volumes, museums offer another excellent source of ancient art. Many museums allow visitors to take photographs of artifacts on display, with some allowing access to archived materials. An increasing number of museums are making their entire collections accessible on the internet. The British Museum, the Louvre, and the Israel Museum (among others) offer searchable online databases, complete with high resolution photographs. The Bibel+Orient Museum in Fribourg

---

3   Many other publications dedicated to certain kinds of corpora might be mentioned, especially seals and seal impressions. Note, e.g., Christian Herrmann's three volumes on the amulets from ancient Israel/Palestine (1994, 2002, 2006).

4   The first volume was coauthored with Othmar Keel.

(Switzerland) offers an especially helpful database called Bibel+Orient Datenbank Online or BODO (www.bible-orient-museum.ch/bodo/).[5]

One final remark: Most publications of ancient Near Eastern iconography include only black-and-white photographs or line drawings and so it is easy to forget that ancient artists frequently used color. Seals, amulets, and gems exist in a kaleidoscope of colors. Egyptian paintings on walls or papyri have their own palette, but statues, too, could be painted or adorned with precious metal and gems. The use of glazed tiles (as on the famous Ishtar gate) and the rich colors used for dyes are other ways the ancient world was every bit as colorful as our own.

4.3. Analyzing Images

Scholars working with art have often found it helpful to think about and describe images in a way that is analogous to how scholars speak of texts and language. Iconographic exegetes do the same. So, for example, contributors to the current textbook occasionally refer to "reading" images, speak of the "visual vocabulary" of a certain region or time period, or analyze the "iconographical syntax" of an artistic tableau. These kinds of remarks rightly recognize that images, much like texts, are designed to communicate information between senders and receivers. However, in order to understand the "language" of images, interpreters must know and be able to assess the rules, tendencies, and styles that influenced how images were produced in the ancient world. As an example, it is important to take note of the *quality* of a given image (what level of workmanship it reflects) as well as its *provenance, style, medium, function,* and *display context.* Whenever possible, it is also helpful to consider the *artist* or *workshop* from which an image originates, its *precursors* and *subsequent development* (*or reception*), and how it *relates to any associated text* (if such exists) like an accompanying inscription or a label.

Note that none of these questions engage what would otherwise seem to be an obvious point of inquiry – namely, whether the artifact in question should, properly speaking, be referred to as "art." This is because the distinction between "art" and "non-art" or between "high art" and "low art" is mostly anachronistic when applied to the ancient Near Eastern world.[6] Still further, even if an object is (presently) judged to be "low art" or even "non-art," the image(s) it carried may still be of great use in the task of iconographic exegesis.

Although there is no one, single way to interpret visual data, many scholars who work with ancient images employ a method of analysis originally pioneered by Erwin Panofsky in the late 1930s (see Panofsky 1972; cf. Strawn 2008a). In Panofsky's under-

---

5   More useful data appears on the web all the time. See, *inter alia,* http://archeologiepalestina.blog-spot.fi/2010/07/sources-for-use-of-ancient-images-in.html (accessed 6/6/2015).

6   This same distinction is now increasingly called into question even with respect to contemporary images (cf. Elkins 2003; Davis 2011).

standing, iconography is a branch of art history aimed at identifying three levels of meaning in an image, each determined through different analytical operations:

1. at the *pre-iconographic* level, one describes the basic subject matter of an image (in Panofsky's example, a male figure on a street, holding a hat raised slightly above his head);
2. at the *iconographic* level, one identifies the conventional meaning expressed by certain pictorial motifs or themes (a male figure removing his hat); and
3. at the *iconological* level, one interprets the symbolic meaning(s) expressed (a polite gesture of greeting/welcome).

These three levels of analysis are guided, respectively, by an interpreter's knowledge about:

1. *the history of style* (is the given subject matter represented similarly in other contexts?);
2. *the history of types* (how are themes or concepts known from literature characteristically displayed in visual form?); and
3. *the history of symbols* (how do the symbolic meanings expressed reflect culturally conditioned principles or values?).

Though interpreters might organize their analysis of an image according to these three levels of meaning, Panofsky admits that they are not completely discrete and, in fact, overlap and intersect in various ways. A chart summarizing Panofsky's approach to image analysis is found in **fig. 9.**

Interpretive Object	Interpretive Task	Interpretive Method	Interpretive Control
Primary or natural subject matter: the world of artistic motifs	Pre-iconographical description of motifs	Practical experience: familiarity with objects/motifs and events	History of style: insight into why objects and events were expressed by specific forms at certain times
Secondary or conventional subject matter: the world of images and image complexes (stories, allegories)	Iconographical analysis in the narrow sense	Knowledge of literary sources: familiarity with themes and concepts at work in an image	History of types: insight into why specific themes or concepts were expressed by objects and events at certain times
Intrinsic meaning or content: the world of "symbolical" values reflected/present in the work	Iconographical analysis in the deeper sense or, better, what might be called iconographical interpretation/synthesis ("iconology")	"Synthetic intuition": familiarity with tendencies of the human mind	History of cultural "symbols": insight into why tendencies of the human mind were expressed by specific themes and concepts at certain times

Fig. 9. Summary of Panofsky's approach to image analysis. Source: Strawn 2008a:310

Panofsky's method "remains the most important starting point for methodological reflections" in iconographic exegesis (de Hulster 2009a:70). Nevertheless, alternative approaches to analyzing the meaning of ancient images are also possible. For instance, in his book *Das Recht der Bilder gesehen zu werden* (1992a), Keel develops the notion of motif analysis, which places special emphasis on understanding how certain ideas are conventionally expressed through iconographic "constellations," or patterns of motifs in a given artistic composition. Others, such as Annette Weissenrieder and Friederike Wendt (2005) and Zainab Bahrani (2003) offer a more radical departure from Panofsky's method by highlighting the utility of semiotic approaches for understanding ancient images.

While biblical scholars need not be experts in any of these methods before pursuing iconographic exegesis, it is nevertheless important that they be aware of and give attention to the fundamental questions of *visual hermeneutics* – the orienting principles and underlying perspectives that govern the questions we ask about what images mean and how they function. At a bare minimum, when consulting iconographic sources one should obtain as much information as possible about the image in question. The many aspects of an image should also be kept in mind: artist(s) and workshop(s), material, technique, image carrier, genre, motifs, relation to other works of art (thematically and materially), and the various use(s) of the image (cf. Baetschmann 2009 and 2003).

4.4. Presenting Images

One final practical matter in working with images concerns how they are best presented in works of iconographic exegesis. Several important questions must be considered. These include which type of image is used, what is needed in order to secure copyright permission (in the case of publication), and a number of other details such as how to reproduce images, what information should be included in accompanying captions, and so on and so forth.

Line Drawings and/or Photographs

Line drawings and photographs are used in academic publications, though not in equal measure. Each type of reproduction has its advantages and disadvantages. Photographs are, to some degree at least, more "objective" and can capture elements of style (e. g., color, texture, medium) that are not readily available in a line drawing. But it can be difficult to secure permission for photographs, and, depending on the condition of the artifact or capabilities of the printer, it can sometimes be difficult to make out details of the object. This leads directly to discussing the advantages of line drawings, which make the basic content of an image easy to see. However, line drawings are an artist's interpretation of an image and thus are even more subjective than photographs. Even if highly detailed, line drawings will not reproduce every aspect of the object and will no doubt reflect the style and assessment of the artists who make the drawings. Compare, for instance, the photographs of the following seal (with its impression, **fig. 10**) with two different line drawings of the same (**figs. 11–12**). The differences between the two line drawings is quite marked, which underscores the interpretive nature of any artist's rendering by means of a line drawing. It is always best, therefore, to compare line drawings with the original artifact or a high-resolution photograph whenever possible.

Fig. 10. Hematite cylinder seal with golden frame, 22 (42) × 10 (14) mm (including frame), ca. 1800–1750 BCE; provenance unknown, presently in the Louvre (AO1634). The seal depicts the weather god in smiting position (on two mountains) above a mongoose, ape, or guenon; a water god with fish in a stream; four animals (caprid, hare, bird, scorpion); and an inscription reading "Ḫaqata, son of Patala, servant of Ḫatniadou." Source: Delaporte 1923: Pl. 96 no. A914, items 12a–b

Fig. 11. Line drawing of **fig. 10**. Source: Ward 1909: Fig. 881

Fig. 12. Line drawing of **fig. 10**. Source: El-Safadi 1974: Pl. VII fig. 61

For those wishing to produce line drawings themselves but who lack an artist's hand (or recourse to a professional artist), certain software programs allow one to convert a photograph into a line drawing. If one does not have access to such programs, or the result is somehow unsatisfactory, a photograph can be printed (with light contrast) with the main characteristics then traced with a pencil or pen. The resulting marked-up photograph can be scanned and saved as a line drawing after increasing the contrast and removing leftovers from the low-contrast image that was originally traced.[7]

Permissions and Copyright

One of the more confusing issues in presenting the results of iconographic exegesis concerns copyright law. Fair use policy allows for the reproduction of images without infringement of copyright in not-for-publication products like teachers' handouts, in-class presentations, student papers, and the like. Reproducing images in publication venues has to be negotiated on a case-by-case basis with the publisher in question. The authoritative *Chicago Manual of Style* (16th ed.; § 4.77–87) advocates for the extension of fair use to include academic publication as well, but, in our experience, different publishing houses have different policies, and so iconographers will have to work directly with their publishers to ensure the requisite standards have been met. It is not unusual for a publisher to require the author to obtain explicit statement of permission. Such permission can sometimes cost money; publishers usually expect such costs to be paid by the author.

Images published before 1917 are usually considered to be in the public domain and can be used without obtaining copyright permission. As noted above, some museums are now granting access to and use of their images via their websites; many other websites house images that can be used in presentations and publications. Making one's own line drawings is perhaps the most expeditious – but not always easy – way to avoid having to obtain permissions, especially if those are costly. Whenever a previously published image is used, a bibliographic citation should be provided, just as one would cite a quotation from an article or a book. For some presses, this type of "footnoting" suffices for publication, with no further permissions needed.

Additional Details

The inclusion of images in a paper, especially one for publication, involves a number of details that deserve brief discussion. These include how best to reproduce the image and what information should be included in any accompanying caption. In the case of reproduction, the minimum requirement to produce a good, readable image is a scan of 300dpi (for a color image), though for publishing purposes, the threshold may be as high as 600dpi (for grey-scale) or 1200dpi (black-and-white). There are various software programs that can capture and reproduce quality scans of images, which can be saved, in turn, in different formats (e. g., pdf, jpg, tiff, etc.) depending on what is required.

For captions, the best practice is to include as much pertinent information as possible, though different contexts or use will no doubt mean that not every caption is as fulsome as others. A listing of some of the information that might be included in a caption follows:

---

7   See Adkins and Adkins 1989, Dorrell 1994, and Steiner and Allason-Jones 2005 for more on professional photographs and line drawings in archaeological illustration.

Description of the image
Source of image (catalogue, book, photographer, etc.)
Museum inventory number (if pertinent)
Size (try to be consistent in metric system used)
Material (terracotta, bone, ivory, stone, metal, etc.)
Kind of image carrier (statue, seal, relief, papyrus, etc.)
Date
Provenance
Bibliography (other publications that reproduce or discuss the object)

Finally, it should be emphasized once more that the images one works with and ends up presenting should be relevant, generative, and illuminating. Including images that are intended to serve only as illustrative visual aids or as nice-looking "eye candy" is a far cry from the way iconographic exegesis pursues the study of images and texts.

5.   A "Textbook" on Iconographic Exegesis

Over the past few decades, iconographic exegesis has steadily gained a seat at the table of accepted methods for biblical interpretation. While there have been many insightful studies in this area – essays, journal articles, and monographs – there has yet to appear an accessible introduction to the method and practice of iconographic exegesis. This volume intends to fill this gap.

As a textbook designed for students new to the field, it does *not* aim to provide a comprehensive overview of the methodological and theoretical issues pertaining to the study of visual materials. Neither does it present an exhaustive catalogue of ancient Near Eastern art. Instead, what is offered here is a series of examples or case studies in iconographic exegesis. Each of the chapters employs the artistic evidence to answer specific exegetical questions. Insofar as the chapters are oriented toward the tripartite structure of the Hebrew Bible, with one chapter focusing on the book of Judith from the Greek Old Testament, they show how iconographic exegesis is pertinent to a wide array of biblical texts.

But iconographic exegesis can be practiced in more than one way – the preceding discussion has shown that it has various aspects and nuances – and several of these are on display in the chapters that follow. While each study exhibits its own unique interests and strategies, a few common goals are evident throughout. First, priority is placed on methodological clarity. Despite different approaches or nuances, contributors frequently reflect explicitly if not extensively on the nature of their adopted approach and on why it is useful in light of the particular exegetical problem at hand. Second, rather than offering a comprehensive, commentary-like treatment of a given biblical text, each essay attempts to shed light on a specific aspect of a text (or texts), such as the meaning of a metaphor or the background of a particular concept.

Among other things, this means that the chapters do not provide a lengthy literature review, and contributors have kept documentation (especially footnotes) to a bare minimum. This streamlined style is intended to enhance the accessibility of the textbook (especially for students who are new to iconographic exegesis) and to highlight as clearly as possible the "payoff" of working with images when interpreting biblical texts. Third, each chapter ends with an assignment/exercise that provides the reader with an opportunity to further explore the ideas and/or to practice the method(s) presented in that chapter. This should allow beginners as well as expert researchers to integrate iconographic exegesis into their toolbox of interpretive skills.

In conclusion, the goal of this textbook is to provide readers with a template for doing iconographic exegesis and for incorporating images into *all* of their subsequent interpretive work. It is our hope that the sort of research exemplified in this volume will motivate and inspire readers to pursue working with images in a field that has been traditionally (and often unfortunately) defined by an exclusive focus on words and texts. If so, we may come to *see* the text in a new perspective, with *eyes* freshly opened to all things *visual*.

Bibliography

Baetschmann, Oskar. 2009 [1984]. *Einführung in die kunstgeschichtliche Hermeneutik: die Auslegung von Bildern.* 6th ed. Darmstadt: Wissenschaftliche Buchgesellschaft.

Bonfiglio, Ryan P. 2014. "Reading Images, Seeing Texts: Towards a Visual Hermeneutics for Biblical Studies." Ph.D. diss. Emory University.

Hulster, Izaak J. de. 2009a. *Iconographic Exegesis and Third Isaiah.* Forschungen zum Alten Testament II/36. Tübingen: Mohr Siebeck.

Hulster, Izaak J. de. 2009b. "Illuminating Images: A Historical Position and Method for Iconographic Exegesis." In *Iconography and Biblical Studies. Proceedings of the iconography sessions at the joint EABS/SBL conference: 22–26 July 2007, Vienna, Austria,* edited by Izaak J. de Hulster and R. Schmitt, 139–162. Alter Orient und Altes Testament 361. Münster: Ugarit-Verlag.

Keel, Othmar. 1992b. "Iconography and the Bible." In *Anchor Bible Dictionary,* edited by David Noel Freedman, 3:358–74. New York: Doubleday.

Keel, Othmar. 1997b. *The Symbolism of the Biblical World. Ancient Near Eastern Iconography and the Book of Psalms.* Winona Lake, IN: Eisenbrauns.

LeMon, Joel M. 2009. "Iconographic Approaches: The Iconic Structure of Psalm 17." In *Method Matters: Essays on the Interpretation of the Hebrew Bible in Honor of David L. Petersen,* edited by Joel M. LeMon and Kent H. Richards, 143–68. Society of Biblical Literature Resources for Biblical Study 56. Atlanta: Society of Biblical Literature.

Panofsky, Erwin. 1972 [1939]. *Studies in Iconology: Humanistic Themes in the Art of the Renaissance.* Boulder, CO: Westview.

Schroer, Silvia. 1987. *In Israel gab es Bilder: Nachrichten von darstellender Kunst im Alten Testament.* OBO 74. Freiburg: Universitätsverlag; Göttingen: Vandenhoeck & Ruprecht.

Weissenrieder, Annette and Friederike Wendt. 2005. "Images as Communication: The Methods of Iconography." In *Picturing the New Testament: Studies in Ancient Visual Images,* edited by Annette Weissenrieder, Friederike Went, and Petra von Gemünden, 1–59. Wissenschaftliche Untersuchungen zum Neuen Testament 193. Tübingen: Mohr Siebeck.

Part I: The Torah/Pentateuch

Chapter 1
Picturing Ancient Israel's Cosmic Geography:
An Iconographic Perspective on Genesis 1:1–2:4a

Izaak J. de Hulster

1. Introduction

The creation account in Genesis 1:1–2:4a offers a fitting starting point for a textbook that explores the intersection between ancient Near Eastern iconography and biblical exegesis. For one, the canonical organization of this volume makes it quite natural to begin with the opening verses of the Pentateuch. Moreover, Genesis 1:1–2:4a, which is attributed to the Priestly source (P), is a promising candidate for iconographic exegesis because it is densely layered with descriptive language about the pre-creation conditions, the ordering of the heavens and earth, and the creation of humanity in God's image. While this language is already familiar to many readers, what it attempts to picture can be better understood if seen in light of ancient images.

The purpose of this chapter is to analyze how the priestly creation account visualizes and simultaneously conceptualizes "cosmic geography" – that is, the structure and layout of God's creation, including the ordering of the heavens and the earth as well as the underlying theologies and perspectives that inform this view of the world. In addition to highlighting points of similarity and difference between biblical and ancient Near Eastern cosmic geographies, this foray into iconographic exegesis addresses the place and presence of God in Genesis 1:1–2:4a.

2. Picturing Cosmic Geography in Ancient Images

Before turning to specific images of ancient Near Eastern cosmic geography it will be helpful to consider several questions about how these images work. For instance, how does an image represent a subject matter like cosmic geography, which consists of an abstract idea and/or is not fully visible to the human eye? To what extent must an image of, say, the heavens or the netherworld be interpreted differently than, say, an image of a king, an animal, or other "earthly" subjects? And more broadly, to what degree do most ancient images intend to look like or resemble that which they represent?

2.1. Conceptual Images

Most images from the ancient Near Eastern world do not attempt to represent their subject matter in a realistic or direct fashion. Rather, they serve as visual signs that signify through culturally conditioned patterns of artistic motifs. Instead of providing a type of historical photograph or exact portrait, they function as a type of pictogram. Put in a slightly different way, ancient images tend to represent concepts (e. g., kingship, tribute scenes, lamentation, etc.) rather than the actual physical likeness of individual people, places, or events.

Yet it does not follow from this observation that there is a complete absence of resemblance between a given image and that which it represents. Indeed, some images of animals, weapons, cultic instruments, and so forth tend to represent their subject matter in ways that, broadly speaking, would appear quite realistic to the observer. This type of image is often referred to as a "visual-picture" (*Sehbild*) insofar as the pictorial representation of the object more or less corresponds to its visual form (i. e., how it would appear to the human eye). However, especially when dealing with representations of abstract ideas or concepts associated with the divine world (both of which apply to cosmic geography), ancient images are best interpreted as a type of "thought-picture" (*Denkbild*). Not unlike a schematic diagram, a thought-picture represents ideas and (sometimes invisible) phenomena in a highly conceptual or symbolic fashion. As such, there is not necessarily, nor even typically, a mimetic correspondence between a thought-picture and the object/idea it represents. This category of images would include, among other things, the personification of air, heaven, and earth (see **fig. 1.4** and the comments in § 2.3).

The conceptual nature of ancient art has important implications for image analysis and, in particular, depictions of cosmic geography. When dealing with such images, one must not only identify the intended subject matter of the picture but also interpret the symbolic meaning of the concepts expressed by that picture. This interpretive process requires knowledge of iconographic conventions – that is, the customary way(s) of communicating themes and ideas in pictorial form.

In contemporary settings, understanding iconographic conventions is widespread and typically automatic for viewers. Examples abound: a hand with an extended thumb inside a circle with a line through it clearly signals "no hitch hiking;" a red octagon (even without writing) means "stop;" and a set of concentric, semi-circular lines indicates the presence of a Wi-Fi signal. Knowledge of these and thousands of other iconographic conventions is so widely assumed that it is easy to forget that they are based on culturally-conditioned codes, at least some of which might be foreign to viewers from different times and places.

In a similar fashion, many ancient Near Eastern images are also based on conventions, though these conventions are often far less familiar to modern observers. For instance, scale is often used to indicate the relative importance of individuals or objects in a scene, even if the proportions of the resulting image are not realistic. Kings are often depicted twice as tall as their subjects while some animals that are perceived to be dangerous, such as the hippopotamus, are represented in small scale in order to symbolically minimize their threat. In these cases, scale is an iconographic convention used to communicate abstract concepts (importance, danger, etc.).

Some images can represent multiple concepts simultaneously in order to construct a fuller or more comprehensive picture of the idea being represented. This convention is evident in the ceiling painting of Ramses VI's tomb, which depicts the various stages of the sun god's travels during the day and the night (**fig. 1.1**). Horizontally, the sun god's bark is represented in successive stages during both the day (marked in the middle of the picture with multiple phases of the sun) and the night (also marked in the middle of the picture, but with stars). While this synchronicity of day and night might appear strange to the modern viewer, it was common in Egyptian iconography to combine multiple, and sometimes mutually exclusive, vantage points in a single, unified frame of reference. A similar phenomenon is evident in Egyptian images that depict human beings in profile except for the shoulders, which are depicted frontally.

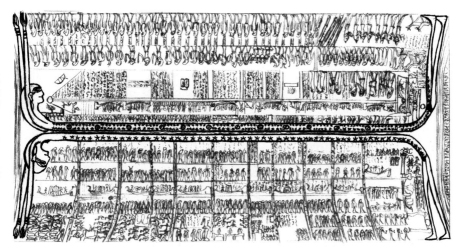

Fig. 1.1. Ramses VI's tomb ceiling painting, Valley of the Kings, 12th c. BCE. Source: Line drawing by Mathis Kreitzscheck and Izaak de Hulster based on various photos

One final example involves divine images. Since ancient Near Eastern gods were often depicted in anthropomorphic form, it can be difficult for the untrained observer to distinguish between humans and deities. However, an ancient viewer would have readily recognized certain conventions as indicating divinity. For instance, in Mesopotamian art the horned crown and flounced robe are typically attributes of deities, though occasionally they may appear on humans (especially kings) in order to imply their super-human or divinized status.

These observations about iconographic conventions apply to a wide range of investigations involving iconographic exegesis. However, they are especially important for this chapter's focus on depictions of cosmic geography, which, as already noted, frequently entail the use of various types of thought-pictures.

2.2. The Horizontal and Vertical Axes of the Cosmos

In ancient Near Eastern thought, the cosmos was perceived along two axes: the horizontal axis, which consists of topographical and geophysical features of the earth, and the vertical axis, which reflects the tripartite division of the heavens, the earth, and the netherworld. Taken together, these two axes comprise the multi-dimensional layout of cosmic geography.

A representative depiction of the horizontal axis of cosmic geography is displayed in **fig. 1.2.** This image is best understood as a type of map or atlas that provides a conceptual (rather than geographically accurate) depiction of topographical features as perceived in Babylonian thought. For instance, the city Babylon lies near the center of the image, thus reflecting its privileged place in geo-political affairs. Likewise, the names of other cities, mountains, bodies of waters, etc., surround the center, as if held in place by the centripetal force of Babylon's influence and power. The two concentric circles mark the ocean, while the triangles indicate distant regions (probably mountain islands). This latter aspect of the map reflects a similar concept as is found in Isa 41:5 and 42:10, where islands (NRSV: "coastlands") are associated with "the ends of the earth." This map, and others like it, was not made for navigation, even though it reflects an ancient geographical perception. Rather, as a conventionally coded "thought-picture," it represents – and reinforces – an ideologically motivated view of the world.

Fig. 1.2. Tablet with Babylonian world map, 12.2 cm × 8.2 cm, 6th c. BCE (BM 92687); composition and line drawing (based on various photos and Horowitz 2011:20–42; cf. Finkel 2014:261–297) by author. The original map contains cuneiform text explaining what is represented. In the figure these words are replaced with numbers. The legend is as follows: 1. Mountain; 2. city; 3. Urartu; 4. Assyria; 5. Der; 6. [undecipherable]; 7. swamp: 8. Susa; 9. channel: 10. Bit Yakin; 11. city; 12. Habban; 13. Babylon; 14–17. Ocean; 18. Great Wall, six leagues in between where the Sun is not seen; 19. region/district, six leagues in between; 20. [regi]on/district; 21. [re]gion/district; 22. region/district, eight leagues

A depiction of the vertical axis of cosmic geography is exemplified by the ninth-century tablet of King Nabu-apla-iddina, which is also known as the "Shamash Tablet" or "Sun-god Tablet" (**fig. 1.3**). On the left, the tablet shows the Babylonian king, the middle of the three small figures, with an interceding goddess (left, see the divine tiara) and a priest. On the right is an anthropomorphic depiction of Shamash seated upon his throne in his shrine. Shamash appears just beneath three celestial symbols. The text below the image refers to the reinstallation of an anthropomorphic cult statue of Shamash after a period in which the sun disk emblem stood in its place within the temple.[1] The sun disk with altar is depicted in the middle, perhaps having just been reinstalled in its new location (Woods 2004).

Fig. 1.3. Shamash Tablet of Nabu-apla-iddina, ca. 29 cm × 18 cm, early 9th c.; Sippar (BM 91000); image compilation (obverse and reverse in the background, obverse image foregrounded) by author based on King 1912: Plates XCVIII–XCIX

There are several takes on the relation between the parts of the representation: cosmic-spatial, narrative, cultic. A crucial question concerns the identification of the water, depicted here as wavy lines, at the bottom of the image and above which the cult-reinstallation scene takes place. It is quite possible that this ocean (*apsu*) represents the heavenly ocean, especially since four orbs (likely planets or other celes-

---

1   That an anthropomorphic cult statue would be reinstalled in this context is noteworthy since Mesopotamian art of this period was generally characterized by a tendency to move away from anthropomorphisms and toward abstraction, i. e. the use of divine symbols (cf. Ornan 2005b).

tial bodies) appear within the wavy lines near the very bottom of the register. If this is the case then the image seems to merge a temple scene with a heavenly scene, thus making it out of place to inquire whether the reinstallation of the cult statue is taking place in the temple *or* in heaven. A similar dynamic might be evident in Isaiah 6. In this case, the temple is on earth, but because Yhwh dwells in it, it is one and the same with heaven (*SBW*:174).

Reasoning in this fashion, many scholars have used this image to argue for a certain degree of "symmetry" between heaven and earth insofar as the earthly temple (on the left) mirrors the deity's dwelling place in heaven (on the right). A more refined position would be to identify the left part as the earthly temple with the sun disk and the right part as heaven. In this view, the image would be understood as displaying two spaces in one visual frame.

However, two caveats must be registered about this interpretation. First, it is equally possible that, rather than representing simultaneous scenes from two different spatial realms, **fig. 1.3** depicts two successive scenes in a narrative sequence: the scene on the left depicts the temple during the time in which the sun-disk emblem was still in place while the scene on the right pictures the temple after the cult statue had been reinstalled. Such an interpretation would make it difficult to sustain the above-mentioned argument about a temple/heaven symmetry. Second, although the earthly temple is not an exact "copy" of the heavenly shrine, heaven and earth can both be said to be the deity's dwelling place. Alternatively, the sanctuary can be thought of as actualized by God's presence: "The sanctuary is the place where the distinction between heaven and earth, between 'this world' and 'the other world,' is annihilated" (Metzger 1971:144, author's translation).

An alternative, and perhaps more plausible, interpretation is that the wavy lines represent the subterranean waters. If the wavy lines are indeed subterranean waters, then the stars indicate that it is daytime, when the stars were thought to descend to the netherworld. Interpreted this way, the *apsu* might be seen as being conceptually analogous to the biblical *těhôm* or "deep" (e. g., Deut 33:13 and Ps 135:7). Furthermore, the *apsu* also refers back to the temple, as it could also indicate the temple water basin (like the "molten sea" in 1 Kgs 7:23–26).

This understanding of the *apsu* could sustain a reading of the Shamash Tablet representing three cosmic realms: the heavens (the scene on the right), the earth (the scene on the left), and the netherworld (represented by the *apsu* beneath both of the other scenes). Alternatively, Woods (2004:77) suggests that this image reflects a cultic tripartition between human/worshiper, symbol, and (main) deity. Although these interpretations draw on existing tripartitions in ancient Near Eastern thought, the most straightforward interpretation is to understand the space of the whole relief as the temple precincts.

2.3. The Tripartite Cosmos

As the Shamash Tablet seems to imply, Mesopotamia shared the general ancient Near Eastern conception of a tripartite (or three-tiered) cosmos, comprised of the heaven, the earth, and the underworld. In other images, the solid "sky" (similar to the "dome," "firmament," or "expanse" in Gen 1:7) separates heaven (where deities live) and earth while simultaneously keeping apart the waters above and the waters below. The celestial bodies hang in the air below the sky. The sun god would spend the night in the underworld and then at dawn would rise and make his tour along the firmament throughout the day (for Egypt, see **fig. 1.1**). The center of the cosmos was located in the temple and is often represented with a "world tree" or a mountain. This mountain, with its roots in the underworld and its top reaching into the heavens, is a fitting depiction of the divine dwelling places (cf. Horowitz 2011).

This tripartite cosmic geography was also prevalent in Egyptian iconography as is seen in **fig. 1.4**. This papyrus drawing brings together various aspects of the Egyptian view of cosmic geography. The goddess Nut represents the sky. In this figure, she is pictured arched over the world, with toes and fingertips touching the ground. She is covered with stars and can be seen parallel to the idea of the (night) sky as a ceiling with stars. Nut is sustained or supported by Shu (the "air god"), who appears in a kneeling position with upraised arms. She grasps an *ankh*-symbol in each hand. Shu separates the sky from the earth, which is represented anthropomorphically in the form of Geb. This deity is in a nearly reclined position with symbols of plants adorning his body.

Fig. 1.4. Papyrus depicting Shu separating the sky (Nut) from the earth (Seb), New Kingdom (second half of the second millennium). Source: http://isis.houseofneteru.com/Geb_Nut.png (cited 12 August 2011); cf. *SBW*: Fig. 32 for a line drawing

The sky in this image can also be understood as a heavenly ocean, which the sun bark crosses during the course of the day (Hornung 1977). Specifically, in the upper right hand corner, the sun bark appears in the day sky while in the upper left hand corner the sun bark appears crossing the night sky, indicated by the multitude of small circles. In terms of cosmic geography, it is important to note that the night sky probably represents the concept of the netherworld since this is the place where the sun was thought to descend each day in Egyptian cosmologies. Thus the spatial placement of the netherworld (upper left hand quadrant) does not correspond in a one-to-one fashion with the conceptual placement of the netherworld in cosmic geography (beneath the heavens and earth). This convention underscores the conceptual nature of ancient images of cosmic geography.

3.   Cosmic Geography in Genesis 1:1–2:4a

This section focuses on the cosmic geography described in Genesis 1:1–2:4a. Rather than providing a thorough exegesis of the text as a whole, attention is focused on similarities and differences between ancient Israel's view of cosmic geography and that which is presented in ancient Near Eastern images.

3.1. The Structure(s) of Creation

Understanding ancient Israel's cosmic geography first involves assessing the highly structured account of creation found in Genesis 1:1–2:4a. Several different structuring principles can be discerned. First, creation is structured in terms of time. The most obvious aspect of this is the delineation of seven discrete days. Specific acts of creation are linked to each of the first six days while the seventh day is set apart as a Sabbath. Thus, by both instituting and sanctifying time, a chronological framework is provided for all of creation.

Second, within this chronological structure there is also a spatial structure that can be divided into two cycles: Days 1–3 and Days 4–6. In the first three days, God creates living spaces or realms[2] by "separating" various elements of creation and ascribing certain names for them. In Days 4–6, God creates various types of inhabitants to fill or rule over these spaces. Taken together, the chronological and spatial structuring of Genesis 1:1–2:4a can be summarized in the following table (adapted from Deist 1987):

---

2   God creates the conditions for life. As such, he also creates plants on the third day and designates them as food for humans on the sixth day. Food for the animals might be implied by the creation of their spaces.

Day	Creation of spaces	Day	Creation of inhabitants
1	Separating: light and darkness; Naming: "Day" and "Night"	4	The two great lights
2	Separating: waters above and waters below Naming: "Sky"	5	Birds above and fish below
3	Separating: land and waters under the sky Naming: "Earth" and "Sea(s)"	6	Animals, humans
	----	7	Institution of Day of Rest

John Walton (2011) offers a similar line of interpretation. However, instead of speaking about chronological or spatial structures he contends that functionality is the main organizing principle of creation (cf. de Hulster 2012a and 2012b). In this view, Genesis 1:1–2:4a can be summarized in terms of the creation of functions on the first three days: time (Day 1), weather and cosmic space (Day 2), and fertility, food production, and earthly space (Day 3). On the next three days, "functionaries" are created that act with respect to the functions outlined in Days 1–3. These functionaries include: sun, moon, and stars (Day 4), living beings in the water and air (Day 5), and land animals and humans (Day 6).

This interpretation plays a role within Walton's overarching interest in reading the seven-day creation account of Genesis 1:1–2:4a in light of Mesopotamian texts on temple inauguration rituals. Reading Genesis 1:1–2:4a in light of Gudea's seven-day temple dedication ceremony, Walton understands the creation of the cosmos in Genesis 1 as the building, dedication, and putting into use of a temple – thus implying that the cosmos as a whole is itself a temple (2011:118, 179).[3]

3.2. Tripartite Cosmology

The tripartite division of the cosmos discussed above (§ 2.3) was prevalent throughout the ancient Near East, and as such, it is likely that biblical authors had some exposure to this way of thinking about the cosmos. In fact, numerous interpreters have concluded that ancient Israel's understanding of cosmic geography also was based on a tripartite division. In particular, Keel (1985) and Cornelius and Deist (2002) have synthesized literary descriptions of cosmic geography found in Genesis 1 and other parts of the Hebrew Bible into schematic diagrams. While no single verse or passage makes reference to all of the elements depicted in **fig. 1.5** (from Keel) or **fig. 1.6** (from Cornelius and Deist), these diagrams present a helpful way of visualizing the descriptions of cosmic geography in the Hebrew Bible.

In **fig. 1.5**, the upper sphere of the cosmos (heaven) is marked with God's presence, symbolized by the cherub throne and the seraphs (the latter is lacking in the drawing by Cornelius and Deist). God's heavenly throne is depicted as being over "the waters

---

3   Reading Genesis 1 as part of the Priestly writing highlights the importance of the relation between the cosmos and the sanctuary/temple/tabernacle (cf. Janowski 1990; Levenson 1984; Morales 2012; Morrow 2009; Weinfeld 1981).

that were above the dome" (Gen 1:7). The placement of God's throne recalls references in the psalms to Yʜwʜ sitting "enthroned over the flood" (Ps 29:10) or God watching "all the inhabitants of the earth" from where he sits enthroned (Ps 33:14). But, as argued above, the flood could also indicate the *apsu* below, and Yʜwʜ's watching the whole world may be granted by the concept that his throne is in his temple on the (cosmic) mountain at the center of the earth.

In the middle of **fig. 1.5** is a depiction of the earthly temple, complete with the cherub throne and seraphs (cf. 1 Kings 6; Isaiah 6). Not unlike the above rejected interpretation of the Shamash Tablet, the earthly temple seems to intentionally mirror the heavenly realm. Above the temple but still under the dome of heaven (sky, firmament) are emblems of the (winged) sun and the moon, which represent the two great lights mentioned in Gen 1:14–16. The trees flanking the temple, which recall the floral imagery of the Solomonic temple (1 Kgs 6:29), and perhaps also the pillars referred to as Jachin and Boaz (1 Kgs 7:21), indicate the fecundity of the earth.

What is perhaps most striking is that the earth is threatened by powers of chaos, personified by the serpent in the upper region of the subterranean waters (cf. Job 3:8; 41:1; Ps 74:14; Isa 27:1). God's wisdom, symbolized by a Torah scroll from which come two outstretched arms, is pictured as upholding the foundations of the earth. This idea reflects Prov 3:19, which states "The Lᴏʀᴅ by wisdom founded the earth; by understanding he established the heavens."

The schematic diagram by Cornelius and Deist (**fig. 1.6**) reflects many of the same elements as are found in **fig. 1.5**. However unlike Keel, Cornelius and Deist do not explicitly mirror heaven and temple (the latter is pictured without the cherub throne). Also of note is the fact that instead of depicting a winged sun disk, **fig. 1.6** represents God within creation as "a combination of the sun god and the storm god with a bow" (Cornelius 2002:203, no. 3 in the figure). By including an animal, a human, and a bird in their diagram, Cornelius and Deist emphasize the world as a space for living beings (cf. Days 4–6 in Genesis 1). Finally, these interpreters also explicitly picture the underworld as a dark pit (no. 7). This depiction corresponds with numerous references to "the Pit" in the Hebrew Bible, including Ps 88:6 [Heb. 7], which describes the Pit as a "dark and deep" region.

Despite the numerous similarities between biblical descriptions of cosmic geography and that which is reflected in ancient Near Eastern images, several points of difference can be noted. For instance, the Hebrew Bible has relatively little to say about the particularities of the netherworld. This is especially true of the priestly creation account, whose reference to "the Sea(s)" is not likely an allusion to the netherworld. The lack of such references puts the particularities of Genesis 1 into perspective. Rather than focusing on the netherworld or even death itself, the priestly creation account is about God creating circumstances that foster life and overcome chaos.

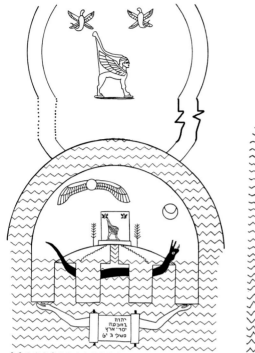

Fig 1.5. Schematic reconstruction of the biblical conception of cosmic geography by Keel. Source: Keel 1985:161 (adjusted with dotted lines and zigzags by Izaak J. de Hulster)

Fig. 1.6. Schematic reconstruction of the biblical conception of cosmic geography by Cornelius and Deist. Source: Cornelius 1994b:218 fig. 10

4. Mapping God's Presence in Genesis 1's Cosmic Geography

As a final step in this example of iconographic exegesis, I turn now to one theological implication of the above discussion. Namely, how can one talk about God's place and presence within ancient Israel's cosmic geography? Is God's activity localized in one realm or is it operative in multiple realms, or even beyond and outside of creation itself?

4.1. Heavenly Coordinates

The NRSV renders the Hebrew term *šāmmayīm* as "heavens" in Genesis 1:1. This translation rightly reflects the fact that *šāmmayīm* is grammatically plural by virtue of its dual ending. It also suggests a parallel situation with Egyptian and Mesopotamian cosmologies, both of which make reference to multiple heavens as distinct regions and/or distinct realms of different gods. Nevertheless, Genesis 1 deals only with a singular heavenly region ("heaven") despite the plurality of its grammatical form. According to the schematic diagrams discussed above (**figs. 1.5–6**), God's presence is localized in heaven, as indicated by the presence of the cherub throne and seraphs.

However, the situation is potentially more complicated in Genesis 1. In verse 6, God creates a "dome" (*rāqîʿa*) to separate the waters. This dome is often interpreted as the vault of heaven, a solid expanse or firmament that supports the waters above. In this view, the dome seems to be located just beneath heaven, the upper water storage. What is important to note for the purposes of this inquiry is that some interpreters, such as Walton (2011), have suggested that the dome could be the location of the heavenly council because the word *rāqîʿa* is used in Ezek 1:22–26 in reference to God's throne room.[4] This interpretation would lead to the conclusion that God (and the heavenly council) would have a place within the cosmos.

Walton's interpretation of the dome as a place for the heavenly council is at odds with other statements in his book, such as: "In Genesis [1], God is outside the cosmos, not inside or part of it" (177). He contrasts this observation with the ancient Near Eastern deities who are explicitly located inside the cosmic system. Thus, it might be better either to reject Walton's thesis that God is *only* outside the cosmos or to revise our understanding of cosmic geography in order to accommodate God's place outside the heavenly realm. Either adjustment would help foster an awareness that the Hebrew Bible contains different perspectives on the place of God, many of which are not easy to synthesize together. Furthermore, contra Walton, it appears that the dome in Genesis 1 (called "Sky" in v. 8) does not refer to a divine dwelling place but rather a region for celestial bodies. Therefore, in contrast to both Keel and Cornelius and Deist (§ 3.2), God cannot be assigned a dwelling place above the "dome" in Genesis 1 and thus have his presence located there.

Although heaven can be taken as God's domain, it is hard to locate. Rather than approaching heaven as a location, it is better to see it as a "thought-picture." In other words, ancient Israel's cosmic geography is not about localizing objects, but proclaiming Yhwh as ruler from heaven and among his people (cf. Houtman 1993). In Genesis 1, God, properly speaking, is beyond creation. In fact, the focus of this creation account is on the human realm. Nevertheless, while Yhwh is active within creation he can also be said to be "beyond" creation in a spatial sense (cf. Schmid 2012:89).

Ancient Near Eastern iconography can express such a "beyond" with a positioning "above" as in **fig. 1.7,** which depicts an ivory plaque from Megiddo with a Hurrian-Hittite perspective on the cosmos. The lower register represents wild bulls fighting each other in the mountains as a symbol for chaos. The middle registers are inhabited by heroes, mountain gods, and various hybrid figures. In the center one sees the vegetation goddess, and above her one more mountain god. The figures in the middle, and the last mentioned mountain god in particular, together carry the sun deity who is dressed like the king, depicted twice (possibly as morning and eve-

---

4   Furthermore, Walton refers to Job 37:18, which speaks about "spreading out" (*rqʿ*) "the sky" (*šaḥaq*), and Psalm 89:6–7, which locates the (heavenly) "council of holy ones" (*sôd-qĕdōšîm*) in this *šaḥaq*.

ning sun), and flanked by two double-headed figures that are (in a way like all the other figures with their hands lifted) "porters of heaven." The many figures carrying the sun deity and the figures next to the sun deity carrying the sun disk stress the supremacy of the sun deity and, by implication, the king. Thus, the positioning above implies the concept of "beyond." In a modern thought-picture, the notion of "beyond" might be expressed by two dotted lines or perhaps by a zigzag line (as added to **fig. 1.5**), both of which would imply a spatial and/or conceptual disjunction between two objects/ideas.

Fig. 1.7. Reconstruction of an ivory representing Hittite cosmology and royal ideology, found at Megiddo but probably produced in Hatti, ca. 1350–1150 BCE. Source: *IPIAO* 3: Fig. 978

4.2. Locating God's Presence: Beyond and Inside

In the ancient Near Eastern world, most deities were thought to reside inside the cosmos. In some respects, Genesis 1 also underlines God's active presence within the cosmos (cf. Smith 2010:11–37). For instance, a series of active verbs (making, blessing, and naming) implies God's involvement with creation "from the inside." Likewise, the work of "separating" that occurs in Days 1–3 might also be understood as activity that occurs within creation. Yet, in other respects, God might be said to be outside or beyond creation in ways that are different than what is found in ancient Near Eastern cosmologies. As an example, Genesis 1 does not deal with theogony (the birth of deities) or with theomachy (combat among deities). In addition, the fact that God speaks creation into being may suggest that he is localized in a place other than creation itself. These two ways of viewing God's spatial relationship with creation suggests God's supremacy (through the metaphors "outside" and "beyond") as well as his proximity (through his acts within creation).

God's "wind/spirit" (Heb. *rûaḥ*) is another way of speaking about divine presence in creation. As a prelude to the first act of creation, Gen 1:2 describes how the spirit of God "swept over the face of the waters." If the waters here are understood in light of the primordial ocean known from other ancient Near Eastern creation accounts, then a combat theme might be implied. The idea that God's creative activity entails (or is enabled by) combat with the seas/water is far more pronounced in Ps 74:12–17. The clear echo of Genesis 1 in the prologue to the Gospel of John also might imply a combat theme, for John 1:5 states: "The light shines in the darkness, and the darkness did not overcome it" (Feldmeier and Spieckermann 2011:271, 534). A third way in which God can be perceived as being present in the cosmos of Genesis 1 is through his "image" – that is, humankind (see chapter 2).

God's presence is not only beyond geographical location but also beyond chronological location. Whereas especially the Egyptian sun deity Aten's cult could not be practiced during his absence (**fig. 1.8** shows an open-air sanctuary during the day), Yhwh is active day and night (although in Genesis 1 Yhwh creates during six days), and can be praised at night as well (cf. Psalm 134). Even if someone experiences God's absence in a (metaphorical) night, God is present through the songs that he provides (Ps 42:8 "at night his song is with me;" cf. Spieckermann 2007). Irrespective of philosophical discussions about "space" (cf. Beuttler 2010), Yhwh is "the One who is actively present" (cf. Exod 3:14; Vriezen 1950). This conclusion of Genesis 1's cosmic geography has consequences for theology (cf. Janowski 2001:15–18): the creation is humankind's abode, Yhwh's sphere of life-giving action and blessing.

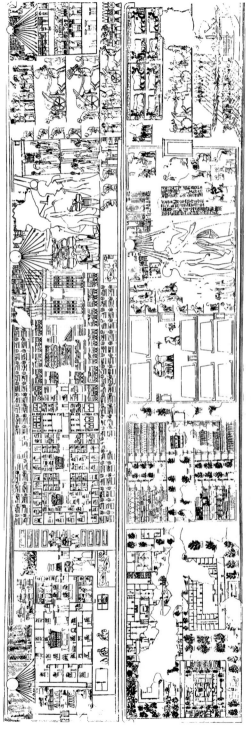

Fig. 1.8. Drawing (in the tomb of Meryra at Amarna) of the sun deity Aten's open-air sanctuary, 14th c. BCE, Amarna (Egypt). Source: Davies 1903: XXV

5. Conclusion

This chapter has compared the priestly creation account with ancient Near Eastern images of cosmic geography. The chapter shows how Genesis 1:1–2:4a focuses on the earthly realm, seemingly leaving aside not only the netherworld, but also the heaven(s). This has consequences for the way God's place and presence is perceived in Genesis 1. If God's relationship to creation were to be depicted in visual form today, one might separate the two with a dotted line or zigzag in order to indicate a conceptual distinction between God and creation.

Ancient images, of course, do not use dotted lines or zigzags. However, other conventions are present that indicate an analogous conceptualization for YHWH's "beyond" in Genesis 1, a text that also emphasizes how God is active within his creation. In numerous images discussed above, the arrangement of elements in the pictorial frame are not meant to depict what a subject would naturally look like to the observer (*Sehbild*), but rather to represent a thought-picture (*Denkbild*) that symbolically conveys an underlying concept. For instance, the Babylonian world map (**fig. 1.2**) presents Babylon at the center of the earth, marking the "end of the earth" with triangles representing islands. Likewise, in the schematic diagrams of biblical cosmic geography (**figs. 1.5–6**), it is possible to interpret the spatial location of heaven "above" the earth as an iconographic convention that indicates the way in which God's presence is "beyond" or "outside" of the cosmos. This observation about the nature of conceptual images not only aids the interpretation of ancient art but it also helps one better visualize the underlying concepts that inform descriptions of cosmic geography in Genesis 1:1–2:4a.

Assignment/Exercise

1. Hartenstein (2008:25–37) distinguishes three phases of how the Old Testament views God in relation to his temple:
    a. Temple as center of the world, the place of God's throne/dwelling (Isa 6:1–11; Ps 93:1–5).
    b. God's throne in heaven and heaven as God's throne (Isaiah 66; Psalms 103–104).
    c. God's transcendence beyond the world; this is related to the ban on images and also brings forward ideas about God's incomparability (Isa 40:12–23; Deut 4:11–13).
    In which of these would you place Genesis 1?
2. Study Psalm 113 and make a schematic drawing (*Denkbild*) of how it expresses (polarities within) cosmic geography. Compare your results with Eccl 5:1 and Isa 66:1–2 and discuss what theological consequences these verses imply with their cosmic geographies.

Bibliography

Cornelius, Izak. 1994b. "The Visual Representation of the World in the Ancient Near East and the Bible." *Journal of Northwest Semitic Languages* 20: 193–218.

Keel, Othmar. 1997b. *The Symbolism of the Biblical World: Ancient Near Eastern Iconography and the Book of Psalms.* Winona Lake, IN: Eisenbrauns.

Walton, John H. 2011. *Genesis 1 as Ancient Cosmology.* Winona Lake, IN: Eisenbrauns.

Chapter 2
The Image of God: Comparing the Old Testament with Other Ancient Near Eastern Cultures

Brent A. Strawn

1. The Problem of the *Imago Dei*

The concept of the "image of God" (*imago Dei*) is a problem. It is, of course, a very famous doctrine and has had a lively reception in the history of interpretation, especially in Christian theology. The *imago Dei* has been taken as referring to or as somehow having to do with everything from humanity's spiritual likeness to God, to our mental endowment, our external appearance, our upright posture, even our capacities for relating – and this is only to name a few of the possible interpretations (see, e. g., Westermann 1994:147–55; Jónsson 1988). But upon closer inspection, the problem of the *imago Dei* is actually two-fold: (1) Since it cannot possibly mean all of these things – at least not all of them *simultaneously* and probably also not *originally* – which, if any, of these interpretations is correct? The second, more fundamental problem is that (2) the image of God notion is notoriously un(der)defined in the Hebrew Bible – it appears only rarely and is never explained fully. This situation is no doubt what has led to so many different and distinct interpretations. Because, that is, the *imago*-notion is proverbially "open to interpretation" – it is a text in search of a context, to borrow language from Nathan MacDonald (2013) – exegetes have filled in the open space or rounded out the context with a vast host of explanations, some more likely than others. But if one is interested – even if only at the start of an investigation – with what the image of God might have meant in its original context (or *contexts*), then attention to *that* context(s) is crucial. Enter the comparative method and, for the purposes of the present volume, the study of ancient Near Eastern iconography.

The current chapter will employ iconography as a comparative tool that can be used to address a particular exegetical problem – namely, how to best understand unique or low-frequency terms, concepts, or motifs in the Hebrew Bible. As already noted, the *imago Dei* is one such instance. According to Claus Westermann,

> What is striking is that one verse about the [human] person, almost unique in the Old Testament, has become the center of attention in modern exegesis, whereas it has no such significance in the rest of the Old Testament. (1994:148)

Lacking extensive literary context on which to base an analysis, interpreters must, as it were, "construct" one. Whenever possible, contemporary biblical scholars have tended to focus heavily on the ancient world – the original historical context(s) of the biblical text – even in the case of motifs that are widely attested or occur with high frequency. Especially in the case of low-frequency concepts, the ancient context must move beyond the biblical text proper, which means the exegetical endeavor becomes a comparative exercise.

Before turning to a discussion of how scholars conduct such comparative inquiries (§ 2), one more "constructed" context should be acknowledged: in the absence of extensive literary context, readers (especially lay readers) often interpret the text in question in light of their own immediate contexts. In the modern period this means many readers read the early chapters of Genesis vis-à-vis scientific developments, whether appreciatively or antagonistically (cf. Gould 1999; White 1967). Seen from an historical perspective – one that prizes most highly the *original context(s)* of a biblical text, idea, or image – reading a text in light of today's contemporary context is not always wise and perhaps the worst option imaginable – at least at first. And yet, as we will see, this kind of reading also represents a kind of comparative approach, and thus can be justified, if it is carefully done.

2.   Comparative Approaches *in Nuce*

The comparative study of religion has a long and distinguished career, tracing back at least as far as the lectures Friedrich Max Müller gave to the Royal Institution of London in 1870 (see Müller 1893). Müller, depending on a famous statement by Goethe, argued that, in the case of religion, *"He who knows one, knows none"* (Müller 1893:13; his emphasis). Knowing only one religion will simply not suffice if someone wishes to discern "those elements, patterns, and principles that could be found uniformly in the religions of all times and places" (Pals 2006:4). The way to reach such conclusions was precisely via *comparison*. Writing in the early twentieth century, not too long after Müller, Otto Pfleiderer put it this way:

> It is a fact that only he really knows one religion who knows more than one religion. Not only does the study of comparative religions make us tolerant … it also teaches us to understand our own religion better because of the clearer differentiation between the essential and the accidental, the perennial and the temporary. (1907:65–66)

The clear emphasis on the common, universal, or essential vs. the different, local, or accidental is pronounced and noteworthy in early articulations of comparative religion.

Comparative approaches in the study of religion and its numerous subfields have, of course, developed in various ways since Müller's famous lectures and the work of those who followed after him. In the case of biblical studies proper, most comparisons have focused on common items with the assumption that these are likely to be related somehow, even in a rather direct ("genetic") fashion. So, among the principles that have guided biblical comparativists are the virtues of "geographical proximity" and "historical propinquity" (see Talmon 1991:386). The closer the two exemplars are in time and space, the more likely they are to be not only similar but related. In many ways, this valorization of proximate time and space in comparative methodology explains the great emphasis placed on ancient Near Eastern languages, literatures, and history in modern study of the Hebrew Bible.

The history of the discipline reveals that the search for similarity occasionally ran amok, leading to situations where everything in the Bible was seen as derived (both too simply and too directly) from this or that culture. "Pan-Babylonianism" was the term used for the attempt to trace everything back to Mesopotamia; "Pan-Ugariticisim" was another scholarly fad for some time after the discovery of the Late Bronze Age city-state of Ugarit in 1929. These sorts of (overly) enthusiastic approaches prompted a reaction among more sober-minded scholars who worried about "parallelomania" (Sandmel 1962), with some going so far as to argue that each civilization had its own "conceptual autonomy" (*Eigenbegrifflichkeit*) (Landsberger 1976). In its most extreme form, the latter understanding could be taken to mean that civilizations are, in the end and at root, simply *not* comparable. But if similarities (parallels) could be overstressed, so also could differences. One should beware parallelomania, to be sure, but one need not be "parallelo-noid" about similarities (Eilberg-Schwartz 1990:87–102).

In a number of important essays, William W. Hallo attempted to offer a synthesis of the thesis provided by "similarity" and the antithesis offered in "contrast," advocating what he calls a "contextual approach" (see, e. g., Hallo 1980, 1990; COS 1:xxv; COS 2:xiii). In this approach, both contrast (*difference* or "negative" comparison) and comparison (*similarity* or "positive" comparison) play important roles. To quote from one particularly important passage:

> The goal of the contextual approach is fairly modest. It is not to find the key to every biblical phenomenon in some ancient Near Eastern precedent, but rather to silhouette the biblical text against its wider literary and cultural environment and thus to arrive at a proper assessment of the extent to which the biblical evidence reflects that environment or, on the contrary, is distinctive and innovative over against it. (1990:3)

Hallo's contextual approach represents a real advance over studies that overemphasize either similarity or difference. But unfortunately even Hallo's improved approach is not foolproof. As I noted in § 1, the practice of contextualized comparison is an exercise in construction and creativity insofar as it inevitably entails selecting certain contexts for comparison while excluding others. So, as Howard Eilberg-Schwartz has noted, "determining just what is 'the context' is itself always an interpretive act. ... The twentieth-century refrain that cultural items have to be interpreted 'in their context' hides more than it reveals" (1990:95). Eilberg-Schwartz's second sentence may be overstated; but the interpretive nature of comparison is not in doubt, and is readily revealed by the politics that have so often been involved in scholarly comparisons (see Strawn 2009a:122–23).

Comparison is, then, a deeply hermeneutical enterprise. In Jonathan Z. Smith's memorable formulation, it is "by no means an innocent endeavor" but rather "a disciplined exaggeration in the service of knowledge" (1990:34, 52). This should not be taken as an invitation to total subjectivity, but it does suggest that even the most dispassionate comparisons are, in the end, quite personal. To again quote Smith, comparison "provides the means by which *we* 're-envision' phenomena as *our* data in order to solve *our* theoretical problems" (1990:52; his emphases). This is because identifying similarities and differences is "the result of mental operations undertaken by scholars in the interest of their intellectual goals" (J. Smith 2000:239). This means, of course, that no comparative exercise is value-free or completely "objective." It also means that the purpose(s) motivating the comparison should be made as transparent as possible. Comparisons, furthermore, should also be interesting and important (Strawn 2009a:127–29).

3. Comparative Data and the *Imago*

The application of comparative data to the opening chapters of Genesis is long-standing, going back to George Smith's remarkable discoveries regarding the flood story in the Epic of Gilgamesh and its relationship to Genesis 6–9 (see G. Smith 1876:1–18). From there, comparative work spread to other parts of the Primeval History (Genesis 1–11) and to the rest of the Bible. Easily one of the most famous of the textual details found in Genesis 1–11, comparatively-speaking, is the creation of humans in "the image/likeness of God" (*ṣelem/děmût ʾĕlōhîm*), which appears not only in Gen 1:26–27, but also in 5:1 (see also 5:3) and 9:6 (cf. Col 1:15; 2 Cor 4:4; Wis 2:23; Sir 17:1–13).

While an important notion, the *imago* is also an un(der)developed one in the Old Testament, as noted in § 1 above (see also Briggs 2010). Once again, this situation has led, somewhat ironically, to a secondary literature that seems "limitless" (Westermann 1994:148). It must suffice here to note four points of widespread scholarly agreement on the *imago Dei*:

1. There is a general consensus that the precise meaning of the *imago Dei* in its biblical context is unclear. There is not enough detail presented to know what, exactly, it signifies. A few scholars would suggest that this ambiguity may be intentional, but most assume that the *imago* did mean something specific at some point in time (and space). The question then becomes how to get at that specific "something." Various approaches have been employed, but comparative analysis has been a favorite one.
2. Comparative investigations have turned up much useful material from both Egypt and Mesopotamia that might apply to the biblical notion of the image of God. In brief:
    a. *Egyptian materials* speak of images (i. e., depictions) of *gods* and also speak of *Pharaoh* as the image of God/gods (cf. **fig. 2.1**);

b. *Mesopotamian materials* speak of *divine images* (i.e., depictions) and of the *king* as the image of God/gods, as is the case in Egypt, but they also speak of the *king's own image* as (i) *a votive object* within a temple or other worship setting (van der Toorn 1996:115) or (ii) as a *physical representation (statue)* of the king, especially in subjugated territories (cf. **fig. 2.2**; see Strawn 2009a:130; Middleton 2005:93–145).

Fig. 2.1. Diorite statue (ca. 42 cm [section height]), Khafre, Fourth Dynasty (2600–2480 BCE). Source: *SBW*: Fig. 260

Fig. 2.2. Stele (3.22 m) from Zinjirli, Esarhaddon, 680–669 BCE. Source: *SBW*: Fig. 407

3. Probably for linguistic reasons, most scholars have aligned the Hebrew *imago* more closely with the Mesopotamian materials.[1] The Hebrew term used for "image" (*ṣelem*) is, after all, cognate with the Akkadian term for the same (*ṣalmu*).

4. There is, furthermore, rather widespread agreement that the *imago Dei* in the Old Testament is a notion that is related to or derived from ancient Near Eastern royal ideology (which is not, of course, limited solely to Mesopotamian exemplars, despite the third point immediately preceding). In this light, the biblical image of God, par-

---

1 Most Mesopotamian texts are written in Semitic languages that are more closely related to Hebrew than is Egyptian, which belongs to a different language family.

ticularly in Genesis 1, is seen as a royal image, which designates the human being as unique in some way, elevated over the rest of creation. Still further, the ancient Near Eastern practice of placing images (*ṣalmū/ṣalmāni*) in subjugated regions could be seen as indicating that human beings exercise a similar sort of representative function for the deity vis-à-vis creation, which can in turn be viewed, in this particular comparative construction, as a territory that has been conquered or otherwise subdued.[2] So, for example, John T. Strong writes: "Humankind … was set up after God's victory and to declare God's dominion in a conquered region" (2008:631).

And yet, while there seems to be general agreement that the *imago Dei* is a royal image that presents the human being as a monarch figure, there is still much more to wonder about. Just *what kind of king* is the human being who is made in the image of God? It is at this point that the dialectic of similarity and difference that is so crucial to proper comparison must enter the picture. How does the biblical *imago* compare with the royal *imagines* (plural of *imago*) of the ancient Near East?

4. *Imagines* of the *Imago*?

The word "image" is, of course, a rather slippery one (Strawn 2008a). There are textual "images" as much as there are physical ones like those found in the iconographical record. Both are important when describing the "royal image" in antiquity. In some cases, the two types of images are found concurrently. For example, in celebrating the military exploits of his first regnal year, the Neo-Assyrian king Ashurnasirpal II (883–859 BCE) recorded that "I made an image of myself (and) wrote thereon the praises of my power" (Grayson 1991:197–98). A bit later in the same inscription he continues:

> fear of my dominion reached as far as Karduniaš [Babylonia], *awe* of my weapons overwhelmed Chaldea; I unleashed my brilliance upon the mountains on the banks of the Euphrates. I made an image of myself (and) wrote thereon (an account of) my victory and strength. I erected (it) in the city Suru. (The inscription reads): "Ashurnasirpal, the king whose strength is constantly praiseworthy, whose face is turned towards the desert, who delights in loosing his javelin." (Grayson 1991:214; his italics)

This is but one example of a myriad of other, similar inscriptions that could be adduced. Altogether, these images and inscriptions, typically made after military victories, functioned to declare the might and power of Assyria and its king(s). The enemies of Assyria and its ruler(s) constitute, therefore, a primary and proper audience for this royal rhetoric. The Assyrian *ṣalmu*, with or without inscription, thus *re*-presents

---

2   In point of fact, Genesis 1 is rather notable for its *lack* of any sort of combat mythology (see further below).

the king – his persona, dominance, and braggadocio – amidst those who have been defeated or who might consider throwing off the yoke of Assyria, even long after the king had returned to his capital city. This explains why the king's statue in colonized areas was a locus of obeisance and care by his dutiful subjects, or, conversely, something to be destroyed and defaced by rebels when they revolted.

The royal image, especially in Mesopotamian garb, has been the "comparable" most favored by scholars interested in comparing the biblical *imago Dei* to other *imagines*. Peter Enns, for example, has summarized the relationship of the ancient Near Eastern image to the biblical *imago Dei* in a discussion that is also concerned with the contemporary, scientific context that occupies so many modern readers (see § 1):

> [A]lthough what "image of God" means in its fullest biblical witness may be open for discussion, in Genesis it does not refer to a soul or a psychological or spiritual quality that separates humans from animals. It refers to humanity's role of ruling God's creation as God's representative. We see this played out in the ancient Near Eastern world, where kings were divine image-bearers, appointed representatives of God on earth. This concept is further reflected in kings' placing statutes of themselves (images) in distant parts of their kingdom so they could remind their subjects of their "presence." Further, idols were images of gods placed in ancient temples as a way of having a distant god present with the worshippers.
>
> Genesis 1:26 clearly operates within the same thought world. ... The image of God is not that spark in us that makes us human rather than animal – like reason, self-consciousness, or consciousness of God. In Genesis it means that humans represent God in the world, nothing less but certainly nothing more. This is not to dismiss the question of what makes us human and how humanity uniquely reflects God, especially given the challenge of evolution; but "image of God" is not the biblical way of addressing those ideas. (2012:xv)

Upon closer inspection, at least two distinct comparisons seem to be at play in Enns' remarks (widely shared by others), which may be outlined as follows:

	Ancient Near East		**Hebrew Bible**
(1)	Ancient Near Eastern monarch : Statue (*ṣalmu*) of the monarch in subjugated territory	»	Yʜwʜ : Human being as God's image (*ṣelem ʾĕlōhîm*) on earth
(2)	Ancient Near Eastern god(s) : Monarch	»	Yʜwʜ : Human being as God's image (*ṣelem ʾĕlōhîm*) on earth

These two ancient Near Eastern comparisons are not completely unrelated, given the ubiquitous presence of the gods in ancient Near Eastern royal theology, but they can be profitably differentiated insofar as the first (1) is concerned with the person of the monarch alone whereas the second (2) operates with the royal figure as representing the deity. The common denominator in the ancient Near Eastern analogy of god : monarch :: monarch : ṣalmu is, of course, the king. If one wishes to compare the ancient Near Eastern ṣalmu to the biblical ṣelem, then one needs further insight into the image of the ancient Near Eastern king.

The rhetoric of ancient Near Eastern rulers – and this is as true for the Ramessides of the New Kingdom in second-millennium Egypt as it is for the Neo-Assyrian kings of the first millennium (see Strawn 2005a:161–63, 174–78) – is often violent, especially in inscriptions meant for public display or dissemination. The violence in question, furthermore, was not limited to the human variety. Victories on the field of battle were often preceded by, juxtaposed with, or metaphorically referenced by victories in another field: the arena of the royal hunt (see Watanabe 2002; Strawn 2005a:161–74). Ancient Near Eastern monarchs loved to boast of their hunting successes. One example, again from Ashurnasirpal II, suffices to illustrate this claim:

> The gods Ninurta (and) Nergal, who love my priesthood, gave to me the wild beasts and commanded me to hunt. I killed 450 strong lions. I killed 390 wild bulls from my … chariot with my lordly assault. I slew 200 ostriches like caged birds. I drove 30 elephants into an ambush. I captured alive 50 wild bulls, 140 ostriches, (and) 20 strong lions from the mountains and forests. (Grayson 1991:291)

The royal hunt was, then – to borrow from William P. Brown's words – "a military campaign in miniature" (1999:358). The close connection between the hunt and military victory is reflected on numerous iconographic objects, including small seals from ancient Israel/Palestine (**figs. 2.3–4**; cf. Keel 1990).

Fig. 2.3. Scarab, LBA or early IA I (Ramesside). Source: Strawn 2005a: Fig. 4.139

Fig. 2.4. Steatite seal, LBA or early IA I (Ramesside). Source: Strawn 2005a: Fig. 4.142

Fig. 2.5. Clay bulla, Samaria, 7th c.
Source: Strawn 2005a: Fig. 4.109

As noted above, the king's enemies are sometimes depicted as animals to be vanquished in the inscriptions describing military battles. The animals that are metaphorically employed in this way include both domestic species that are decapitated or butchered, and various other wild animals – as is clear from Ashurnasirpal II's inscription. This metaphorical use of animal imagery "serves to stress the flight, fear, and subordinated status of the king's enemies" (Brown 1999:352). It also draws a parallel between the king's military prowess and his hunting prowess. These are *directly* (inter)related. Success *out in* the field (countryside) implies success *on the field* (of battle), and vice versa. It is thus no accident that the official seal of the Neo-Assyrian Empire depicts the king in hand-to-hand combat with a raging lion (**fig. 2.5**).

More could be said about the royal *imagines* in the ancient Near East, but even this much can be profitably compared with the biblical *imago Dei*. What happens when that is done, especially in a contextual approach that pays equal attention to similarity and difference?

Several of the key similarities have already been noted above, beginning with the close linguistic relationship between Akkadian *ṣalmu* and Hebrew *ṣelem*. This, along with other considerations, has led most scholars to argue that the biblical notion of humanity in the image of God is related to, if not actually derived from, ancient Near Eastern royal models. If so, the biblical presentation "figures" YHWH as the Great King who places humanity as his representative image in creation in order to govern for him in his stead. But at this very juncture, close attention to the typically violent rhetoric of ancient Near Eastern royal ideology (and theology) suggests some points of marked distinction (difference) between the biblical *imago* and, for example, the Neo-Assyrian *imagines*. Whether on the field of battle or in the hunt, the Neo-Assyrian king was master predator/hunter, "top of both the food chain and the chain of command" (Brown 1999:359). Still further, all of the king's killing – whether as warrior or huntsman – was sanctioned and supported by the gods.

It is striking how *non*-violent the biblical *imago* is in comparison. The human beings who are made in the image of God are immediately given a vegetarian diet (Gen 1:29; so also 2:16), which remains in place until the flood is over (Gen 9:2–3). Even when the shedding of blood for the purposes of eating meat is later permitted by God, it is carefully circumscribed and closely tied to the image of God:

> God blessed Noah and his sons, and said to them, "Be fruitful and multiply, and fill the earth. The fear and dread of you shall rest on every animal of the earth, and on every bird of the air, on everything that creeps on the ground, and on all the fish of the sea; into your hand they are delivered.

> Every moving thing that lives shall be food for you; and just as I gave you
> the green plants, I give you everything. Only, you shall not eat flesh with its
> life, that is, its blood. For your own lifeblood I will surely require a reckon-
> ing: from every animal I will require it and from human beings, each one
> for the blood of another, I will require a reckoning for human life. Whoever
> sheds the blood of a human, by a human shall that person's blood be shed;
> for in his own image [ṣelem ʾĕlōhîm] God made humankind." (Gen 9:1–6)

Neither should one miss the fact that, according to this understanding that the human
being is the image of the Divine King, the creational activity of this deity in Genesis 1 is
also devoid of violence, in strong contrast to so many other ancient Near Eastern creation accounts (see Middleton 2005:235–69; Garr 2003:191–211; Levenson 1994:122,
127). That is, not only is *God's royal image* (i. e., humanity) non-violent, so is the literary image (depiction) of *God, the Divine King.* Indeed, it is likely that the non-violence of the latter is what leads to the non-violence of the former. The non-violent
imago reflects the non-violent *Deus.* That is to be expected, given the *re*-presenta-
tional nature of *imagines.* To be sure, violence occurs elsewhere in the Hebrew Bible,
and elsewhere in the Primeval History – amidst both humans and God – but "in the
beginning" it was not so. The image (i. e., depiction) of God in Genesis 1 is peaceful,
with God's image (i. e., representative) at one with creation and its creatures. Admittedly, some interpreters have concluded that this peaceful portrait is complicated by
humanity's commission to "subdue" (*kbš*) and "have dominion" (*rdh*) over creation
(Gen 1:28). But even if these verbs often have violent connotations elsewhere (a point
that is not certain and debatable), here their meaning is carefully qualified with the
more peaceful language of "serving" (*šmr*) and "preserving" (*ʿbd*) in Gen 2:5, 15.

Both similarity and difference, then, are at work in a contextualized comparative
approach to the biblical *imago Dei* amidst its ancient Near Eastern congeners. The
biblical *imago Dei* may be a royal image but it is no monarch like the Neo-Assyrian
kings. More must be said, then, beyond asserting straightforwardly, "the biblical *imago
Dei* is derived from ancient Near Eastern royal ideology and theology," especially as
that assertion traffics almost exclusively in similarity. The statement is accurate as far
as it goes, but the question that immediately presents itself is: But *what kind of royal
image* (i. e., king) is the biblical *imago?* At this juncture, crucial points of dissimilarity
(difference) prove to be as important as what is the same or similar.

Before taking leave of this section, one further distinction should be noted between
the two datasets being compared here. In the Bible, the image of God is consider-
ably democratized vis-à-vis the ancient Near Eastern royal image. The conception of
the image does not apply only to the top of the food chain, solely to the master and
commander, uniquely to the king himself. It applies to human beings *more generally*
(*ʾādām,* "humankind," in Gen 1:26–27a) as well as in their differentiated parts (*zākār
ûnĕqēbâ,* "male and female" in Gen 1:27b) (see Middleton 2005:204, 20, 214, 227–28,
254). This is a noteworthy difference between what one finds in the biblical *imago*
and in the ancient Near Eastern *imagines.*

5. Imag(in)ing the *Imago/Imagines*

In conclusion, I wish to revisit the constructed nature of comparative endeavors and their purposes. What motivates a comparison like the one pursued here? Or, put differently, to what end(s) might such a comparison be pursued? To borrow (and alter slightly) Smith's formulation cited above, how has the preceding essay "re-envisioned phenomena as *my* data in order to solve *my* theoretical problems" (cf. J. Smith 1990:52)? What are the theoretical problems I am trying to solve? Given the very personal, even *interested* nature of comparison, transparency seems the best policy at this point.

So, first, one theoretical problem I am concerned with has to do with violence in the Bible. There is a good bit of that, both human and divine, but the comparative exercise conducted here suggests that in the broader (canonical) vision, this was not always so and was not by divine design – it was never intended to be that way "in the beginning" (Chapman 2013:64). This is a very important point, one that is readily available upon even a surface reading of the Bible, but one that becomes even more obvious and nuanced when viewed comparatively. It changes how one imagines (or, indeed, how one might "image") the biblical *imago* – both its human instantiation and its divine reflex.

A second theoretical problem concerns sustainability, especially in light of the blame that has often been laid at the door of the Bible for humanity's wanton destruction of the environment (cf. White 1967). The argument is that Genesis presents humans as in charge, ruling and subduing (*kbš* and *rdh*), and this has led to irresponsible management of creation and its resources. Such a reading of the biblical materials is, however, quite poor (see further E. Davis 2008). Be that as it may, iconography – a key tool in the comparative enterprise – proves helpful with this theoretical problem as well.

For example, **figs. 2.6–7** can be understood as evoking the kind of royal image that rules or dominates, like a monarch or mighty hunter, but with significant limitations. There is, then, both similarity and difference at work in these depictions and the biblical *imago* and ancient Near Eastern *imagines*. To be more specific, the rule or domination that may be operative in the biblical *imago* is not willy-nilly, but exercised *on behalf of* those who need assistance and help. Here too there are similarities, not just differences, between the biblical *imago* and ancient Near Eastern *imagines*. It pays to recall that a frequent metaphor for kingship throughout the ancient Near East is that of the shepherd (see Good 1983; cf. also 1 Sam 17:34–37; Psalm 23).

In these two seals, the needy entities in question are, notably, *animals* – the caprids directly in front of the human figure and directly underneath the lion's paws. If violent action is required, that is, it is to be performed *for the sake of the weak to protect them from certain death at the hands (or paws) of deadly and chaotic predators.* Such violence is not sport – killing for fun – nor does it serve primarily to underscore the essential power of the hunter. It is, rather, quite pragmatic and protective, in defense of those that need help. Once again, imaging or imagining the biblical *imago* in this comparative light has significant payoff in hermeneutical and ethical arenas.

Fig. 2.6. Seal, Middle Assyrian Period (1350–1000 BCE). Source: Strawn 2005a: Fig. 4.22

Fig. 2.7. Seal, Neo-Assyrian Period (9th–7th c. BCE). Source: Strawn 2005a: Fig. 4.55

To be sure, including iconography stretches the work of comparison as it has traditionally been pursued. The same is true when it becomes clear – perhaps for the first time – that any comparative analysis is influenced by contemporary concerns. The present essay is no exception, as it has been colored by sustainability issues. But, as noted above, a purpose that guides or somehow motivates a comparison does not invalidate either the comparison itself or the comparative data because *all* comparisons are motivated, purposed in some way. Far from invalidating the comparison, the motivation or purpose for which it is undertaken make it and the comparative data *interesting*, not to mention potentially helpful, even and perhaps especially to present day readers in their contemporary contexts with their particular concerns.[3] The latter, too, are "comparables" that can profitably be compared to the biblical material. In the end, after all, *we* are the ones that conduct our comparisons and we ought to do so about *things that matter* to us. Otherwise, the comparative endeavor loses much of its *raison d'être* and significance for all but the most committed of antiquarians.

Assignment/Exercise

The present chapter conducted a comparative analysis of the biblical *imago Dei* that was motivated by and concerned with matters of violence and non-violence, ecology and sustainability. Conduct your own investigation of the image of God with reference to a different concern, purpose, or motivation (see § 1 for some different interpretations of the *imago,* or perhaps consider the nature of humans in God's image as created both "male and female"). How are your results different? Does the comparison work as well? Alternatively, consider another low-frequency motif or notion that you are aware of in the Bible that lends itself to comparative analysis. Try a comparative approach to better understand it and try to incorporate ancient Near Eastern iconography in your study.

---

3   As an interesting counter-example, see Zenger's too-easy dismissal (in Hossfeld and Zenger 2011:663) of Strawn and LeMon 2007.

Bibliography

Briggs, Richard S. 2010. "Humans in the Image of God and Other Things Genesis Does Not Make Clear." *Journal of Theological Interpretation* 4:111–26.

Garr, W. Randall. 2003. *In His Own Image and Likeness: Humanity, Divinity, and Monotheism.* Culture and History of the Ancient Near East 15. Leiden: Brill.

Jónsson, Gunnlaugur A. 1988. *The Image of God: Genesis 1:26–28 in a Century of Old Testament Research.* Coniectanea biblica: Old Testament Series 26. Lund: Almqvist & Wiksell.

MacDonald, Nathan. 2013. "A Text in Search of Context: The *Imago Dei* in the First Chapters of Genesis." In *Leshon Limmudim: Essays in the Language and Literature of the Hebrew Bible in Honour of A. A. Macintosh,* edited by David A. Baer and Robert P. Gordon, 3–16. Library of Hebrew Bible/Old Testament Studies 593. London: Bloomsbury.

Middleton, J. Richard. 2005. *The Liberating Image: The* Imago Dei *in Genesis 1.* Grand Rapids: Brazos.

Strawn, Brent A. 2009a. "Comparative Approaches: History, Theory, and the Image of God." In *Method Matters: Essays on the Interpretation of the Hebrew Bible in Honor of David L. Petersen,* edited by Joel M. LeMon and Kent Harold Richards, 117–42. Society of Biblical Literature Resources for Biblical Study 56. Atlanta: Society of Biblical Literature.

Westermann, Claus. 1994. *Genesis 1–11: A Continental Commentary.* Translated by John J. Scullion. Minneapolis: Fortress.

Chapter 3
The "Pagan" Prehistory of Genesis 22:1–14:
The Iconographic Background of the Redemption of
a Human Sacrifice

Thomas Staubli

1.   Introduction

For centuries, interpreters have puzzled over Gen 22:1–14, which is often referred to as the binding of Isaac, or the Akedah. The story itself is fraught with ambiguity, and questions abound concerning the theological and ethical implications of its portrayal of God and Abraham. A full treatment of these issues lies far beyond the scope of the present chapter. Instead, the purpose of this inquiry is to demonstrate how an evaluation of a particular motif in ancient Near Eastern iconography can shed new light on the prehistory of a key theme in Genesis 22 – namely, the notion of divine redemption of a human sacrifice.

Before turning to the iconographic data, it will be helpful to briefly discuss one aspect of the interpretation of Gen 22:1–14. In many popular readings, the binding of Isaac story is thought to play a central role in the self-understanding and theological distinctiveness of monotheistic traditions. For instance, in Jewish and Christian circles Abraham is widely understood as a model of faith, responding without hesitation when he encounters "a God of love, a God of mercy, to whom each life is precious" (Berman 1997:57). Early Jewish and Christian communities drew on this story as an essential background narrative for the discontinuation of the sacrificial system after the destruction of the Second Temple. In the New Testament, what Abraham ended up not having to do (i. e., sacrifice his son) is ultimately thought to be accomplished by God himself, who gave his own son, Jesus, as a type of redemption offering. Muslim interpreters go one step further when they point to Ibrahim (Abraham in Arabic) as the first Muslim, ready for a total *Islam* (which means "submission") to God's will (Quran Sura 37,100–11).

The story of the binding of Isaac is also deeply embedded in the liturgical memory of Jewish, Christians, and Muslim traditions. Jews blow the *Shofar* on Rosh Hashanah (the New Year), thereby recalling God's provision of the ram and salvation of Isaac at twilight on Sabbath eve. Christians read the story of the Akedah during the Easter vigil service as a landmark on the way to God's redeeming work for humankind. Muslims remember the story of Ibrahim during the main festival of the year, a three-day feast called Eid al-Adha ("feast of the sacrifice"), by praying and, for those who can afford it, slaughtering a ḥalal (ritually pure) domestic animal.

Furthermore, Gen 22:1–14 is often thought to underscore a sharp contrast between ancient Israelite religion and so-called "pagan" traditions, especially as it pertains to practices of human/child sacrifice. While Abraham is, at first, called to sacrifice his only son, God ultimately intervenes, sparing Isaac by providing an alternative sacrifice in the form of a ram. In this sense, the Akedah might be understood to repudiate paganism and/or reflect "a transformation of pagan values, specifically, the idea that the pagan gods of nature, embodying as they do projections of human emotions and desires, need to be assuaged and flattered and, as a result, became recipients of the ultimate pacification by human beings, by the periodic sacrifice of their own kind" (Lippman 2005:68).

In these ways, Gen 22:1–14 constitutes an important reference point for various beliefs and practices in monotheistic religions (Gellman 1994). Its view of both God and sacrifice is presumed to be distinctly monotheistic, or at least generative for later monotheistic conceptions about divine redemption. Yet, this line of interpretation does not tell the whole story. What if it turns out that divine redemption in a moment of near sacrifice is not a concept unique to monotheistic religions? What if rather than offering a contrast to so-called "pagan" notions of sacrifice, Genesis 22 actually builds on an already existing pattern within these systems? In other words, what if the binding of Isaac story is not the starting point of something totally new in religious history but rather reflects a motif that long predates the Hebrew Bible itself?

Iconographic exegesis offers a promising tool for investigating these and related questions about the binding of Isaac story. As will be shown below, an analysis of ancient pictorial sources reveals that the most central feature of the story – the divine redemption of a human sacrifice – was known in the form of certain iconographic constellations, or patterns of pictorial elements through which a given theme is expressed.[1] As such, it is possible to identify a visual – and one might add, "pagan" – prehistory of the divine redemption motif in Genesis 22. The following analysis demonstrates the value of applying iconographic methods to the study of religious history and the conceptual background of biblical literature.

2. Redemption Scenes in Mesopotamian and Syrian Art

The earliest known iconographic expression of the substitution of a human sacrifice with an animal offering is found in the form of Old Babylonian art from the nineteenth century BCE. Less than one hundred years later this constellation is also attested in the western parts of the ancient Near Eastern world, albeit in a slightly different form.

---

1   For further discussion of the idea of constellations, see Assmann 1977:29 and 1982:14.

2.1. Old Babylonian Cylinder Seals

A nineteenth-century BCE Babylonian cylinder seal, likely from Sippar, displays what might be characterized as a redemption scene (**fig. 3.1**).

This seal, which resides in the British Museum, has been described by Dominique Collon (1986:169) as follows:

> Five figures stand before the ascending Sun god who rests his foot on a trapezoidal, scale-patterned mountain. From left to right these are: a figure resembling the king with a mace, but with a high-crowned head-dress and his hair in a fish-tail denoting divinity, who stands on a scale-patterned dais or mountain; a smiting god who is similarly attired, who brandishes a *harpe*-sword and who tramples one enemy under foot while grasping another by the shoulder – this figure is half kneeling, and turns back to look at the god, while a bird of prey dives towards him; the suppliant goddess; a small kilted priest who stands on a two-tiered, paneled dais and holds a cup and pail; and the robed king with an animal offering (damaged by a chip).

The smiting god (or mythic victor) is also represented in a very similar constellation on another seal (**fig. 3.2**) where, in addition, he holds a whirling mace in his left hand. The sequence of the smiting god, the suppliant goddess (*lama*), and the robed king with an animal offering is similar to that seen in **fig. 3.1**. The fifth figure with cup and pail behind the ascending Sun god (Shamash) corresponds to the small standing figure with the cup in **fig. 3.1**, but **fig. 3.2** lacks the royal figure on the mountain. A similar constellation appears on an Old Babylonian seal impression (**fig. 3.3**), this time with the inscription ᵈEN.ZU (*Su'en,* "moon-god") between the first figure on the left and the smiting god. A dog and a goat-kid appear above the menaced human and a lunar symbol and a head appear between Shamash and the king, who bears the offering.

Fig. 3.1. Cylinder seal, Old Babylonian period (19th c. BCE), Sippar (?), BM26180. Source: Author's drawing after Collon 1986: Pl. XXXI no. 424

Fig. 3.2. Cylinder seal, Old Babylonian period (19th c. BCE), Mesopotamia, BM89103. Source: Author's drawing after Collon 1986: Pl. XXXI no. 421

A condensed version (**fig. 3.4**) of the same constellation, which still contains the lunar symbol but lacks the fifth figure, presents an enthroned Shamash. The legend reads Na-ra-am-ì-lí-šu. A vervet monkey appears to the left of the smiting god and another animal, perhaps a lion, stands on the dais before the smiting god. Another variant (**fig. 3.5**) has what appears to be a dog behind the throne as well as a scale between the suppliant goddess and the king. On other seal impressions a smiting god, who stands over a human in a ready-to-strike position, is accompanied by fighting hybrid creatures, gods, men, and lions (**figs. 3.6–8**). Though in fragmentary form, several seal impressions depict the smiting god with the whirling mace (**figs. 3.9–10**).

Fig. 3.3. Seal impression, Old Babylonian period (19th c. BCE), Mesopotamia, BM 92649. Source: Blocher 1992: Abb. 36

Fig. 3.4. Seal impression, Old Babylonian period (19th c. BCE), Mesopotamia, BM 82463. Source: Blocher 1992: Abb. 12

Fig. 3.5. Seal impression, Old Babylonian period (19th c. BCE), Mesopotamia, BM 80110. Source: Blocher 1992: Abb. 7

Fig. 3.6 Seal impression, Old Babylonian period (19th c. BCE), Mesopotamia, BM 82447. Source: Blocher 1992: Abb. 225

Fig. 3.7. Seal impression, Old Babylonian period (19th c. BCE), Mesopotamia, BM 80140. Source: Blocher 1992: Abb. 61

Fig. 3.8. Seal impression, Old Babylonian period (19th c. BCE), Mesopotamia, BM 22704. Source: Blocher 1992: Abb. 153

Fig. 3.9. Seal impression, Old Babylonian period (19th c. BCE), Mesopotamia, BM 82449. Source: Blocher 1992: Abb. 111

Fig. 3.10. Seal impression, Old Babylonian period (19th c. BCE), Mesopotamia, BM 78760. Source: Blocher 1992: Abb. 158

The full version of the constellation on the seals and seal impressions of the early-nineteenth century BCE seems to represent the substitution of the life of the menaced human (i.e., the one about to be struck by the smiting god) with a goat-kid, thanks to the intervention of the suppliant goddess before Shamash, the master of justice. The more condensed versions constitute a type of recapitulation of the full version. These interpretations are based on the following observations about the visual syntax, or arrangement, of this iconographic constellation:

1. The smiting god threatening (or menacing) a human figure, the suppliant goddess, and the offering of a four-footed animal (lamb or goat-kid) form a horizontal sequence in front of the Sun god (**figs. 3.1–5**).[2]
2. In condensed versions of the constellation (**fig. 3.7**), the menaced human figure and the redemption offering are placed in a vertical line. The animal is located in the upper register of the image, in what might be called the "celestial" area insofar as it is on the same level as the astral symbols of the highest gods (cf. **fig. 3.3**).
3. The substitution offering (in the form of the recumbent goat-kid) is found only in this specific constellation on Old Babylonian seals. In an interesting variant of the constellation, the goat-kid is emphasized by its triple representation, where it appears between the suppliant goddess and the smiting god, in its usual place in the celestial area, and under the foot of the second representation of the smiting god. In the latter case, the goat-kid appears in the place of the menaced person, who is now standing naked before the smiting god in a gesture of supplication (**fig. 3.11**).
4. In certain seals, multiple figures with nearly identical headdresses appear. Most likely, this indicates the same person in different acts within the same iconographic constellation. This is especially clear in **fig. 3.11**, where the smiting god

---

2 For a smiting god menacing a human in front of three suppliant goddesses but without a substitution offering, see Teissier 1984:235 no. 455.

is represented twice, once in front of the suppliant goddess and once in front of the suppliant naked figure.

5. The position of the suppliant goddess between the smiting god and the offering king indicates an intervention in favor of the threatened figure. This is again especially clear from **fig. 3.11** where the goddess and the naked figure are back-to-back and form a central pair between the doubled smiting god.

6. The gesture of the suppliant goddess resembles that of the menaced human under the smiting god's hand or foot. This formal correspondence suggests that the goddess and the human express similar attitudes.

7. The whirling of the mace may indicate that the act is one of menacing and not (yet) killing – that is, the mace is being wielded, but it has not yet delivered the deathblow.

8. The presence of a priestly figure in certain versions of the constellation implies a cultic context for the scene (see also Collon 1986:139).

In sum, the visual syntax of this iconographic constellation suggests a motif in which the life of a human figure is threatened by a smiting god. Instead of receiving the deathblow, the human figure is spared when a suppliant goddess intervenes, offering a lamb or goat-kid in his place. A cultic setting is suggested in some, but not all, versions of this constellation.

2.2. The Constellation Spreads North and West

Admittedly, the iconographic constellation described above is rather rare. However, when it does occur the visual syntax is relatively consistent, and as we will see, the constellation has a wide geographic distribution, especially in sanctuaries and dynastic seals. After the collapse of the Old Babylonian culture, the motif appears in Hittite (**fig. 3.12**) and Old Syrian glyptic art, both in the East (Mari; **fig. 3.14**) and the West (Alalakh; **fig. 3.15**), and it persists also in northern (Nuzi; **fig. 3.16**) and southern (**fig. 3.13**) parts of Mesopotamia.

On a cylinder seal from Kültepe (**fig. 3.12**), the substituting animal is positioned beneath a Janus, or double-faced, mediator. The angular orientation of the animal's body mirrors that of the menaced person below the smiting god's foot. This visual feature underscores the animal's function as a substitute for the menaced person who appears on the other side of the suppliant goddess in the center of the scene. The suppliant goddess appears in her Syro-Hittite manifestation as a naked goddess. The goddess also replaces in some way the Sun god, who is absent in this northern variant of the constellation. The original three-part constellation (smiting god, *lama*, Sun god) is reduced to a two-part constellation here (smiting god, naked goddess).

Fig. 3.11. Cylinder seal, Old Babylonian period (19th c. BCE), Mesopotamia. Source: Author's drawing after Porada 1948: No 427E

Fig. 3.12. Seal impression, Kültepe, ca. 18th c. BCE. Source: Winter 1983: Abb. 82

The contrast with the southern concept is illuminated by **fig. 3.13,** where all the elements of the traditional constellation (smiting god with whirling mace, menaced human with suppliant gesture, substitute animal above him in the celestial realm, a scale, and an offering before Shamash) appear with the exception of the traditional *lama* figure, who is replaced by the naked goddess as suppliant. In the West the naked goddess typically appears on a bull instead of on a lion (see below **fig. 3.17b, register 2, side A**). A seal from Mari (**fig. 3.14**) at the frontier of the Old Babylonian and the Old Syrian cultures combines the traditional southern and the new northern traditions by juxtaposing the *lama* and the naked goddess, both of whom demonstrate the same supplicating gesture.

Fig. 3.13. Cylinder seal, Mesopotamia, mid-second millennium. BCE. Source: Winter 1983: Abb. 166

Fig. 3.14. Cylinder seal, Mari, 18th c. BCE. Source: Winter 1983: Abb. 266

A dynastic seal from Alalakh (**fig. 3.15**) may be understood as a very abbreviated form of the constellation under consideration. The ruling king in his best clothes (far left) embodies the smiting god. The likewise richly enrobed protecting goddess of the city takes on the role of the suppliant goddess on behalf of the suppliant under the king's foot. The Egyptianizing *ankh*-symbol in the goddess's right hand may signify life not only for the ruling king (horizontal axis) but also for the one dominated by him (vertical axis). The king's staff, which marks the vertical axis, probably symbolizes his power to decide life and death.

Fig. 3.15. Seal image, reconstructed from different impressions, from Alalakh Level VII (17th c. BCE), found in Level IV (15th c. BCE). Source Collon 1975:12 f., 170f, Pl. XII

Fig. 3.16. Seal impression, Nuzi, 15th–14th c. BCE. Source: Stein 1993: No. 381

2.3. The Stele from Sanctuary G3 at Ebla

This iconographic constellation is also found in a sophisticated Middle Bronze Age Syrian artifact – namely, the basalt stele from the forecourt of sanctuary G3 in the temple of the city goddess of Ebla (**fig. 3.17a–b**).[3] The banquet scene on the front of the stele (A3) is divided into two sub-registers (a, b), with the sacrifice in the upper register and the scene of entertainment before the seated ruler in the lower register. This central scene is framed by a visual chiasm in which images on side B, registers 2 and 4, mirror images on side C, registers 4 and 2, respectively (i. e., B2/C4; B4/C2).

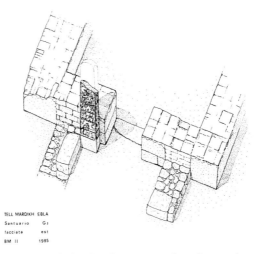

TELL MARDIKH EBLA
Santuario   G₃
facciata   est
BM II   1985

Fig. 3.17a. The basalt stele in its secondary place on the left side of the entrance of the sanctuary G3, the temple of Ebla's city goddess. Source: Matthiae 1987: Fig. 2

---

3   The stele was moved here during a temple renovation. In the first phase of the temple, it was probably located in a place where it was visible from all sides (Matthiae 1987:454).

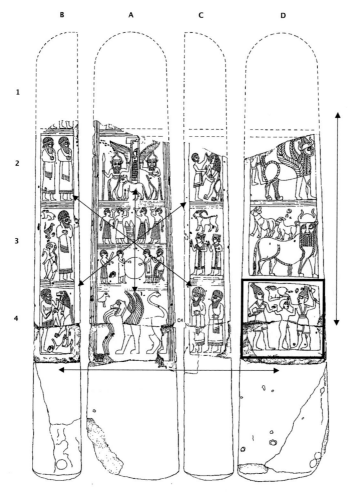

Fig. 3.17b. Basalt stele with reliefs, Ebla, forecourt of sanctuary G3, early 18th c. BCE. Source: Idlib Museum 3003

The same scene is similarly depicted on a cultic basin from two other Eblaite sanctuaries: B (= Matthiae, Pinnock, and Scandone 1995:422 Fig. 291) and D (= *IPIAO* 2 Nr. 497). In the uppermost preserved register (A2), the image of the goddess appears in the winged shrine, above a bull, flanked and protected by bull-men. In a more compressed form, the constellation of the banquet in front of the goddess with her divine entourage (A2) can be found on a contemporary cylinder seal in the BIBLE+ORIENT collections at the University of Fribourg (**fig. 3.18**).

The lowest scene on the front side of the stele shows a water-spewing dragon (A4). This creature is the old carrier-animal of the rain goddess and the storm god during the Akkadian period as well as in the ancient Babylonian period (cf. **fig. 3.19**). The positioning of the goddess (A2) over the dragon (A4) suggests the important function of the cult in controlling chaotic forces and appeasing, stimulating, and praising benevolent powers. The diagonally placed scenes in which a human figure subdues a lion (C2/B4) emphasize the goddess's control over nature. Furthermore, a cultic context is implied by the diagonally placed priests (B2/C4) as well as what appears to be an additional priest and two demi-gods (?) in B3 and C3, respectively.

Fig. 3.18. Cylinder seal, Kültepe Level II-seal, early 18th c. BCE, Syrian style. Source: Keel-Leu and Teissier 2004: Nr. 306

Fig. 3.19. Cylinder seal, Akkadian period (2340–2193 BCE). Source: Keel-Leu and Teissier 2004: Nr. 79

The upper registers on the backside (D2–3) depict two different hybrid creatures, one with wings (D2) and one without (D3). In an analogous manner to the investiture image of Mari (*IPIAO* 2, Nr. 434), the upper registers (D1) probably contained an additional hybrid creature in the form of a winged sphinx. Taken together, these hybrid creatures represent three guarding and protecting beings, of which the highest one protects the heavens (most probably represented by celestial emblems and their venerators in the destroyed scenes B1, A1, and C1), the second one protects the sphere of the goddess (B2, A2, C2), and the third one (B3, A3, C3) protects the herd, out of which comes the sacrificial animals.

Recognizing this progression can help us to interpret the lowest image on the reverse side (D4). It most likely depicts the protection of the human sphere. Indications can be found in the lion-fighting scene of this register (B4), showing a threatened human-headed (?), four-legged creature saved by the hero in contrast to the diagonally arranged complementary scene (C2), where this element is missing. In D4 the active protecting power is not a hybrid but the twice-appearing smiting god, armed once with a dagger and once with a battle-axe. The doubling of the smiting god recalls **fig. 3.11.** The person being threatened is naked. In the contemporary glyptic art of Alalakh, this person is sometimes depicted in a victorious pose, sometimes in a fight with other naked people, and sometimes subordinated, but never dead. He takes an intermediate role between the hero and the enemy or the demon, respectively (Collon 1975: Pl. 37).

The goat-kid above the threatened figure is the substitute animal from our constellation. It is an animal from the sacred flocks of the goddess (A2), protected and blessed by priests and a bull-man in register 3 (B, C, D). In this sense, the goddess saves the life of the endangered person by offering an animal from her own sphere of protection (the herds) for sacrifice.

The representation of the redemption constellation as part of a complex composition depicting the realm of the goddess and the various liturgies (banquet, music, singing and performing, offering) that occur within her sacred precinct suggests that redemption ceremonies took place in the context of the main sanctuary of the city-state. They were not only acts of public importance but were also theologically linked to the realm of the goddess – the compassionate one, the protector of the life of animals and humans.

3. Excursus: Egyptian Redemption Scenes

Before switching to the story of Isaac's redemption, I would like to mention two Egyptian evocations of redemption as an important cultic institution during the Eighteenth and Nineteenth Dynasties. In those imperialistic days of Egypt's history (i.e., sixteenth through twelfth centuries BCE), we find images of sacrificial cattle in funeral and cultic contexts with the heads of foreigners/enemies depicted between their horns instead of the usual floral decorations. Sometimes they are illustrated in such a way that their horns become the supplicating arms of those figures. The motif is first attested in the Tomb of Huy (**fig. 3.20**). Examples of Nubians and Asians are found in the procession reliefs of the Luxor-temple (**figs. 3.21–22**). Further evidence of this motif comes from Kawa and Bet el-Wali. This is a concise iconographic way of expressing that the sacrificial animal is identified with the foreigner/enemy and represents his substitution.

Fig. 3.20. Wall painting, Tomb of Huy, Thebes West, Tutankhamun, 1333–1323 BCE, in situ. Source: Davies and Gardiner 1926: Pl. 30

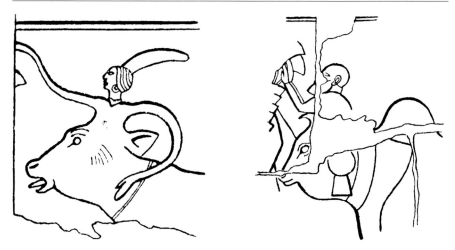

Figs. 3.21–22. Reliefs, Temple of Luxor, procession, Ramses II, 1279–1213 BCE, in situ. Source: Leclant 1956: figs. 10–11

Furthermore, there is evidence for the redemption of a near sacrifice as part of important official ceremonies in main temples. In an analogous placement to that of the stele in front of the Ishtar temple of Ebla, we find redemption scenes in front of the entrance to the great Amun temple in Karnak. The oldest one is from the time of Sethos I (1273–1279 BCE; **figs. 3.23a–b**), who conquered the rural Canaanite population of the Levant, called the Shasu, and consecrated a great number of his prisoners of war to Amun.

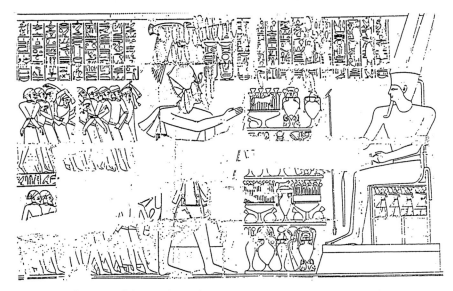

Fig. 3.23a. Redemption of Shasu in front of Amun. Source: Staubli 1991: fold-out plate I (scene V)

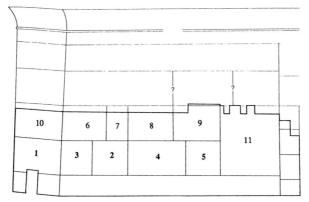

Fig. 3.23b. Schema of the military campaign against Palestine under Sethos I, 1290–79 BCE, in the northeastern corner of the Hypostyle hall of the great Amun temple in Karnak (fig. 23a corresponds to scene no. 5). Source: Staubli 1991:49 fig. 1

They are depicted on the exterior northeastern corner of the Great Hypostyle Hall. The battle and triumphant scenes are arranged in such a way that the consecration of the prisoners of war before Amun forms the conclusion of the image sequence. They constitute a link between the story of the military campaigns and the ritual of the consecration and redemption, which was probably enacted at this location. The redemption is expressed visually by the heavy tribute of the conquered, depicted *between* the deity and the Pharaoh, while the prisoners are standing *behind* the Pharaoh. A further indication for the redemption is contained in the words coming from the mouths of the prisoners:

> Hail to thee! How great is your name, how mighty your power! Blessed is the land that acts in partnership with you, and miserable those who attack your borders – enduring your Ka. We knew nothing of Egypt; our fathers had not entered into it. Give us the breath that you give. (Staubli 1991:56)

The prisoners are presented in a borderline situation between condemnation and redemption by virtue of the fact that they are presented as praising the name and power of Amun, condemning Egypt's enemies, claiming to be the first of their people to enter Egypt, and asking for breath.

Two generations later under Merneptah (1213–1203 BCE) an analogous sequence of images is created closer to the front on the so-called "Cour de la Cachette." Here too, the redemption scene creates the conclusion, as well as an equivalent to the peace treaty of Qadesh (Staubli 1991:58 with **fig. 2**).

The Egyptian depictions illustrate that, here as well, humans were not sacrificed before the deity but were instead redeemed. The redemption was depicted iconographically and, most likely, also enacted ritually at a prominent location as a sign not only of victory but also of the philanthropic nature of the deity.

4. The Pattern of the Redemption Constellation in Genesis 22

Turning now to Gen 22:1–14, the next step in iconographic exegesis is to explore whether aspects of the binding of Isaac story are congruent with the iconographic constellation of divine redemption scenes found in the artwork discussed above (§ 4.1). In doing so, additional questions can be raised about the possible association of Gen 22:1–14 with the sanctuary of a redeeming goddess (§ 4.2) and the significance of the placement of this story as the culmination of the Abraham cycle (§ 4.3).

4.1. Redemption and a Multi-Figurative Divinity

According to Gen 22:1–14, it is God (*'ĕlōhîm*) who asks for the sacrifice, and it is the angel of the YHWH (*mal'ak yhwh*) who stops it. The unfolding of these events creates a tension for purely monotheistic interpretations. Namely, God's actions do not seem to be coherent: he asks for something that, in the end, he prevents from happening.

Indeed, early retellings of the story try to resolve the contrasting behavior of the two divine actors (i. e., God and the angel of YHWH). For instance, the book of Jubilees (17:16) ascribes Elohim's role to Mastema, a figure similar to Satan in the book of Job: "And the prince Mastema came and said before God, 'Behold, Abraham loves Isaac his son, and he delights in him above all things else; bid him offer him as a burnt-offering on the altar, and Thou wilt see if he will do this command, and Thou wilt know if he is faithful in everything wherein Thou dost try him.'" While Mastema takes on God's role, an unnamed figure (the "I" in 18:9–10) takes on the role of the angel of YHWH: "And I stood before him, and before the prince Mastema, and the Lord said, 'Bid him not to lay his hand on the lad, nor to do anything to him, for I have shown that he fears the Lord.' And I called to him from heaven … " (18:9). Jubilees enlarges the repertoire of figures in the older constellation of the Old Babylonian cylinder seals. The conflict between the smiting god (Prince Mastema) and the interceding figure (the "I" in 18:9) plays out before the highest god (YHWH). Benno Jacob pursues this line of interpretation when he suggests that the tempter is not God but, similarly to the scenario in the book of Job, "one of his heavenly servants, an overzealous subordinate, doubting perfect human submission to God" (Jacob 2000:492).[4]

In Pirqe de Rabbi Eliezer (ch. 31), God's role as tester is not questioned, but the role of interceding angels is accentuated, and again an additional deity appears: "Like a high priest he brought near his meal offering, and his drink offering; and the Holy One, blessed be He, was sitting and beholding the father binding with all (his) heart and the son bound with all (his) heart. And the ministering angels cried aloud and

---

4   My translation of Jacob 2000:492: "… einer seiner himmlischen Diener, ein übereifriger, vollkommene menschliche Gottergebenheit bezweifelnder Untergebener." The sentence is not to be found in the English edition of his commentary (cf. Jacob 2007:142).

wept, as it is said, 'Behold, the Erelim[5] cry – without; the angels of peace weep bitterly' (Isa 38:7). The ministering angels said before the Holy One, blessed be He, 'Sovereign of all the worlds! Thou art called merciful and compassionate, whose mercy is upon all His works; have mercy upon Isaac, for he is a human being, and the son of a human being, and is bound before Thee like an animal.'" Just as the variant of the constellation from Mari (**fig. 3.14**) features multiple goddesses, here, too, the angels appear in the plural.

One gets the impression that these (and other) midrashim are not based on the biblical text alone but were influenced by oral traditions that more closely correspond to the original Canaanite constellation than the story portrayed in Genesis 22. But the biblical story itself is by no means purely monotheistic. Attempts to understand it in a purely monotheistic manner have only created psychological and moral problems, which consequently produced a wide array of explanations. In those explanations we encounter the tendency to interpret the angel of YHWH as a later addition to the story.[6] In light of the now known iconographic background, this is not at all plausible.

Genesis 22 is not the only biblical narrative developed on the background of the constellation of redemption of an individual before a life-seeking God. In the case of the flood story, YHWH takes on the role of the goddess who intercedes on behalf of Noah (Gen 6:8; 8:20ff), but he also acts as an angry destroyer (Gen 6:5–7) side-by-side with God ('ĕlōhîm; Gen 6:11–13). Therefore the multi-figured concept is less clear, at least at the level of the final redaction. In Job 33:23ff, however, the mercy and the substituting action of a messenger (mal'āk) in favor of a just (or even unjust) person are mentioned explicitly. In Zech 3:1–7 Joshua is justified by the angel of YHWH in front of Satan and the others standing before him. In this sense, the scene contains even more figures than in Genesis 22 but lacks the redemption offering. Nevertheless, it is clear that all these (and many other; Staubli 2010a:93ff) stories function on the background of a similar matrix.

4.2. Sanctuary of a Redeeming Goddess as *Sitz im Leben*

What has been suggested thus far is that the angel of YHWH in Gen 22:1–14 acts in way that is analogous to the role of the goddess in some ANE iconographic constellations that predate the Hebrew Bible. Beyond this thematic congruence, it is also possible that the biblical text shares with the pictorial sources a similar *Sitz im Leben* –

---

5   The Jewish commentators Qimhi and Ibn Ezra explain this word as "messenger, angel," while modern exegetes explain it as "offering-hearth." In the latter case, it would represent a personified altar that cries against God in favor of the innocent victim.

6   See, e.g., Boehm 2004 and 2007. His main argument for the interpretation of the angel's speech as secondary derives from Jewish commentators who propose a conversation between the two different actors. He points to Tanhuma Wajjera Gen 4.128: "*But an angel of Yhwh called unto him* (Gen 2:12). Abraham said to him: Who are you? He said to him: I am an angel. Abraham said to him: When the holy one told me to sacrifice, he told me to himself. So now I ask that he himself tell me [to stop]" (Boehm 2007:83).

namely, that each was originally associated with a holy place, or more specifically, the sanctuary of a redeeming goddess.

As the example from Ebla demonstrates (**fig. 3.17a–b**), the main sanctuary of a city goddess likely represented the setting for the redemption ceremony. Does Gen 22:1–14 share a similar *Sitz im Leben*? There is much to suggest so. On the one hand, the story of the binding of Isaac was, among other things, also understood as an etiology for a place called Moriah (Gen 22:2), because Abraham called that place "Yнwн will provide" (*yhwh yirʾeh*). By the time of the Chronicler at the latest (2 Chr 3:1), the Jewish tradition identified Mount Moriah as the place where the Jerusalem temple was built (see also Josephus, *Ant.* 1.244). Thus, a connection between Gen 22:1–14 and a sanctuary setting is plausible, even in the minds of later interpreters.

On the other hand, the sender of the Jerusalemite letters in the Amarna archive (fourteenth century BCE) is named Abdi-Hepa ("servant of [the goddess] Hepa"), probably pointing to the importance of this Hittite goddess in the early city pantheon. The goddess Hepa is possibly still present in the Bible in the name Eve (*ḥawwah*), the mother of all living.[7] According to Hittite sources, Hepa was the head of the pantheon. Almost a thousand years later, hundreds of pillar figurines with the ancient gesture of the local goddess were in use in Judah, attesting to the continued importance of the goddess in this area. Aside from these figurines, some form of cultic activity associated with the Asherah was likely present in the Jerusalem temple well into the monarchic period, as is evident in the reforms of both Hezekiah and Josiah. Even the quasi-divine status of Zion as a female personification of the city may be understood as an outgrowth of the local goddess tradition. Considered together, these factors – the goddess Hepa domesticated to Eve, a very popular but persecuted Asherah-cult, and the tradition of Zion as an almost deified personification of Zion – suggest a deeply rooted cult of the goddess in Jerusalem.

From the preceding we may prudently conclude that Yнwн or his messenger in Genesis 22 adopted the part of an older city goddess, once connected to redemption rites in Jerusalem – a merciful goddess who offers a substitute sacrifice from among her own property, a goatling of her holy herd still called *ʾaštěrōt* (the name of the goddess Ashtarte!) in biblical Hebrew (cf. Deut 7:13; 28:4, 18, 51).

4.3. The Place of Genesis 22 in the Abraham Cycle

As a final step in the process of iconographic exegesis, it is necessary to explore the place of Genesis 22 in its larger literary setting – namely, the cycle of Abraham stories. The Mishnah already notes that the binding of Isaac is the last and most difficult of ten trials for Abraham, the endpoint and climax of which is redemption (m. *Avot* 5.3). A similar pattern is evident in other literary settings. For instance, the end of the book of Job presents an analogous case. Job's friends turn out to be accusers rather than friends, believing that Job is a sinner and has to confess his sins. In order to save them

---

7   See Gen 3:20; cf. Keel 2007:116–18 and *DDD* 316, 319.

from the anger of God, Job proves his justness one last time by praying for his friends and thereby redeeming them from death (Job 42:9–10).

In some important Greek eposes, redemption scenarios also conclude long and complicated stories. At the end of the Iliad, the corpse of Hector is redeemed. The driving force behind this act of piety is the nymph Thetis, mother of Achilles, sent by Zeus, who acts like a Mesopotamian *lama* goddess and moves her son to agree to give the corpse to Priam, Hector's father (Iliad 24.561f). Another example is the famous Golden Fleece, the pelt of the miraculous ram Chrysomeles, which was sacrificed by Prixos as an offering of gratitude, because he had been saved by Zeus through this ram from King Aietes of Colchis.

From these examples, together with the aforementioned redemption scenes on prominent places in the temples of Ebla and Karnak, we may conclude that while the composers of Genesis 22 formed their story carefully and with many original elements (such as the dramatic father-son relationship of the offerer and his offering), they did so by drawing upon a rich stock of Eastern Mediterranean traditions. Thus it is possible to conclude that the Akedah was not originally intended as a polemic against pagan beliefs.

5. The Iconic Constancy of Redemption

The binding of Isaac is a favorite motif of Jewish, Christian, and even Muslim art. Such representations are the focus of ongoing research into the story's reception history.[8] While I will not present an analysis of the passage's reception history here, I would like to underline that the semantics and syntax of this artwork is sometimes quite close to those of the Canaanite prototypes. The presence of this congruence is perhaps not surprising in light of the above observations. That is, just as the visual elements of the iconographic constellation are reflected in Genesis 22, so too are the textual themes found in the binding of Isaac story transposed into later works of art. This is not to say that later artists had direct knowledge of, say, Old Babylonian seals that depict scenes of divine redemption of human sacrifice. Rather, the points of similarity discussed below are suggestive of a common conceptual background that links image and text.

Specifically, the transposition of the narrative into art produces, in many cases, a combination of the four main visual elements found in the iconographic constellations discussed above: the threatened human, the sacrificer, the deity, and the substitute sacrifice. We find this quartet already on the Torah shrine of the synagogue from Dura-Europos (**fig. 3.24**), where they form a vertical line with the saving hand of God on top and the ram at the bottom. On Christian oil lamps from northern Africa (**fig. 3.25**) the scene is even more condensed, but still with Abraham holding the knife as a main figure. In a mahzor of the thirteenth century CE (**fig. 3.26**) the saving ram is separated from the three other figures by the illuminated characters of a heading.

---

8   See for instance U. Schubert 1977:197f and K. Schubert 1991. For the Akedah in Jewish art, see
     Milgrom 1988; for the offering of Ibrahim in Islamic art, see Milstein 2005:72–75; Gutmann 2001.

Fig. 3.24. Menorah, Etrog, Lulav, temple façade, binding of Isaac on a fresco over the torah shrine, Dura Europos, 3d c. CE. Source: Damascus, National Museum

Fig. 3.25. Binding of Isaac, Christian oil lamp, Northern Africa, 5th c. CE. Source: Collections of BIBLE+ORIENT Museum, Freiburg CH, G 2005.4

Fig. 3.26. Binding of Isaac, illumination for Rosh HaShanah in a mahzor, southern Germany, 13th c. Source: Oxford, Bodleian Library, MS Laud Or. 321, fol. 184r

Despite its theological significance, the motif does not appear in Islamic art before the fifteenth century CE. According to Rachel Milstein, the first Islamic representations of the Akedah stood under the influence of older representations of Mitras slaughtering the bull (for this and the following see Milstein 2005:73). In a Persian manuscript of the late sixteenth century CE (**fig. 3.27**), the arrangement of composition lines (drawn as green lines over the painting) functions as a visual exegesis of the story. Specifically, the gazes of Ibrahim and his son meet in the eyes of the winged messenger, who functions as the divine redeemer. The gaze of the victim also crosses the eyes of the substituting goat-kid in the hands of the angel, which underlines the goat-kid's function as a heavenly substitution. Those lines are in turn antithetically crossed by the diagonal horizon of the mountain, which separates the painting into heavenly and terrestrial sections. Thus, the arrangement indicates that redemption happens for Abraham but all the more for Isaac via the gift of a heavenly messenger. No less impressive is a children's drawing of the twentieth century CE (**fig. 3.28**) in which a palm tree and the knife form the central axis, flanked by the angel and the ram on the left and Ibrahim and his son on the right. This composition strongly recalls the ANE prototypes with their tendency to symmetric composition, creating a relationship between the victim and the ram and between the offerer and the redeemer by vertical and horizontal arrangements (see **figs. 3.3, 11, 13–15**).

Fig. 3.27. Offering of Ibrahim, illumination in Qisas al-anbiyā, late 16th c. Source: Bibliothèque nationale française, suppl. persan 1313, f. 40r

Fig. 3.28. Offering of Ibrahim, Islamic drawing of a child, 20th c. CE. Source: unknown

6. Human Sacrifice:
Not a Common Practice in the Ancient Levant

If redemption rites are so deeply rooted in ancient Near Eastern cultures, what, then, is to be said about human sacrifices? A traditional view of religious history still holds that human sacrifices were a common practice among ancient Mediterranean cultures. This view is found, for instance, in the otherwise well informed and masterful synthesis on the Mediterranean by David Abulafia (2011). But a closer look at the sources reveals most theories about child sacrifices to be groundless and based on misperceptions.

With the rise of farming societies during the Pottery Neolithic Age (6400–4500 BCE) in the southern Levant, we observe special burials of young children, infants, and fetuses in jars. The most ancient of these have been found in the excavations of Naḥal Zehora II in the Carmel hills (Gopher and Eshed 2012: **Fig. 36.1–6**). Orrelle (2008) considers that the earliest infant burials of the Pottery Neolithic Age could involve ritually killed infants, although she is forced to admit that "no signs of disease or violence were reported on the skeletons." Her arguments are a mixture of more or less relevant and reliable information from all over the world. She mentions an alleged tradition of killing a human victim to placate the divine forces and to assure seasonal regeneration as especially relevant for the Levant with its unpredictable rainfall (Orrelle 2008:74). Unfortunately we are not told from which source such a "tradition" might be known.

Much more reasonable is the assumption that the earliest farmers were confronted with stillbirths and high infant mortality, maybe at least partly as a consequence of their new sedentary lifestyle, which facilitated the emergence and diffusion of infectious disease. It is possible that preindustrial sedentary life put high demands on human labor, and with it, elevated the value of life, the grief associated with death, and the desire for the replacement of lost life. These values may have been expressed by new ritual practices made possible by the invention of pottery. As such, it is quite plausible that the burial of infants in pots symbolized the restitution of the dead body to the motherly womb, which was seen in strong parallelism with the earth – both of them giving birth to life.[9]

The most recent example of the child offering theory is that of Garbini (2012), who claims that the Philistines brought this special form of sacrifice as an Aegean-Anatolian custom to the Levant, where it was supposedly adopted by the Israelites. At the same time, he portrays the Israelites as antagonists of the Philistines and is forced to admit that direct documentation of child offerings in the Levant is totally lacking (Garbini 2012:229).

Fig. 3.29. "Child-eater," i. e. Saturn (= Kronos) as a Jew (identified as such by hat and ring), woodcut, Nürnberg, 1492. Source: Schreckenberg 1996:343

More credible than the theory about a culture adopting from its antagonists the rite of murdering its own offspring is the assumption that stories about child offerings were used to demonize the enemy, as is known to be the case in antique pagan stories against Christians (Tertullian, *Apol.* 7–9) and in medieval Christian stories against

---

9   Keel (1989a) demonstrates that the most ancient stamp seal amulets of the Levant (nineteenth c. BCE) show a sign in the form of an omega, the symbol of the Mesopotamian goddess Ninkhursanga (and perhaps representing a uterus). Many of these amulets have been found in burials of embryos and infants.

Jews (Schreckenberg 1996:285–303). The same may be true for the Greek stories about Phoenicians, which are conspicuously absent in the works of Herodotus, Thucydides, Plato, Xenophon, and Aristotle, but which can be found in the writings of later historians (Simonetti 1983:91–111; Day 1989:86–91; Moscati 1991:55–62), not one of whom was an eyewitness. Notably, Quintus Curtius Rufus (IV, 3, 23; mid-first century CE) writes that during the siege of Tyre under Alexander the Great, the council of Elders, facing grave danger, refused to reanimate an old custom, abandoned centuries ago, of offering a free-born boy to Saturn (Kronos). The late medieval motif of the "child-eater" (**fig. 3.29**), referring to the old story of Kronos or Saturn devouring his own children, marked at that time as a Jew, is a sad testimony to a long tradition of defamation of the "other" as a child murderer.

Cleitarchus (third century BCE) and the several biblical passages that speak about a rite in which children were passed (*'br*) through fire for Molech concur in describing a vow and not a sacrifice.[10] The inscriptions on the famous Tophet-stele mention a vow as well, but never specify what has been vowed. The persistent interpretation, however, that the inscriptions "may well point to child sacrifice" (McCarty 2011:203 n. 2) is highly speculative and tells more about human fantasy than history. The same is true for a forced connection between Molech-offerings and the story in Genesis 22. The archaeological verification of the four-step rite (sacrifice, incineration, deposit, stele erection), which took place in the Punic Tophet of North Africa, "begins at the pyres upon which the sacrificial victims were incinerated" (McCarty 2011:212). To speak of "sacrificial victims" is already highly speculative for it implies that humans were being sacrificed. While it is more than probable that animals were offered to the gods, it is not at all probable that children were offered as well.

In the first rigorous analysis of the largest sample of cremated human skeletal remains from the Carthaginian Tophet, Schwartz et al. (2010) examined tooth formation, enamel histology, cranial and postcranial metrics, and the potential effects of heat-induced bone shrinkage of 540 individuals. The results show an age distribution that ranges from the prenatal period to six-month-old babies. This is consistent with perinatal mortality up to the present day. Numerous diseases known from other large cities in the ancient world are responsible for this mortality rate: smallpox, vaccinia, listeriosis, viral infections, malaria, cholestasis, hypertension, toxemia and renal disease, cholera, dysentery, gastroenteritis, infectious hepatitis, leptospirosis, typhoid, and parasitic intestinal infestations, most of which result in severe dehydration, a common proximate cause of infant death. The analysis does not support "the contention that all humans interred in the Tophet had been sacrificed" (Schwartz et al. 2010:10). Rather, the Carthaginian Tophets were more likely cemeteries for infants who died as a result of various disease and ailments.

---

10   "To burn" is used for non-Israelites and not together with the word Molech. Only Ezekiel uses the verbs "to offer" (*zbḥ*) or "to slaughter" (*šḥṭ*). See Bieberstein's list in Keel 2007:497. Collecting all relevant information, Keel opts for the possibility that the Judean fire-rite was a vow of children for their protection (ibid. 501).

To summarize: Since the existence of the earliest farming societies in the Levant about 8,000 years ago, stillbirths, infants, and young children received special attention in funeral rites. Positive data indicating that those human beings were victims of a sacrifice is lacking. Instead, it is more likely that these practices reflect ways in which societies sought to overcome grief over the loss of infants and children due to natural causes.

Nevertheless, some scholars still conclude that widespread child sacrifice existed in ancient Mediterranean cultures, especially in the Levant and in Phoenician northern Africa. This conclusion is, at least in part, based on a problematic understanding of "paganism" and "cult." Rather than being an instrument to manage situations of crisis with non-violent methods, cult is perceived as a problematic, antiquated, and obsolete part of a conflict-ridden society. But what may be true for some modern contexts can't necessarily be applied to the Levant in antiquity.

This is true also for those human offerings (not necessarily child offerings), which in extreme situations may have been carried out by representatives of an urban elite. For them, human sacrifice was a measure of last resort in a desperate situation, either to demonstrate to a large public that they were not acting for their own profit (as in the case of Mesha, offering his firstborn as a precondition of the founding of a new city), or to avoid a greater disaster (as in the case of the siege of Abel-Bet-Maacha, following the council of a wise woman of the city), or to legitimize an abnormal status or abnormal warlike acts (as in the case of Jephthah, offering his daughter in accordance with a vow [Judg 11:29–40]).

7.   Conclusion

What I believe I have demonstrated through this examination of pictorial sources is the existence of an ancient Babylonian, Syrian, and Canaanite tradition of redeeming and thereby saving humans dedicated as victims for a sacrifice; a tradition of saving from death by the substitution of an animal; a tradition, in other words, of combining *a priori* the possibility of human sacrifice (as an unsurpassable measure of devotion) with the redemption of it by a divine gift (as an unsurpassable measure of grace). I highlighted a constellation that included four figures: (1) a god, menacing (2) a human being, before (3) a goddess, with (4) a recumbent sheep or goat above the human victim. Sometimes in addition to and/or in place of the goddess one finds a man bringing a sheep or goat as an offering. It was also shown that the story of Genesis 22 is likely founded on the same constellation: (1) a deity (*'ĕlōhîm*) asking for (2) a human sacrifice, and (3) another deity, represented by its messenger (*mal'ak yhwh*) providing (4) an animal substitute. In the biblical tradition the multi-figurative aspect of the deity has not been denied, and in Jewish literature it has sometimes even been reinforced.

The constellation of the redemption of a human in grave danger as the representation of the crucial moment of salvation was part of the central iconography of the main sanctuary (for Ishtar) of the Syrian metropolis Ebla, and it was quite possibly connected to the YHWH-sanctuary at Jerusalem. The prehistory of the Jerusalemite constellation reveals the absorption of qualities of the goddess by YHWH.[11] It shows that the pagans of the ancient Near East were able to confront and to question mighty human feelings, conceived of and shaped as gods: righteous zeal with its willingness to murder; compassion and love with its willingness to find a less violent solution. In a stimulating paper, Mayer I. Gruber (2007:3) calls attention to an interpretation of the Binding of Isaac canonized in the rabbinic liturgy of the New Year, which suggests that the story illustrates "justifiable anger [being] conquered by unconditional love." This idea – "Love Conquers Anger" – would be a perfect title of the iconographic constellation discussed above, which points to an old tradition (starting around 1850 BCE at the latest) of redeeming human victims by virtue of intervention by the goddess. This clearly challenges still-existing notions of there being a sharp contrast between, on the one hand, pagan Canaanite, Phoenician or Punic cults that supposedly practiced human sacrifices, and, on the other hand, Jewish, Christian or Muslim cults without such sacrifices.

The method applied in this study is founded on the assumption that the biblical literature is part and parcel of ancient Near Eastern culture and participates therefore in its symbolic system. This is to deny neither the singularity of the biblical canon in its function for religious communities over centuries nor its unique importance for the history of humanity as a consequence of this. It is also not to deny a theological understanding of the text as part of a permanent process of divine revelation to humankind. But it is a rejection of an elitist interpretation of the text as part of an *a priori* higher culture or higher religion of a higher God over and above pagan culture – an interpretive presupposition that often surfaces, especially with Genesis 22.

On this basis, and by meticulous analysis of the semantics and syntax of the studied images, a constellation of two gods, one of them asking for a human sacrifice, the other one redeeming it by a substitution offering, was shown on Old Babylonian (§ 2.1) and Old Syrian cylinder seals (§ 2.2), but also on the stele of a central sanctuary of the northern Levant (§ 2.3), which is crucial for the iconological interpretation of the images. Further iconographic evidence was found in artifacts from Egypt (§ 3). The constellation in the biblical text itself could additionally be supported by examples from the exegetical history of the text (§ 4.1), by a historical argument (§ 4.2), and by an analysis of the text in its larger literary context, which corresponds to the larger iconographic context of the images possessing the same constellation (§ 4.3). Looking at the iconographic reception history of the Akedah revealed an astonishing – conscious or unconscious – continuity of the discovered constellation (§ 5). Finally, I emphasized the importance of neutralizing the notorious claim of widespread child

---

11 Keel 1989b points to several examples of this phenomenon: YHWH in the role of a mother goddess (Ishtar in the epos of Gilgamesh, Nintu in the version of Atrahasis) in the biblical flood-story (Gen 8:20ff); the image of motherly care in Hosea (11:8–9, 13); and the motherly metaphors in Second Isaiah (54:9–10).

offerings in the pagan ANE by pointing to facts rather than to pure speculation based only on loose pieces of information (§ 6).

Assignment/Exercise

1. Using **figs. 3.2, 3, 11–14** and **17a**, try to identify: (1) the menacing king/god; (2) the victim; (3) the goddess; (4) the substitute offering; and (5) the enthroned or highest deity. Number each of these visual elements.
2. Using the same figures, mark by strokes and arrows the relation of the visual elements (i. e., visual syntax). How is a relation expressed on the limited space of the cylinder seals and on the stele? What does the visual syntax suggest about the meaning of the figures?
3. Using the bibliographic references listed in § 5 and/or the internet, select one example of the reception history of Genesis 22 in Jewish, Christian, or Muslim art. What similarities and differences do you see between this piece of art and the Mesopotamian, Canaanite, and Egyptian iconographic constellations discussed in this chapter? What conclusions can you draw about how this piece of art interprets the binding of Isaac story?

Bibliography

Berman, Louis A. 1997. *The Akedah: The Binding of Isaac.* Northvale, NJ: J. Aronson.

Boehm, Omri. 2007. *The Binding of Isaac: A Religious Model of Disobedience.* Library of Hebrew Bible/ Old Testament Studies 468. New York: T&T Clark.

Gruber, Mayer I. 2007. "Love Conquers Anger: The Aqedah in the Rabbinic Liturgy." In *Unbinding the Binding of Isaac,* edited by Mishael Caspi and John T. Greene, 1–8, Lanham, MD: University Press of America.

Gutmann, Joseph. 2001. "The Sacrifice of Abraham in Timurid Art." *The Journal of Walter's Art Museum* 59: 131–135.

Milgrom, Josephine. 1988. *The Binding of Isaac (the Akedah): A Primary Symbol in Jewish Thought and Art.* Berkeley: Bibal.

Staubli, Thomas. 1991. *Das Image der Nomaden im Alten Israel und in der Ikonographie seiner sesshaften Nachbarn.* Orbis Biblicus et Orientalis 107. Freiburg/Göttingen: Universitätsverlag/Vandenhoeck & Ruprecht.

Staubli, Thomas. 2010. "Alttestamentliche Konstellationen der Rechtfertigung des Menschen vor Gott." In *Biblische Anthropologie: neue Einsichten aus dem Alten Testament,* edited by Christian Frevel, 88–133. Quaestiones disputatae 237. Freiburg: Herder.

Chapter 4
"With a Strong Hand and an Outstretched Arm": On the Meaning(s) of the Exodus Tradition(s)

Brent A. Strawn

1. Introduction

There can be little doubt that the book of Exodus, and the great departure from Egypt for which it is named, is at the very heart of the Old Testament – in terms of both its literature and its theology. But even when this point is granted – and so far it is nothing more (or less) than a claim about the importance of the Exodus tradition throughout the Bible (see Houtman 1993–2002: 1:190–212) – more needs to be said. The Exodus tradition is, after all, a complex one. Indeed, it would be better to refer to the Exodus as a macro-tradition, comprised of a number of other, smaller traditions: the plague tradition, for instance (see Exod 7:8–11:10; 12:29–36), or the traditions surrounding the crossing of the Re(e)d Sea (see Exod 13:17–14:31; 15:1–21) or Passover (see Exod 12:1–28; 13:3–10; cf. also Num 9:1–14; Deut 16:1–8; 2 Kgs 23:21–23; Ezek 45:21–24). Depending on how widely one circumscribes the Exodus "macro-tradition," one could also include the wilderness wanderings (Exod 15:22–18:27), or, within these, the provision of food in the desert (Exod 16:1–36; cf. Num 11:1–35). One could go so far as to include the giving of the law (Exod 20:1–24:18) and the tabernacle construction (Exod 25:1–31:18; 35:1–40:38) as part of the larger Exodus tradition. But even if these various traditions are discrete units or blocks (cf. Noth 1981), they are nevertheless now found within the larger book of Exodus and, for that reason, play a role in the larger "Exodus macro-tradition" as it now stands, even if, for the sake of clarity, one prefers to restrict the most immediate referent of the Exodus tradition to the actual departure from Egypt.

In addition to larger or mid-sized blocks of tradition, other, smaller bits and pieces frequently play important roles in the Exodus tradition, whether they are well attested or more infrequent. Stock phrases that are used to describe the Exodus are a case in point. So, for example, the departure is often described as YHWH's bringing (usually the verb *bw'* in the Hiphil [causative] stem) Israel "out of Egypt, out of the house of bondage" (e.g., Exod 13:3, 14; 20:2; Deut 5:6; 6:12; 8:14; 13:10; Josh 24:17; Judg 6:8; Jer 34:13; cf. Deut 13:5; Micah 6:4).[1] Or, one could note how Egypt is called "a furnace" or "smelting pot" (Deut 4:20; 1 Kgs 8:51; Jer 11:4). Repeated terminology like these items suggests a pattern of usage that likely depends on preexisting mate-

---

1 The inclusion of texts from outside of the book of Exodus demonstrates how tradition-units are not necessarily restricted to the boundaries of a single biblical book.

rial. That preexisting material could be variously deployed in different texts, units, or even biblical books. Study of these recurrent tropes, as well as their different implementations in various periods or texts, is part and parcel of what biblical scholars call tradition history, which is the study of different traditions and their history of use (see, e. g., Knight 2006).

The present chapter looks at one piece of repeated terminology that belongs to the Exodus tradition, analyzing it with reference to ancient Near Eastern iconography in an attempt to gain exegetical insight on both the meaning of the phrase itself and the meaning of the larger Exodus tradition to which it belongs and to which it contributes. The phrase in question is "the strong hand and the outstretched arm" (*hayyād haḥăzāqâ wĕhazzĕrō[a]ʿ hannĕṭûyâ*),[2] which often describes YHWH's action in the exodus.[3] I will first discuss the textual instances of this phrase along with previous studies of it, though the data and the scholarship have often led to distinct conclusions that seem hard to reconcile (§ 2). This conundrum leads to a consideration of another dataset, or perhaps better, image-set – namely, ancient Near Eastern iconography – which casts further light on the situation and may help decide the conundrum, one way or another (§ 3). But iconography has its share of traditions no less than texts do, and there are at least two viable iconographical traditions that can make good sense of YHWH's strong hand and outstretched arm (§§ 3.1–2). In conclusion, I try to merge the two "tradition-sets" – the textual and the artistic – to gain greater purchase on the meaning, or perhaps better, *meanings* of the Exodus tradition(s) in the Hebrew Bible (§ 4).

2. The Tradition of the Strong Hand and Outstretched Arm of YHWH in the Hebrew Bible: Perspectives and Problems

While the Old Testament speaks of God's hands and arms quite frequently, and with various connotations (oftentimes deleterious; see Roberts 1971), the motif of the outstretched arm can be isolated and treated separately given its specific and distinctive formulation. The outstretched arm (*zĕrô[a]ʿ nĕṭûyâ*) is conjoined with "strong hand" (*yād ḥăzāqâ*) eleven times: Deut 4:34; 5:15; 7:19; 11:2; 26:8; 1 Kgs 8:42; Jer 32:21; Ezek 20:33, 34; Ps 136:12; and 2 Chr 6:32. The outstretched arm is accompanied by "great power" (*kō[a]ḥ gādôl*) four times: Deut 9:29; 2 Kgs 17:36; Jer 27:5; and 32:17 (cf. Bar 2:11). In Exod 6:6, the outstretched arm is found with "great judgments" (*šĕpāṭîm gĕdōlîm*). Finally, Jer 21:5 is an especially intriguing instance of the motif since it also occurs with "strong" and "hand," but reverses the usual sequence of the nouns and adjectives so as to produce "with an outstretched hand and a mighty arm" (*bĕyād nĕṭûyâ ûbizrô[a]ʿ ḥăzāqâ*). Most commentators agree that this reversed sequence in

---

2   This exact spelling occurs only in Deut 7:19 (where it is actually preceded by the conjunction). Many constructions are anarthrous, and, in most instances, *zĕrô(a)ʿ* is spelled *plene*.

3   Indeed, some scholars argue that every instance of the phrase refers to a subset of that divine activity – namely, YHWH's capacity to cause disease and plague (so Martens 2001).

Jeremiah is used to transform the normal, benevolent sense of the phrase into a highly negative sentiment that announces judgment on Judah (see Holladay 1986:569–72).

The various formulations that involve *zĕrô(a)ʿ nĕṭûyâ* are not identical – Jer 21:15 is proof enough of that – but they all share the motif of YHWH's outstretched arm. Previous studies have shown they have other things in common as well, which is another way of saying that they appear to be (or belong to) a unit of tradition. For one thing, the majority of the texts that mention YHWH's outstretched arm have to do with the exodus from Egypt. Second, most of the instances of the full phrase, "with a strong hand and an outstretched arm," are either Deuteronomic, Deuteronomistic, or found in literature that is typically thought to be influenced by Deuteronomy or the Deuteronomistic History (so, in sum, the references in Deuteronomy, 1–2 Kings, Jeremiah, and 2 Chronicles). It comes as no surprise, then, to find most scholars saying that the terminology is Deuteronomi(sti)c in origin (e. g., Weinfeld 1991:212). But such a judgment may hold true only for the origin of the phrase; even within the Deuteronomi(sti)c realm, the phrase is not consistently employed. A good bit of variation persists in the specific instances of the outstretched arm, as delineated above.

Scholars who have investigated the Hebrew motif from a comparative perspective have also tended to agree that the construction "(a) strong hand and (an) outstretched arm" is best tied back to Egyptian antecedents, specifically Egyptian royal typology (Weinfeld 1991:212). Mention of the pharaoh's mighty arm (Egyptian ʿ) is as early as the Pyramid texts and inscriptions dating to the Fourth and Fifth Dynasties, but it is only in the Middle Kingdom that expressions referring to the conquering arm of Pharaoh begin to appear (see Hoffmeier 1986). For its part, the *flourit* of Egyptian *ḫpš* ("strong arm"; "strength, power") takes place during the reigns of the militaristically-minded Thutmoside and Ramesside kings of the Eighteenth and Nineteenth Dynasties (see Hoffmeier 1986; Görg 1986). Two examples from Dynasty 18 are illustrative: Thutmose IV (1400–1390 BCE) is called "Possessor of a strong arm" (*nb ḫpš*) and "Mighty of Arm Who Subdues the Nine Bows" (*wsr ḫpš dr psḏt*), whereas his predecessor, Amenhotep II (1427–1400 BCE), is known as the one "who smites foreign rulers of the far north" and "a god whose arm [*ḫpš*] is great" (Hoffmeier 1986:381).

One additional piece of textual evidence is noteworthy: the strong arm of the Egyptian king is attested four times in three different Amarna letters, all from king ʿAbdi-Ḫeba of Jerusalem (EA 286:12; 287:27; 288:14, 34). It is quite significant that in each case, the scribe writes *zu-ru-uḫ*, which is the syllabic spelling for the word known in biblical Hebrew as *zĕrô(a)ʿ*, rather than the usual Akkadian term for "hand," which is *qātu* (though often written in these letters with the Sumerogram ŠU). That the Pharaoh's conquering arm is mentioned in Amarna letters from Jerusalem, and in the indigenous language of the Canaanite scribes who wrote them, "demonstrates that the concept surrounding pharaoh's conquering arm was already known in Canaan by the 15th century B.C." (Hoffmeier 1986:386). It can also be taken as further evidence for "seeing Egyptian influence behind the Hebrew use of *zĕrôaʿ*" for God's victorious arm in the Hebrew Bible (Hoffmeier 1986:384).

But it is precisely here that one encounters a problem. How can the motif of God's strong hand and outstretched arm be (1) stock Deuteronomi(sti)c phraseology that dates, presumably, to the seventh or sixth century BCE (at the very earliest according to many scholars), and also (2) be influenced by or derived from Egyptian sources, especially from the New Kingdom dating to the mid-second millennium BCE? If the second point is accurate, it seems that the Hebrew tradition must be dated much earlier than Deuteronomy or the Deuteronomistic history. Alternatively, if the first point is accurate, it is hard to see how the motif could be traced – and certainly not directly – back to New Kingdom Egypt. One could, of course, posit a very early borrowing and a very long memory in the source material (i. e., a long perdurance of the outstretched arm tradition) utilized much later by Deuteronomy and the Deuteronomistic history. Or perhaps one could look to texts from the Late Period in Egypt for traces of Pharaoh's arm. There are, to be sure, a few of these latter texts, but according to Hoffmeier subsequent Dynasties witness "a discernible decline" in use of the motif (1986:383–84).

There are still other problems besetting these two conclusions, their interrelation, and their application to understanding the motif of Yhwh's outstretched arm in the Old Testament. Perhaps the largest problem is that none of the Egyptian formulations are precisely cognate with the Hebrew phrase *běyād ḥăzāqâ ûbizrô(a)ʿ něṭûyâ*. In one sense, this comes as no surprise since Egyptian is not Semitic; but it does pose some difficulties nevertheless, especially for any argument that wants to relate the Hebrew motif to Egyptian exemplars exclusively at the level of linguistic or literary borrowing. It seems that such an exclusively linguistic/literary approach cannot account for all of the evidence and encounters several significant problems. Another type of evidence should be considered, therefore – namely, the iconographic.

3.   The Image-Traditions

Previous scholarship has, with good reason, drawn attention to the motif of Pharaoh's strong arm in literary texts from Egypt. It is hardly a surprise to learn that there are artistic depictions of the same. In point of fact, however, there are two image-traditions that are quite pertinent to the discussion of Yhwh's outstretched arm. The most frequently discussed of the two has been the conquering arm of the pharaoh. Given its (pre)dominance, this tradition deserves to be considered first (§ 3.1). The second, less oft-discussed but equally relevant, image-tradition concerns the life-giving deity in a gesture of blessing (§ 3.2).

3.1. The Strong Arm of Pharaoh

The image of Pharaoh's smiting/conquering arm is a very early one. It is found on the famous Narmer Palette, dating to the Nagada III period (ca. 3100–2920 BCE) but is already attested in Tomb 100 at Hierakonpolis (**fig. 4.1**), which is 300 years earlier still (Strawn 2009b:171–72). The image is established early on, then, and proved remarkably stable, enduring well into the Late Period and even into the Greco-Roman era (see Hall 1986).

Egyptian texts referring to Pharaoh's smiting arm suggest that particular attention should be paid to the New Kingdom period, where artistic representations of the notion are also found in abundance. So, for example, **fig. 4.2** depicts Ramesses the Great (1279–1213 BCE) smiting a Semitic victim while the god Atum looks on approvingly.

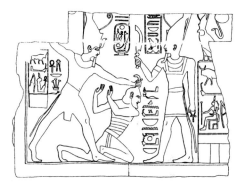

Fig. 4.1. Detail from painted wall of Decorated Tomb (100) at Hierakonpolis, Nagada 2 (ca. 3400–3300 BCE). Source: Kemp 1989:50 fig. 16

Fig. 4.2. Relief from the temple at Tell el-Retaba, Ramesses II (1279–1213 BCE). Source: Kemp 1989:224 fig. 77

Is this the (kind of) image that would have been evoked by the Hebrew motif of YHWH's outstretched arm? Many scholars have thought as much, and not without good reason, especially if the Hebrew motif is related to Egyptian antecedents, and if the Hebrew motif is, like the Egyptian one, primarily one of (militaristic) domination. If so, it would follow that the Hebrew motif is heavily ironic – perhaps by design – insofar as YHWH's outstretched arm wreaks havoc *on Egypt,* the very location that made so much of its own king's mighty arm that was so often touted as wreaking havoc on all foreigners.

One could, on the basis of the happy confluence of New Kingdom literary texts and New Kingdom iconography, declare the quest complete at this juncture: the Hebrew motif of God's strong hand and outstretched arm belongs to Egyptian royal ideology (cf. Weinfeld 1991:212). What is imag(in)ed in the Hebrew phrase, then, is YHWH smiting Egypt just as Pharaoh is shown smiting his enemies – which is, again, ironic, since in the Hebrew formulation, it is Pharaoh who is being smitten, getting a taste of his own medicine, as it were!

While such irony is both rich and biting, the quest should not be ended prematurely because this conclusion encounters a potential problem – namely, that of relating non-contiguous images and texts. In this specific case, the problem is found in connecting an earlier New Kingdom image-tradition with the (much) later biblical attestations of a text-tradition. Equally if not more important, however, is the fact that there are some marked differences between Pharaoh's conquering arm and the arm of Yhwh in the Hebrew Bible. For one thing, in Egyptian depictions, the pharaoh almost always holds a weapon of some sort. But no passage in the Old Testament indicates that Yhwh's outstretched arm brandishes an object (see Strawn 2009b:172 and n. 40). A second consideration is even more telling: Yhwh's outstretched arm is not unequivocally violent or destructive in the Bible. So, for example, Yhwh's outstretched arm can be connected with the themes of creation and redemption, or with prayer offered by foreigners (see, e. g., Jer 27:5; 32:17; Exod 6:6; 1 Kgs 8:42; 2 Chr 6:32). To be sure, the outstretched arm is often referenced in combination with "great terrors" or "signs and wonders" and the like (see, e. g., Deut 4:34; 7:19; 26:8; Jer 32:21) – all of which seem to have destructive connotations, especially if these are somehow related to the plague narrative (so Martens 2001). But if the outstretched arm was, by itself, sufficient to connote excessive violence, these additional complements would be unnecessary. Still further, the more "positive" uses of the motif with reference to creation or redemption, too, would be unexplainable if, all by itself, the outstretched arm was coterminous with terror.

There are still other things that do not align perfectly when comparing Yhwh's outstretched arm and the conquering arm of Pharaoh. Most obvious among them, perhaps, is that in Egypt it is the king's arm that is the focus of attention whereas in the Old Testament it is Yhwh's arm. This is no small difference.[4] Altogether, these considerations suggest that while the image-tradition of Pharaoh's powerful arm may be the most dominant comparative datum (especially among scholars), it is not the only option. There are sufficient differences between the Hebrew tradition of Yhwh's outstretched arm and Pharaoh's conquering arm to urge one to consider other comparative materials that might prove instructive and useful.

3.2. The Life-Giving Deity Who Blesses

Interestingly enough, it is again precisely in the New Kingdom, especially in the Amarna Age of Dynasty 18 (ca. 1352–1336 BCE), that there are numerous depictions of a god – not just a king – with outstretched arm, thus resolving one (the last mentioned) of the difficulties faced in relating Pharaoh's conquering arm to Yhwh's outstretched arm.

The depictions in question are the highly formalized presentation of the Aten (*itn*), a special manifestation of the sun-god Re-Harakhti in this period. Adoration of the Aten had been on the rise since the beginning of Dynasty 18, but increased dramatically in the reign of Amenhotep III (1390–1352 BCE), climaxing in the reign of his successor, Amenhotep IV (1352–1336 BCE), who changed his name to Akhenaten[5] and who relocated his capital from Thebes to present day el-Amarna, naming

---

4   Notwithstanding the divine or semi-divine nature of the pharaoh. For studies on the latter, see O'Connor and Silverman 1995; Abitz 1995; Strawn 2003.

5   The name change is indicative of the religious change: "Amun is content" (*imn-ḥtp*; Amenhotep) to "radiance of Aten" or "he who is useful to Aten" (*3ḫ-n-itn*, Akhenaten). See Reeves 2001:101; Hornung 1999:50.

it Akhetaten ("horizon of the sun-disk"). The name change and the city relocation reflected Akhenaten's drastic religious transformation as he moved from initial tolerance of other Egyptian deities to a systematic removal of all of the same, save the Aten.

Akhenaten's new religion was accompanied by a new artistic style. For the purposes of the present chapter, the iconography of the Aten within that style is of greatest importance. H. A. Groenewegen-Frankfort describes the artistic changes:

> [T]he old repertoire of royal scenes had to be scrapped, and instead of repeating the classical robot figures which, though dull, had at least the dignity of beings engaged in symbolical acts or confronting deities on a footing of equality, artists were now commanded to depict the king as a single person in relation with a divine power which transcended human or animal form. This was done by the simple device of showing the [Aten] orb above and the life-giving rays stretching toward the royal figure. (1951:99)

While the device may well be "simple," iconography of the Aten is ubiquitous and consistent, with the sun-disk's rays everywhere and always beaming down on the main subjects in a composition – these are typically the king and members of the royal family (**figs. 4.3–4**).

Fig. 4.3. Limestone relief, Amarna. Source: Beyerlin 1978:17 fig. 1

Fig. 4.4. Limestone stele, Amarna. Source: Kemp 1989:282 fig. 94

The rays of the Aten often terminate in hands that extend the *ankh,* the symbol of life, to the noses of the royal figures. These rays are nothing less than arms, then, since they terminate in hands, and they are agents of blessing, offering life to the figures in the scene, or alighting on a crown or pausing above the head (**figs. 4.5–6**) in a gesture that is at once both intimate and benevolent. The human figures in these depictions are waiting for life and blessing – anticipating those things and receiving them from the Aten and its outstretched arms.

Fig. 4.5. Relief fragment, Amarna. Source: Shafer 1991:78 fig. 48

Fig. 4.6. Detail of *talalat* from Hermopolis depicting Kiya, Amarna. Source: Aldred 1988: Pl. 37

While some aspects of Aten iconography in the Amarna age seem to correspond nicely with certain elements in the Hebrew motif of Yhwh's outstretched arm – most especially the fact that in both cases it is a matter of a *deity* with an outstretched arm – there is still much that needs discussion. For one thing, the Aten's hands seem delicate, hardly strong – and it is strength and power that are at work in Pharaoh's smiting arm and in so many understandings of Hebrew *yād ḥăzāqâ.* But then again, the basic meaning of the Hebrew root *ḥzq* (from which *ḥăzāqâ* is derived) is "to seize, take hold, grasp" (see BDB 305; *HALOT* 1:303–304). The Aten's hands *do* often grasp something: the *ankh*-symbols that are extended to the monarchs.

More significant than the arms and hands of the Aten, however, may be the fact that creation is ascribed to the Aten. A particularly important passage is found in the Short Hymn to the Aten, which connects the Aten's power and strength with his creative activity and, notably, his rays:

> Your power, your strength, are firm in my heart;
> You are the living Aten whose image endures,
> You have made the far sky to shine in it,
> To observe all that you made.
> You are One yet a million lives are in you,
> To make them live <you give> the breath of life to their noses;
> By the sight of your rays all flowers exist,
> What lives and sprouts from the soil grows when you shine.
> (*AEL* 2:92; emphasis added)[6]

Similar themes are found in the Great Hymn to the Aten, which many scholars believe may have directly influenced Psalm 104 (see Auffret 1981:133–316; Dion 1991). Whatever the case, the Aten's creative arms bear close comparison with Yhwh's outstretched arm that is also associated with creation in the Old Testament:

- Jer 27:5: "It is I myself who by my great power (*běkōḥî haggādôl*) and by my outstretched arm (*ûbizrô'î hannětûyâ*) have made (*'śh*) the earth, humankind, and the animals that are upon the earth; I give it to whomever is pleasing in my eyes."
- Jer 32:17: "Ah my Lord Yhwh! Look: you have made (*'śh*) the heavens and the earth by your great power (*běkōḥăkā haggādôl*) and by your outstretched arm (*ûbizrô'ăkā hannětûyâ*); nothing is too difficult for you." (author's translation)

These texts from Jeremiah are important in confirming that the outstretched arm of Yhwh is not beyond positive connotation, especially when it is conjoined with *kō(a)ḥ gādôl*. So, again, the text-tradition of Yhwh's outstretched arm need not be compared only with the text- and image-tradition of Pharaoh's conquering arm. Instead, Aten iconography may be a better "match" – at least in the instances that have to do with creation. But, even so, one must admit that there are a number of texts in the Hebrew Bible that mention Yhwh's outstretched arm and that do seem to carry connotations of destructive strength altogether in line with Pharaoh's mighty arm.

At this point, then, we face another question: which image-tradition – the life-giving arm of the Aten or the vanquishing arm of the pharaoh – is best suited as a means to understand the Hebrew motif of Yhwh's outstretched arm? We must turn to that question next, but before doing so, two additional points must be mentioned:

First, the Amarna period was short lived and subsequent pharaohs took care to erase Akhenaten and his heresy as completely as he had attempted to eliminate traces of other worship prior to his rule. To posit a direct connection from the Aten iconography of the Amarna Age to the Old Testament's use of Yhwh's outstretched arm, then, will have to overcome some significant hurdles, not simply in terms of chronology, but also in terms of availability of the imagery and the mechanisms that would permit any interrelationship. Is there, that is, sufficient reason to believe that Amarna

---

6   See also *AEL* 2:91; Murnane 1995:158–59; Strawn 2009b:181–82.

motifs survived long enough to be received into the Hebrew Bible? And what is the nature of the connection(s) between the two tradition-sets that would have permitted and facilitated such a reception?[7]

Second, while the problems outlined in the previous point are important, they are not finally definitive insofar as the iconography of a deity who extends life to a royal figure is not limited solely to the Amarna Age. So, for example, **fig. 4.7** depicts the goddess Maat presenting the *ankh* to the nose of Seti I (1294–1279 BCE). The motif of a divine outstretched arm with a hand that grasps life, extending that to the worshipper and/or king, is thus not restricted to Akhenaten's Aten religion, but is found elsewhere in Egyptian art (see Strawn 2009b:189 and n. 115). Nor is this kind of presentation found only in Egypt. The famous Broken Obelisk of Tiglath-Pileser I (ca. 1110 BCE) depicts two divine hands extending from a solar symbol that probably represents the god Ashur (**fig. 4.8**). One hand holds a bow, the other is open and outstretched in what is apparently an expression of "divine approval of the king's glorification" (Frankfort 1996:134). The ultimate significance of the Amarna data, then, may not lay in the specifics of Aten iconography, but in how those images recommend attention to *deities – not just kings – with outstretched arms that hold symbols for and/or that make gestures of blessing, life, and salvation.*

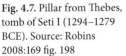

Fig. 4.7. Pillar from Thebes, tomb of Seti I (1294–1279 BCE). Source: Robins 2008:169 fig. 198

Fig. 4.8. Broken Obelisk of Tiglath-Pileser I from Nineveh (ca. 1110 BCE). Source: *SBW:* Fig. 297

---

7   See Strawn 2009b:185–88 for fuller discussion of these points.

4. Merging Text- and Image-Traditions to Produce Meaning(s)

Both image-traditions represented in the Egyptian iconography discussed above can be profitably compared to the motif of YHWH's outstretched arm. But is one more helpful than the other? Is YHWH's arm more akin to Pharaoh's strong arm, ready to bash another Asiatic? Or is YHWH's arm most similar to the outstretched arms of gods like Maat or the Aten, extending life and blessing to adorants?

Coming to a definitive decision between the two options seems ill-advised since both have clear contributions to make. It is better to ask, then, what each particular image-tradition contributes to understanding the tradition of YHWH's strong hand and outstretched arm. So, as noted above, there are certain points, especially in some collocations with *yād ḥăzāqâ*, where YHWH's outstretched arm seems to be closely similar to the strong, bashing arm of Pharaoh.[8] This important point granted, in several other passages, YHWH's outstretched arm is connected with the act of saving/redeeming Israel or with creating the world. Hence, an exclusively negative, destructive, or war-like interpretation of the Hebrew motif is unwarranted, and, at this point (or at least with these particular texts), the divine arms that extend life and blessing in Egyptian iconography, whether at Amarna or elsewhere, seem the most helpful in understanding the Hebrew motif. It is worth noting, furthermore, that both image-traditions are known in ancient Israel/Palestine: **figs. 4.9–10** reflect the conquering arm of Pharaoh, while **figs. 4.11–12** showcase the life-giving arm of the deity.

Fig. 4.9. Scarab from Beth-Shean, Ramesses II (1279–1213 BCE). Source: *GGG*:91 fig. 114a

Fig. 4.10. Scarab from Tell el-Far‘ah (South), IA I. Source: *GGG*:121 fig. 114c

---

8 And deities, of course, since the smiting posture is also attested of them. See, e.g., **figs. 4.13–15** below; further Cornelius 1994:255–56; Keel 1997a:532–533 (Akko no. 5), 600–601 (Akko no. 199).

Fig. 4.11. Mekal stela from Beth-Shean (stratum IX), 15th–early 14th c. BCE. Source: *GGG*:85 fig. 102

Fig. 4.12. Stela of goddess from Beth-Shean (stratum VII), 14th c. BCE. Source: *GGG*:87 fig. 107

To be sure, one might choose to identify one image-tradition with a particular textual instance of Yнwн's outstretched arm, and then relate the other image-tradition to other textual instances. While that is possible, the Hebrew Bible seems to employ the tradition about Yнwн's outstretched arm in a flexible fashion. At the highest literary level (the Old Testament as a whole, that is), the tradition of Yнwн's outstretched arm integrates more than one aspect – or, at least, it can be said to incorporate *both* of the aspects that are well captured in the two image-traditions: that of military violence and dominance, on the one hand, and that of blessing and benevolence, on the other. In point of fact, a number of small seals from ancient Israel/Palestine represent this very same sort of integration by depicting the aggressive outstretched arm of the god along with a symbol of life (**figs. 4.13–15**).

Fig. 4.13. Plaque of a god, MBA (unprovenanced). Source: Keel 1995:209 Abb. 411

Fig. 4.14. Scarab of a god from Tell el-Farʿah (South), LBA/IA I. Source: Keel 1995:209 Abb. 412

Fig. 4.15. Scarab of weather god from Tell el-ʿAǧul no. 1041, 1630–1522 BCE. Source: Keel 1997a:458–59

In the final analysis, then, Yнwн's strong hand and outstretched arm is, despite its relative concision, something of a macro-tradition itself, though certainly on a small, even miniature, scale. It seems best in the light of the comparable traditions found in both text and art (some of which may have had direct impact on the deployment of the Hebrew motif), not to understand this "mini-macro" tradition regarding Yнwн's arm in just one way – whether violently or benevolently – but rather to see *both at work at one and the same time*. Defeating an enemy or outsider, after all, is crushing to the opponent and simultaneously a beneficent act for the one(s) needing deliverance or protection. The two different aspects that are ably attested in the different image-traditions – and in various instantiations of the Hebrew text-traditions – may be closer than they at first appear.

While this more integrated interpretation is no doubt helpful, it is nevertheless very important to underscore the benevolent aspects of Yнwн's outstretched arm, especially in the Exodus tradition and in light of the Egyptian image- and text-traditions. In the Exodus event, it is not simply or merely a matter of a God of Asiatics who wreaks destruction on Egypt, bashing it and its king in an ironic reversal of typical Egyptian royal ideology; it is also and equally a matter of a God who blesses, protects, and cares for Israel – like a single, solitary ray of light dawning on a people long oppressed and enslaved (cf. **fig. 4.5**). The arm that was outstretched in creation according to the prophet Jeremiah is the very same one that saved, blessed, and created Israel in the Exodus (cf. Exod 15:16 and its use of *qnh*). Israel is, after all, Yнwн's firstborn son (Exod 4:22), and at Sinai Yнwн claims to have brought the people "to myself" (Exod 19:4), indicating that the divine self is deeply, even personally involved in what took place in the Exodus. No wonder, then, that we find in the Exodus tradition not only divine anthropopathism – Yнwн's care and concern (see Exod 2:23–25) – but also anthropomorphism: Yнwн's outstretched arm.

Assignment/Exercise

Despite the integrated interpretation offered in the present study (see § 4), try to make a case for aligning just one of the image-traditions outlined above with a particular text (or set of texts) from the Hebrew Bible that have to do with Yнwн's outstretched arm. Does a one-to-one correspondence make good sense of the text(s) in question? Or is something crucial left out that is readily apparent only if the other image-tradition is considered? Make sure to pay attention to the specific context of your tradition-historical comparison: Are you focusing *only* on the specific verse in which Yнwн's arm appears? Or are you considering that verse *and* its surrounding context? In the case of the latter, how many verses are you working with – just one or two, or are you interpreting a larger paragraph or other unit of discourse? These different contextual levels can impact how you assess the question, even if the tradition per se under investigation is limited to the motif of Yнwн's outstretched arm.

Bibliography

Görg, Manfred. 1986. "Der starke Arm Pharaos: Beobachtungen zum Belegspektrum einer Metapher in Palästina und Ägypten." In *Hommages à François Daumas,* edited by H. Altenmüller, 1:323–30. 2 vols. Montpellier: Université de Montpellier.

Hoffmeier, James K. 1986. "The Arm of God Versus the Arm of Pharaoh in the Exodus Narratives." *Biblica* 67: 378–87.

Martens, Karen. 2001. "'With a Strong Hand and an Outstretched Arm': The Meaning of the Expression ביד חזקה ובזרוע נטויה." *Scandinavian Journal of the Old Testament* 15: 123–41.

Roberts, J. J. M. 1971. "The Hand of Yahweh." *Vetus Testamentum* 21: 244–51.

Strawn, Brent. 2009b. "Yahweh's Outstretched Arm Revisited Iconographically." In *Iconography and Biblical Studies: Proceedings of the Iconography Sessions at the Joint EABS/SBL Conference, 22–26 July 2007, Vienna, Austria,* edited by Izaak J. de Hulster and Rüdiger Schmitt, 163–211. Alter Orient und Altes Testament 361. Münster: Ugarit-Verlag.

Chapter 5
Figuring Yhwh in Unusual Ways: Deuteronomy 32 and Other Mixed Metaphorsfor God in the Old Testament

Izaak J. de Hulster and Brent A. Strawn

1. On Mixed Metaphors

In their classic textbook on proper English usage, *The Elements of Style,* William Strunk and E. B. White warn against using mixed metaphor in writing:

> When you use a metaphor, do not mix it up. That is, don't start by calling something a swordfish and end by calling it an hourglass. (2000:80)

But, with all due respect to this standard volume, the fact of the matter is that many speakers and writers continue to use mixed metaphors, sometimes intentionally. To be sure, some mixed metaphors may be the result of carelessness, but others are by design, and, regardless of intent, mixed metaphors can often have significant impact or achieve remarkable effects. Indeed, other writers have noted that the problem is not so much with mixed metaphors as with *poor* or *bad* mixed metaphors (Elbow 1998:54). In fact, James Wood goes so far as to assert that, since "metaphor is already a mixing of disparate agents," a mixed metaphor is "the essence, the hypostasis, of metaphor" (Wood 2008:205).

The Old Testament has its fair share of mixed metaphors, especially with reference to Yhwh. Genesis 49:24 is one of many examples. Here "[t]he God of Jacob is Steer, Shepherd and Stone within one and the same verse" (Korpel 1990:634). The present essay investigates how the Hebrew Bible often figures Yhwh in unusual ways such as this. We will first outline the mixed description of Yhwh in a more extended example taken from Deuteronomy 32 (§ 2) before turning for help to developments in metaphor theory and conceptual blending (§ 3). Insights from these two areas of inquiry, along with the fact that the mixed nature of biblical metaphorical descriptions of the divine is reminiscent of mixed divine creatures in ancient Near Eastern iconography, leads to a consideration of the visual evidence (§ 4). These two lines of inquiry – metaphor, on the one hand, and iconography, on the other – are then brought back to bear on Deuteronomy 32 so as to cast light on the theology of mixed metaphors for God in the Old Testament (§ 5). A short conclusion rounds out the study (§ 6).

2. Mixed Metaphors in Deuteronomy 32

Deuteronomy 32 is a famous text within the Torah and has many different facets worthy of extended study. The present essay focuses on the varied metaphorical descriptions of Yhwh in this chapter. There are many of these in Deuteronomy 32, several of which seem to be incongruous. So, for example, the poem begins by describing God as a rock (v. 4; see also vv. 15, 18, 30–31) and then as a parent with "degenerate children" (v. 5) – an odd juxtaposition since procreation and parenting are not qualities proper for an inanimate object like a rock! The parent image is further specified in v. 6 as that of a "father who created you," but the imagery of this same verse immediately shifts by describing Yhwh as "maker" (*ʿśh*, also in v. 15) and "establisher" (*kwn*) – both of which are verbs that are not restricted solely to parental or paternal domains. As one continues to read the poem, still more metaphors are utilized: Yhwh is provider, protector, and nurturer (v. 10), which are additional images that may not be parental, but, even if they are, need not be paternal (cf. Claassens 2004; Strawn 2008b). Verse 13 seems unambiguously maternal in its mention that YHWH "nursed" (*ynq*) his people, but v. 18 mixes maternal and paternal imagery in almost hermaphroditic fashion within the same parallel line of poetry:

> You were unmindful of the Rock that fathered you;
> you forgot the God who gave you birth.

Even this robust list of divine metaphors in Deuteronomy 32 is not complete as it has not yet mentioned the zoomorphic imagery that is also found here. Verse 11 portrays Yhwh as an eagle hovering over its young, taking them up and bearing them aloft. As elsewhere in the chapter, the grammar here is masculine with reference to Yhwh but the imagery may well be derived from female subjects. If v. 11's imagery is drawn from the behavior of mother birds, it might explain the presence of maternal imagery in v. 13 (see above). Whatever the case, even this brief discussion suffices to show that Deuteronomy 32 abounds in metaphors for Yhwh, all of which are predicated of this one divine subject. At the level of the whole literary unit, then, Deuteronomy 32 offers us an extended example of what might be called a *mixed* or *complex metaphor*.

Once again, Deuteronomy 32 is not alone in offering such an unusually dense metaphorical depiction of Yhwh. And, while it may not be as stark a shift as Strunk and White's movement from a swordfish to an hourglass (see above), the course of the divine metaphors in Deuteronomy 32 (and elsewhere) is nevertheless often quite abrupt, striking, and jarring to modern sensibilities. Is this contemporary assessment an indication that good, ancient (Hebrew) style is just different than good, modern (English) style? Perhaps ancient (Hebrew) style simply had a higher tolerance for mixed metaphors. Even if so, these mixed divine metaphors deserve careful consideration precisely as an entrée into that ancient (Hebrew) style and the authors responsible for it.

Two avenues of inquiry seem profitable in this pursuit: first, developments in metaphor theory and the notion of conceptual blending, and, second, the existence of mixed divine creatures in ancient Near Eastern iconography. We take up each in turn.

3. Metaphor Theory and Conceptual Blending

Among the many possible definitions of metaphor, the following is instructive: A metaphor is a "picturing" or "visualized" identification (see de Hulster 2009a:109).[1] Both aspects of this definition require further discussion. First, in terms of "identification," metaphor is an instance of figurative language that connects two concepts or entities by identifying them, "A is B," but without necessarily explaining which characteristics, qualities, aspects, and so forth make this identification apt. To use a famous example from metaphor theory (see, e. g., Black 1962), "man is a wolf" identifies these two entities but does not say how, exactly, "man" is wolf-like. There exists, then, alongside this metaphorical identification, a good bit of tension or lack of identification. That is, A and B are identified but not entirely equated. "A is B" is the not the same as "A=B," because, in the case of metaphor, "A≠B" is also true. Human beings may be metaphorical wolves (somehow wolf-like) but they also have many not-so-wolf-like characteristics despite the metaphorical identification. It is thus the special power of metaphor to identify A with B even though A and B remain different, never fully equated. If A and B were exactly identical, after all, the formula would not be "A=B" but "A=A" or "B=B." So, alongside the "*is*-ness" of metaphorical identification there remains a resolute "is-*not*-ness" (cf. Fretheim 1984:7).

Second, the "picturing" or "visualized" aspect of the definition offered above deserves comment. In the description "A is B," B is usually known (or concrete) – to some degree, at least – whereas A is not (perhaps because it is abstract). Because B is known and concrete, it can be applied, even visually, to A by means of metaphor. One way metaphors function, then, is by picturing A as (or in terms of) B so that one who hears or receives a metaphor can visualize or "see" (i. e., comprehend and understand) the point. For example, if one does not know what an elephant is, one might portray it metaphorically:

A: unknown	metaphorical identification	B: known and pictured
an elephant	is	a gray bus on four tree trunks with a hose for a nose

---

1   Here is not the place for a full review of metaphor theory. Within biblical studies, among many others, see Korpel 1990; Strawn 2005a; and de Hulster 2009a.

The (A) is unknown but identified (through the metaphorical *is*-ness) by something (or things) that is known and can be visualized by the recipient of the metaphor (B).

Or, to use a more abstract example (with additional wordplay):

A: unknown	metaphorical identification	B: known and pictured
love	is	a verb

Presumably the one who hears this sort of metaphor knows something about love (A) but the metaphorical construction now depicts it (pictures it) as something else – in this case a verb, with the result that love is now seen in a different way.

3.1. Conceptual Metaphors

Metaphor theorists have determined that not every metaphor is created equal, which is to say that some metaphors are far more extensive and powerful than others. The most powerful and generative metaphors are often called *conceptual metaphors*. These types of metaphors reflect concepts that are often extensive and complicated. Conceptual metaphors are frequently (inter)related to other metaphors and therefore allow people to talk about large and complex topics like those relating to worldview or ideology. Conceptual metaphors are thus typically more profound than the kind of metaphors that serve largely for aesthetic effect (though these, too, can frequently be very powerful!). In point of fact, until relatively recently, many scholars felt metaphor to be largely decorative. This changed dramatically when George Lakoff and Mark Johnson introduced the idea of conceptual metaphors: metaphors we live our lives by (1980, 2003[2]).

According to Lakoff and Johnson, conceptual metaphors have the capacity and the structures to organize our thinking about various things, but all within their metaphorical identification of "A is B." Three of their examples are: TIME IS MONEY, LIFE IS A JOURNEY, and ARGUMENT IS WAR.[2] Each of these conceptual metaphors hosts many others that depend on them. So, for example, the existence of the conceptual metaphor TIME IS MONEY explains (sub)metaphorical expressions like "she was living on borrowed time," "he is spending time," "they save a lot of time," each of which depends on the conceptual metaphor that identifies time and money. Similarly, ARGUMENT IS WAR explains (and generates) expressions like "she demolished his argument," "he defends his position," or "they couldn't agree so ended up calling a truce."

---

2   We follow Lakoff and Johnson's practice of putting conceptual metaphors in all capital letters.

3.2. Conceptual Blending

Lakoff and Johnson's work has found wide acceptance and it has been profitably combined with other studies that have furthered our understanding of the way metaphor works. An important example for present purposes is found in Gilles Fauconnier and Mark Turner's model of conceptual blending. In their book, *The Way We Think: Conceptual Blending and the Mind's Hidden Complexities* (2002), they offer a cognitive explanation for how two different concepts or entities interact. They call the interaction between donor and recipient fields (like A and B above) "blending." This interaction takes place in the imagination and is expressed in the "blended space" of metaphor. These blends can quickly become highly complex – further blended, as it were.

An example from 1 Kings 22 may be used to illustrate blending. In this chapter, the prophet Zedekiah is said to have made iron horns for himself, after which he told the king of Israel:

> This is what the LORD says: With these horns you will gore the Arameans until there's nothing left of them!" (v. 11; CEB)

What seems to be a relatively straightforward sign-act on the part of the prophet (cf. Friebel 1999) is actually quite complicated at the conceptual and metaphorical levels. The various types of interaction that can be traced in this one verse are presented in the following chart (**fig. 5.1**).

The complexity of the chart and its multiple interrelations is exactly to the point. The prophet "metaphorizes" the king (or at least the king's military activity) as a bull, a referent that is itself not without its own history (see further below), including, perhaps, an allusion to zoomorphic metaphors for Aram's weather god, Hadad, as bovine. Iconographic depictions of a violent encounter between a bull (often a symbol for the king) and a human enemy (**fig. 5.2**) indicate the graphic nature of this "goring" (*ngḥ*). The fact that horns are often used as symbols for divinities – including for Hadad – lends force to the king's military action, especially because these horns are a peculiar conceptual blend: they are made not of bone but of iron. Othmar Keel rightly describes these iron horns as a "powerful symbol of victory" (see 1974:123–34), virtually guaranteeing God-given success (see 1 Kgs 22:12).

Isaiah 63:1–6, discussed briefly in the Introduction of this textbook, is another example of how blending can often operate with more than just two inputs. In this text, God is represented not only as a grape-treader but also as a warrior, and as someone dressed in splendid garments. The latter detail suggests YHWH's presentation as either a priest, a judge, or a king, though the latter seems most likely. Whatever the case, this well-dressed YHWH is represented metaphorically as a grape-treader, which "metaphorizes" God as a human agent with the grapes turning into God's enemies. Using different metaphors within one "image" – that is, blending more than two input fields – creates a complex metaphor or what is sometimes called a "megablend."

In many ways conceptual blending is a common, daily practice, which Faucon-

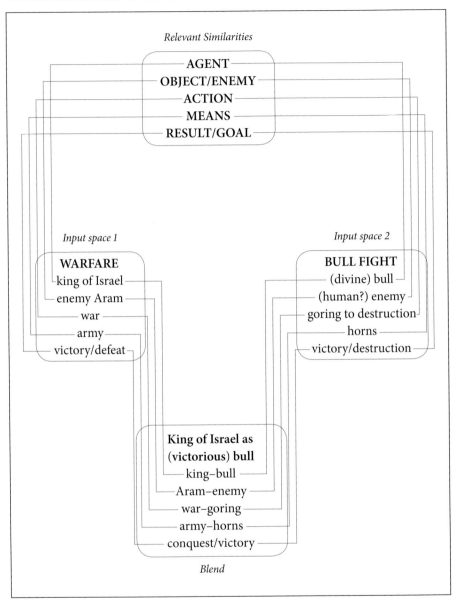

Fig. 5.1. Conceptual blending in 1 Kgs 22:11 (created by Izaak J. de Hulster)

nier and Turner (2002) think began as a part of human evolution 50,000 years ago. Even so simple a sentence as "Emma is visiting Athens today," blends various inputs: the *subject* domain "Emma," the *temporal* domain "today," and the *spatial* domain "Athens." But blending is even more apparent in metaphor since metaphor functions precisely to mix source and target domains into something new (see Croft and Cruse 2004:193, 203–204, 207; cf. § 3.1 above).

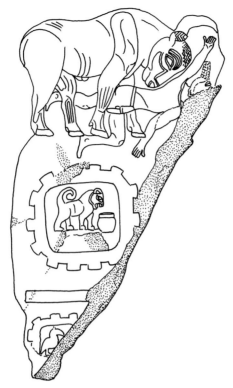

Fig. 5.2. Bull Palette (reverse), Predynastic Period,
Egypt. Source: Strawn 2005a: Fig. 4.155

3.3. Metaphor, Blending, and Ancient Near Eastern Iconography

Much of the theoretical work mentioned above has been carried out with reference
to modern metaphors within one primary language. To be sure, contemporary metaphors are every bit as complex as ancient ones – if not more so – but are far more
readily explained than metaphors from antiquity. When the user and receiver of a
metaphor are contemporaries who speak the same language, any problems or questions can be quickly resolved. The situation is vastly different when the metaphor is an
ancient one and/or is in a language that has not been used for millennia. The study of
ancient metaphors like those found in the Bible is, therefore, *a cross-cultural endeavor.*

When translating an ancient metaphor into a contemporary idiom, it is ideal to
explore the full range of the metaphor in the target (modern) language so as to find
the best-fitting equivalents (cf. Kroneman 2004), but the antecedent and still more
fundamental task is to comprehend the ancient metaphor itself in its original (source)

language. It is imperative, that is, to investigate the full range of the metaphor in its ancient context if one is to understand it at all now. Such an investigation involves understanding the *ancient user's sign-context* – the mental map, as it were (both individual and cultural) – that, among other things, reveals the system of associated commonplaces pertaining to the domains or inputs (A and B, etc.) that go into the construction of a metaphor. Paul Henle puts the matter memorably:

> There is a narrow sense of understanding a language in which one may be said to understand a language when he knows the grammar, the literal meanings of all the terms, and even the meaning of the idioms. Such knowledge does not suffice for the understanding of the metaphors of the language. … [For that,] one must know something of the linguistic conventions … and even of minor facets of the general culture, such as what characteristics of bears are uppermost in people's minds. (1965:185–86)

Or, to shift from bears to wolves, Korpel writes:

> The reader of the metaphorical expression "man is a wolf" should know the *system of associated commonplaces* belonging to the world "wolf." (1990:46; her emphasis)

It is this kind of knowledge of the user's sign-context – what characteristics of bears are uppermost in people's minds (cf. Sperber and Wilson 1995) when they speak of, say, Yhwh as a bear (see Hos 13:8) or the associated commonplaces of wolves (ferocious, cunning, frightening?) when they identify human beings as the same – that allows a receiver to grasp a metaphor most fully and accurately.

Once again, when the user and receiver of a metaphor are contemporaries who share a common language, clarification can (theoretically, at least) be quickly sought for and received if anything about the metaphor is unclear. The situation is much more complicated when the user is an ancient (text) and the receiver a modern (reader), and that is precisely the case with metaphors in the Hebrew Bible. Thankfully, repositories exist that cast significant light on the ancient user's sign-context, one being ancient Near Eastern textual remains, another being ancient Near Eastern iconography.

As noted in the Introduction to the present volume, textual remains have long been the favored comparative instrument within the field of biblical studies. Only recently has the largely untapped resource provided by ancient Near Eastern iconography been explored. But art, no less than text, offers irreplaceable access to cognitive products like metaphorical language. Indeed, if metaphor is "a 'picturing' or 'visualized' identification" (see above), then iconography may be the preferred tool – above and beyond text (alone) – in gaining access to the mental images and imagining that go into the construction of metaphors. Iconography, in a way distinct from and at times superior to textual remains, allows one to "picture" or "visualize" a metaphor. The artistic data instantiate many of the commonplaces associated with a given metaphorical source domain, and (once again) can do so in a way that surpasses an investigation via text alone. It would take a significant amount of text to explain **fig. 5.2**, for example, but, as the old saying goes, "a picture is worth a thousand words"! A picture communicates a great deal of information quickly, virtually instantaneously, even to those who cannot read or write (or draw!) for themselves.

It is clear, then, that iconography can help one "see" the associated commonplaces of a metaphor's source domain, but artistic presentations also seem able to capture conceptual metaphors (§ 3.2). This may be the case in certain portrayals of heroic combat or heroic control (**fig. 5.3**). Especially in the Achaemenid (Persian) period, images like these may have communicated something not just about the figures in question (an anthropomorphic hero/king encountering a threatening beast), but something much larger and more complex: the hero/king as a symbol for the empire, the animal(s) as symbolizing subjugated peoples. In this view, the image instantiates a larger conceptual metaphor for imperial control – THE EMPIRE IS A DOMINATING HERO.

Fig. 5.3. Bulla, Wadi Daliyeh, IA III/Persian Period. Source: Strawn 2005a: Fig. 3.122

Finally, the visual arts are a place where conceptual blending is frequently on display insofar as images often combine several inputs into the construction of an altogether new mixture. Contemporary advertising makes extensive and clever use of visual blending (see Forceville 1996; Zhang and Gao 2009), but blends are also known across a variety of artistic media (Turner and Fauconnier 1999:407), including ancient Near Eastern iconography, to which we now turn.

4.   Mixed Divine Creatures in Ancient Near Eastern Iconography

Since the concern of this article is complex metaphorical descriptions of YHWH in the Old Testament, we may focus our attention on visual blends in iconographical depictions of divine beings. Two well-known examples might be considered.

The first of these are the mixed forms that are commonly used for Egyptian deities, where the gods are portrayed with human bodies but their heads are replaced by the heads of these deities' attribute animals and/or by symbols associated with them (**figs. 5.4–5**; cf. *ANEP*:191 fig. 573). Such depictions show visual blending of anthropomorphic and zoomorphic qualities – and also inanimate symbols – within a single divine entity. These figures are instructive for and comparable to complex metaphors for YHWH like that found in Deuteronomy 32 insofar as they are: (1) used even of high gods in the Egyptian pantheon; and (2) blends that depict the majority of the figure in the most familiar (to humans) form – namely, anthropomorphically – even though the animals or symbols used for (or with) the heads are also clearly recognizable.

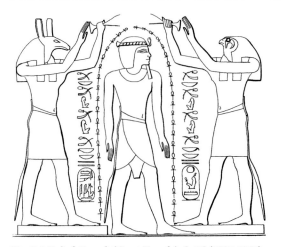 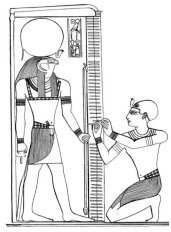

Fig. 5.4. Relief, Karnak (Great Temple), Seti I (1317–1301). Source: *SBW*: Fig. 345

Fig. 5.5. Limestone relief, Abydos, temple of Seti I (1317–1301). Source: *SBW*: Fig. 229

The second example of mixed divine or semi-divine creatures well-attested in ancient Near Eastern iconography is the so-called *Mischwesen* (see, e. g., Wiggerman 1993–1997; Green 1993–1997; Aston 2011), and these are quite different than the first example. *Mischwesen* are frequently far less anthropomorphic and their admixture of various elements – anthropomorphic, zoomorphic, and/or symbolic – is not nearly as clearly delineated, recognizable, or regularized as it is in the first example of Egyptian god-animal-symbol blends. Instead, the *Mischwesen* are complex, frequently frightening conglomerations of a number of different elements and creatures.

A Neo-Babylonian Lamashtu plaque may serve as a representative example (**fig. 5.6**) of these *Mischwesen*. It shows the demon Lamashtu known (among other things) for sudden infant death syndrome, but it also depicts her counterpart who is capable of driving her away: Pazuzu, the king of the wind demons (see also *SBW*: Figs. 93–94). Both figures – in this instance, one malevolent, the other beneficent – are complex blends of many different inputs. Pazuzu, for instance, has talons for feet, two sets of wings, a scaly body, and a snake-headed phallus. Lamashtu also has bird talons in addition to a hairy body, a lion head, and donkey ears; she nurses a pig and a dog while grasping two snakes.

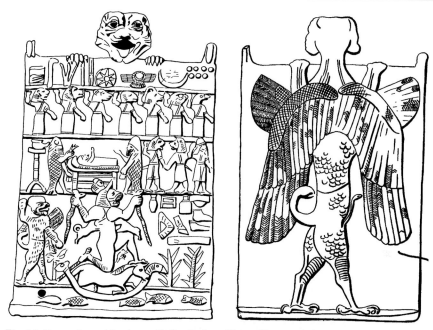

Fig. 5.6. Bronze Lamashtu plaque, IA (beginning of first millennium). Source: Strawn 2005a: Fig. 4.68

The dense combination of visual inputs into one subject/referent has a number of effects, one of which is to overwhelm the senses. Unlike the clearer and cleaner images of the Egyptian gods in **figs. 5.4–5**, the *Mischwesen* are far more confusing. Like other instances of the monstrous, they function as category-jamming figures (Beal 2001:52, 74–75, 106, 183). One simply cannot categorize them easily or at all. Indeed, this inability to adequately contain such figures is what makes them monsters in the first place – fear-inspiring but also awe-inspiring. There is a relationship, then, between the monstrous *Mischwesen* and the divine experience of awe and fear common to the high gods (*mysterium tremendum et fascinans;* cf. Otto 1950).

That is as it should be because the *Mischwesen,* too, are divine or at least semi-divine. The latter may be the most appropriate designation since, in Mesopotamia, this type of heavily-mixed form seems primarily to have been used for supernatural entities lower on the ladder (e. g. monsters, demons, divine servants) than the highest gods in ancient Near Eastern pantheons. When the high gods were blended in some way, the majority of their figures (or parts thereof) were identifiable and thus "parsable" (**fig. 5.7**; cf. **figs. 5.4–5**). And yet, the very unusual, highly complex forms of the *Mischwesen* also depict – in unambiguous fashion – their otherworldly, supernatural status. They cannot be categorized – not *en masse* or *en bloc* at any rate – and so *instantly embody and signal the presence of the divine.* It comes as no surprise, then, that the *Mischwesen* were frequently employed as guardians of sacred objects, as bearers of divine thrones, or otherwise served as divine attendants (**figs. 5.8–11**). This explains, in turn, why such creatures were frequently used in liminal architectural spaces, whether at the gates of cities, temples, or palaces (**figs. 5.12–14**). Their capacity to overwhelm viewers and manifest supernatural presence makes the *Mischwesen* ideally suited to threaten those they face and/or protect those they guard. Either way, they mark the space they inhabit or guard as set apart in some way, and do so primarily by their own unique and curious combination of imagery.

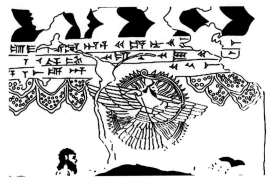

Fig. 5.7. Glazed tile of Tukulti-Ninurta II, 888–884 BCE. Source: LeMon 2010: Fig. 1.4

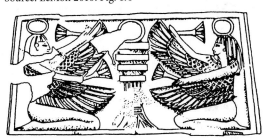

Fig. 5.8. Ivory, Samaria, IA IIB. Source: LeMon 2010: Fig. 1.1

Fig. 5.9. Wall relief from Tell Ḥalaf, 9th c. Source: LeMon 2010: Fig. 2.21

Fig. 5.10. Seal of *ddbw*,
IA. Source: LeMon
2010: Fig. 5.3

Fig. 5.11. Ivory plaque from Megiddo, 13th c. Source: LeMon 2010: Fig. 3.12

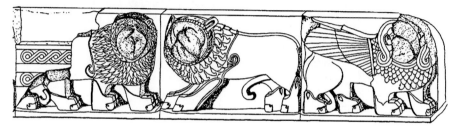

Fig. 5.12. Relief, ʿAin Dara (temple staircase), ca. 1300–740. Source: Strawn 2005a:493 fig. 4.296

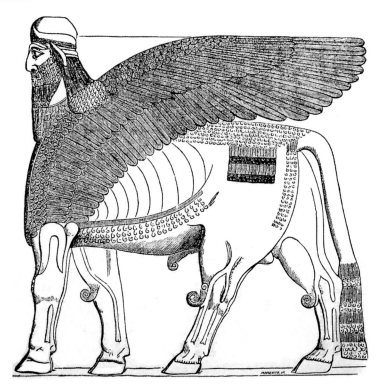

Fig. 5.13. Winged bull guarding an entrance at Nineveh. Source: Layard 1852:86

Fig. 5.14. Relief, Sakjegözü, second half of 8th c. Source: Strawn 2005a: Fig. 4.307

5. "Mischmetaphors": Mixing the Data

The insights from metaphor theory, conceptual blending, and ancient Near Eastern mixed creatures can now be mixed together and brought to bear on the complex metaphors used to describe Yhwh in the Hebrew Bible. We might begin by noting that a text like Deuteronomy 32 does indeed present a kind of conceptual blending. The various metaphors used of Yhwh here occur sequentially, to be sure – as one would expect from reading a text linearly, "from left to right" (or in Hebrew, from right to left) – but insofar as all of these metaphors are predicated of one divine referent, they present Yhwh as a complex and mixed divine entity, not unlike those discussed previously. Still further, if one were forced to choose between the two primary types delineated in § 4 above – the mostly-anthropomorphic Egyptian deities with animal and/or symbolic heads, or the more complex *Mischwesen* – the latter seem more akin to what is found in Deuteronomy 32's textual presentation of Yhwh. Perhaps it would not be going too far to call such a presentation a "Mischmetaphor" (cf. Strawn 2005a:271–73), not only because it is a complex string of images predicated of the same referent, but because the end result bears a striking relationship to the category-jamming, sense-overwhelming *Mischwesen*. Yhwh in Deuteronomy 32 just cannot be captured or easily categorized.

Conceptual blending theory has shown how blends allow one to make something new out of something old – to make new meanings out of old inputs, for example (cf. Turner and Fauconnier 1999:397). And, despite the fact that the various inputs in Deuteronomy 32 are ascribed to one divine entity, the singularity of that referent should not be used to impose coherence on the presentation as a whole. Blends create something new but they are not solely or primarily a mechanism of consistency. Instead, the *dynamic nature of blending* must constantly be kept in mind. Any one *Mischwesen* can be seen, of course, and absorbed – to some degree at least – but the mixture functions to simultaneously resist coherency, easy imaging, or even imagining at all. The *Mischwesen* are and remain *otherworldly* creatures that are, as such, beyond comprehension and, similarly, cohesion – or at least that is what their complex presentation suggests. They represent, in Beal's terms, instances of "classificatory obfuscation" (2001:52). *Mischwesen* struggle to portray what in effect cannot be portrayed: the supernatural realm that is ultimately beyond human comprehension.

The same is true for "Mischmetaphors" like the one found in Deuteronomy 32. In light of the iconography examined above, they, too, seem to function to facilitate or mediate an encounter with something that ultimately cannot be grasped, even as it must somehow be discussed. In the particular case of Deuteronomy 32, that "something" is Yhwh, who is portrayed as a rock-turned-parent-turned-father-turned-maker-turned-protector-turned-nusing-mother-turned-eagle-turned-rock (see § 2). Yhwh is all of these things sequentially, but also, and ultimately, simultaneously. On analogy with the iconography of the *Mischwesen,* the Mischmetaphorical presentation of Yhwh in Deuteronomy 32 functions as a literary instantiation witnessing to Yhwh's otherworldly divine nature. Yhwh simply cannot be located in just one image and so God cannot be easily imag(in)ed, if imag(in)ed at all. The presentation of Yhwh in complex divine metaphors like that of Deuteronomy 32 is "too much" (see Beal 2001:195), overwhelming the senses and exploding all familiar categories (cf. also Chapter 9).

A final point must not be missed, however. It is simply this: in blending so many inputs, Mischmetaphors not only function to mediate or reveal their divine referent, they also serve to protect the deity's divinity by constraining the imagination even as they transgress all imaginative categories. This is to say that their "too-muchness" communicates crucial data about God even as that quality simultaneously functions to prohibit mastery of the divine Subject. In this way, Mischmetaphors are entirely similar to the *Mischwesen,* only in the literary realm. In the final analysis, then, complex divine metaphors serve not only as ways to image/imagine the divine but as ways to chasten such imaging/imagining, especially if that imaging/imagining is confined to one particular image or one set of images (this chastening function is primary). In this way, Mischmetaphors appear to be literary enactments of the image-ban, even though they are ironically themselves *overfull* with images. Perhaps they also somehow enact the incomparability formula by showing that no one and no thing – not by itself at any rate – can be compared to Israel's God (cf. Exodus 15:11; Isa 40:25; Labuschagne 1966; Strawn fc [b]). To come full circle, Mischmetaphors are in this way fully in line with other instances of metaphor, insofar as they testify to both the "*is*-ness" and "*is-not*-ness" of all metaphorical constructions.

6. Conclusion

Max Black once wrote that "[e]very metaphor is the tip of a submerged model" (1962:30) – the tip of an conceptual iceberg, as it were. The possible meanings and ramifications of any given metaphor, that is, are vast. Metaphors are remarkably open-ended: it is possible to draw ever more implications from their expressions (cf. Gutt 2000). If these things are true of metaphor generally, they are even truer of mixed metaphors, complex conceptual blends, what Wood calls the very hypostasis of metaphor (2008:205). The present essay has demonstrated that ancient Near Eastern iconography is helpful in assessing metaphorical constructions, affording crucial insight into the source domains used in metaphorical constructions (what a wolf was like, for example, or showing the primary characteristics of bears). In this way, iconography helps one "see" metaphors more clearly. In the particular case of unusually complex, mixed-metaphorical depictions of Yhwh like the one from Deuteronomy 32, the iconographic data have also proven helpful in better understanding this epitomization of metaphor. Here, too, ancient Near Eastern iconography helps us "see" Yhwh even as the Mischmetaphorical construction ultimately functions to partly obscure our view.

Assignment/Exercise

Consider another unit of text where metaphors appear in dense concatenation and so appear to be mixed. Hosea 13:4–8 is an example from the prophets. In this text, God is described as a savior (v. 4), then a knower or feeder (v. 5; perhaps also v. 6), then a lion, then a leopard, then a bear bereaved of cubs, then a lion again, and then a non-descript wild-animal (vv. 7–9). The Psalms, too, have their fair share of passages where the metaphorical descriptions of God occur in dense formations (e. g., Psalm 17; see LeMon 2009, 2010). After selecting a suitable unit, explore it along the lines of the essay above. Is this a case of mixed metaphor and conceptual blending? What comparable images exist, if any, that help us imagine or visualize the complex presentation of the metaphorical subject? What new insight is generated by assessing the individual images and what seems to be the function of the new blend?

Bibliography

Aston, Emma. 2011. *Mixanthrôpoi: Animal-human Hybrid Deities in Greek Religion.* Liège: Center International d'Étude de la Religion Greque Antique.

Fauconnier, Gilles and Mark Turner. 2002. *The Way We Think: Conceptual Blending and the Mind's Hidden Complexities.* New York: Basic Books.

Hulster, Izaak J. de. 2009a. *Iconographic Exegesis and Third Isaiah.* Forschungen zum Alten Testament. II/36. Tübingen: Mohr Siebeck (esp. 105–18).

Korpel, Marjo C. A. 1990. *A Rift in the Clouds. Ugaritic and Hebrew Descriptions of the Divine.* Ugaritisch-biblische Literatur 8. Münster: Ugarit Verlag.

Kövecses, Zoltan. 2010. *Metaphor: A Practical Introduction.* 2d ed. Oxford: Oxford University Press.

Lakoff, George and Mark Johnson. 2003 [1980]. *Metaphors We Live By.* Chicago: University of Chicago Press.

Strawn, Brent A. Forthcoming (b). "'Mischmetaphors': Complex Divine Images, Conceptual Blending, and Ancient Near Eastern *Mischwesen.*"

Wiggermann. Frans A. M. 1993–1997. "Mischwesen." In *Reallexikon der Assyriologie und vorderasiatischen Archäologie,* vol. 8, edited by Dietz Otto Edzard, 222–46. Berlin: de Gruyter.

Part II: The Nebiʾim/Prophets

Chapter 6
Royal Construction in the Book of Kings: Architecture and/as Iconography

Rüdiger Schmitt

1. Introduction

Not unlike ancient images, architecture is a form of material (and visual) culture that participates within a given culture's symbol system. As such, architecture can have a communicative function, having the capacity to express ideas, order social relations, structure human experience, and situate ritual or performative actions. Thus construed, iconographic exegesis includes the interpretation of the symbolic meaning of architectural structures and how they relate to corresponding descriptions in biblical texts.

Be that as it may, reconstructing the cultural and social significance of architectural features in an ancient culture is no easy task. Doing so requires assistance from other comparative sources, such as texts and other iconographic materials. While the general purpose of various kinds of structures can be determined from biblical texts and iconographic evidence, it must be kept in mind that these sources do not provide "blueprints" or literal renderings of architectural remains. Because of this, the exact relation of architectural structures to biblical texts may be somewhat ambiguous. In some cases, biblical exegetes have been too quick to identify archaeological discoveries with specific objects referenced in the biblical text. As but one example, the tripartite storehouses discovered at Megiddo and elsewhere were originally thought to be the "stables of Solomon" mentioned in the account of the king's building activities in 1 Kgs 9:15–20. More recent research, however, has questioned this conclusion based not only on a reassessment of the function of these structures but also on more advanced dating methods, which suggest an Iron Age II B context for the structures in question (well after the time of Solomon). This example illustrates the potential methodological challenges encountered when relating the biblical text and archaeological findings.

As a form of iconographic exegesis, this chapter aims to carefully interpret the function of certain architectural features. In doing so, the chapter follows Amos Rapoport (1990), who identifies three basic categories by which architectural features communicate meaning:

1. *Fixed feature elements* of the architectural layout (e. g., walls, floor plans, doorways, etc.), which do not change or only slowly change.
2. *Semi-fixed feature elements* of the architectural layout (e. g., decorative elements, gardens, landscapes, and furniture).

3. *Non-fixed feature elements* related to human behavior (e. g., domestic activities, representative and/or ritual use, etc.), which are dependent on the purpose(s) of the structure and are linked to fixed and semi-fixed elements.

In addition to analyzing artifactual remains that fit into each of these categories, the present chapter also explores how these features relate to literary descriptions in the book of Kings that describe the construction of the temple and various royal structures.

2. Fixed Feature Elements

Fixed feature elements consist of various architectural features, including the size and geometric layout of a structure. For instance, royal Israelite architecture, like the Omride structures at Samaria, Megiddo, and Jezreel (as well as the Judean palace-fort at Lachish), differ from non-official architecture mainly by their monumental size. For instance, the southern palace 1723 in Megiddo (**fig. 6.1**) measures 20 x 22 m (equal to 38 x 40 royal cubits, each of which has sides measuring 52.5 cm in length). The building is surrounded by a nearly perfect square compound of about 57 x 58 m. The royal compound in Samaria (**fig. 6.2**) is built in the form of a rectangular enclosure in a ratio of 2:1 (178 x 89 m) so that the whole structure consists of two squares of 89 x 89 m. At Jezreel, a square compound enclosed by a casemate wall and equipped with four monumental square towers at the corners measures about 289 x 157 m, again in a (roughly) 2:1 ratio much like what is found in Samaria. In both cases, the broad side of the building is oriented to the north. Because the excavated western side is almost exactly 300 royal cubits long (just over 150 m), the whole structure may have been planned as two squares of 300 x 300 cubits each. The sophisticated geometrical plans of these structures is in contrast with domestic and other utilitarian structures. Their massive size was likely intended to inspire awe among visitors and is perhaps best interpreted as signifying order and superiority of the king and/or his royal regime.

Another important fixed feature element is the arrangement of a building with respect to its surroundings. The Megiddo palace 338 and the Lachish palace-fort, both of which were built on an artificial podium at the highest point in their respective cities, are positioned so as to overlook, perhaps even dominate, the surrounding area. In the case of Jezreel, the monumental appearance of the enclosure is emphasized by its positioning on a small hill on the ridge of the Jezreel Valley that overlooks the whole area. In Megiddo and Lachish, the palatial or official structures were additionally secluded from the city by separate, monumental gate entrances. The fortified structures inside cities, as at Omride Megiddo, Samaria, and Judean Lachish, functioned to segregate the social and/or administrative elite from the common people by means of horizontal and vertical distance.

Additionally, there was no direct access to palatial buildings but rather circuitous entries. Here again the fixed element features underscore the social distinction

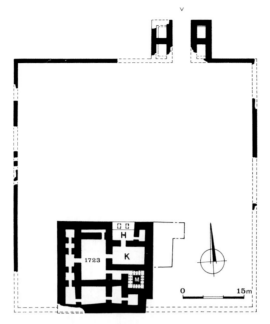

Fig. 6.1. Palace 1723 in Megiddo, Iron Age II B. Source: Kempinski and Reich 1992:204 fig. 2

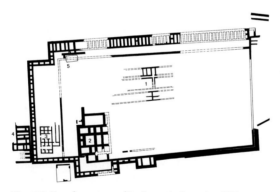

Fig. 6.2. Royal compound in Samaria, Iron Age II B. Source: Kempinski and Reich 1992:249 fig. 14

between elites and their subjects by means of architectural design. In the cases of Megiddo palaces 1723 and 388, a visitor or petitioner would have had to pass a wide courtyard to the palace at the opposite of the gate. The monumental impression of official buildings is further emphasized by the quality of the building, including its use of fine ashlar masonry, which consists of large cut and dressed stone blocks of rectangular shape that are mostly laid alternately as headers and stretchers.

Temples demonstrate similar aspects of monumental architecture, as shown by the Iron II B Israelite sanctuary at Tell Dan. The Stratum II sanctuary complex (**fig. 6.3**) comprises a rectangular casemate structure of about 45 x 60 m, effectively separating the holy precinct from the town. A large podium structure of 18 x 18 m and preserved to a height of approximately 2 m (built of ashlar with a monumental staircase 8 m wide in the northeast corner) was most likely the podium of the temple building proper. With the monumental platform and the (proposed) entrance in the south, the sanctuary emphasizes the aspect of distance both horizontally and vertically. A walled court before the podium of 14 x 12.5 m is assumed to have been the place of the large altar. The wall served to segregate the cultic personnel from the cultic audience, again highlighting social status by means of architectural distance.

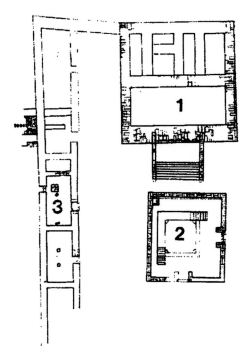

Fig. 6.3. Iron II B Israelite sanctuary at Tell Dan. Source: Biran 1994: Fig. 163

The First Temple in Jerusalem most likely had the same features. Note, for example, that the temple was built on top of mount Zion, overlooking and dominating the surrounding city. However, the lack of archaeological evidence for the temple in Jerusalem has led many scholars to rely completely on the account of Solomon's temple-building activities in 1 Kings 6 as "evidence" of its size and architectural design. While the witness of these biblical texts need not be dismissed, interpreters must carefully take into account both the late date and idealizing tendency of the text (especially regarding the temple's size). Nevertheless, the layout of the temple described in the book of Kings generally corresponds to that which is found in other Iron Age temples known from the archaeological record. But even with this point granted, numerous questions remain unresolved, including the temple's actual dimensions and the positioning of the columns referred to as Jachin and Boaz (cf. 1 Kgs 7:21; 2 Chr 3:17).

Much of what has been said about official structures can be applied to the fortifications of a city more generally. Cities are often built at places dominating the surrounding area, such as on hills or other elevated terrain. The size of the fortification walls and massive gate towers were likely meant to give the impression of impenetrability. The area in front of the gate or in between a double-gate area has highly symbolic value as the threshold between the city and its surroundings. Such places are often used for religious and/or other public activities. For instance, features like standing stones (at Tell Dan) and figurative steles (at Bethsaida) were used for offerings and other ritual activities. The gate plaza was a public place and as such was used for communal gatherings (cf. Job 29:7), judicial decisions, and ritual activities.

The fixed feature elements of architecture can be thus neatly categorized: the use of ashlar masonry; a separated compound with gate tower and non-direct access; the use of a roughly square ground plan based on the royal cubit; and a dominating position (either horizontal or vertical) in relation to other buildings, the city plan, or the landscape in general.

3. Semi-Fixed Feature Elements

The most prominent semi-fixed (decorative) feature of monumental buildings in ancient Israel and Judah are the proto-aeolic capitals (**fig. 6.4**). Their architectural context indicates their communicative purpose: as they flanked doors and gates or served as balustrades for official buildings, the proto-aeolic capitals stood as an icon of power, marking the realm of the royal and administrative elites. Additional evidence for the communicative meaning of the proto-aeolic capital comes from iconographic sources. The minor arts from the Levant and both minor and monumental art from Mesopotamia show a close relation between proto-aeolic capitals and the so-called sacred tree with its symbolic meanings of fertility and prosperity.

Fig. 6.4. Proto-aeolic capital. Source: *SBW*: Fig. 145

The sacred tree motif also relates to ancient Near Eastern kingship ideology, symbolizing the king as guarantor of fertility. This particular connection is reflected in Ps 72:5–16:

> [5] May he live while the sun endures, and as long as the moon, throughout all generations.
>
> [6] May he be like rain that falls on the mown grass, like showers that water the earth.
>
> [7] In his days may righteousness flourish and peace abound, until the moon is no more.
>
> [8] May he have dominion from sea to sea, and from the River to the ends of the earth.
>
> [9] May his foes bow down before him, and his enemies lick the dust.
>
> [10] May the kings of Tarshish and of the isles render him tribute, may the kings of Sheba and Seba bring gifts.
>
> [11] May all kings fall down before him, all nations give him service.
>
> [12] For he delivers the needy when they call, the poor and those who have no helper.
>
> [13] He has pity on the weak and the needy, and saves the lives of the needy.
>
> [14] From oppression and violence he redeems their life; and precious is their blood in his sight.
>
> [15] Long may he live! May gold of Sheba be given to him. May prayer be made for him continually, and blessings invoked for him all day long.
>
> [16] May there be abundance of grain in the land; may it wave on the tops of the mountains; may its fruit be like Lebanon; and may people blossom in the cities like the grass of the field.

In Psalm 72 the king is addressed as the guarantor of prosperity and welfare in general, but more specifically as the one who guarantees nature's fertility by his righteous maintenance of his office. This aspect of royal ideology is also witnessed in ancient Near Eastern texts from Ugarit and first-millennium Syria and Mesopotamia (cf. Schmitt 2004:41–46).

In addition, the proto-aeolic capital and the stylized palm tree both appear on seals belonging to members of the Judean royal family and administration (**fig. 6.5**), as well as on ivory inlays from furniture and other household items from Samaria. These paraphernalia reproduce features of kingship in miniature within the king's dwelling. The proto-aeolic capital communicates the claims of royal ideology to be responsible for the positive aspects of the fertility of nature. The positioning of the proto-aeolic capitals as symbols of royal power in gateways is to be understood as a demarcation of the king's realm, which is entered by visitors or petitioners. Thus, the

Fig. 6.5. Seal of Pedayahu, son of the king, un- provenanced, Iron Age II C. Source: Schmitt 2001: Fig. 99

capitals mark the threshold between two distinct realms: the secluded administrative/royal realm and the realm of the subjects of the king.

Decorations on furniture like ivory inlays also belong to Rapoport's category of semi-fixed features. These ivories communicate a sense of luxury, perhaps of an excessive variety (cf. Amos 3:15; 6:4), and with it, the prosperity of the court. The combination of iconographic designs carved on the ivories themselves (the so-called "iconographic program") reinforces the legitimacy and divine protection of the king, the protection of the divine order by the king, and the prosper- ity of nature guaranteed by the king. The ivories communicate these aspects predominantly to those who would have had access to the royal court – namely, the administrative elite.

When it comes to the consideration of semi-fixed furnishings in the First Temple, the same methodological problems obtain as with the fixed-fea- ture elements. For instance, 1 Kgs 6:23–38 describes the Solomonic temple as hav- ing monumental freestanding cherubs 5 m in height. The general description of these creatures corresponds to the appearance of sphinxes known from the archaeological record. Indeed, cherubs/sphinxes are well attested in the Israelite and Judean glyp- tic repertoire, and monumental sphinxes and other mixed creatures are well known from northern Syria (Zincirli) and Mesopotamia (Nimrud and other places) from the first millennium BCE. However, in comparison to the 1 m high sphinxes from Zincirli, the description of the massive size of the cherubs (and other furnishings) in 1 Kgs 6:23–38 seems to be exaggerated, especially for a small and mostly rural king- dom that would have lacked vast economic resources. In addition, an Iron Age II A date of such furnishings seems unlikely since the bulk of comparative material from northern Syria dates to a later period. Thus, the analysis of semi-fixed architectural elements in comparison with textual evidence can make an important contribution to exegesis. Comparing the architecture with the texts can contribute to an understand- ing of the furnishings but cannot firmly establish details about the size and position of the semi-fixed objects mentioned in the texts; nor can it definitively prove that such objects actually existed in the First Temple.

4. Non-Fixed Feature Elements

The third category of architectural features consists of non-fixed feature elements such as human behavior and usage patterns (living space, food preparation, and con- sumption, as well as other domestic activities, including representative and/or ritual usage). These are obviously more difficult to trace. Additional evidence from other iconographic sources as well as textual sources is thus required. So, for example, bib- lical texts give evidence that the king carried out certain activities in the gates or gate plazas mentioned earlier. In the context of Absalom's *coup d'état,* the book of Samuel describes specific acts of David at or near the gate. In 2 Sam 18:1–5, David reviews his troops at Mahanaim. While he stands at the side of the gate his troops parade in front of him as they depart into battle. In 2 Sam 19:5–8 [Heb. 6–9], Joab demands tribute for himself and his troops and threatens David openly by insinuating that he will revoke his support for the king. David gives in and finally acquiesces to Joab's request, taking his place in the gate and receiving the recognition of his army and the population.

A similar royal act for the preparation of a battle is witnessed in 1 Kgs 22:10–12. The kings of Israel and Judah are sitting on their thrones presenting themselves at the city gate at Samaria while a prophet, Zedekiah, is performing a ritual (consisting of aspects of divination and execration) by presenting iron horns to assure victory. Likewise, in Jeremiah 19, the prophet performs an execration ritual against Jerusalem by smashing pots at the dump gate in the presence of the elders and the senior priests. These performances at the gate were intended not only to publically legitimize the ruler but also to reinforce the relationship between the king, the army, and the population, especially in situations of political crisis.

Iconographic evidence for ritual acts occurring at or near the gate appears in Palestine, Syria, and Mesopotamia. The Late Bronze Age/Iron Age I ivory panel in **fig. 6.6** shows (from left to right) an architectural structure – either a palace or a stylized city – with the enthroned ruler under a canopy receiving dignitaries and tribute-bearers. In first-millennium Assyrian art, comparable scenes are quite frequent. A scene from the White Obelisk of Assurnasirpal I shows the king sitting at a ritual banquet in or rather before the gate (**fig. 6.7**). Another scene from the same object (**fig. 6.8**) shows a procession of musicians, dignitaries, and chariots carrying standards with divine emblems to a city gate. A ritual scene between two towers is found on a seal from the collection of the Pierpont Morgan Library. The relief of the enthroned queen from Zincirli under an arch may also be interpreted as a celebration at a gate. This iconographic evidence from Megiddo, Assyria, and northern Syria confirms what is seen in the biblical texts – namely, that ritual and/or performative actions often took place in the gate area.

Fig. 6.6. Late Bronze Age/Iron Age I ivory panel from Megiddo. Source: Loud 1939: Pl. 32: 106b

Fig. 6.7. Scene from the White Obelisk of Assurnasirpal I (Nineveh, last half of 11th c. BCE). Source: Magen 1986: Pl. 26: Reg. VII D

Fig. 6.8. Scene from the White Obelisk of Assurnasirpal I, Nineveh, last half of 11th c. BCE. Source: Magen 1986: Pl. 26: Reg. VI D, A, B

5. Conclusion

In sum, while iconographic exegesis focuses primarily on the interpretation of images and their relationship to biblical texts (and vice versa), this method can also be fruitfully employed with another form of material (and visual) culture: architectural structures. Attention to architectural features is predicated on the fact that these, too, belong to a given culture's symbol system, and thus are capable of communicating in a variety of ways. They are, as it were, large-scale "icons."

As a way of organizing the communicative function of different architectural features, this chapter relied on Rapoport's distinction between fixed, semi-fixed, and non-fixed features of the built environment. These categories not only provide a helpful way of organizing diverse architectural features but they also provide a starting point for interpreting the cultural and social significance of material remains in the ancient world.

Understanding the relationship between biblical texts and architectural remains from the ancient world is no less difficult than other areas of iconographic exegesis. While no single methodological procedure can solve every problem, interpreters should be aware of certain pitfalls. The most important consideration is this: just as archaeologists should be cautious about making technical judgments about biblical texts, so also should biblical scholars refrain from facile use of textual data in the interpretation of the chronology and function of archaeological artifacts. Architectural remains, like any other object of study from the ancient world, are best interpreted in light of various lines of comparative evidence as well as a judicious awareness of insights from other disciplines and fields.

Assignment/Exercise

Do one or both of the following: (1) Read Ezek 4:1–3 and analyze the symbolic meaning of his actions. How would knowledge of various architectural elements (fixed, semi-fixed, and non-fixed) inform how you interpret the meaning of this ritual or performative act? (2) Examine the scene in **fig. 6.9** in which tribute-bearers carry miniature models of a city. How could this iconographic representation inform an interpretation of Ezek 4:1–3?

Fig. 6.9. Tribute-bearers with city models from a relief of Sargon II from Khorsabad, last quarter of 8th c. BCE. Source: Uehlinger 1987: Fig. 13

Bibliography

Finkelstein, Israel. 2000. "Omride Architecture." *Zeitschrift des deutschen Palästina-Vereins* 116: 114–38.

McCormick, Clifford Mark. 2002. *Palace and Temple: A Study of Architectural and Verbal Icons.* Beihefte zur Zeitschrift für die alttestamentliche Wissenschaft 313. Berlin: de Gruyter.

Rapoport, Amos. 1990. *The Meaning of the Built Environment: A Nonverbal Communication Approach.* 2d ed. Beverly Hills, CA: Sage.

Schmitt, Rüdiger. 2009. "The Iconography of Power: Israelite and Judean Royal Architecture as Icons of Power." In *Iconography and Biblical Studies: Proceedings of the Iconography Sessions at the Joint EABS/SBL Conference, 22–26 July 2007, Vienna, Austria,* edited by Izaak J. de Hulster and Rüdiger Schmitt, 75–96. Alter Orient und Altes Testament 361. Münster: Ugarit-Verlag.

Chapter 7
Of Angels and Iconography: Isaiah 6 and the Biblical Concept of Seraphs and Cherubs

Izaak J. de Hulster

1. Introduction

What, exactly, is an angel? This question has long captured the imagination of readers of the Bible. Indeed, there is no shortage of Jewish and Christian art and literature that has attempted to portray what angels are and how they appear. At least some of these portrayals are derived from the Hebrew Bible's descriptions of angel-like beings known as seraphs (*śĕrāpîm*) and cherubs (*kĕrûbîm*). Among other things, these creatures are pictured as guardians of the Garden of Eden (Gen 3:24), attendants to God (Isaiah 6), and bearers of Yhwh's mobile throne (Ezekiel 1, 10). Moreover, visual representations of seraphs are found on Moses's staff (2 Kgs 18:4), and those of cherubs appear in the temple and on cultic furnishings (Exod 25:18–20; 1 Kgs 6:23–36).

Yet questions remain. Where do the Hebrew Bible's concepts about seraphs and cherubs come from? How do these ideas develop over time? And what influence do they have on how later interpreters understand the appearance and function of angels? The purpose of this chapter is not to offer a detailed cultural history of angels (see the popular publications by, e. g., Rees 2013; Schlieper 2006; and Jones 2011) nor even a robust survey of their background (see Keel 1992c; Savignac 1972). Rather, as another avenue of iconographic exegesis this chapter demonstrates how biblical portrayals of seraphs and cherubs draw on and adapt certain aspects of ancient Near Eastern visual culture.

Beginning with Isaiah 6, this chapter explores the role seraphs and cherubs come to play in the growth and development of the biblical concept of angels, and, in a few instances, its reception history in post-biblical art and literature. In order to scrutinize the seraphs in Isaiah 6 from an iconographic perspective, one needs to be aware of ancient visual culture and how Isaiah's vision, its imagery (with its religious-cultural background), and his proclamation can all be studied as a type of *image*.

2. Seraphs in the Vision of Isaiah 6 and Other Biblical Texts

Isaiah 6 reports the prophet's call and can be dated to around 730 BCE. It is replete with vivid descriptions of God, the prophet's commission, and, most relevant for our purposes, seraphs:

[1] In the year that King Uzziah died, I saw the Lord sitting on a throne, high and lofty; and the hem of his robe filled the temple. [2] Seraphs were in attendance above him; each had six wings: with two they covered their faces, and with two they covered their feet, and with two they flew. [3] And one called to another and said:

"Holy, holy, holy is the LORD of hosts (ṣĕbā'ôt);
the whole earth is full of his glory."

[4] The pivots on the thresholds shook at the voices of those who called, and the house filled with smoke. [5] And I said: "Woe is me! I am lost, for I am a man of unclean lips, and I live among a people of unclean lips; yet my eyes have seen the King, the LORD of hosts!"

[6] Then one of the seraphs flew to me, holding a live coal that had been taken from the altar with a pair of tongs. [7] The seraph touched my mouth with it and said: "Now that this has touched your lips, your guilt has departed and your sin is blotted out." [8] Then I heard the voice of the Lord saying, "Whom shall I send, and who will go for us?" And I said, "Here am I; send me!"

Before turning to the seraphs, the dynamics of Isaiah's presentation of the vision needs to be addressed. The text simply tells us "I saw my Lord ('ădōnây)." What is the nature of this vision? It might be thought of as the pictorial equivalent of language about God insofar as it expresses the reality of God by means of concepts humans can grasp. Isaiah skilfully plays with the ways reality is conceived of not by saying that he had a vision, but by simply stating "I saw" and by becoming part of that reality himself. One might compare this vision with an animated cartoon that shifts into a videogame or a computer game: while seeing the vision (the cartoon) Isaiah becomes part of it (the computer game) and this experience permeates Isaiah's reality (like a performative speech act). Whatever the take on image and reality, he *really* got cleansed and commissioned for a new task, a ministry among flesh-and-blood people (see also § 2.2).

2.1. Seraphs

Though seraphs play a central role in the prophet's vision, Isaiah 6 does not offer much explanation about what these creatures are. They are said to have six wings, two of which are used for flying. As they attend to the Lord seated upon his throne they utter a doxology that is known in later liturgical usage as the *trisagion* ("thrice-holy"). The seraphs also take part in Isaiah's commission. One of the seraphs carries out the purification ceremony by which Isaiah's guilt and sin is blotted out. Thus cleansed, the prophet is prepared to respond to the Lord who calls for a messenger.

As in the Septuagint, most modern versions of the Bible transliterate rather than translate the Hebrew term *śārāp*. The verbal form of this root means "to burn," thus suggesting that seraphs can be understood as "fiery ones" or "burning ones." In fact, when the root *śrp* is used in combination with *nāḥāš* (serpent), it functions adjectivally to describe a "fiery" or "poisonous" serpent. In Num 21:6, God sends these fiery/poisonous serpents as a punishment against Israel. When the people acknowledge their sin to Moses, he prays for them. In response, Yнwн provides Moses with this curious instruction: "Make a poisonous serpent *[śārāp]*, and set it on a pole; and everyone who is bitten shall look at it and live" (Num 21:8). Although in this verse *śārāp* is not used in association with *nāḥāš*, it still seems to refer back to the kind of fiery/poisonous serpent that is referenced in Num 21:6.

Most scholars link Moses's seraph staff in Numbers 21 with the object known as "Nehushtan" (a proper name related to the Hebrew word for serpent, *nāḥāš*) that appears in the temple. As part of his cultic reforms, King Hezekiah breaks this object, which is described as "the bronze serpent (*nĕḥaš hannĕḥōšet*) that Moses had made" (2 Kgs 18:4). While the author of 2 Kings 18 does not use the term *śārāp*, it is likely that the bronze serpent serves as a pejorative reference to the seraph staff made by Moses. While this does not necessarily imply that Moses instituted a cult around the bronze serpent, it is certainly possible (and clearly implied by 2 Kings 18) that the seraph staff had eventually obtained some sort of problematic function in the Jerusalem cult. Since Hezekiah's reforms can be dated to sometime between 720–701 BCE, Moses's bronze serpent likely still would have been in the temple at the time of Isaiah's commission. However, it is not possible to clearly determine the extent to which the Nehushtan might have influenced Isaiah's vision.

Seraphs also appear in Isa 14:29 and 30:6. Though they are not said to have wings in these verses, their description as "flying" (*mĕʿôpēp*) creatures surely implies a winged-form. Isaiah 6 makes this connection explicit because it relates how one of the winged seraphs "flew" (*ʿwp*) to the prophet. In either case, the parallelism with different snakes in Isaiah 14 and 30 corroborates the notion that the seraphs in Isaiah 6 can be understood as serpent-like beings with wings.

2.2. Isaiah's Address of His Contemporaries

Again: what did Isaiah see? Let's apply the comparison with the animated cartoon and the video game to the seraphs. Initially, the seraphs in Isaiah 6 function only as a literary device. It should not be overlooked, however, that part of Isaiah's audience would have seen the seraphs as powerful beings, which is why they would have worn for protection amulets with images of seraphs on them. In this sense, they would have understood Isaiah's description as a supernatural reality, not as a mere literary device.[1] In either case, employing seraphs as a literary device does not deny the existence of angels (either good or bad). Rather, the vision initially appears as a clear statement

---

1 For demons as a literary device see Blair 2009 and Anthes-Frey 2007. From a conservative point of view, one could keep this argument for the demons, or at least for their derivation from deities outside Israel. For the seraphs one could make a different argument and state, assuming angels were an accepted part of Yнwн's entourage in Isaiah's day, that Isaiah describes *angels in the disguise of seraphs*. However, for the purposes of this chapter an awareness of angels as heavenly beings is not assumed for Isaiah and his audience.

about their hypothetical, "if-they-would-exist" status but then incorporates the seraphs actively into the scene (see § 3).

What needs to be considered here is the relation between amulets and supernatural powers. If read in light of the Isaianic theme of the incomparability of YHWH and, in particular, idol polemics (e. g., Isa 40:18–20; 44:9–20), one can also read Isaiah 6 as ridiculing idol beliefs. It does so not by pointing out the futility of the material form of idols but by putting into perspective the power projected onto them by the people. Even this supposed power is rendered naught in the presence of YHWH. The direct denial of any supernatural power by the idol polemics could be understood as a later fruit of the ongoing dispute about powers and idols.

Thus, Isaiah's address describing his vision employs the visual culture of his day in order to engage his audience in familiar language. The seraphs we read about are presented as part of the imaginary entourage of YHWH. They play a role within the setting of the divine king insofar as they contribute to the visual communication of the majesty of God. In what follows, I discuss not only the visual culture of Isaiah's day as an important backdrop for this text (§ 3) but also the later developments of seraphs (and cherubs) in relation to angels (§ 4).

3. The Iconographic Background of Isaiah's Seraphs

The description of winged-serpents, or seraphs, in Isaiah 6 is likely influenced by the prominence of uraei (singular uraeus) in ancient Egyptian art. In most cases, the uraeus appears as a cobra in an upright position and serves as a symbol for Wadjet, the patron goddess of Lower Egypt. As a sign of his/her divinely authorized sovereignty, the uraeus was worn by the Pharaoh or his wife as a crown or diadem (fig. 7.1). The uraeus could be depicted as an ornament on the forehead of either pharaoh (fig. 7.2) or various deities (figs. 7.3–4). During times when Lower and Upper Egypt were unified, the uraeus appears on the royal crown along with the white vulture, the symbol of Nekhbet, the patron goddess of Upper Egypt.

The uraeus also had a protective function insofar as it was displayed in order to ward off evil. For this reason, friezes (horizontal bands on a building or in an image) were often completely filled with uraei. The wings of the uraeus were likely thought to increase its power and ability to protect the name of the king or certain gods (figs. 7.5– 7). The protective function of the uraeus was also employed in amulets (fig. 7.8). Their association with fire is iconographically expressed on scarabs that depict the pharaoh as the sun, with a seraph coming from his mouth as a symbol of scorching heat (fig. 7.9). Sometimes uraei appear in pairs (figs. 7.7, 10). This motif might have influenced Isaiah 6, which speaks of multiple seraphs.

As a result of Egypt's extensive influence in the Levant, uraei with a single set of wings also appear on seals and amulets in Syro-Palestinian iconography (cf. figs. 7.6– 7). Towards the time of Isaiah, a development becomes clear: in addition to the uraeus with two wings (figs. 7.10–11), one finds a four-winged uraeus (figs. 7.12–13).

Doubling the number of wings is usually understood as a way to increase the creature's protective power. The same might be true of the six-winged seraphs in Isaiah's vision, though very few six-winged beings (and no uraei at all) are known from the archaeological record.[2]

To summarize thus far: Isaiah's vision of seraphs likely draws on common ancient Near Eastern imagery of uraei. The fact that Isaiah's seraphs have six wings as opposed to the more common two- or four-winged uraei can possibly be understood as a way of enhancing the protective power of these creatures.

Despite these points of connection between image and text, differences also obtain. Specifically, Isaiah 6 ascribes to these creatures a role that is not clearly present in iconographic sources. Rather than protecting the deity as is the case in Egyptian iconography, the seraphs cover their faces in the presence of God; this suggests that they – not God – need protection. Subsequently (vv. 6–7), these winged serpents turn out to be servants of the deity. They attend to God, are preoccupied with declaring his praise, and are called on to carry out Isaiah's purification. In either case, if Isaiah's seraphs are presented as powerful creatures, then their power pales in comparison to that of the holy God whose glory fills the earth (Beuken 2004).

Fig. 7.1. The diadem of Lady Sat-Hathor-Junit with a uraeus to be worn at the forehead, ca. 1887 BCE (Cairo Museum: JE 44919 = CG 52841). Source: Tiradritti and de Luca 2000:139

Fig. 7.2. Wall relief depicting a uraeus at the forehead of pharaoh Ramses II, Beit el-Wali, 13th c. BCE. Source: Keel 1977: Fig. 41

Fig. 7.3. Wall relief depicting a uraeus at the head of the goddess Sachmet, Medinet Habu, 12th c. BCE. Source: Keel 1977: Fig. 39

---

2   One such example is a 10th–9th c. BCE six-winged goddess from Tell Ḥalaf (present-day Northern Syria), kept at the Walters Art Museum in Baltimore: http://art.thewalters.org/detail/26585/slab-with-six-winged-goddess/(cited 18 March 2014).

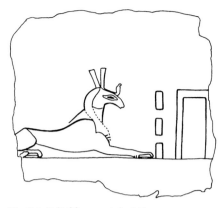

Fig. 7.4. Relief fragment depicting a uraeus at the head of Seth as theriomorphic king of the gods, El-Qubeibeh (northwest of Jerusalem), 17th–16th c. BCE. Source: *IPIAO* 2: Fig. 320

Fig. 7.5. Winged uraeus protecting the name of Pharaoh Ramses III, Medinet Habu, 12th c. BCE. Source: Keel 1977: Fig. 50

Fig. 7.6. Scarab depicting a winged uraeus protecting a sun disk and a sphinx, Lachish, 13th c. BCE. Source: Keel 1977: Fig. 80

Fig. 7.7. Scarab depicting a winged uraei protecting sun disks and flanking a beetle (Khepri) above a crocodile (Sebek), Megiddo, 14th–13th c. BCE. Source: Keel 1977: Fig. 83

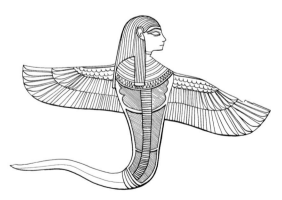

Fig. 7.8. Winged uraeus as amulet, found in the tomb of Pharaoh Tutankhamun, 14th c. BCE. Source: Keel 1977: Fig. 29*

Fig. 7.9. Scarab depicting Pharaoh with the scorching heat of the sun coming from his mouth as a uraeus, enthroned between falcon wings, under the wings of a sun disk, probably from Philistia, 9th–10th c. BCE. Source: Keel 1982:408–415 fig. 1

Fig. 7.10. Seal with two two-winged uraei and a winged cherub belonging to ʾElʿamar, 8th–7th c. BCE. Source: Keel 1977: Fig. 84

Fig. 7.11. Seal with a two-winged uraeus belonging to the priest of Dor, mid-8th c. BCE. Source: Keel 1977: Fig. 87*

Fig. 7.12. Red jasper seal with four-winged uraeus, belonging to Jahmoljahu (ben) *m'sjhw*, 8th–7th c. BCE. Source: Keel 1977: Fig. 88

Fig. 7.13. Bulla from Shekanyahu (ben) ʾElʿasa depicting a four-winged seraph, 720–640 BCE. Source: Deutsch 1999: No. 86

Fig. 7.14. Winged snake with legs on the Mythological Papyrus of Amen-hotep, 1100–950 BCE. Source: Keel 1977: Fig. 31*

Fig. 7.15. Two of three snakes with legs holding a snake which tows a bark on the Mythological Papyrus of Amen-hotep, 1100–950 BCE. Source: Keel 1977: Fig. 32*

In addition to praising God, the seraphs interact with the prophet through the ritual of purification. In this context, another element of seraph representation comes into play: the seraph that approaches Isaiah is said to have a "hand." Iconographically, while uraei typically have wings they occasionally are also depicted with hands or legs/feet (**figs. 7.14–15**). Furthermore, one of the seraphs in Isaiah 6 uses tongs to take a burning coal from the altar. This imagery picks up on the association of the Hebrew root *śrp* with burning or fire. It is striking, though, that these fiery creatures use (or perhaps even need) tongs to pick up a burning coal. Perhaps this detail underscores the efficacy of the coals as instruments of cleansing and judgment, both of which play a role in Isaiah's commission.

It is also important to note that the context in which the seraphs appear is a vision of God's glory. The Lord sits high and exalted on his throne. The fact that the hem of his robe fills the temple (*hêkāl*) often is taken to mean that Isaiah's vision is of the Holy of Holies, or some other place within the cultic sphere. Yet, the Hebrew term *hêkāl* can also indicate a royal palace. If this is the case, then the Lord sits upon a royal throne, and even the hem of his robe is enough to fill the divine palace completely. Worshiped by humans and non-humans alike, God is presented as the exalted Lord, the King of Kings.

It is possible that the inclusion of seraphs in Isaiah 6 is meant to enhance the presentation of Yhwh's glory and holiness. Indeed, when they praise God with their voices the pivots of the thresholds shake and smoke fills the house. This latter reference seems to imply a theophany (cf. Gen 15:17; Exod 19:18; 20:18), but it also is consistent with the suggestion that seraphs are "fiery" or "burning" ones. In either case, Isaiah is overwhelmed by what he sees. In the presence of Yhwh he is briefed regarding the message he is to deliver – a message of disaster (vv. 9–12) and, perhaps, future hope (v. 13).

Thus, when Isaiah 6 is read against its iconographic background, it is evident that the biblical description of seraphs draws on knowledge of uraeus imagery in the visual culture of ancient Egypt. However, it is also evident that Isaiah 6 adapts uraeus imagery in order to make its own point. Specifically, while Isaiah 6 makes the seraphs even more powerful with the addition of wings, it relativizes that power by juxtaposing these creatures next to a holy and supreme "Lord of hosts." The seraphs encountered in Isaiah 6 are not so much God's protectors (as Isaiah's audience might assume) as they are members of his heavenly entourage. They play a role within the setting of the palace/temple, and through their well-known doxology, proclaim the holiness of God. Beyond that, they minister to Isaiah.

4. Seraphs, Cherubs, and the Biblical Concept of Angels

Having briefly discussed the biblical and iconographic background of the seraphs of Isaiah 6, it is now possible to return to the broader thematic concern of this chapter: the development of the biblical concept of angels. A full treatment of this topic lies beyond the scope of this chapter, especially with respect to the proliferation of angelic figures and speculation about the heavenly realm in Jewish literature of the Second Temple period (cf. Mach 1992). As such, the present inquiry focuses on how seraphs and cherubs – creatures who were not, strictly speaking, angels in their earliest manifestations – later came to be interpreted as specific types of angelic beings.

4.1 From Seraphs to Anthropomorphic Angels

While an association between winged-serpents and angels is not evident in ancient art, their description in Isaiah 6 might encourage such a connection at a general level. For instance, the seraphs of Isaiah 6 are linked with theophany, as their "thrice-holy" praise causes the pivots of the thresholds to shake and the house to fill with smoke. Likewise, in Exod 14:19 the angel of God is associated with the manifestation of God's presence in the pillar of cloud. As noted above, the term seraph suggests concepts like "fiery" or "burning," an association that might call to mind the description of the heavenly being in terms of fire or flames in Dan 10:5–6.

Furthermore, the seraphs also help commission an important person to a task, much like the angel of YHWH commissions Moses in Exod 3:2. Though less directly than in the case of Elijah's encounter with an angel in 2 Kgs 1:15, the seraphs in Isaiah 6 participate in the communication of God's word to a prophet. In these latter two capacities, the seraphs of Isaiah 6 might be understood as carrying out an intermediary role as a type of divine messenger. Though not used in this passage, the Hebrew term for divine messenger (mal'āk) can also be translated as "angel." Taken together, these elements of Isaiah 6 have contributed to – and perhaps encouraged – a history of interpretation that understands seraphs as a class of angelic beings (cf. 1 Enoch 61:10).

Two further details in Isaiah 6 also might contribute to the eventual connection between seraphs and angels. First, the seraphs here are described as being part of YHWH's entourage or royal court. As is the case elsewhere in the ancient Near East, Israel imagined its God enthroned as king and being served by a host of heavenly beings, collectively known as the divine council. Much like these heavenly beings, the seraphs attend God as he sits upon his throne, high and lofty. That the seraphs become part of the divine council is also implied by Isa 6:8, in which the voice of the Lord poses the question, "Whom shall I send, and who will go for us?" In 1 Kgs 22:19–22, YHWH poses a similar question to the divine council.

Second, the seraphs of Isaiah 6 also seem to have some connection to YHWH's heavenly host, or army. Admittedly, Isaiah 6 does not specify that the seraphs are part of YHWH's heavenly host, but they do declare in v. 3 "Holy, holy, holy is the LORD of hosts (yhwh ṣĕbā'ōt)." What is interesting to note is that in other contexts it is evident that YHWH's heavenly host is an angelic army (cf. Deut 33:2). This is also suggested in Josh 5:14, where a mysterious man with a drawn sword is said to be "commander of the army of the LORD" (śar-ṣĕbā'-yhwh). Thus, the description of seraphs in Isaiah 6 might prompt later interpretations of seraphs as angelic beings.

Beyond these observations, it should also be noted that the fascination with angelology in the late Second Temple period led to a great expansion of the category of angels. In many cases, this involved concretizing certain forces or concepts as distinct angelic beings. This is evident in the reference to the "angels of the presence" and the "angels of holiness" in Jubilees 2:2 as well as the inclusion of "thrones" and "authorities" among the ten classes of angles in the *Testament of Levi* 3:5–8. The angelic dualism found in the Qumran literature moves in a similar direction insofar as it conceives of forces of light and darkness in terms of good and evil angels. An analogous process may have been at work with seraphs, who in 1 Enoch 61:10 are listed (along with cherubs) among various classes of angels.

What is unclear, however, is whether the seraphs were still considered to have serpent-like bodies in their later interpretation as angels. For instance, Rev 4:8 clearly alludes to Isaiah 6 (and also Ezekiel 1) when it describes four living creatures, each with six wings, singing the "Holy, holy, holy" doxology in the presence of God's throne. Though the imagery of seraphs clearly informs Rev 4:8, this text does not describe these creatures as having serpent-like bodies. In fact, over time the perception of angels became increasingly anthropomorphic and, as a result, focus shifted from their appearance to their ranks and tasks. This is evident in much later Christian art, where seraphs appear with a human head with one pair of wings above and one pair of wings below and one pair to fly (**fig. 7.16**).

Fig. 7.16. Wall painting of a seraph at the outside of the Moldoviţa monastery, Bucovina, Romania, built in 1532 CE. Source: Photograph by author, adjusted for black-and-white presentation

For Isaiah's contemporaries, such anthropomorphic depictions likely would have seemed foreign if not inappropriate. Not only was the notion of seraphs clearly informed by uraeus imagery (see above), but, as Keel and Uehlinger note, "to imagine creatures in human form above the enthroned, anthropomorphically depicted king YHWH would have been gross and an unpardonable breach of ancient Near Eastern court etiquette" (*GGG*:273). Ancient Israelites, much like ancient Egyptians, supposed that the complex nature of the divine world was best expressed with composite or hybrid forms. Thus, a winged, serpent-like creature would have been a more fitting way to represent an attendant to God than, say, the chubby, child-like depictions of angels common in much contemporary religious visual culture.

4.2. Cherubs

As with seraphs, cherubs are not strictly speaking angels. In fact, they are limited to two specific functions: they can serve as a winged mount for (or perhaps an attribute of) the deity or they can serve as protective guardians of certain places or things. Both aspects of cherubs are also known from ancient Near Eastern art and literature.

Perhaps the clearest biblical example of cherubs as a winged mount for the deity comes from descriptions of YHWH being "enthroned upon the cherubim" (Ps 80:2 [Eng. 1]; 99:1; 1 Sam 4:4; 2 Sam 6:2). This imagery likely refers to the two giant cherubs placed in the inner sanctuary (1 Kgs 6:23–28; the ark was placed under their wings, 1 Kgs 8:6–7), which were understood to function as a resting place, or throne, for God's enormous, yet invisible, presence.[3]

Psalm 18:11 [Eng. 10] draws on a similar idea when it relates how YHWH "rode on a cherub, and flew; he came swiftly upon the wings of the wind." This verse depicts YHWH in the guise of an ancient Near Eastern weather deity riding upon a cherub. In one manifestation, the cherub is the descendent of the winged lion-griffin who accompanied the weather god Adad as a flood monster (**fig. 7.17**). In addition, the association of YHWH's cherubim throne with the storm and lightning (Ezek 1:4; cf. Eichler 2011:185) seems to recall features of a weather deity.

---

3   In 2 Chr 5:7 the ark was put under the wings of the cherubs in the Jerusalem temple. This descrip-
    tion might reflect an older tradition of cherubs as porters of heaven (as on the Megiddo ivory
    plaque, the relief of Megiddo, or the relief of Eflatun Pinar; cf. Beyer 2001:41) whose new function
    was to protect the ark.

Fig. 7.17 Seal depicting the weather god and the moon
god before Enlil, from LUGAL.DÚR found in burial 14 of
level XII in area WF at Nippur (18N174), ca. 2000 BCE.
Source: Gibson and McMahon 1995:13

For the Syro-Palestinian context, one needs to take into account a potential line
of influence from the bull that accompanied the weather god in Ugarit and – perhaps
even more importantly – in the Aramaean-Luwian areas (such as modern-day Syria;
cf. **fig. 7.18**). This association is made more plausible in light of the identification of
the cherub and bull/ox in the description of the four faces of the living creatures in
Ezek 1:10 (lion, human, eagle, ox/bull) and 10:14 (lion, human, eagle, cherub). These
observations corroborate traces of an early perception of the cherub as a (sometimes
winged) mount of a weather god, perhaps in a bull-like form.

Fig. 7.18. Orthostatic relief from Aleppo, weather god named "god of the mace,"
entering his cart, 11th c. BCE. Source: Used with permission by the Mission
Archéologique d'Alep/Kay Kohlmeyer

However, the cherub, especially when conceived as a winged-bull, did not only
function as a mount for the deity. In Assyria, the winged-bull also functioned as a
protective guardian in front of the entrances to temples or palaces (**fig. 7.19**). In this

capacity, the cherubs mark "the border between heaven and earth, the sacred and the profane" (Staubli 2012:55). Thus, they not only guard doors, but they also protectively flank the sacred tree, like the winged creatures in **fig. 7.20.** These cherubs might also be related to the Assyrian *apkallu,* a winged being with similar protective powers (**fig. 7.21**). Likewise, the cherub shares much in common with the Egyptian sphinxes, which also function as fierce guardians. The cherub imagery incorporated into the temple/tabernacle, especially in relation to the ark of the covenant, is usually understood to function along the lines of the protective guardian motif. The same applies to Gen 3:24, where a cherub is posted at the entrance to the Garden of Eden.

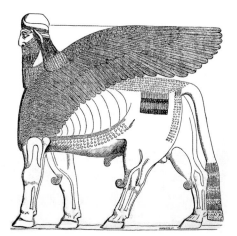

Fig. 7.19. Winged bull guarding an entrance at Nineveh. Source: Layard 1852:86

Fig. 7.20. Cylinder seal from Gaza depicting two winged beings flanking a tree and next to them a lion, ca. 1800–1400 BCE. Source: Nougayrol 1939:32–33 Pl. VIII

Fig. 7.21. Alabaster relief from Nimrud, 883–859 BCE. Metropolitan Museum of Art (32.143.4). Source: LeMon 2010: Fig. 2.19

4.3. Angels as Winged-Creatures

In ancient Near Eastern iconography, seraphs and cherubs are winged beings, often portrayed in composite or hybrid form. Wings on these or other creatures often indicate an association with the wind (**fig. 7.22**) or testify to their tempestuous character and speed. Later, wings function as a sign of the creature's protective quality (for more on wings, see chapter 14).

The inclusion of cherubs and seraphs among the ranks of angels likely catalysed the conception of angels as winged beings. However, another development may have played an even larger role. Namely, angels could be understood as messengers who traversed the heavenly and earthly realms to act as God's agents (cf. Dan 10:13) and to carry out God's will. This task presupposes some means of transportation. Jacob's dream in Genesis 28 imagines the angels ascending and descending on a ladder, perhaps picking up on the idea of a Mesopotamian *ziggurat* (**fig. 7.23**). This text notwithstanding, the attribution of wings to angels is a far more common way of visualizing the mobility of divine messengers.

Fig. 7.22. The four winds depicted on a seal from Sippar, late 19th c. BCE. Source: Wiggermann 2007:142

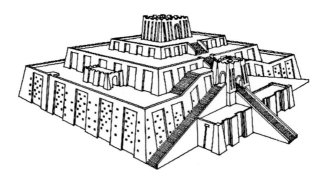

Fig. 7.23. Reconstructed drawing of the ziggurat at Ur, a Mesopotamian 'stairway to heaven.' Source: http://public.csusm.edu/aitken_html/m330/Meso/ziggurat.jpg (cited 13 March 2014)

Fig. 7.24. Reverse of a silver coin minted by Lysimachos, ca. 280 BCE. Source: Imhoof-Blumer 1871: Pl. IX

In its later reception in the Christian tradition, the iconography of winged angels might be traced to yet another theme. According to scholarly consensus, the Christian angels received their wings on the basis of Greco-Roman depictions of the victory goddess Nike (the Roman equivalent is Victoria; cf. **figs. 7.24–26**) in the 4th c. CE (Keel 2010). In light of this background, wings still imply mobility. But the connection to Nike/Victoria suggests that the purpose of the wings was to deliver the "good news" of victory. It is likely that this motif was influenced by winged cherubs and seraphs.

Fig. 7.25. Oil lamp depicting Victoria carrying a tablet listing the virtues of the emperor above an altar flanked by laurels, 1st c. CE. Source: http://www.bible-ori-ent-museum.ch/bodo/search_einfach.php?id=55bfaee78c231#&bomid=13748 (cited 3 August 2015)

Fig. 7.26. Tunesian oil lamp depicting Christ as the one treading on the lion and the adder (Ps 91:13), flanked by two angels, ca. 500 CE. Source: http://www.bible-ori-ent-museum.ch/bodo/search_einfach.php?id=55bfafb1727eb#&bomid=13607 (cited 3 August 2015)

4.4. From Cherub and Seraph to Angels

In light of the above observations, the development of the biblical concept of angels can be broadly traced as follows. Angels were not the novel creation of biblical authors but were born, so to speak, out of the plethora of composite beings known in ancient Near Eastern iconography. For instance, the winged lion-griffin who accompanied the weather god Adad was likely one of the precursors to the biblical cherub (cf. Metzger 1985:322) while the Egyptian uraei likewise informed descriptions of seraphs in Isaiah 6 and other places in the Hebrew Bible. Over time, seraphs, and perhaps also cherubs, came to be seen as members of the divine council over which God reigned supreme. A polytheistic heavenly council could be occupied by several tiers of deities and God could still preside amongst the gods, as in Ps 82:1: "God has taken his place in the divine council; in the midst of the gods he holds judgment." Then the idea of only one supreme deity obtained a foothold in Syro-Palestine and probably led to a (theological/scriptural) phase in which YHWH was "alone" – that is, without divine or heavenly beings.[4] The increasing emphasis on YHWH's supremacy called for an alternative kind of mediated interaction with God. In this sense, angels as intermediary figures could "refill" the divine council (cf. Westermann 1978:93–97). Part of this is reflected in the Septuagint's occasional translation of "gods" with "angels" (Pss 97:7; 138:1). The special "angelic" roles of cherubs and seraphs already had made them easy candidates to fill the ranks of angels together with all kind of heavenly messengers, singers, and other representatives of the heavenly council.

The notion that seraphs/cherubs were special classes of angels was solidified in the late Second Temple period. The last stage of this development was not only a function of the biblical and iconographic connections discussed above. Rather, it also reflected a clear increase in speculation about heavenly beings in various genres of literature, but especially apocalypses and the sectarian writings of the Qumran community.[5]

4.5. The Reason for Angels

What forces, both theological and historical, may have contributed to the interpretation of creatures such as seraphs and cherubs as a special class of angels? And why are angels needed at all?

This phenomenon is not fully understood, but several reasons might be noted. First, increased interest in intermediaries may have been a function of the emergence of monotheism. Specifically, stressing YHWH's incomparability and universality may have had the consequence of enhancing divine transcendence, thus distancing God from human affairs. In this context there arose a need for intermediaries,

---

4   This is the impression one gets from common descriptions of monotheism in Second Isaiah and is related to the Babylonian and Persian periods.

5   Part of this speculation included increased interest in categorizing angels accoring to their location, number, name, appearance, and so forth.

or divine messengers, who could function as God's agents in the earthly realm. Carrying out this role, angels mediate divine revelation (Zech 1:9), commission people for certain tasks (Judg 6:11–24), intervene in decisive moments in individual lives (Gen 22:11–12), announce births (Gen 16:11–12), and serve as agents of divine protection (Num 20:16) and punishment (2 Samuel 24). By fulfilling these tasks, angels provide God with "face-to-face" contact with human beings (e.g., Genesis 18). Hilbrands (2006) elaborates on this last point with regard to the book of Exodus when he concludes that angels can be a literary device that function to speak about a creational form of YHWH's appearance. Or, as Anselm Grün puts it, "Through the idea of angels who stay at our side, God's healing and loving closeness become concrete for us. From the beginning, angels have opened a horizon of experience" (2000:10).

Second, reference to angels can help emphasize both the presence and absence of God. This is especially evident with the angel of YHWH (mal'ak yhwh). In many instances, the angel of YHWH seems to be used interchangeably with YHWH and may have been seen as a functional equivalent to, or perhaps even a hypostasis of, the deity. In this sense, an angel manifests God's authority and presence in tangible ways. Yet, at the same time human contact with the angel of YHWH stresses that there is no unmediated encounter with God. Similarly, after the golden calf affair, God withholds his presence as a punishment, sending instead an angel to go before the people (Exod 33:2–3). By emphasizing both divine presence and absence, angels underscore the supremacy of God.

A third possibility – and surely there are others – is that the emergence or emphasis of angels in biblical thought reflects changing socio-historical and theological contexts. For instance, increased speculation about angels in the exilic and postexilic periods might have resulted from greater contact with Babylonian and Achaemenid religious traditions, though biblical interest in angels can nevertheless be traced to the preexilic period as well. The emphasis on angels as powerful agents of God's will in both the heavenly and earthly realms might also constitute a response to the problem of the exile, the ever-present threat of neighboring empires, the failure of human institutions, and the hope for restoration in the eschatological future. While the details are not always clear, discussions about angels likely proved to be one way in which biblical authors negotiated important theological and historical issues.

5. Conclusion

As an example of iconographic exegesis, this chapter has demonstrated how biblical descriptions of seraphs and cherubs were informed by the visual culture of Egypt and the ancient Near East. Exploring the iconographic background of these creatures sheds light on what they are and how they might have been imagined in texts such as Isaiah 6 (in its composition and reception as text). This analysis also revealed that common attributes of our understanding of angels today – such as their winged-form – can be traced, at least in part, to visual depictions of seraph- and cherub-like creatures in ancient art. Building off these observations, this chapter has also shown how seraphs and cherubs, while not strictly speaking angels, came to be understood as special classes of angelic beings. The motivating factors behind this development are numerous but can likely be understood as a response to changing theological and socio-historical circumstances. These observations present only a small portion of the overall picture of the biblical concept of angels. Nevertheless, this chapter underscores the valuable role that iconographic exegesis can play in the study of the growth and development of important biblical concepts.

Assignment/Exercise

1. Compare the texts discussed in the present chapter with those discussed in chapter 1 of this volume (on Genesis 1). What differences or similarities do you see between issues related to heavenly beings, the division between earthly and heavenly realms, and the nearness/transcendence of God?
2. How do angels or other heavenly beings function in the prologue of the book of Job (1:1–2:13)? Or in the mysterious revelations in Daniel 7–12? What are some new things you learn from these texts about what angels are, how they function, or what they look like?
3. Claus Westermann wrote in 1978: "Powerful machines, human works replace the theriomorphic mythical powers in our world. God cannot shrink before these powers. He can employ these powers in his actions, like he once conquered the mythical powers and made them his servants" (25, author's translation). In your present cultural context, what sorts of things are considered "powerful" and how can you express God's power in a way that exceeds these things? What expressions of God's supremacy fit your culture?

Bibliography

Jones, David A. 2011. *Angels: A Very Short Introduction.* Oxford: Oxford University Press.
Keel, Othmar. 1977. *Jahwe-Visionen und Siegelkunst: eine neue Deutung der Majestätsschilderungen in Jes 6, Ez 1 und 10 und Sach 4.* Stuttgarter Bibelstudien 84/85. Stuttgart: Verlag Katholisches Bibelwerk.
Mach, Michael. 1992. *Entwicklungsstadien des jüdischen Engelglaubens in vorrabbinischer Zeit.* Texte und Studien zum antiken Judentum 34. Tübingen: Mohr Siebeck.
Staubli, Thomas. 2012. "Cherubim: I. Ancient Near East and Hebrew Bible/Old Testament." *Encyclopedia of the Bible and its Reception* 5: 55–58.
Westermann, Claus. 1978. *Gottes Engel brauchen keine Flügel.* Berlin: Kreuz.

Chapter 8
Thrones in Sheol: An Ancient Near Eastern Motif in Isaiah 14:9

Regine Hunziker-Rodewald

1. Introduction

The word "throne" (*kissē'*) occurs in numerous contexts throughout the Hebrew Bible. While this term can simply refer to a piece of ordinary furniture, more often than not it suggests a seat of honor for an important person, as is the case with the priest Eli in the Shiloh temple (1 Sam 1:9) or Haman in Xerxes's court (Esth 3:1). The most common usage, however, is to denote authority and power in connection to the royal throne. As such, one finds references to the thrones of earthly rulers such as Pharaoh (Exod 12:29), David (2 Sam 3:10), Solomon (1 Kgs 1:46), and various other kings of Israel and Judah. In many of these cases, the throne functions as a metonym for the king and/or his rule (2 Sam 3:10). In this sense, to sit on a throne conveys royal sovereignty (1 Kgs 1:13; 2 Chr 9:8), and the promise of an eternal throne symbolizes the establishment of a perpetual dynasty (2 Sam 7:13, 16). By way of analogy, the divine king, YHWH, is also said to have a throne (Isa 6:1; Pss 9:8 [Eng. 7]; 11:4; 45:7 [Eng. 6]; 103:19). In each of these uses, the term *kissē'* occasions few interpretive problems.

However, this relatively straightforward word – and its typical deployment – undergoes a surprising twist in Isa 14:9:

> Sheol below stirs for you
> to meet your coming;
> It rouses for you the Rephaim[1]
> all the chiefs of Earth;
> It raises from their thrones
> all the kings of the nations.
> (translation modified from Alter 2011:184)

This verse is part of a larger taunt song (vv. 4b–23) aimed at the defeated and executed king of Babylon. The strange scene in v. 9 pictures the Babylonian ruler's descent into Sheol. As he arrives, deceased kings of the nations are roused from their thrones as a type of "welcoming committee" (Shipp 2002:150). Much of the scholarly literature on the taunt has focused on the identity of the specific Babylonian king in question (Blenkinsopp 2000:286–87). But equally intriguing, and perhaps even more enigmatic,

---

1   See § 2.2 below for further discussion of this word.

is the reference to the thrones. Typically one would not expect to find thrones in this context since the very things symbolized by thrones – earthly power and status – are rendered meaningless in Sheol (cf. Job 3:19; Ezek 31:14, 18; 32:32; Ps 49:11–12). What, then, are these thrones doing in Sheol?

Unfortunately, the larger context of Isaiah 14 provides no further details about what these thrones are or how and why they came to be in the Netherworld. Broadening one's study to the larger context of the Hebrew Bible does little to help. Some texts describe circumstances that only partially overlap with aspects of Isa 14:9. For instance, Ezek 32:21 refers to apotheosized heroes (*'ēlê gibbôrîm*) who will welcome the coming of a tyrant (in this case, Pharaoh) into Sheol. But, in contrast to Isa 14:9, no mention is made of thrones. Likewise, Ezek 32:27 describes how fallen warriors "went down to Sheol with their weapons of war." These deceased warriors, much like the deceased kings in Isa 14:9, enter the Netherworld with an object that symbolizes status and power, but once again the specific motif of thrones is absent. In fact, the topic of Sheol itself is addressed only rarely in the Hebrew Bible and even then in very general terms (see, e.g., Amos 9:2; Ps 139:8; Job 26:6; Prov 15:11). Complicating matters further, texts such as Ps 49:18 give the impression that *no* earthly objects accompany the deceased into the Netherworld.

The meaning and significance of the thrones in Sheol in Isa 14:9 thus remains an open question, especially if one limits the scope of analysis to the biblical material. However, it is possible – and, as will be shown, profitable – to broaden the scope of analysis so as to include evidence outside the Hebrew Bible, including pictorial materials from the ancient Near East. This type of comparative approach can offer new insight into what is a particularly vexing interpretive problem in Isa 14:9. As is amply demonstrated elsewhere in this textbook, iconographic exegesis is an especially helpful tool in assessing these sorts of textual cruxes. Even so, caution must always be exercised when it comes to relating (biblical) texts and (ancient Near Eastern) images. Each medium conforms to its own conventions of meaning, and it is thus best if each is studied separately at first. It is only in a subsequent analytical step that textual and iconographic data can be correlated with one another in order to clarify the meaning of a motif that finds expression in both word and image.

In what follows, I will first offer a literary analysis of Isaiah 14, focusing on the opening verses of the taunt song (§ 2). Turning next to non-biblical sources of underworld thrones, I will survey representative examples from Syro-Palestinian art (§ 3). I will then relate the images and the text, beginning first with relevant ancient Near Eastern materials (§ 4) and then proceeding to Isaiah 14 (§ 5). In this last step, I pay special attention to the rhetorical function of the ancient Near Eastern throne motif in Isaiah 14, arguing that it is a case of sarcastic re-use of the image to make a particular theological point.

2. Isaiah 14:4b–11: A Literary Analysis

At the outset of Isaiah 14 (vv. 1–4a) the prophet announces that YHWH will once again have compassion on Israel by restoring them to their land (v. 1), enabling them to rule over their oppressors (v. 2), and giving them rest from their pain and servitude (v. 3). A similar tone is struck in vv. 22–23, although there the emphasis is on YHWH's punishment of Babylon. The decidedly theological focus of these verses contrasts with the descriptive style of the taunt song in vv. 4b–21 (Sweeney 1996:232). The possible exception is v. 5. In referring to how YHWH has broken the staff of the wicked and the scepter of rulers, this verse echoes the theme of YHWH's initiative that is so clearly on display in vv. 1–4a and 22–23. In either case, breaking the staff and scepter refer figuratively to the defeat of the king of Babylon along with his oppression and insolence (v. 4b). While Isaiah 14 does not identify the specific king in question, in its final form this chapter alludes to the end of the Babylonian exile and so must be dated to a time after 539 BCE (Berges 2012:140–41). The focus of the present study, however, is not on the identification of the king, but rather on the shocking scene of his humiliation, which is described in vv. 4b–11.

2.1. Syntax and Sarcasm

The taunt itself can be divided into two poems: vv. 4b–11 and vv. 12–21. Each of these is introduced by the elegy formula "How is … ". The first poem, which contains the reference to the thrones and is thus the main focus of this chapter, reads as follows:

> 4b How is ended the taskmaster
> at end is oppression!
> 5 YHWH has broken the staff of the wicked
> the rod of rulers.
> 6 Who struck against peoples in fury
> a blow unrelenting,
> Who reigned in wrath over nations,
> ran them down unsparingly.
> 7 All the earth is calm, quiet,
> they burst forth into song.
> 8 Even the evergreens rejoice over you
> the cedars of Lebanon:
> "With you now laid down
> the woodsman won't come up against us."
> 9 Sheol below stirs for you
> to meet your coming;
> It rouses for you the Rephaim
> all the chiefs of Earth;
> It raises from their thrones

wilted flower may indicate that, after the king's natural body had ceased to exist, the king's body politic alone is left and needs sacrificial "care" (**fig. 8.2**).

Fig. 8.1. Ivory plaque (detail), Megiddo, 1350–1150 BCE. Source: *SBW*: Fig. 233; see also Fig. 14.1 in this volume

Fig. 8.2. Limestone sarcophagus, Byblos, 1250–1150 BCE. Source: *IPIAO* 3:389 fig. 962

3. "Throne" (*kissē'*). This Hebrew word is borrowed from Akkadian *kussû* ("chair"), which itself is taken from Sumerian ^{giš}gu-za. As noted at the outset of this chapter, the Hebrew Bible most often uses this word in reference to a royal throne. The only detailed description of a throne in the Old Testament, however, refers to a gilded lion throne in Egyptian style with ivory inlay and arm rests (1 Kgs 10:18–20). The terminology connected with *kissē'* – such as "to sit or to be installed on a throne," "to make the throne secure," and "to set up/overturn a throne" – is almost the same in Hebrew as in Akkadian and in Phoenician texts. This common cultural background and its iconographical manifestation in Middle and Late Bronze as well as Iron Age Syria-Palestine must now be examined in greater detail, with special attention paid to the motif of the enthroned ruler.

3.   Thrones in Sheol: Iconographic Evidence

In the ancient Near East, the motif of dead rulers sitting upon thrones is well established in iconographic sources. In what follows, I will present representative examples of this motif from ancient Syria-Palestine during the second and first millennia BCE. I pay particular attention to principles of composition, expression, impact, and find context. I deliberately exclude discussion of enthroned rulers in glyptic art because a specialized methodology is needed when assessing the function of enthroned rulers on seals.

3.1. Examples from the Middle and Late Bronze Ages

Sculptures of enthroned rulers with hands clasped at the chest or waist are attested in ancient art since the Early Dynastic period. However, sculptures of enthroned rulers with arms bent at a 90-degree angle and held close to the side of the body first appear at the end of the Middle Bronze Age (Bonatz 2000). In most cases, the right hand, which rests on the right leg near the knee, grasps a cup. This is evident in a series of statues from nineteenth-century BCE Ebla (western Syria). Four such statues in sitting posture, all fragmentary and with the heads missing, are attested. A fifth statue, the only one that is complete, also presents a cup in the right hand, while the left hand holds a weapon in front of the upper chest (**fig. 8.3**). The garment of this statue shows the typical padded fringes of the Syrian ruler's dress. A sixth statue of the same type, now in the Cleveland Museum of Art, probably also originates from Ebla. The fact that five of the statues were found buried in a group under the floor of a temple porch suggests that they had been used as objects of worship. The cup in the right hand identifies the statues, especially in the immediate vicinity of a temple, as recipients of (drink) offerings.

Fig. 8.3. Basalt statue, Ebla, about 1850 BCE, h. 1.05 m. Source: Bonatz 2000:48 fig. 6

In Qaṭna (western Syria), two almost identical seated statues (see **fig. 8.4**) have been found and date to around the nineteenth or eighteenth century BCE. They were excavated in situ 13 m below the royal palace at the end of a 40 m long corridor in an antechamber where they flanked the entrance to the dynastic tombs. The typological similarity with the statues found in Ebla is striking. These statues all include a low throne, the holding of a cup, and the royal garment with padded fringes. The left clenched fist placed in front of the chest recalls

Fig. 8.4. Basalt statue, Qaṭna, about 19th–18th c. BCE, h. 0.85 m. Source: *IPIAO* 2:293 fig. 532

the gesture of the complete Ebla statues mentioned above, but the bowls held in the right hand are bigger than those in the Ebla statues. The positioning of these bowls gives the impression that they are being held out in order to invite someone to fill them up. The statues are much older than the last use of the tomb complex (fourteenth century BCE). Ceramic bowls on the floor in front of the statues bear witness to the constant practice of sacrifice over time and thus the importance of these statues in the context of ancestor worship.

A fragmentary and much smaller figure in the same sitting posture as those found at Ebla and Qaṭna has been excavated from a temple in Hazor that dates from the seventeenth century BCE (**fig. 8.5**). The fragmentary figure sits on a cube-like stool, wears the royal garment with a padded fringe, and holds a damaged bowl in the right hand. While the find context is cultic, the garment and the throne suggest a royal motif. It might also be possible that, typologically speaking, the fragment points to a concept of ancestor cult. If so, Hazor would be the southernmost site in Syria-Palestine where this concept is attested.

From the beginning of the fifteenth century BCE, another enthroned figure is attested in Alalakh (northwest Syria). In the twelfth century BCE, the statue has been partially destroyed and buried in a pit below the temple annex courtyard (**fig. 8.6**). The lower cubic part of the body was originally inserted into a lion/sphinx throne, which was found not far from the statue together with an altar. The figure wears the typical royal garment with padded fringes. This figure bears an inscription that references King Idrimi. Unlike the statues discussed above, the king depicted here does not hold a cup. A possible explanation of this fact can be gleaned from the content of the inscription. In line 89, we learn that Idrimi had reinstated the tradition of liquid (*niqû*) offerings for the ancestors. This suggests that before Idrimi's reign, such offerings had been interrupted. It is possible that the interruption of this practice was reflected in the local tradition of sculpturing statues in which the cup was not included.

Fig. 8.5. Basalt statue, Hazor, about 17th c. BCE, h. 0.31 m. Source: *IPIAO* 2:293 fig. 533

Fig. 8.6. Stone statue, Alalakh, about 1500–1480 BCE. Source: *IPIAO* 2:391 fig. 965

3.2. Examples from the Iron Age

The tradition of portraying deceased rulers in an enthroned position continues into the Iron Age. Compared to the Middle and Late Bronze age funerary statuary, the artifacts from the northern Levant during this time period show no significant typological modifications.

From the thirteenth–twelfth century BCE, at the meeting point of Egyptian and Aramaic influences in Byblos, the portrait of an enthroned Phoenician ruler has been found in the form of a bas-relief on a sarcophagus (**fig. 8.2**). The bearded king depicted on one of the long sides of the sarcophagus wears a headband/diadem, is dressed in a long robe, and sits, with his feet placed on a footstool, on a high-back sphinx throne in front of a table. With the left hand he presents a lotus blossom hanging downward and with the right hand he holds out a small bowl as if wanting it to be filled. The king receives a delegation of dignitaries: the first arrives with one or two crook-like instruments, followed by figures carrying bowls and others displaying their respect with uplifted arms and palms facing the king. On the other long side of the sarcophagus, men and women furnish supplies of food and drink for the celebration. They are accompanied by additional figures performing gestures of respect. Concurrently, on the short sides of the sarcophagus, women are depicted in mourning.

The whole iconographic display on this sarcophagus represents two phases of a drama. First, disempowered by death (symbolized by the lotus) the enthroned king is symbolically brought to life by an opening of the mouth ritual (using the crook; cf. Bunnens 1995). This enables him to receive a drink offering (see the figures carrying bowls) and to join the glorious ancestors of the dynasty (cf. *KAI* 13:8; 14:7). Second, when the king is ready to receive these offerings and join the ancestors, he may be addressed as follows: "Lo! May Rapiʾu, King of Eternity, drink!" (cf. *KTU* 1.108:1).

By around 1000 BCE, the sarcophagus was re-used and an inscription was added (on the rim of the coffin and on the lid). Through its re-use the scene of the enthroned king with a cup from the thirteenth–twelfth century BCE became a kind of "type scene." What is important is not the story of a particular king, but the quasi time-transcending strategies of royal commemoration within a context of assuring dynastic succession.

The ancient tradition of portraying enthroned rulers holding a cup is prominent for the last time in the Syro-Hittite states between the end of the tenth and the eighth centuries BCE. Twelve complete or fragmentary statues of different sizes (0.20 m – 1.92 m), mainly from Taftanaz, Karkamish, and Tell Ḥalaf, have been recovered (Bonatz 2000). These sculptures are typologically identical with those from the second millennium BCE.

Innovations at Tell Ḥalaf include two large statues of enthroned women/queens found in situ above the grave shafts containing their urns (**fig. 8.7**) as well as the double figure of a sitting royal couple (or of a king with his divine guardian). In the latter image, the king wears a garment with padded fringes and the queen (or goddess) wears a crown. The couple has been carved from a single stone in a ponderous geometric style with a table-like lap. They sit on a low bench with their left hands placed on their knees and their right fists clenched as if they were holding a cup (**fig. 8.8**). The double figure was found next to the statue of a standing, armed god on a podium in front of which was an altar and a slab with a slight indentation used to receive libations (Niehr 2014).

Fig. 8.7. Basalt statue, Tell Ḥalaf, about 900–800 BCE, h. 1.42 m. Source: Bonatz 2000: Pl. V fig. B 4

Fig. 8.8. Basalt statue, Tell Ḥalaf, about 900–800 BCE, h. 80 cm. Source: Bonatz 2000: Pl. V fig. B 9

The find context suggests that both the royal couple and the standing god received customary sacrifices. This observation offers strong evidence for the existence of ancestor worship in Tell Ḥalaf (note the wish that the deceased king Panamuwa might eat and drink with the god in *KAI* 214:17, 21–22). As a local development, the practice of pouring libations on specially prepared slabs in front of the gods has replaced the usual cups or bowls in the right hand of the statues of deified kings. Interestingly, the posture of the hands has been maintained.

Funerary steles from between the end of the tenth and the eighth centuries BCE found in northern Syria/southeast Anatolia reflect very similar features as those found in earlier images of enthroned rulers. The similarities in presentation are especially evident in the positioning of the hands, the holding of a cup or bowl, and the garment with padded fringes. Even so, these funerary steles constitute something of an innovation in two respects. First, the inscriptions applied on some of them identify the deceased as members of the upper class of Syro-Hittite society, but not necessarily kings. A similar conclusion can be drawn from the design and layout of the scenes themselves. This development may reflect a new awareness among aristocracy (not just the monarchy) of personal identity and of the desire for perpetuity by accentuation of the self (Bonatz 2000). Second, in these steles one finds a revival of the ancient banquet scene that has a long heritage in the ancient Near East. In the Syro-Hittite city-states, steles with a banquet motif functioned as a type of status symbol among the privileged. In these images, there is no evidence of any sacrificial or cultic practice. In the end, however, the locally restricted nature of these steles and their lack of connection to royal ideology make them less relevant for the understanding of the thrones in Isa 14:9.

3.3. Summary of Iconographic Evidence

To summarize, the following insights can be gleaned from this short survey of the enthroned king motif in Syro-Palestinian iconography:

- In the Middle Bronze Age (early-second millennium BCE), a new type of smaller-than-life-size statues appeared in the northern Levant: the enthroned king with arms bent at a 90-degree angle and held close to the side of the body. The tradition continues into the first millennium BCE.
- Apart from rare local variations, the enthroned king always holds a cup or bowl in his right hand. The combination of throne and royal garment indicates royal identity.
- In most cases, the find context of the statues indicates that a sacrificial practice was performed in connection with these statues.
- Evidence of inter-generational use and of ritual burials of these statues attests to a distinct concept of ancestor cult that took shape in the enthroned-king-with-a-cup statues for at least 1000 years in the ancient northern Levant.

4. Correlating Image and Text

Understanding the compositional features and find contexts of the artifacts surveyed above is a necessary starting point for iconographic exegesis. To understand more about their implied ideas and symbolic meanings, one must next correlate this data with related textual materials from the ancient Near East. For instance, a host of Mesopotamian literary traditions from third–first millennia BCE refers to the Netherworld as a subterranean city-state with a hierarchical social order in which deceased monarchs held distinguished positions (Katz 2003). This is evident in the Death of Ur-Namma (Flückiger-Hawker 1999:115–125). Upon his arrival to the Netherworld, Ur-Namma was welcomed by famous kings. He, in turn, gave a banquet for them, offered gifts to the Netherworld gods, and was finally seated on the great dais where he joined the court of Ereshkigal, the "Lady of the Great Earth."

Several other textual materials, including statuary inscriptions and an Ugaritic ritual text, offer even more historically proximate data for comparison with the images discussed above.

4.1. Statuary Inscriptions

As already noted, some monuments of enthroned rulers are accompanied by inscriptions. One such artifact is the previously discussed fifteenth-century statue from Alalakh, which bears an autobiographical report of Idrimi (**fig. 8.6**). Another example is the thirteenth–twelfth century BCE sarcophagus from Byblos (**fig. 8.2**) that bears the ʾAḥiram inscription, which itself dates from around 1000 BCE and attests to the re-use of the earlier decorated sarcophagus (and thus the transition of the dead-ruler-with-cup motif from the LBA to IA I; see Niehr 2006).

These inscriptions contain curses against anyone who tries to remove the statue or desecrate the coffin, respectively. In both cases, the matter is one of life and death. The removal of the statue shall be punished by the extinction of one's name (Idrimi, lines 92–98) and the uncovering of the coffin shall be punished by the extinction of one's memorial inscription (*KAI* 1:2). To delete one's name and memory means to completely erase their identity and definitively cut them off from all their connections with life. And yet one can deduce from these same inscriptions that, if the removal of the image results in death, then the image itself, as long as it is sufficiently supplied with drink offerings, guarantees the enduring existence of the king's spirit in the Netherworld. Such notions may lie very near the center of the concept of ancestor cult that seems to be implied by the statues that depict an enthroned king holding a cup.

4.2. A Ritual Text from Ugarit

One of the questions for Isa 14:9 is how (and why) the kings' thrones came to be in the Netherworld. An Ugaritic ritual text from around 1200 BCE provides one possible answer (*KTU* 1.161:20–23). This text gives a set of instructions for successfully performing a funeral ceremony on the occasion of the death of King Niqmaddu III. At the beginning of the ritual, different groups of men and women, probably incantation priests, call to each other that the Rapi'ūma[2] of the Netherworld shall be invoked and invited to the feast. These Rapi'ūma are the deified ancestors of the royal dynasty (cf. *KTU* 1.113 where the listed kings' names are preceded by the determinative *'il,* meaning "god"). At the end of the first part of the ritual, King Niqmaddu himself is called to join the assembly.

As the ritual continues, Niqmaddu's throne, footstool, and table are invited one by one to weep. Next, the Sun Goddess is called on in order to fulfill her role in the ceremony. She cries out:

> [20] After your lord, O Throne!
> [21] After your lord, to the Netherworld descend!
> [22] To the Netherworld descend!
> [23] And go down to the dust!
> (Author's translation; cf. *TUAT* 3.2.3; Tropper 2012)

In the dusty Netherworld, the throne will meet the ancient Rapi'ūma and will be reunited with the deceased king. The text closes with sacrifices in honor of the new Rapi'u – King Niqmaddu himself – who is now installed on his throne in the Netherworld.

The high importance attached to the throne in this text is striking. Unfortunately, there is no archaeological evidence for the existence of furniture (or ancestor statues) in the Ugaritic royal tombs as they were all plundered long before modern excavators arrived. And yet, though no statue of an enthroned king with a cup is preserved at Ugarit, the ritual described in *KTU* 1.161 provides textual evidence for the idea that a king takes his rightful place on a throne even in the Netherworld and that such a king received funerary offerings.

Armed with these pieces of visual and textual data, we can now relate them to our knowledge of the culture and history of the ancient Levant in order to better understand the rhetorical function of the thrones-in-Sheol motif in Isaiah 14.

5.   Thrones, Sheol, and Satire in Isaiah 14

At first sight, the fact that the kings of the nations are sitting on thrones in Sheol in Isa 14:9 seems to be of little consequence for the meaning of this text. Indeed, most previous scholarship on Isaiah 14 has passed over the detail. Instead, scholarly attention has focused on a variety of other topics, including deciphering the identity of the Babylonian king or finding in the taunt's unbalanced rhythm evidence of the

---

2   This is the likely vocalization of Ugaritic *rp'm/rpum* (alternatively, *Rāpi'ūma*), which is equivalent to Hebrew *Rĕpā'îm.*

qinah-meter, which is characteristic of biblical laments. Scholars have also frequently discussed the mythological motifs (e. g., vv. 12–15), noting the different puns in this "deadly serious poetic satire" (Alter 2011:189). Although the detail of the thrones has often been overlooked, the iconographic data amassed and discussed above suggests that the remark concerning these kings on their thrones in v. 9 is not inconsequential. To the contrary, the thrones-in-Sheol motif functions as yet another satirical element that heightens the rhetorical poignancy of the taunt against the defeated Babylonian king. Several aspects of this satire can be noted.

First, the author of Isaiah 14 seems to draw on the enthroned-king-with-a-cup motif only to sever it from any connection to ancestral cults. For instance, while divinization was one of the pillars of ancestor cults, Isa 14:13–14 seems to mock the tyrant's inclination toward self-deification:

> [13] And you once thought in your heart:
> "To the heavens will I ascend
> above God's stars I'll raise my throne."
> [14] I'll sit on the mount of divine council
> in the far reaches of Zaphon.
> (translation by Alter 2011:185)

But instead of reaching such lofty heights, the king ultimately is brought down "to Sheol … to the far reaches of the Pit" (v. 15). This is a cruel end to a king who was the master of nations (v. 12). Thus, what Isaiah 14 pictures is a fallen king, not an exalted and divinized one.

Second and closely related, Isaiah 14 strips the Babylonian king of the two markers of royal identity found in the enthroned ruler statues discussed above: namely, the garment and the throne. Instead of being adorned in kingly regalia, the king is covered with maggots and lays on a bed of worms (v. 11). Even more significantly, while the thrones of the nations' rulers are present in Sheol, no specific mention is made of the Babylonian king's throne. This is especially striking in light of the Ugaritic text in which Niqmaddu's throne accompanies him into the Netherworld. In effect, the Babylonian king's royal stature is no longer recognizable in Isaiah 14 – he has been robbed of both robe and throne.

Third, the author of Isaiah 14 can be seen as subverting – or better yet, completely upending – the notion that the "enthroned king" is the object of honor, respect, and worship. In sharp contrast to the Ugaritic ritual text, Isaiah 14 shows little concern for the Babylonian king receiving a proper funeral ceremony. In fact, vv. 18–19 describe how the Babylonian king, unlike the kings of the nations, is cast out from his grave and is left prostrate on the battlefield like a trampled corpse. Furthermore, that the king is said to be "like a corpse trampled underfoot" (v. 19; NRSV) is especially jarring in light of the ʾAḥiram inscription on the Byblos sarcophagus, which describes the severe consequences of disturbing the king's coffin. When the Babylonian king of Isaiah 14 is envisioned according to the image of the enthroned ruler, he is a particularly tragic version thereof. While he joins the ranks of the Rephaim, his pernicious acts in life rob him of an honorable burial in death.

In sum, the author (or more likely a later exilic redactor) of Isaiah 14 completed the mock elegy in vv. 1–4a, 5, and 22–23 with references to Yʜᴡʜ, on the one hand, and the King of Babylon, on the other. The tyrant is no longer simply "brought down," "fallen," and "cut down" (vv. 11–15); instead, it is Yʜᴡʜ who has broken the king's staff (v. 5). Theology triumphs, evidently because mythological ideology alone (vv. 4b–21) was insufficient to convince the author's audience. The tyrant was strong – but he fell. Death was strong – but the power of Yʜᴡʜ does not end at the gates of the Netherworld and faith is stronger than any tyrant (vv. 1–4a, 22–23). Seen in this way, within the framework provided by vv. 1–4a, 5, 22–23, the ancient Rephaim became nothing more than poor "shades." There may still be thrones, but no more gods, in Sheol!

6. Conclusion

This chapter has demonstrated how iconographic exegesis that employs a comparative approach can provide new insights on the meaning of puzzling literary imagery in the Hebrew Bible. The strange reference to thrones in Sheol in Isa 14:9 is best read in light of a well-established tradition in ancient Near Eastern iconography of representing deceased kings as enthroned figures who often hold a cup. I argued that this motif was not only known by the author of Isaiah 14 but was reworked (along with other motifs) in service of a biting satire against an unnamed Babylonian king. This conclusion recognizes that the imagery used in Isaiah 14 reflects a high level of cross-cultural contact. This is true not only of the thrones-in-Sheol motif, but also the mythological themes concerning the ascent to heaven, the falling star, and the Mount of Assembly (vv. 12–14). Terms like "Rephaim" and "Zaphon" also indicate borrowings from northern Levantine cultures. This contact was likely fostered by the political situation in the second half of the eighth century BCE. In the context of Assyrian pressure and violence, political coalitions were formed between vassal-states and kingdoms to the north of Egypt and to the southwest of Assyria (cf. Isa 14:28–32). Thus, even if Isaiah 14 shows evidence of later (exilic or postexilic) redaction, the political situation of the eighth century provides a plausible setting for understanding the conceptual background that informed the taunt song in Isaiah 14. The iconography, in turn, helps us see this song in a fresh light.

Assignment/Exercise

For this exercise, you should begin with a literary analysis of 1 Samuel 28, investigating key terms, syntactical elements, and important themes. Then, using study helps or commentaries, reflect on the different consultations of God referred to in the chapter. To what extent is the practice of the woman in Endor a divinatory practice? What is the character of revelation in 1 Samuel 28? How can prophetic phenomena be compared to divinatory practice?

As your next step, try to identify visual depictions that seem to be related to 1 Samuel 28 using books that contain representative samples of ancient Near Eastern iconography (*ANEP, IPIAO, GGG, SBW*). You might want to look specifically for the motif of righteous kingship sanctified by the gods, which is commonly expressed through images with a "rod-and-ring symbol." Create a list of these images, being sure to note their compositional features, their provenance, and their find contexts. What aspects of this imagery stand out to you? Do the motifs show variation over time or geographical context? If so, what developments do you see?

Finally, try to correlate the information gleaned from your textual and iconographic analyses. What points of similarity do you see between these images and the practices described in 1 Samuel 28? Are there aspects of the iconography not reflected in 1 Samuel 28? Are there themes in 1 Samuel 28 that do not appear in the images? How does this comparative analysis clarify what is ultimately at stake in 1 Samuel 28? To what extent does including ancient Near Eastern images help to advance our knowledge of specific characteristics of theology in the Hebrew Bible (e. g., divination, monarchy, kingship)?

Bibliography

Bonatz, Dominik. 2000. *Das syro-hethitische Grabdenkmal. Untersuchungen zur Entstehung einer neuen Bildgattung in der Eisenzeit im nordsyrisch-südostanatolischen Raum*. Mainz: P. von Zabern.

Bunnens, Guy. 1995. "The So-called Stele of the God El from Ugarit." In *Actes du IIIe congrès international des études phéniciennes et puniques, Tunis, 11-16 novembre 1991*, edited by Mhamed Fantar and Mansour Ghaki, 1:214-221. Tunis: Institut National du Patrimoine.

Kantorowicz, Ernst H. 1957. *The King's Two Bodies: A Study in Medieval Political Theology*. Princeton: Princeton University Press.

Katz, Dina. 2003. *The Image of the Netherworld in the Sumerian Sources*. Bethesda, MD: CDL.

Lewis, Theodore J. 1992. "Dead, Abode of the." In *The Anchor Bible Dictionary*, edited by David Noel Freedman, 2:101–105. 6 vols. New York: Doubleday.

Rouillard, Hedwige. 1999. "Rephaim." In *Dictionary of Deities and Demons in the Bible*, edited by Karel van der Toorn et al., 692–700. 2d ed. Leiden: Brill.

Schmidt, Brian B. 1996. *Israel's Beneficent Dead: Ancestor Cult and Necromany in Ancient Israelite Religion and Tradition*. Winona Lake, IN: Eisenbrauns.

Shipp, R. Mark. 2002. *Of Dead Kings and Dirges: Myth and Meaning in Isaiah 14:4b–21*. Academia Biblica 11. Atlanta: Society of Biblical Literature.

Chapter 9
"A Monument and a Name": Isaiah 56 and the Aniconic Image

Izaak J. de Hulster

1. Introduction

Yad Vashem ("a monument and a name") is the name of a Holocaust memorial in Jerusalem that consists of a museum and an educational center. Taken from Isaiah 56:5, this name serves as an apt description of the center's goal of preserving the memory of victims and the "righteous among the nations" who aided their cause during the Second World War. One of the ways the *Yad Vashem* does this is by displaying the names and photographs of victims in the "Hall of Names" and those of the righteous on the "Wall of Honor." These exhibits, along with a variety of photo archives, art displays, and video testimonies, offer a moving – and one might add, visual – reminder to visitors of the importance of never forgetting those whose lives were lost in the Holocaust (www.yadvashem.org).

The *Yad Vashem* memorial is an example of how Isa 56:5 has been received and interpreted in contemporary contexts. While much more could be said about the *Yad Vashem* in its own right, this chapter considers the historical phenomena that informed the biblical text from which the name of this museum is derived. Specifically, what does the phrase "a monument and a name" (*yād wāšēm*) refer to in Isa 56:5? In what sense is the *yād wāšēm* an "image" and how can we understand its place within a religious tradition known for its strictures against certain forms of visual representation? By addressing these and related questions, this chapter demonstrates how iconographic exegesis can not only clarify the meaning of a difficult phrase in Isaiah 56 but also elucidate aspects of ancient Israel's aniconic tradition.

2. Isaiah 56: Materializing Memory

Before turning to both lexical and archaeological modes of analysis, it will be helpful to situate the Hebrew phrase *yād wāšēm* within the broader context of Isa 56:1–8 (cf. de Hulster 2009a:144–68).

> [1] Thus says the LORD:
>   Maintain justice, and do what is right,
>   for soon my salvation will come,
>   and my deliverance be revealed.

[2] Happy is the mortal who does this,
   the one who holds it fast,
who keeps the sabbath, not profaning it,
   and refrains from doing any evil.
[3] Do not let the foreigner joined to the LORD say,
   "The LORD will surely separate me from his people";
and do not let the eunuch say,
   "I am just a dry tree."
[4] For thus says the LORD:
To the eunuchs who keep my sabbaths,
   who choose the things that please me
   and hold fast my covenant,
[5] I will give, in my house and within my walls,
   a monument and a name
   better than sons and daughters;
I will give them an everlasting name
   that shall not be cut off.
[6] And the foreigners who join themselves to the LORD,
   to minister to him, to love the name of the LORD,
   and to be his servants,
all who keep the sabbath, and do not profane it,
   and hold fast my covenant –
[7] these I will bring to my holy mountain,
   and make them joyful in my house of prayer;
their burnt offerings and their sacrifices
   will be accepted on my altar;
for my house shall be called a house of prayer
   for all peoples.
[8] Thus says the LORD God,
   who gathers the outcasts of Israel,
I will gather others to them
   besides those already gathered.

Verses 1 and 2 set the tone of this passage and show how closely justice and cultic observance are related (cf. Hrobon 2010). In this context, the exhortation to do justice before YHWH is aimed not only at Israel but also observant people who were traditionally excluded from the cultic community: foreigners and eunuchs. Reference to the *yād wāšēm* occurs within the promise made to eunuchs in v. 5: "I will give, in my house and within my walls, a monument and a name (*yād wāšēm*) better than sons and daughters; I will give them an everlasting name that shall not be cut off."

   What does this phrase mean? Some scholars have understood *yād wāšēm* as a hendiadys, which is an expression of a single idea by two independent words connected with "and" instead of a noun and its modifier (e. g., "nice and warm" instead of "nicely warm"). In this reading, *yād wāšēm* might be translated as "everlasting name" (Japhet 1992:69). Yet, even if the phrase is interpreted as a hendiadys, it is still important to study both words independently in order to find out what they express together.

To begin with, it is worth noting that the use of *yād* in Isaiah 56 does not reflect its normal meaning of "hand." Neither does it imply the most common figurative meanings of *yād,* such as "power" or "strength." Rather, in this context *yād* has the rare sense of "monument." This meaning is evident in 2 Sam 18:18 where *yād* is found in parallel with *maṣṣēbâ,* a stone pillar often used as a monument or personal memorial. The parallel arrangement of *yād* and *maṣṣēbâ* in 2 Sam 18:18 suggests that these two terms can be used as near synonyms. While this observation helps to clarify the basic meaning of *yād* in Isa 56:5, it does not yet clarify why this text opts for this special sense of *yād* instead of using a more common term such as *maṣṣēbâ.*

The unusual word choice in Isa 56:5 is likely motivated by a common Hebrew euphemism in which *yād* can refer to the penis. This usage of *yād* – along with a possible allusion to a stone pillar or stele[1] – is found in Isa 57:7–8. Commenting on these two verses, Johnston notes:

> In this portrayal of promiscuity, several terms have both sexual and death cult allusions, e. g. "bed" (*miškāb*) can mean "grave" (as in v. 2), and the word translated "nakedness" (*yād,* "hand," here a euphemism for "penis") can also mean "mortuary stele" (as in Absalom's stele, 2 Sam 18:18). (2002:177)

Similar connotations are active in Isa 56:5. In this context, the promise of a monument (*yād*) is given to eunuchs (individuals who were castrated at a young age) or to those who were impotent or willingly celibate. Thus, while the basic (though atypical) meaning of *yād* in this verse is "monument," ancient readers would also have picked up on how the promise of a *yād* (in its euphemistic sense) was fitting given the situation of a eunuch.

At first glance, the basic meaning of *šēm* in Isaiah 56:5 is more straightforward. Here and elsewhere in the Hebrew Bible, this term means "name." However, *šēm* can also surface wider-ranging connotations. For instance, Isa 66:22 parallels words for offspring and name (here italicized): "For as the new heavens and the new earth, which I will make, shall remain before me, says the LORD, so shall *your descendants and your name* remain." A similar parallel is also present in 56:5, which states that "a monument and a name" is "better than sons and daughters."

On the one hand, this parallel implies that children are a means by which one's name is perpetuated. This is evident in the use of patronymics as well as the more general sense that children carry on the name (or memory) of their parents through their appearance, character, occupation, and so forth. On the other hand, the connection between *šēm* and descendants points to the well-known ancient custom in which

---

1   A stele is an erected stone usually inscribed with text and/or figures while a *maṣṣēbâ* generally lacks writing and pictorial depictions.

children erected stone monuments as memorials for their parents. This practice was carried out for both fathers and mothers since erected stones were not thought to be gender-specific (Uehlinger 1991:877–78).

In the ancient Near East, kings were also interested in the preservation of their names. They often did so by setting up a stone monument, which in certain cases were inscribed with their names (**fig. 9.1**). In other cases, kings undertook large building projects as a way to "'establish their name[s]' in view of eternal remembrance" (Becking 1999:764). Though without an overtly royal context, an analogous situation seems to be in view in Genesis 11:4a: "Then they said, 'Come, let us build ourselves a city, and a tower with its top in the heavens, and let us make a name for ourselves."

Fig. 9.1. Standing stones with the names of Tiglath-Pileser III and Ashur-resh-ishi II, Ashur, 8th c. BCE.
Source: Andrae 1913: Pl. XIV, 1

Thus, erecting stone monuments or larger buildings were common ways to assure that one's name would not be cut off. The same applies to the *yād wāšēm* in Isa 56:5. It is intended to be an everlasting memorial, a way of preserving an individual's name through the setting up of a physical and visible object. Thus, it might be concluded that the *yād wāšēm* is a way of materializing memory. The name and the material form of the monument are fused. To borrow and slightly adjust Marshall McLuhan's well-known phrase, the medium is the memory.

3. Material Evidence: The Aniconic Image

What did such a monument look like? To answer this question, one needs to turn to both archaeology and iconography. The previously noted parallel between the *yād wāšēm* and *maṣṣēbâ* points to the possibility of interpreting this object as an erected stone pillar that functions as a monument. Also referred to as "standing stones," these pillars have a long history in the (southern) Levant, even though an indisputable example cannot be presented for every single century. **Figures 9.2, 3, 4,** and **5a–b** show a few examples from the archaeological record of Syria-Palestine.

Fig. 9.2. Standing stones in a desert sanctuary near Eilat, ca. 5000 BCE. Source: Avner 2001:30–31

Fig. 9.3. Standing stones at Gezer, 18th c. BCE. Source: Modified from Macalister 1903:29 pl. VII

Fig. 9.4. Standing stones at Hazor, northern Israel, 14th–13th c. BCE. Source *GGG:* Fig. 47

Figs 9.5a–b. Standing stones at Tell Dan, northern Israel, ca. 8th c. BCE. Source: Photograph by author

A *maṣṣēbâ* generally consists of an unhewn or crudely shaped stone (cf. Deut 27:5; Josh 8:31) that stood in an upright position. These stones are often found in special contexts, such as sanctuaries, and are often arranged in pairs or groups. Usually these stones are understood as representatives of ancestors who are thought to have joined the divine ranks. Bloch-Smith (2005:36) has outlined the following criteria for identifying a *maṣṣēbâ* in the archaeological record:

> (1) the stone's shape and size conform to expectation; generally, height exceeds width, (2) the stone does not bear a striking resemblance to a functional item such that its cultic status is not evident, and (3) the context and accompanying assemblage support the identification if the stone is functioning as a *maṣṣēbâ*.

Having generally discussed what this type of stone pillar looks like, it is necessary to consider why people would have used them. A *maṣṣēbâ* can have numerous functions, including representing a deity, serving as a memorial, marking a boundary, bearing an inscription about a victory, or taking on the role of a covenant witness. According to Graesser (1972:37), these stone pillars fall into four functional categories: memorial (related to a person), commemorative (related to an event), legal, and cultic. In either case, de Moor notes, "the function of all standing stones is to keep memory of something or someone alive" (1997:360). In other words, the commemorative function of the standing stones means that they are capable of recalling someone's presence or memory.

However, it is also important to note that the commemorative function of *maṣṣēbôt* (plural of *maṣṣēbâ*) does not typically involve pictorial representation. In fact, *maṣṣēbôt* are imageless or "aniconic" objects insofar as they are not typically marked with any form of figural representation. Yet at the same time, the stone pillars themselves are surely meant to be seen, as is indicated by the care given to their placement and arrangement, not to mention their size. They are, in a sense, a special type of image (broadly conceived) insofar as they have a communicative function. In this sense, a *maṣṣēbâ* (or the *yād wāšēm* in Isa 56:5) might be considered an aniconic image – that is, a communicative, visual sign that lacks figural depiction.

Interestingly, this type of aniconic image is sometimes depicted on other forms of visual representation. For instance, **fig. 9.6** is a Nabataean rock carving that depicts several upright stones: a large one near the center with three smaller stones in the lower right corner. Some large carved stones, like the one here, bear a memorial inscription, corroborating the practice of using these as memorial steles (known as *nepeš,* in distinction to a *betyl,* which represents a deity; cf. e. g., Wenning 2001). The three small upright stones to the right have been interpreted as representatives of the spirits protecting the funerary memorial. In **fig. 9.7** is a Phoenician stele, which happens to depict what appears to be a *maṣṣēbâ.* Likewise, some coins also depict upright stones. In the example shown in **fig. 9.8,** the *maṣṣēbâ* is located in a sanctuary.

Fig. 9.6. Standing stones hewn in a rock relief, near Petra, Jordan, Hellenistic period. Source: Dalman 1908:344–345 fig. 313

Fig. 9.7. Phoenician stele depicting another stele, Motya, 6th or 5th c. BCE. Source: Moscati 1988:317, 648 fig. 380

Fig. 9.8. Coin from Byblos with a *betyl* in a temple, Hellenistic period, BMC Phoenicia XII 13. Source: Mettinger 1995:107 fig. 5.12

4. The Place of the Monument in Isaiah 56:5

As the previous section has shown, erecting a stone pillar was a way to materialize memory. Yet, where would such a monument be placed? Isaiah 56:5 refers to the *yād wāšēm* being given "in my house and within my walls."

Reading this reference against the background of the reconstruction of Jerusalem in the Achaemenid period, "within my walls" indicates a location within the city. However, the mention of the monument being "in my house" gives added specificity. The monument is not only within the city, but is within the walls of the rebuilt temple precinct. A temple setting would further underline the close relationship between God and the eunuch: by erecting a monument within the temple, the eunuch's acceptance by God is marked for eternity. A stone monument would be the most appropriate form of commemoration in this context since burials were prohibited in the temple precinct. In addition, the monument in the temple was thought to represent or replace the presence of the eunuch serving before Yhwh. In other words, the eunuch's worship and praise is perpetuated – and indeed, petrified – in the form of this monument.

Seen in this light, other aspects of Isaiah 56 can be brought into focus. For instance, the eunuch identifies himself with a dry tree. This tree, like the *yād*, will not be cut off. Now even more of the word play on *yād* appears. The imagery of a "dry tree" suggests that the eunuch will lack offspring, a metonomy of *yād* in its euphemistic sense. Yhwh's remedy is to give the eunuch a *yād* that is better than sons and daughters. One could interpret this *yad* as a sign of the tree prospering.

In conclusion, *yād wāšēm* indicates a monument and a name. This memorial can be interpreted in light of archaeological and iconographic evidence as an upright stone pillar (*maṣṣēbâ*) that had a commemorative function. God places this monument for a childless eunuch within the temple courtyard as a sign of recognition of the eunuch's devotion to Yhwh and as an act of God's open-heartedness.

5. The Image Ban and the Aniconic Image

If the previously introduced idea of an "aniconic image" (or "imageless image;" cf. de Hulster forthcoming [a]) sounds somewhat paradoxical, it effectively picks up on a persistent tension in the history of Israelite religion. On the one hand, the Hebrew Bible prohibits the production of certain types of images, especially those used to represent Yhwh or other deities. Such images are ridiculed by the prophets and declared to be idols in legal materials. In view of these texts, aniconism – the practice of avoiding divine images or other pictorial representations in the context of worship – is often thought to be a distinguishing characteristic of Israelite religion. Yet on the other hand, it is abundantly clear from archaeological discoveries that there *were* images in Israel throughout its history, as Silvia Schroer so aptly puts it in the title of her important book, *In Israel gab es Bilder* (1987). How can these two observations hold together? What types of images might have been allowed and how did the ban on images develop over time? The following sections begin to address some of these questions.

5.1. Types of Aniconic Images

Even in its most programmatic forms (see below), the ban on images in the Hebrew Bible never prohibited the use or production of *all* forms of visual representation. In fact, two broad categories of aniconic images can be identified (Mettinger 1995).

First, instead of representing a deity in anthropomorphic form (as was common in the ancient Near East), one could use a symbol (cf. Ornan 2005b). These symbols could consist of depictions of the "divine standard" (*ANEP* 293, 625), a weapon, or an object or attribute associated with the deity (as *ANEP* 246, 453). In the Hebrew Bible, examples may include the ark of the covenant or the menorah. This form of divine representation is also known in Mesopotamian glyptic art, especially in the first half of the first millennium. It is important to note that while not representing the physical (or anthropomorphic) form of the deity, divine symbols were thought to covey the presence or power of the deity in special circumstances.

Fig. 9.9. Taanach cult stand. Source: Vriezen 1998:55 fig. 9

Fig. 9.10. Empty cart on a stele from Urartu, 800–750 BCE. Source: Keel 1977:186 fig. 129

Fig. 9.11. Large footprints in the temple of ʿAin Dara. Source: Abū ʿAssāf 1990:14 Pl. 11a

The second category of acceptable images is often referred to as "empty space aniconism." These images function as indexical signs, referring to the deity indirectly by metonymic extension or by logical implication. References to Yhwh being "enthroned upon the cherubim" (Ps 99:1; 1 Kgs 6:23–28) call to mind one such form of empty space aniconism. In this example, the cover of the ark is adorned with cherubs, the wings of which functioned as a throne for the invisible presence of Yhwh. Other examples can be found in ancient Near Eastern iconography. For instance, the hole in the Taanach cult stand between the two sphinxes (second register from below, **fig. 9.9**) has been interpreted as an expression of empty space aniconism, perhaps because the deity referred to could not be depicted. Another example might be found in **fig. 9.10**, where an empty cart is depicted on a battlefield. Perhaps most impressive are the massive footprints (97 cm x 35 cm) sculptured in the floor of the sanctuary in the temple of ʿAin Dara (**fig. 9.11**). The footprints testify to the presence of a god without representing the image of that deity directly (Abū ʿAssāf 1990:14).

Taking the *maṣṣēbôt* as the third category,[2] we might point to a fourth possibility: the open-air sanctuary of Aten lacks a cult image because Aten the sun "himself" is present during the day (see chapter I,1, figure 8).

5.2. The Development of Aniconism

There is considerable disagreement in the scholarly literature concerning exactly when and why ancient Israel's aniconic tradition began. However, there is a broad consensus that different forms of aniconism developed over time.

In earlier stages, Israel likely expressed what Mettinger calls *de facto* aniconism. This form of aniconism involves a general preference for aniconic representations of the deity without expressly prohibiting the use of iconic objects, such as anthropomorphic cult statuary (Mettinger 1995). In part, this type of aniconism might be related to the semi-nomadic background of Israel, since nomadic tribes would have had limited means to make material images. Similar tendencies existed among some of Israel's neighbors, none of whom observed an explicit ban on images (Köckert 2008).

Perhaps as late as the exilic or postexilic period, a more programmatic form of aniconism likely developed. This form of aniconism demanded an imageless cult and probably expanded the scope of what was included in the image ban. For instance, if a cult statue of Yhwh had existed in the Jerusalem temple at this time, it would have been dismissed and denounced as a form of idolatry. A more programmatic form of aniconism likely motivated the idol parodies of Second Isaiah, and, over time, more sharply differentiated Israelite religion from the beliefs and practices of its neighbors.

This shift from *de facto* aniconism to programmatic aniconism may have evolved slowly over time or it may have been the product of a more rapid "revolution" in per-

---

2   Mettinger (1995:167) considers *maṣṣēbôt* only as images of deities; as pointed out above (§ 3), this chapter draws on examples of *maṣṣēbôt* representing either divine or human beings, as well as *maṣṣēbôt* used in keeping memories alive.

spectives on images. In either case, this trend was likely embedded in other theological developments (e. g., the rise of more exclusive forms of monotheism) and was the product of certain historical circumstances. Some scholars connect the emergence of more explicit strictures against divine images to Israel's exile in Babylon (Wagner 2005). The loss of the central reality of the land, the king, the temple, and the cult (its rituals) naturally led to new ideas about God and, in particular, a reconceptualization of how the divine presence could be experienced or secured (Hundley 2011).

Other motivations for aniconism are also possible. One line of reasoning is that since it is impossible to adequately represent God in any single image, all forms of divine representation would be deficient in one respect or another. Closely related, it also might be reasoned that if nobody has seen YHWH's form (a point which is somewhat ambiguous in the Hebrew Bible, but cf. Deut 4:12), any image of YHWH would potentially be a misrepresentation, a mere creation of the artist's imagination (MacDonald 2007:21). Alternatively, the ban on images might be motivated out of a fear of reducing God in being, place, or power, or out of a fear of making God's image available for maligning. This latter motivation may be broadly analogous with the mentality behind the strictures against making wrongful use of YHWH's name (Exod 20:7; Deut 5:11).

In sum, the historical development of Israel's aniconic tradition surely moved in the direction of more explicit and severe prohibitions against divine images. Numerous factors contributed to this development, not least of which was the exile, which prompted a theological reorientation at various levels. Regardless of when aniconism firmly took hold, it eventually came to be seen as a defining aspect of early Judaism. Already by the fourth century BCE, Greek sources describe Judaism as a religion characterized by monotheism and aniconism.

5.3. Responses to Aniconism

In many ways, the emergence of Israel's aniconic tradition can be understood as reflecting a change in emphasis from images to words/speech. Indeed, with the role of divine representations restricted or even eliminated, other points of emphasis filled this void, including an increased focus on the law and the written Scriptures in the postexilic period and beyond. In addition, as the deity became increasingly disassociated with images, people would have had to come to terms with alternative means of accessing and assuring divine presence, such as through the architecture of the temple and/or its description (cf. Ezekiel 40–48; Tuell 1996; McCormick 2002), national stability, and the priesthood.

However, the rise of stricter forms of aniconism in Israelite religion and early Judaism never completely severed ties with the visual realm. For instance, visual experience was never considered problematic in theophanies. While not giving full, unmediated access to the appearance of God, theophanies were visually stunning events, meant as much for the eyes as for any other sense. Indeed, the Hebrew Bible continues to give priority to sight as a sensory experience (Avrahami 2012), and visuality and audibility are sometimes synesthetically combined (Ebach 2004).[3] In fact, responses to aniconism are perhaps best understood not as a disavowal of all things visual but rather as an attempt to find substitutes for material images that nevertheless preserved ties to the visual realm.

For instance, one might understand the presence of descriptive imagery in prose and poetry as a type of substitute for material images. Figures of speech paint a picture in the mind of the reader. Not only does this type of language draw on iconographic themes prominent in the visual culture of the ancient Near East, but they also might be considered a type of "verbal iconography" in their own right. As but one example, metaphors can be understood as a way of picturing an association between two seemingly disparate concepts. In this sense, divine metaphors in the Hebrew Bible prompt the reader to "see" YHWH, his actions, and his character in new ways.

While steering clear of any violation of the image ban, metaphors carry their own danger. In some cases, figurative expressions can become so conventional that their metaphorical nature is forgotten. These so-called "dead metaphors" become reified as literal statements, thus potentially narrowing one's perception of God. There are two ways in which this tendency can be countered. On the one hand, texts such as Deuteronomy 32 (see chapter 5) feature an abundance of metaphors that may be purposely incompatible (cf. Brettler 1998 and Brassey 2001 on Isaiah 40–55). The resulting avalanche of imagery dissuades the reader from too closely identifying God with any one figurative description. On the other hand, certain metaphors can exhibit what LeMon refers to as "multistability" (cf. chapter 14) such that a single verbal image can evoke multiple meanings, and with them, multiple visual associations.

Responses to aniconism also involved several other image substitutes (Bauks 2007:§ 8). For instance, it is thought that Israel's aniconic tradition fostered both *shem* (Name) and *kabod* (glory) theologies. In both cases, instead of referring to God as a certain "shaped" appearance, God is referred to in abstract terms that imply formlessness. Yet, even though *kabod* and *shem* theologies are likely motivated by aniconism, they still might have been "visible" concepts in ancient Near Eastern thought. In fact, the concept of *kabod* and *shem* found pictorial expression elsewhere in the ancient Near East. The former might be related to the *melammu*, understood as the equivalent of *kabod* in the sense of awe-inspiring glory (cf. Ps 104:1–2; de Hulster 2009a:176–77). The latter might be related to Egyptian "name fetishes" in which names were conceived of as independent entities deserving veneration. These name fetishes, then, might be understood as the iconographic background for the deuteronomistic expression "where YHWH puts his Name" (Deut 12:21; cf. Staubli 2009 and **figs 9.12–13**).

---

3   Ebach (2004:86) understands, for instance, Deut 4:9 in the sense of taking care not to forget "the *words* that your eyes have seen," interpreting *děbārîm* as "words."

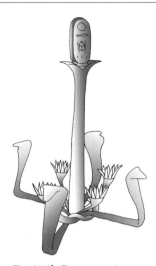

Fig. 9.12. Stamp seal from Ashdod depicting Ishtar with a *melammu.* Source *GGG:* Fig. 288a

Fig. 9.13a. Scarab depicting a cartouche fetish with four uraei and the throne name of Amenophis III, Manachat (Jerusalem region), 1390–1353 BCE. Source: Staubli 2009:109

Fig. 9.13b. Reconstruction, based on stamp seal amulets, of a possible "name fetish" in southern Levantine Temples. Drawing by Barbara Connell. Source: Staubli 2009:110

Another image substitute that retains some connection to the visual realm is human embodiment. Specifically, the creation of human beings in the image of God makes humanity into a type of visual representation of God's presence and power. Although there are various interpretations of the *imago dei* (see chapter 2), humanity is taken here as an embodied reference to Yʜwʜ. The manifold diversity of humanity not only attests to the creativity of the creator, but also warns against associating Yʜwʜ with any single form.

One might also note the presence of what earlier was referred to as aniconic images. Though constituting a type of visual representation, objects such as *maṣṣēbôt* and the *yād wāšēm* of Isa 56:5 lack any figural depiction of the deity and thus are not typically understood to be in violation of the image ban. As van der Toorn (1997; cf. 2009) has suggested, even the Torah scroll itself might have come to be seen as a type of aniconic image insofar as it was often treated as a visible divine symbol rather than merely a repository of words. In this sense, the Torah scroll brings together the visual and the textual in the form of an object that is both read and recited as well as looked at and displayed (cf. de Hulster forthcoming[a]).

6. Conclusion

In its approach to iconographic exegesis, this chapter has focused on the meaning and archaeological background of the *yād wāšēm* in Isa 56:5. This object was interpreted as a standing stone, or *maṣṣēbâ,* that functioned as a monument insofar as it "materialized" the memory of a name (or person). Although the monument described in Isa 56:5 likely was not marked with any figural depictions, it nevertheless can be considered as a visual form of expression. As a type of aniconic image, it probably did not fall under the scope of the image ban. As such, the *yād wāšēm* represents one way in which the visual realm continued to be important long after a more programmatic version of aniconism had emerged.

The *yād wāšēm* is not the only place one encounters the intersection of commemoration, aniconism, and visuality. As van Oorschot (1999) argues, "the *no* to statues of deities" in the Hebrew Bible gave rise to "a *yes* to a culture of commemoration" in later forms of Judaism (318, translation by author). In the case of the *Yad Vashem* memorial in Jerusalem, acts of commemoration involve visual signs, be they in the form of photographs, art exhibits, or digital archives. Something similar might also be said of common Jewish practices, including the display of the Shema on doorframes in Jewish homes (*mezuzah*) or the wearing of *tefillin* (also called phylacteries) during prayers. In each case, memory is materialized – and, one might add, visualized – in forms that are meant to be seen and yet are not in violation of the ban on images. This connection between visible signs and commemoration sheds light on the meaning and function of the *yād wāšēm* in Isa 56:5. At the same time, it highlights the persistence of visuality even within a religious tradition characterized by aniconism.

Assignment/Exercise

1. Read 2 Kings 5 from the perspective of aniconism. How would you assess Naaman's solution for venerating Yнwн?
2. In light of the aniconic image, how would you assess Jacob's stone in Gen 28:19? How does the stone function?
3. In religious contexts, aniconism rarely involves the complete absence of all visual representation. As noted above, photographs of human beings are allowed in the *Yad Vashem,* and in Islam, photos of holy places are included among the souvenirs at Mecca (along with sand, stones, water, and pieces of cloth, etc.; cf. Sui 2008). In the (Continental) Christian Reformed tradition, biblical texts such as the Decalogue are often displayed in churches, while Lutheran, Roman-Catholic, and Eastern Orthodox churches tend to have altar paintings. In these settings two tendencies are of note. First, a kind of hierarchy of "forbidden images" is implied, with divine images at the top, followed by humans, animals, buildings or objects, and non-representative motifs and decorative texts (as in calligraphy). Second, it is often the case that texts can take the place of images, much like how the ani-

conic image replaces realistic representations. Can you think of other examples of how aniconicity is negotiated in religious contexts?

Bibliography

Gaifman, Milette. 2012. *Aniconism in Greek Antiquity.* Oxford Studies in Ancient Culture and Representation. Oxford: Oxford University Press.

Mettinger, Tryggve N. D. 1995. *No Graven Image? Israelite Aniconism in its Ancient Near Eastern Context.* Coniectanea biblica: Old Testament Series 42. Stockholm: Almquist & Wiksell.

Toorn, Karel van der, ed. 1997. *The Image and the Book: Iconic Cults, Aniconism, and the Rise of the Book Religion in Israel and the Ancient Near East.* Leuven: Peeters.

Chapter 10
The Power of Images: Isaiah 60, Jerusalem, and Persian Imperial Propaganda

Izaak J. de Hulster and Brent A. Strawn

1. Starting Points for Iconographic Exegesis

The Introduction to this textbook noted that iconographic exegesis could be pursued in any number of different ways. One way is to begin with an exegetical question or crux and then pursue iconography that might prove illuminating in solving it. In this approach, the text or textual problem leads the way into the iconography which follows. Another option raised in the Introduction was to begin, not with a text or textual conundrum, but with the iconography – perhaps the artistic remains of a particular period – assessing that and then seeing how it may (or may not) relate to biblical texts from the same chronological horizon.

The present chapter is something of a combination of these two approaches. Building on earlier work (de Hulster 2009a; Strawn 2007; Chan 2013), it focuses on iconography of the Persian period (ca. 586–333 BCE) and on Isaiah 60, a text that is typically dated to this era. We begin with a brief discussion of Isaiah 60 in its historical and literary contexts (§ 2) before turning to iconography that is germane to an understanding of its motifs (§ 3). This ordering is obviously most similar to the "text-first" approach to iconographic exegesis, but it has been chosen mostly to simplify the presentation. Ultimately we hope to show that the art and text under consideration here exist in something of a feedback loop, so that even if this one leads for a while, with the other following for a bit, the situation can easily be reversed. Indeed, in the present case both text and art turn out to be instantiations of something anterior to both – namely, Persian imperial propaganda (§ 4). We conclude the study with a few methodological reflections (§ 5).

2. Isaiah 60: Its Content and Its Contexts

Isaiah 60 resides at the center of a unit of text called Third or Trito-Isaiah (Isaiah 56–66), which has been typically assigned to the Persian period. After this rather general consensus, opinions vary widely, especially over the matter of the (dis)unity of these chapters. Most scholars have argued that Isaiah 56–66 is not, in fact, a unified composition and, as a result, parts of it stem from different hands and from more than one period of time. But despite the wide range of opinions that have been offered (see Strawn 2007:91–93), there is still wide agreement that the vast majority of Third

Isaiah, if not the entirety of it, dates to sometime within the Persian period. Many scholars have also agreed that Isaiah 60–62 is the nucleus around which the rest of Third Isaiah took shape (e. g., Westermann 1969:296–308). These three chapters are often thought to be closely related to Second Isaiah (Isaiah 40–55), and, if so, perhaps they ought to be dated similarly, to ca. 520 BCE, if not before (cf. Strawn 2007:93 n. 3).

Thus far, then, it appears justifiable to (a) treat Isaiah 60–62 as a defensible block of text within Third Isaiah; and (b) to locate this unit relatively early in the Persian period. A closer look at Isaiah 60, specifically, reveals a number of motifs that bear striking similarity to Persian period iconography. Three particularly important aspects of the chapter should be noted (see more extensively de Hulster 2009a:169–229; Strawn 2007).

First, Isaiah 60 abounds in *light imagery*. The chapter begins with three verses that are replete with it, and returns to the light imagery toward the end of the chapter (vv. 19–20):

> [1] Arise, shine; for your light has come,
>   and the glory of the Lord has risen upon you.
> [2] For darkness shall cover the earth,
>   and thick darkness the peoples;
> but the Lord will arise upon you,
>   and his glory will appear over you.
> [3] Nations shall come to your light,
>   and kings to the brightness of your dawn.
> …
> [19] The sun shall no longer be your light by day,
>   nor for brightness shall the moon give light to you by night;
> but the Lord will be your everlasting light,
>   and your God will be your glory.
> [20] Your sun shall no more go down,
>   or your moon withdraw itself;
> for the Lord will be your everlasting light,
>   and your days of mourning shall be ended.

The addressed "you" here is Jerusalem/Zion, and YHWH is described as a "light" ('wr, vv. 1, 3) and as an "eternal light" (l'wr 'wlm, vv. 19, 20). Even this may be enough to evoke solar and/or astral connections, indicating that YHWH is (like) the sun (see, e. g., Gen 1:16; cf. Stähli 1985; Taylor 1993). A number of other terms found in Isaiah 60 are also associated with light, whether these be verbs like "dawn" (zrḥ), bodies of light (sun, moon), antonyms to light (darkness), or words that are often metaphorically related to light (e. g., glory). Moreover, YHWH is not the only thing that shines in Isaiah 60: so does Jerusalem, which shines because of God's own shining glory. The light of Jerusalem makes it stand out in the world, and draws nations and kings to its brightness. The prevalence of light imagery, especially with solar/astral connections, suggests that iconography pertaining to the same conceptions will repay careful study.

A second important aspect of Isaiah 60 has already been mentioned in passing: it is the notion that the *nations will stream to Jerusalem/Zion bringing their wealth with them*. This motif (see Chan 2013) is present already in v. 3 where it seems to be the direct result of the light of Jerusalem/Zion and its God. It continues in various ways throughout the rest of the chapter. Note, for example, the following passages:

> [5] Then you shall see and be radiant;
>   your heart shall thrill and rejoice,
> because the abundance of the sea shall be brought to you,
>   the wealth of the nations shall come to you.
> [6] A multitude of camels shall cover you,
>   the young camels of Midian and Ephah;
>   all those from Sheba shall come.
> They shall bring gold and frankincense,
>   and shall proclaim the praise of the Lord.
> [7] All the flocks of Kedar shall be gathered to you,
>   the rams of Nebaioth shall minister to you;
> they shall be acceptable on my altar,
>   and I will glorify my glorious house.
> …
> [10] Foreigners shall build up your walls,
>   and their kings shall minister to you;
> for in my wrath I struck you down,
>   but in my favor I have had mercy on you.
> [11] Your gates shall always be open;
>   day and night they shall not be shut,
> so that nations shall bring you their wealth,
>   with their kings led in procession.
> …
> [13] The glory of Lebanon shall come to you,
>   the cypress, the plane, and the pine,
> to beautify the place of my sanctuary;
>   and I will glorify where my feet rest.

Details that are notable here and that will prove important later include: the listing of gifts (e. g., wealth, camels, gold, frankincense), the listing of various locales (Midian, Ephah, Sheba, Kedar, Nebaioth, and Lebanon; cf. also Tarshish in v. 9.), and the fact that foreigners (*běnê-nēkār,* v. 10) are the ones to build up Jerusalem's walls.

The third important aspect of Isaiah 60 is that the tribute procession found here appears entirely *unforced*. There can be little doubt that this chapter belongs to the broader genre of theophanic texts in the Hebrew Bible (see, e. g., Jeremias 1977; Hiebert 1992:505–11; Cross 1973:147–94). Such texts recount the awesome appearance of Yhwh amidst celestial and atmospheric phenomena; some of them also refer to processions (see, e. g., Psalm 68, Judges 5; 2 Samuel 22 = Psalm 22). But Isaiah 60 should not be too quickly identified with these other theophanies for several reasons. One is that while processions sometimes occur in the other theophany texts, the bringing of tribute is not a dominant theme. Another difference is that most theophanies are dominated by violent imagery associated with the coming of YHWH as divine warrior (Miller 1973). These texts recount the upheaval and withering of nature and are replete with references to war, battle, enemies, and so forth. But this is not the case with Isaiah 60, which witnesses an almost total dearth of militaristic imagery. Unlike other theophanies, YHWH does not come in a storm in Isaiah 60; and, while there is mention of "darkness" (ḥšk) and "thick cloud" (ʿrpl) in v. 2 – stock elements of the theophanic tradition (see, e. g., Exod 19:9; 20:18; Deut 4:11; 5:19–20; Judg 5:4; 2 Sam 22:10–12 = Ps 18:10, 12) – YHWH appears to dawn on Jerusalem as the calm *after* the storm, as it were, rather than appearing within it. There is no mention of YHWH destroying his enemies (see, e. g., Exodus 15, Deuteronomy 33, Judges 5, Micah 1, Habakkuk 3, Psalm 68; contrast Isa 60:9 with Ps 48:7) and, while tribute comes, it seems to be voluntarily brought. The noticeable lack of divine violence prior to the giving of tribute suggests that it is not forced by YHWH or brought out of fear by an intimidated and humiliated foe. Instead, the impression is that the nations and their wealth are drawn to the radiance of Jerusalem and its glorious Lord (Isa 60:1–3), not unlike the way trees extend their branches to the sun.

It must be admitted, however, that two verses in Isaiah 60 seem to undermine the notion that the tribute procession is unforced or altogether non-violent. They are vv. 12 and 14:

> [12] For the nation and kingdom that will not serve you shall perish;
>   those nations shall be utterly laid waste.
>
> …
>
> [14] The descendants of those who oppressed you shall come bending low to you,
>   and all who despised you shall bow down at your feet;
> they shall call you the City of the LORD,
>   the Zion of the Holy One of Israel.

Both verses, however, seem out of place precisely due to their more violent content and their extra long lines, which upset the poetic balance (cf. Loretz and Kottsieper 1987). Both factors indicate that these verses (or parts thereof) may be later additions (see Clements 1997:451–52; Steck 1986; 1991:58–61).[1] Even if these verses are original, however, their brief presence here does not begin to raise Isaiah 60 to the level of violence so prevalent in other divine warrior theophanies. So, while Isaiah 60 may

---

1   See the standard commentators and note the apparatus in *BHS* and *BHK*.

be a theophany, it is not a divine warrior theophany. The final proof of this point is that the bringing of tribute in Isaiah 60 *precedes* vv. 12 and 14.[2]

These three important aspects – light imagery, the wealth of nations, and unforced bringing of tribute – represent a particular constellation of motifs in Isaiah 60 and are crucial elements of its iconic structure (cf. LeMon 2009, 2010; Brown 2000). Armed with these insights, we may turn to Persian period iconography to see how these aspects may be traced there as well.

3.   Persian Period Iconography

Each of these three aspects could be investigated individually in the art of the Persian period, but, as already intimated above, it will be their particular combination in close formation (that is, as a constellation) that will prove most illuminating in comparison with Isaiah 60. We begin, then, with a brief discussion of solar imagery, showing where it is found in the iconography of Persian period Yehud (§ 3.1) before turning to the Apadana reliefs from Persepolis, which showcase the full constellation of solar imagery, the wealth of nations, and the unforced bringing of tribute in a fashion that is remarkably similar to what is found in Isaiah 60 (§ 3.2).

3.1. Solar Imagery in Persian Period Yehud

Solar imagery is, of course, widespread throughout the ancient Near East in both artistic and textual traditions (Strawn 2007:111–17; de Hulster 2009a:214–19). It was frequently associated with deities as a manifestation of their glory or is otherwise ascribed to deities, as when they are depicted with wings, taking on the same splendor as the sun (see LeMon 2010).

Several scholars have argued that Jerusalem has a long tradition of solar symbolism (see, e. g., Stähli 1985; Taylor 1993) as well. There may have been a pre-Israelite solar cult in Jerusalem, and perhaps this is what led to the emphasis on solar metaphors for YHWH there (see Keel 1993, 2007). One piece of evidence for this solar tradition in later periods is the rosette stamp impressions that have been recovered (**fig. 10.1**). These stamp seals are related to the sun and sometimes to royalty as well because they stand in the tradition of other royal seal impressions. The first generation of royal seals, the *lmlk* seals (*lmlk*: "belonging to the king"), depict a winged sun disk or a dung beetle, another solar symbol. Probably during the reign of Josiah and due to Assyrian control of the region, these Egyptian symbols were replaced by the rosette, a solar symbol commonly known in Anatolia and Mesopotamia.[3] After the exile, different symbols were used for official stamps (e. g., the lion image and the

---

2   Note, too, that the verbs in v. 12 are imperfect, apparently designating (or threatening) *future* subjugation, not past defeat. The verbs in v. 14 are *wĕ-qātal*.

3   Note that the same clay previously used for vessels stamped with Egyptian solar symbols was also

inscription *yhd,* "Yehud"), but the rosette continued to be known and the production of at least one type has been attributed to the Persian period (Yellin and Cahill 2004:201). Especially among the Achaemenids, the rosette was frequently associated with the sun and with royalty.

Fig. 10.1. Two rosette stamp impressions, City of David (stratum 9, Persian period). Source: Cahill 2000:88–89

Another important item that may relate to solar imagery for Yʜwʜ in the Persian period is the small silver coin now housed in the British Museum (**figs. 10.2–3**).[4] The reverse of the coin is of particular interest.[5] The bearded figure in the center sits on a wheel with spokes and seems to rest his back on a wing. He wears a long robe. His right arm rests on his leg; with the left arm he carries a bird which faces the same direction he does. Three letters in Aramaic script are written around this figure and the bird: *yhd,* apparently to be read as "Yehud."[6] To the right of the seated figure, slightly beneath it and facing it, is a head in profile.

Fig. 10.2. Coin from Yehud, now in the British Museum (TC242.5/BMC Palestine XIX 29), ca. 380–360 BCE (left: obverse, right: reverse). Drawing by Izaak J. de Hulster

Fig. 10.3. TC242.5/BMC, Palestine XIX 29, 380–360 BCE. Source: D'Albert de Luynes 1846: Tafel IV

    used for vessels stamped later with rosettes, further corroborating the latter as related to solar imagery.

4   Although not from a controlled excavation, the authenticity of the coin is not in doubt. For discussion, see de Hulster 2013, and note also the online publication: http://www.monotheism.uni-goettingen.de/resources/dehulster_tc242.pdf (cited 15 June 2015).

5   The obverse, showing a military figure with a Corinthian helmet, is of less importance here. Note that the odd position of the eye(s) and the nose(s) seems to be evidence that the coin was struck twice.

6   Early studies sometimes read *yhw,* short for "Yʜwʜ."

The seated figure has often been identified as a sun god, especially due to the winged wheel that appears to serve as his throne. The bird may be a falcon, which can also be used as a solar symbol (note, for example, the presentation of the sun god as a falcon in Egypt). The significance of the human head on the right hand side is not entirely clear; perhaps it represents a theophanic encounter with the human seeing a revelation of the sun god (Pilcher 1908). This would be a highly unusual scene for a depiction on a coin, but it should not be too quickly ruled out, if only because the coin itself is rather unique.

Can anything further be said about the seated figure, other than that he appears to be divine? Some have posited that the wing and wheel represent the god's means of transportation on land and in air (cf. **fig. 10.4,** which shows divine transportation over water by means of the winged sea horse; see de Hulster 2013), in which case the deity in question may not be solar per se, but supreme nevertheless. Indeed, according to Mildenberg (1998:68), the coin is syncretistic, and does not represent "a specific god, but a general conception of a deity easily comprehensible to many people in the western part of the Persian Empire." In this view, the seated figure could be any (solar or supreme) god in which case the provenance of the coin would suggest a more precise identification depending on local religious preferences. While the artifact did not come from a controlled excavation, the inscription on the coin indicates that it is from Persian period Yehud.[7] Perhaps, then, the seated figure is a representation of YHWH. If so, such a depiction might have been viewed as a threat by local non-Judean governors (see Barag 1993) but it may have been perfectly acceptable within certain types of Yehudite religion of that day, though certainly not for others (for more on viewer reception, see Bonfiglio 2014; LeMon and Strawn 2015).

Fig. 10.4. Tyrian coin. Drawing by Mathis Kreitzscheck based on Elayi/Elayi 2009: Plate 38, Nr. 1272

To be sure, much remains in doubt about this coin, above all the possible identification of the seated figure as YHWH.[8] If *yhd* is indeed to be read as "Yehud," and if

7 See Mildenberg (1998:70) for a date in the first half of the 4th century, with probable production between 380 and 360 BCE.

8 See note 6 above. Reading *yhw* might identify the seated figure, but would eliminate an explicit connection to Yehud.

the seated figure is indeed a (solar or supreme) deity, then the depiction may well be of Yhwh, who would be the best candidate for the job in this specific time frame and in this specific region, especially since Persians did not represent their own deities on local coins. So, for Yehudite viewers, an association with Yhwh and the seated figure would probably be the one most readily made (assuming one was made at all). If the seated figure is also intended to have solar associations – and this is true regardless of whether it depicts Yhwh – this coin joins the rosettes in supporting the existence of royal and divine solar imagery in ancient Israel/Palestine during the Persian period.

Thus far, then, the iconography has attested to a relationship between solar imagery, divinity, and royalty. Solar deities are well attested in the ancient world (e.g., Shamash, Re) and links between the sun and kingship are equally well known from both ancient Mesopotamia (see, e.g., *Laws of Hammurabi* XI.84) and Egypt (e.g., Maat as the daughter of the sun god). This background, coupled with the rosettes and the coin discussed above, indicate that in Yehud, too, light had royal associations and could also be associated with Yhwh. In the case of the latter process, Yhwh could acquire characteristics associated with other solar deities, such as being a judge, the guarantor of order, and/or the supreme deity.

While the preceding probe of solar imagery has been illuminating, still more light is cast on Yhwh and Jerusalem, as portrayed in Isaiah 60, when we consider (1) solar imagery in tandem with iconography that shows (2) unforced (3) tribute processions. A stunning example of all three of these aspects is found in the Apadana reliefs from Persepolis.

3.2. The Apadana Reliefs from Persepolis

Darius I (522–486) located his capital at Persepolis (**fig. 10.5**) and was apparently responsible for the construction of the platform, cistern, drainage system, central part of the Apadana, and several sections of the Treasury building there (Young 1992:236). Work on the site probably began shortly after his reign began, perhaps around 520 or 518 BCE (see, respectively, Young 1992:236; Root 1989:33v50). Somewhat later, Xerxes (486–465) expanded and completed the work.

For present purposes, the reliefs preserved on the Apadana (**fig. 10.6;** structure J on **fig. 10.5**) are of greatest concern. According to some inscriptions, it would seem that Xerxes' completed the structure, but the foundation inscription found at each corner of the Apadana demonstrates that it was planned and begun under Darius I (Schmidt 1953:70; cf. Root 1979:90).[9] The exact chronology of the building may be left aside, at least for the moment, since it is the program of the Apadana reliefs that is of greatest import for our purposes. These monumental carvings (almost 300 feet in length) are found on the north and east sides of the Apadana and are virtually identical, appearing in mirror opposite. A reconstruction of the north façade is found in **fig. 10.7**. In

---

9   See XPb and XPg (for Xerxex) and DPh (for Darius) in Kent 1953. Updated translations of the latter two may be found in Kuhrt 2007:300–301 and 476–77, respectively.

panel A, which is on the right side of the north façade, contingents of Persian nobles with horses, chariots, attendants, and guards (**fig. 10.8**) process toward the center. The B panel depicts delegations bringing tribute, also proceeding toward the center, each of which is led by a Persian host of some sort. These are arranged according to ethnicity and are presented with enough detail to allow for identification. Delegation 11, for instance, is the Saka Tigraxauda or Pointed-Hat Scythians (**fig. 10.9**).

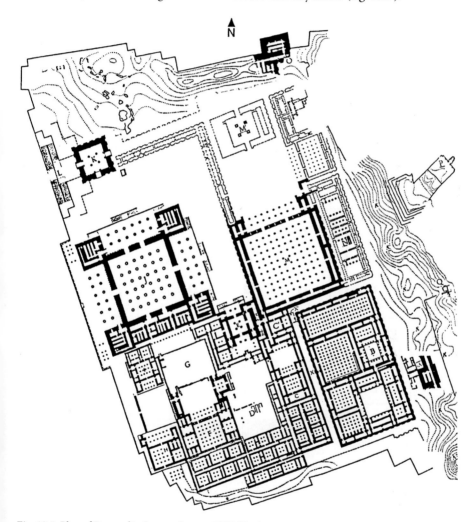

Fig. 10.5. Plan of Persepolis. Source: Strawn 2007: Fig. 1

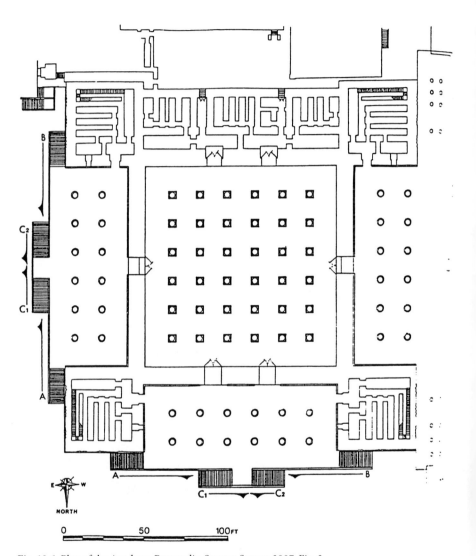

Fig. 10.6. Plan of the Apadana, Persepolis. Source: Strawn 2007: Fig. 2

Fig. 10.7. Reconstruction of the north façade of the Apadana, Persepolis. Source: Strawn 2007: Fig. 3

Fig. 10.8. Detail of Persian troops from the east side of the Apadana, Persepolis. Source: Strawn 2007: Fig. 4

Fig. 10.9. Detail of tribute procession from the east side of the Apadana, Persepolis. Source: Strawn 2007: Fig. 5

The A and B panels move toward the central panel, which is the focal point of the entire relief program. The central panel that is still *in situ* (**fig. 10.10**) is apparently not the original one, which had been moved to the Treasury at some point, probably for safekeeping (Root 1979:88, 94; Schmidt 1953:168). The original central panel (**fig. 10.11**) was recovered there and is far better suited to the theme of the reliefs, since it depicts the king receiving an official who probably announces the arrival of the various groups found on panels A and B. Directly above the central panel is a frieze (depicted in **fig. 10.7** and **fig. 10.10**) with the winged sun-disk (Frei and Koch 1996:161). In the Achaemenid context, this is best understood as a symbol for Ahuramazda (Lecoq 1984). So, immediately above the king's head in the original central panel, was this image of the god as a sun-disk. The king and his god, therefore, are the focal points of this massive, most impressive program.

Fig. 10.10. Replacement central panel of the Apadana, Persepolis. Source: Strawn 2007: Fig. 6

Fig. 10.11. Original central panel of the Apadana (north façade), Persepolis. Source: Strawn 2007: Fig. 7

These reliefs would have been the first thing a visitor saw upon entering Persepolis via stairway L and then through Xerxes' "Gate of All Nations" (structure K on **fig. 10.5**). They were likely to have had a significant impact on all who viewed them, and their beautiful execution, grand scale, and strategic location indicates they were designed to communicate a particular message about the Persian Empire. One aspect of that message was surely the size, extent, and power of the empire. The Persian Empire was, to use Margaret Cool Root's memorable phrase, "a world under control" (1992:446). One aspect of that control, which is manifest on the Apadana reliefs and on other instances of Persian art, is that the nations stream to Persepolis willingly, cooperatively, perhaps even happily. In Root's own words:

> Official Persian art was designed for widespread dissemination and message conveyance, just as the official decrees were. … [T]he overarching message is one of a world under control. … The pervasive image of imperial domain and social hierarchy stresses cooperative – even joyous – service and the virtues of blamelessness. (1992:446)

This notion of joyous cooperation on the part of subjugated peoples is found in inscriptions[10] and in images like **fig. 10.12**. In this depiction, the people who carry the king aloft do so in the "Atlas pose," wherein they bear the weight of the throne effortlessly on the thumb and index finger (see Root 1979:147–61). Root has gone so far as to suggest that the Persians consciously imitated earlier images like the presentation scene (compare **fig. 10.13** with **fig. 10.14**) in order to transform the bringing of tribute "into a scene of pious reverence" (Root 1979:284). If so, the delegations in panel B may be seen as petitioners ushered by Persian officials into the presence of the divine, represented in Apadana program by the king and his deity.

Much more could be said about the Persepolis reliefs (see Root 1979:129–311) – not to mention about other instances of official Persian art – but Young's summary suffices to make the main point:

> [T]he ultimate goal of both the architecture and the decoration of Persepolis was to present to the world the concept of a Pax Persica – a harmonious, peaceful empire ruled by a king who contained within his person and his office the welfare of the empire. (1992:236)

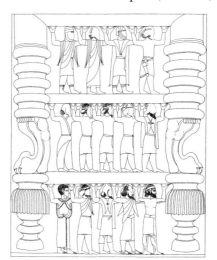

Fig. 10.12. Detail of throne carriers from south door (west side) of the Hundred Column Hall, Persepolis. Source: Strawn 2007: Fig. 8

---

10 See, e. g., DNa, DNb, DPe, and DPh (see Kent 1953; Kuhrt 2007).

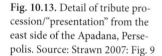

Fig. 10.13. Detail of tribute procession/"presentation" from the east side of the Apadana, Persepolis. Source: Strawn 2007: Fig. 9

Fig. 10.14. Presentation scene from Mesopotamia, Ur III (ca. 2050–1959 BCE). Source: Strawn 2007: Fig. 11

4. Persian Art- and Text-Forms and/in Isaiah 60

The particular combination of solar imagery (the winged sun-disk) with an unforced tribute procession in the Apadana reliefs reflects a constellation of images that is quite comparable to, if not identical with, what was found in Isaiah 60. That text, too, concerned a deity with solar connections "dawning" (note especially *zrḥ* in vv. 1–3; cf. Mal 3:20; Ps 84:12) over a capital city to which the wealth of nations was being brought, apparently voluntarily. But is this similarity more than that? Could it be a case of direct dependence?

To make an argument for direct dependence would be difficult, as it would seem to depend on Isaiah 60 having direct knowledge of the Apadana reliefs – perhaps the author saw them or at least heard about them from some source that had seen them. The latter option, in particular, is not entirely impossible given the cosmopolitan nature of the Persian empire and the way Darius imported both materials and artisans from all over the empire in the work at Persepolis (Collon 1995:177; cf. Root 1985; Strawn 2007:117–21). But the issue of chronology remains vexed, even in that scenario. Schmidt (1953:70) dated the substructure (at least) of the Apadana prior to ca. 513 BCE, and Root (1989:34) dated the foundation inscription (DPh) to 519– 510 BCE. Whether these dates are early enough for the Apadana's program to be known and formative for the nucleus of Third Isaiah, however, is debatable (see § 2 above).

But even if the dependence is not direct, the similarities between Isaiah 60 and the Apadana reliefs are too striking to ignore. As was noted previously, solar imagery is widely attested in ancient Near Eastern texts and artistic remains; tribute processions, too, are well-known and not infrequently encountered (Chan 2013; Strawn 2007:107–17; Bär 1996). But the particular three-fold constellation of solar imagery, the wealth of nations, and the unforced bringing of tribute that is found in Isaiah 60 and in the Apadana reliefs seems unparalleled elsewhere (Strawn 2007:114, 117). If these two "sets" are not directly dependent upon each other, what could explain this remarkable similarity?

One possible answer is that Isaiah 60 and the Apadana reliefs are both dependent on something else, something prior to both that gives rise to both. In this case, that something would seem to be Persian imperial propaganda as manifested in both art- and text-forms. If the Persian Empire was "a world under control" and the Persians went to great lengths to portray it as as such, it is not surprising to find reflexes of that ideology in royal inscriptions and in official Persian art. Indeed, it is these two instruments that helped to create and convey the ideology of a stable empire.

Artistic reflexes of Persian imperial propaganda were not restricted to monumental iconography. The minor arts were a more economical way to disperse such ideology widely (Uehlinger 2000). It is worth noting here that it is precisely in the Persian period that we find a revival of the cylinder seal (Collon 1995:181). One such seal depicting "Darius, the great king" hunting under the aegis of Ahura Mazda was recovered from Thebes (**fig. 10.15**). Other Achaemenid seals showing Ahura Mazda in the winged sun-disk have been recovered from locales as disparate as Turkestan, Sinai, and Marathon – including a host of Levantine sites (e. g., Kamid-el-Loz, Tell el Mazar, Jericho) – demonstrating their widespread distribution. In an important study, Christoph Uehlinger (1999) argued that a number of Persian period seal impressions (especially from Wadi ed-Daliyeh) reflect "powerful Persianisms" – instances of Persian imperial ideology – in a variety of ways (see, e. g., **figs. 10.16–19**). In each instance, the message is one of control, which serves the ideal of the *Pax Persica*. Official Persian imagery like unto that found at Persepolis was probably well known, then, in Yehud – and not only there – whether by eyewitness, by tale, or by mobile art like seals (Strawn 2007:118).

Fig. 10.15. Seal of Darius I (?), Thebes. Source: Strawn 2007: Fig. 14

Fig. 10.16. Bulla, Wadi ed-Daliyeh (WD 17). Source: De Hulster 2009a: Fig. 7.13

Fig. 10.17. Bullae, Wadi ed-Daliyeh (WD 3A, 10A, 11B, 12, 24). Source: De Hulster 2009a: Fig. 7.14

Fig. 10.18. Bulla, Wadi ed-Daliyeh (WD 13). Source: De Hulster 2009a: Fig. 7.15

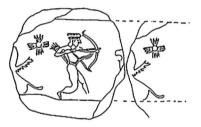

Fig. 10.19. Bulla, Shechem. Source: De Hulster 2009a: Fig. 7.16

In this light, the possible relationship between Isaiah 60 and the Apadana reliefs should be seen as one of dependence – not one upon the other, but both upon Persian imperial propaganda writ large. One is a textual reflex, the other an artistic reflex of that ideology. It is not surprising to find Persian ideology in Persian art and inscriptions but it is somewhat surprising to find it in a biblical text, especially as Third Isaiah is typically interpreted. But the intriguing and unique constellation of images found in Isaiah 60 and elsewhere in the Persian materials suggests exactly that. In Isaiah 60, too, one may see the influence of Persian ideology and theology – this time in Persian period *Yehud*.

The Isaianic reflex of Persian imperial propaganda is not unmitigated, however. In Isaiah 60, that propaganda – its ideology and theology – have been coopted, modified, and reapplied to Jerusalem and to Yʜwʜ. The *Pax Persica* has become the *Pax Jerusalem*. All nations stream, not to Persepolis, but to Zion, bringing their tribute willingly, peacefully, even joyously because they are drawn to its brilliant light. In the absence of a monarch in the postexilic period, Jerusalem's light is democratized and marks the city as a whole. But ultimately Zion's light is due to its God, who dawns on the city, facilitating and enabling its flourishing, including its flourishing by means of and at the hands of foreigners (see vv. 3, 5–7, 9–11, 13, 14b–18).[11] Perhaps the ascrip-

---

11 Even the somewhat odd vv. 12 and 14a (see § 2 above) can be seen to fit with Persian precedent – such sentiments are simply the other side of the *Pax Persica!*

tion of Yhwh as an eternal light that will replace the sun is something of a critique of Persian solar imagery. Perhaps the imperfect verbal forms in Isa 60:2 recognize that the application of the Persian ideal onto a Jerusalemite reality that is superior still lies in the future. Whatever the case, the utilization of Persian imperial propaganda in Isaiah 60 suggests an optimistic and positive assessment of Zion's future by the anonymous prophet responsible for it.

5. Conclusion

Mostly for pragmatic purposes, the present study began with a biblical text dated to a particular era and then explored what LeMon has called "congruent iconography" (2010). To be sure, the sequence might have been reversed, with the investigation beginning with the Apadana reliefs (cf. Strawn 2007). Either starting point could be used in iconographic exegesis. Whichever is chosen, the preceding essay has demonstrated again the importance of a constellation of imagery – in both text and art – for the most profitable iconographic exegetical probes. It also showed that such constellations are to be identified not only by what they contain (e. g., solar imagery, tribute processions) but also by what they leave out (force, violence, war).

Assignment/Exercise

Consider another unit of text typically dated to the Persian period (e. g., Haggai, Malachi) and study its imagery in light of Persian iconography (see Chapter 12 for a further example). In the process you might first look at Persian period art for recurrent themes, images, and motifs and then assess the biblical text(s), or vice versa. The same kind of exercise could be done with a different period – say the Neo-Assyrian or Neo-Babylonian periods and the prophetic texts that date to these eras. Alternatively, you could look at a particular region, especially if it is relatively limited in terms of artistic remains (e. g., Moabite or Edomite iconography), study the visual data from there, and see what they might evoke in terms of similar material from the Old Testament.

Bibliography

Bonfiglio, Ryan P. 2014. "Reading Images, Seeing Texts: Towards a Visual Hermeneutics for Biblical Studies." Ph.D. diss. Emory University.

Chan, Michael J. 2013. "The City on a Hill: A Tradition-Historical Study of the Wealth of Nations Tradition." Ph.D. diss. Emory University.

Hulster, Izaak J. de. 2009a. *Iconographic Exegesis and Third Isaiah.* Forschungen zum Alten Testament II/36. Tübingen: Mohr Siebeck.

Root, Margaret Cool. 1979. *King and Kingship in Achaemenid Art: Essays on the Creation of an Iconography of Empire.* Acta Iranica 19. Leiden: Brill.

Strawn, Brent A. 2007. "'A World Under Control': Isaiah 60 and the Apadana Reliefs from Persepolis." In *Approaching Yehud: New Approaches to the Study of the Persian Period,* edited by Jon L. Berquist, 85–116. Semeia Studies 50. Atlanta: Society of Biblical Literature.

Uehlinger, Christoph. 1999. "'Powerful Persianisms' in Glyptic Iconography of Persian Period Palestine." In *The Crisis of Israelite Religion: Transformation of Religious Tradition in Exilic and Post-Exilic Times,* edited by Bob Becking and Marjo C. A. Korpel, 134–82. Old Testament Studies 42. Boston: Brill.

Chapter 11
What Do you See? Reading Zechariah's Yhwh-Vision (4:1–14) in Light of Southern Levantine Lunar Iconography

Thomas Staubli

1. Describing What We See: Perspectives on Image Analysis

The analytic language commonly used for the interpretation of images shares a striking similarity with that which is used for the interpretation of texts. Interpreters often talk about "reading" images and analyzing the pictorial "syntax" of works of art. Or, they might identify the visual "vocabulary" of a certain artistic program or describe a basic unit of pictorial data as an "iconeme" (on analogy with a lexeme). Using this language in iconographic exegesis certainly has a good deal of heuristic value insofar as it offers those who are primarily trained to work with texts a familiar way to talk about images. Indeed, this similarity of analytic language owes much to the text-centered history of human science (*Wissenschaftsgeschichte*), which has often based its method of interpreting images on categories already in place for textual analysis. Despite its advantages, this methodological tendency can potentially obscure that fact that images convey meaning in ways that are different than texts.

As but one example, in an image every pictorial unit, or iconeme, in the composition is immediately (or at least potentially) related to every other pictorial unit. The meaning of the image as a whole emerges from the complex interaction between these iconemes. As one way of describing the arrangement of elements in an image, one might imagine a kind of invisible grid that demarcates the pictorial space in terms of an above and a below, a left and right, a foreground and a background (if the style of art is able to evoke three dimensions), and even a before and after (if elements of sequential art are used). While in certain instances texts might also be thought to have a visual pattern (see below), image analysis especially requires a keen awareness of the spatial arrangement of elements in a composition.

In a similar way, the analysis of any single image might be said to depend on an awareness of how that image relates to other images. It is only by comparing multiple images with one another that an interpreter is able to detect and describe the presence of artistic conventions, specific styles, cultural variations, and the developments of motifs. This type of comparative analysis has the potential to open up the artistic space of a given image to a wider, diachronic network of visual information. As in a museum where an artifact is presented in an exhibition space along with other related objects, it is possible for those interested in iconographic exegesis to analyze a particular image with respect to a "virtual space" – that is, a set of images understood to be related in some fashion. In my estimation, it is advantageous to construe this "virtual space" in the broadest possible terms, including in it comparative data that comes from historical and cultural contexts that are both contiguous and non-contiguous with the image under discussion. This procedure allows us to "describe what we see" in a given image with respect to broader observations about the history of art in general and, more specifically, the development of particular iconographic motifs.

In this chapter I briefly illustrate some of these methodological suggestions with an example that is already well known from past iconographic research: namely, lunar iconography from the southern Levant and its potential implications for interpreting the YHWH-vision in Zechariah 4:1–14 (Keel 1977; Keel and Uehlinger 1998:298–315; Theuer 2000; Staubli 2003).

2. Describing Texts as Images

While the approach described above is primarily used with images, it can also be helpful when applied to certain aspects of texts. That is, it is sometimes possible to talk about how the meaning of a text emerges from a complex interaction between a network of lexemes and other linguistic elements within a given composition. The arrangement of these basic linguistic units might be said to comprise the visual pattern of a text, or its spatial dimension.

The visual pattern of a text becomes recognizable after analyzing the structure of a given passage. In certain instances, this structure can be made visible through the graphic layout of the text itself. This latter procedure can be seen, for instance, in the Jewish meditative representation called a Shiviti. As a composite "imagetext," a Shiviti

displays the words of a biblical passage in such a way as to create a graphic form that loosely reflects the structure of the passage. In the case of **fig. 11.1,** the forty-nine words of Psalm 67 form a threefold inclusio with a center.

This structure is made visible through the layout of the text in the form of a menorah with seven branches. How the text is visually displayed in the Shiviti reflects and reveals something about its meaning. In the case of the Shiviti of Psalm 67, the central branch of the menorah along with its base displays that thematic center of the psalm itself: "Let the nations be glad and sing for joy, for you judge the peoples with equity and guide the nations upon the earth. *Selah*" (v. 5 [Eng. 4]).

Fig. 11.1. Shiviti, amulet on paper, 17th c. CE, 18.3 x 12.8 cm. Source: Herrmann and Staubli 2011:187 fig. 4 (Courtesy of the Jewish Museum of Switzerland, Basel, Inv. 572)

What the example of the Psalm 67 Shiviti shows is that it is sometimes helpful from an interpretive perspective to describe (or display) texts as images. This approach represents the logical converse of the situation discussed at the outset of this chapter. In addition to talking about images as texts it is also possible to speak of the visual dimensions of a literary composition. As the Psalm 67 Shiviti reveals, doing so can be thought of as a form of iconographic exegesis.

A similar procedure can be applied to the series of visions in Zech 1:8–6:15. This text has a sevenfold, concentric structure (Hanhart 1990:51; Lescow 1993:79; Uehlinger 1994:99; Staubli 2014:290). Specifically, the visions of the riders (1:7–17) and the chariots (6:1–8), which are connected by the motif about the announcement of the rebuilding of the temple, form an outer bracket of the series of visions. Conversely, the visions of the horns and blacksmiths (2:1–4 [Eng. 1:18–21]) and of the elimination of the women in the basket (5:5–11) are connected by the motif of the fight against evil and form a middle bracket. The inner bracket consists of the vision of the man with the measuring cord (2:5–9) and the flying scroll (5:1–4), both of which broach the issue of the material and moral preparation of the temple ground. The thematic center of this sevenfold, concentric structure is the vision of the menorah between the two trees (4:1–14).

Not unlike Psalm 67, the literary structure of Zech 1:8–6:15 has been designed in the form of a menorah (Smyth-Florentin 1992). This structure is important not only because it emphasizes the relevance of the central vision of the menorah (4:1–14) but also because it underlines the symmetric literary structure surrounding it. Furthermore, some Shiviti depict the motif of a menorah flanked by trees (**fig. 11.2**) in a way that echoes the content of Zech 4:1–14. The imagery present in the Shiviti and/or the central vision of Zechariah may also have influenced the design of Israel's state emblem, which includes a menorah flanked by olive twigs (**fig. 11.3**). In this emblem, the two twigs symbolize the governmental and the religious authorities.

3. The Crescent and its Iconographic Associations

In ancient Near Eastern thought, similarities between certain words often provoked speculations about similarities between the realities signified by those words. This is often the case in ancient Near Eastern omen lists in which signs and their interpretations are often linked by a play on similarly sounding words. For instance, an omen in the Assyrian Dream Book reads as follows: "If a man in his dream eats a raven (*arbu*): income (*irbu*) will come in [to him]." A similar logic also applies to pictorial forms, where the basic appearance or shape of one image might provoke an association in the mind of the viewer with other similarly shaped images and the objects they signify. Thus, another way of applying the methodology described at the outset of this chapter is to analyze the associations potentially generated between related images. For the purposes of the present interest in Zech 4:1–14, it will be especially helpful to explore lunar imagery and the various associations it might generate.

Fig. 11.2. Shiviti, amulet on paper (http://www.jewishealing.com/spiri-tuality.html)

Fig. 11.3. State emblem of Israel. Source: Israeli 1999:15

In ancient Near Eastern iconography, the crescent moon, especially when oriented along a horizontal axis, can be associated with the image of a ship (**fig. 11.4,** upper left) or even with the shape of the horns of a bull (**fig. 11.4,** upper right). These associations are known from the epithets of the Sumerian moon god Nannu or the Akkadian moon god Su'en, respectively (Krebernik 1993–1997). The association of the crescent with the bull/horn is also attested in the southern Levant of the tenth century BCE on the door stele from et-Tell. This image is a sophisticated elaboration of the lunar emblem from Haran, which consists of a crescent on a standard with two tassels, combined with a bull pointing to the crescent and with anthropomorphic elements of a warrior, emphasizing the militant character of the moon as a fighter for justice and order (Bernett and Keel 1998). In the late Iron Age Levant the association between the crescent and a ship is found on Phoenician stamp seals while the bull/horn association is evident on various Edomite artifacts.

A further association might be made between the crescent moon and menstrual cycles. In Mesopotamia, a god holding the emblems of the crescent and the uterus-symbol of Ninhursanga in his left and right hand, respectively, expresses this association. This association may also be part of the widespread constellation of the late Iron Age Southern Levant, which combines the crescent with a caprid, tree, and worshiper – elements that all belong to the realm of the goddess. In addition, a loose association between the Omega sign and crescent is found on the pendant on the neck of the goddess from Revadim (**fig. 11.4,** lower right; cf. *IPIAO* 3: Fig. 828). In the arrangement of this figure from the thirteenth century BCE one finds an iconographic constellation that is common in the late Iron Age of the southern Levant: the crescent flanked by trees.

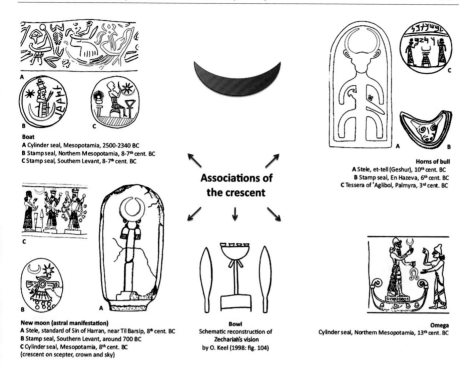

Boat
A Cylinder seal, Mesopotamia, 2500-2340 BC
B Stamp seal, Northern Mesopotamia, 8-7ᵗʰ cent. BC
C Stamp seal, Southern Levant, 8-7ᵗʰ cent. BC

Associations of the crescent

Horns of bull
A Stele, et-tell (Geshur), 10ᵗʰ cent. BC
B Stamp seal, En Hazeva, 6ᵗʰ cent. BC
C Tessera of 'Aglibol, Palmyra, 3ʳᵈ cent. BC

New moon (astral manifestation)
A Stele, standard of Sin of Harran, near Til Barsip, 8ᵗʰ cent. BC
B Stamp seal, Southern Levant, around 700 BC
C Cylinder seal, Mesopotamia, 8ᵗʰ cent. BC
(crescent on scepter, crown and sky)

Bowl
Schematic reconstruction of
Zechariah's vision
by O. Keel (1998: fig. 104)

Omega
Cylinder seal, Northern Mesopotamia, 13ᵗʰ cent. BC

Fig. 11.4. Possible ANE associations of the crescent (collage by the author, based on Staubli 2003)

The crescent flanked by trees motif often appears in a form similar to that which is found in the crescent standard from Haran. As is evident in Southern Levantine glyptic art (see **fig. 11.5**), this symbol entered the local cults and seal workshops through Assyrian influence. It was integrated into autochthonous cults in which trees likely already played a significant role, probably because the moon cycle in the Southern Levant was always connected with the menstrual cycle and therefore with the realm of the goddess. This connection accounts for the association between the goddess and tree imagery. However, the Marduk sign, which the Assyrians juxtaposed with the crescent-standard, was replaced in local seal workshops by trees in spade-like form.

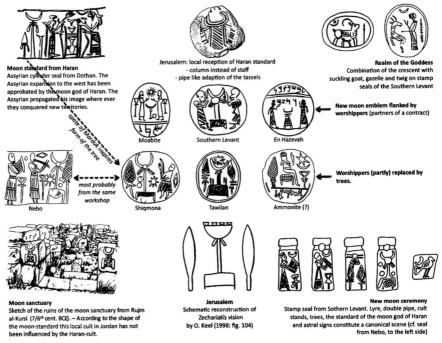

Fig. 11.5. The crescent flanked by trees motif in the context of Southern Levantine New Moon iconography, cylinder and stamp seals, 8th–6th c. BCE (collage by the author)

3.1. The Crescent and Tree Constellation in Image and Text

Lunar imagery can also be found in the fourth and central vision of Zechariah's cycle (4:1–14). As the chapter begins, an angel "wakens" the prophet and asks, "What do you see?" (v. 2). In response, the prophet describes a golden lamp stand (menorah) topped by a bowl. On the rim of the bowl are seven lamps, each of them with seven lips. The candelabrum with its 49 lights is flanked by two olive trees.

Lamp stands, topped by a bowl and lamps with seven lips, are well-known from cultic places in the Southern Levant from the Middle Bronze Age. The setting of the menorah between trees is likely an adaptation of the well-known constellation with the crescent between two trees. However, in the case of Zechariah's vision, the formal association of the crescent is not with the horns of a bull, a boat, or menstrual cycles. Rather, it is with the shape of the bowl and its lights. These lights are interpreted by the angel as the seven eyes of God. This constellation can thus be understood as a type of "lunarized" interpretation of YHWH. However, in view of the fact that the 49 lights encircle the rim of the bowl much like the orbit of the sun, it is also possible that the prominent solar interpretation of YHWH during the eighth and seventh centuries BCE had some impact on Zechariah's vision.

In either case, the angel interprets the trees as symbols of the two "sons of fresh oil" (*bĕnê-hayyiṣhār*) who stand by YHWH. These two figures are most likely the high priest and the king. Rather than pointing to the messianic aspect of these two figures (as is implied in the NRSV's "anointed ones"), the expression *běnê-hayyiṣhār* likely suggests that these two figures are full of fresh power (Willi-Plein 2007:94) – that is, individuals possessing the power of an olive twig or tree with fruits for oil. In view of this observation, the angel's interpretations fit well with the iconography, with the trees being replaced by men flanking a moon standard (for the interchangeability of men and trees see also Pss 1:3; 52:10 [Eng. 8]; 92:13 [Eng. 12]; 128:3; 144:12; Ezekiel 31).

Two rather strange details in Zech 4:12 are, according to Keel (1977:307–311), the main proof that the prophet was inspired by the local lunar iconography. The prophet asks, "What are these two ears of olives, which are in the hand of the two golden pipes which pour out the gold?" (author's translation). The expression "ears of olives" (NRSV: "branches of the olive trees") recalls the often stylized trees on the seals, while the "pipes which pour out the gold" refer to the tassels of the moon standard from Haran, which in the southern Levant sometimes look like pipes. The detail of the tassels/pipes is used for the theocentric argument, implying that the new rulers (the young, powerful, earlike twigs) obtain their radiance and dignity only by (the gold/light of) God. As such, the biblical text adapts and interprets every element of the lunar iconographic tradition discussed above.

4. The Moon Cult in the Southern Levant

Zechariah's lunarized Yhwh-vision is unique in its specific implementation, but as we have seen it adapts a given iconographic constellation (moon god between two trees). In both its visual and textual manifestations, lunar imagery can likely be traced to the long lasting tradition of moon cults in the southern Levant, which prospered especially in the days of the Assyrian and New Babylonian hegemony.

In the Transjordan region, there is strong evidence of a widespread and important veneration of the moon god during the Late Bronze Age. This is especially clear in the Balua stele, where the local version of the Egyptian god with the *was*-scepter and the ankh symbol is characterized as a moon god with crescent on one shoulder and crescent with halo over the other shoulder (*IPIAO* 3: Fig. 886). In an inscription from the moon sanctuary of Rujm al-Kursi at Deir ʿAlla (seventh–sixth century BCE; Hübner 2009), the name of an Ammonite king, Yerakhʿezer ("Moon of Help"), references Shaggar, the new moon. Furthermore, one finds lunar symbols commonly used in Jordanian glyptic art.

In the Cisjordan region, there is evidence of place names like Beit Yerakh or Jericho, both of which reference lunar terminology (*yārēaḥ* = "moon" in Hebrew). Evidence of a moon cult is also found in the Late Bronze Age moon sanctuary of Hazor and the gate sanctuary (*bāmāh*, cf. 2 Kgs 23:8) with a moon-god stele at et-Tell (tenth century BCE). A fragment of a standard of the Moon God from Haran (or rather Harran) from Tell Serʿa offers a direct testimonial for the presence of this Aramaean variant of moon veneration during the Assyrian hegemony. The form of the main stele from En Ḥazevah and another seal (see **fig. 11.5**, middle upper right) point to the veneration of the moon in this sanctuary from the seventh or sixth century BCE. From the ostraca of Tell Arad we learn that on the day of the new moon business ceased (Theuer 2000:501), a significant fact since Tell Serʿa, Arad, and En Ḥazevah all are situated along the caravan corridor between Gaza and Edom.

References to lunar imagery are also present in the theological production of the sages around the sanctuary of Jerusalem. There is evidence for the importance of the new moon festival as a family feast (1 Samuel 20). In certain psalms it is described as a day for blasting the shofar (Ps 81:4 [Eng. 3]), "a statute for Israel, an ordinance of the God of Jacob, he made it a decree in Joseph, when he went out over the land of Egypt" (Ps 81:5–6 [Eng. 4–5]). The moon cycle (4 x 7 days; cf. Hos 2:15 [Eng. 13]; Isa 1:13; 66:23; Ezek 45:17) is a basic element of the calendar, which is based on cycles of seven days. The main festivals of the year, Pesach and Sukkot, are connected with the new moon and the equinox during the first and the seventh months of the year, respectively. It is also possible that before the Babylonian exile Shabbat was a festival associated with the full moon (Theuer 2000:504–6). The day of the new moon was a favorite day to visit a local sanctuary (2 Kgs 4:22).

However, the new moon festival does not appear in the cultic calendar of the Holiness Code (Leviticus 23; but see Numbers 28 and Ezekiel 46) and the commandment about the new moon festival mentioned in Ps 81:5–6 [Eng. 4–5] is not to be found in the book of Exodus. In the deuteronomistic literature, there is also a strong polemic against the worship of celestial phenomena in general and the moon cult in particular. The book of Hosea regards the moon cult as a threat: "Now the new moon shall destroy them along with their fields" (Hos 5:7; cf. Keel 1998:105).

The explanation for the somewhat conflicting evidence presented above can be explained in the following manner. The Yʜᴡʜ-prophets and some priestly circles apparently tried to disconnect Yʜᴡʜ's cult from any veneration of natural phenomena. Yet, at the same time, these same figures did not or could not suppress customs and festivals based on the new moon that were already deeply rooted in the life of the people. As such, while aspects of a lunar cult were sharply critiqued, the importance of the new moon and lunar cycles left a deep imprint on ancient Israel's calendar system, including the timing of certain important festivals.

5. Lunar Imagery and its Iconographic Afterlife

Finally, let me connect the already discussed lunar iconography from the Levant in the eighth – sixth century BCE with an important visual element in later Islamic tradition. While the most zealous forms of Islam traditionally require the destruction of all kinds of divine or spiritual symbols (or at least deny their value as signs of true devotion), lunar imagery is widely accepted. In fact, images in the shape of a crescent moon top most minarets and are a virtually omnipresent symbol in the Islamic world. As such, lunar imagery has had a long and persistent afterlife as a religious symbol in Islam.

Why is it that this iconography has gained such a sure footing in a tradition that is widely considered to be aniconic? According to the Palestinian ethnographer Ali Qleibo, the love of Allah expressed during preparation of Ramadan "is reflected in the great interest in following the successive waxing and waning of the moon to measure the temporal distance towards the holy month of God. The passionate longing for Ramadan intensifies in the two lunar months [Rajab and Sha'ban] preceding Ramadan."[1] Thus, the observation of the cycles of the moon (Qamar) between the crescent (Hilal) and the full moon (Badr) functions not only as a way of marking time but also as a means of meditating on divine beauty in the cosmos. The moon is still today a symbol of beauty, perfection, piety, and virility. Furthermore, the terms Hilal, Badr, Rajab, Sha'ban, and Ramadan are occasionally used in personal names, suggesting that language associated with the moon marks personal identity. This is evident in the story *One Thousand and One Nights,* which features a marriage between the princess Badr Al-Budure ("the moon that outshines all other full moons") and the prince Qamar el-Zaman ("the moon of all time"). In other instances, the full moon is also a common simile for female beauty.

Space does not permit a full treatment of the continuing enthusiasm for lunar imagery in Islamic circles. However, one might tentatively conclude that the use of the moon crescent as a religious symbol in Islam perpetuates a moon piety that was deeply rooted in the religious visual culture of the ancient Near East. This way of imagining or expressing devotion to the divine is manifest in a bronze votive figure, probably from Upper Mesopotamia (seventh century BCE), which shows a perfectly sculpted, aristocratic or royal suppliant with devoutly folded hands under a big crescent (**fig. 11.6**).

Fig. 11.6. Bronze figure depicting a (royal) suppliant under a crescent moon, Mesopotamia, 7th c. BCE, 27.3 cm x 15.5 cm. Source: Collections BIBLE+ORIENT Fig 2011.4 (photo: Primula Bosshard)

---

1   See Qleibo 2012:8, from where also the examples of Islamic moon-enthusiasm are taken.

6. Conclusion

Zechariah 4:1–14 is of double interest for iconographic exegesis. On the one hand, we have explored how literary texts such as Psalm 67 or Zech 1:8–6:15 can be read as a type of image insofar as the arrangement of its various linguistic units can be said to comprise the visual pattern of a text. This visual pattern can be described through close textual analysis or even displayed in graphic form, as is the case with the Jewish Shiviti. On the other hand, Zechariah 4:1–14 offers yet another example of how biblical texts transpose common themes in ancient iconography into literary imagery. Specifically, Zechariah's vision of a lampstand flanked by two figures corresponds with ancient lunar iconography: two men, which can be replaced by trees, flanking a crescent moon emblem. It was also shown that textual and visual manifestations of lunar imagery were associated with the moon cult in the southern Levant, especially during the Assyrian and Neo-Babylonian hegemony. Both analyses benefitted from understanding how the relationship between certain images, or iconemes within a given composition, contributes to the interpretive process.

Assignment/Exercise

1. Study the collages represented in figures 11.4–5. In addition to what is described in this chapter, what other associations can you identify between these various images?
2. Next, peruse other books that present a large amount of ancient Near Eastern iconography, such as *ANEP, GGG,* or *SBW.* Identify images from these volumes that could be added to the collages. In what ways do you think these additional images are related to the images already present in figures 11.4–5?
3. Using the same sources of ancient Near Eastern iconography, try to create a similar collage for another biblical text (e. g., Habakkuk 3; Isaiah 6; Ezekiel 1).

Bibliography

Bernett, Monika and Othmar Keel. 1998. *Mond, Stier und Kult am Stadttor: Die Stele von Betsaida (et-Tell).* Orbis Biblicus et Orientalis 161. Freiburg/Göttingen: Universitätsverlag/Vandenhoeck & Ruprecht.

Keel, Othmar. 1998. *Goddesses and Trees, New Moon and Yahweh: Two Natural Phenomena in Ancient Near Eastern Art and in the Hebrew Bible.* Journal for the Study of the Old Testament: Supplement Series 261. Sheffield: Sheffield Academic.

Smyth-Florentin, Françoise. 1992. "L'Espace d'un chandelier: Zacharie 1,8–6,15." In *Le livre de traverse: De l'exégèse biblique à l'anthropologie,* edited by Oliver Abel, 281–89. Paris: Patrimoines.

Staubli, Thomas. 2003. "Sin von Harran und seine Verbreitung im Westen." In *Werbung für die Götter: Heilsbringer aus 4000 Jahren,* edited by Thomas Staubli, 65–90. Freiburg: Universitätsverlag.

Theuer, Gabriele. 2000. *Der Mondgott in den Religionen Syrien-Palästinas: Unter besonderer Berücksichtigung von KTU 1.24.* Orbis Biblicus et Orientalis 173. Freiburg/Göttingen: Universitätsverlag/Vandenhoeck & Ruprecht.

Chapter 12
Divine Warrior or Persian King? The Archer Metaphor in Zechariah 9

Ryan P. Bonfiglio

1. Presenting the Problem

Zechariah 9 introduces the first of three oracles that comprise what is often referred to as Second Zechariah (chs. 9–14). Typically dated to the late-sixth or fifth century BCE, one of the most striking features of this chapter is the military theophany described in verses 13–14. Here YHWH appears in the guise of an archer, readying his bow for battle and shooting forth arrows like lightning:

> For I have bent Judah as my bow;
>   I have loaded Ephraim as its arrow.
> I will arouse your sons, O Zion,
>   against your sons, O Greece,
>   and wield you like a warrior's sword.
> Then the LORD will appear over them,
>   and his arrow go forth like lightning;
> the Lord GOD will sound the trumpet
>   and march forth on the storm clouds of the south.
> (vv. 13–14; author's translation)

This imagery is by no means an innovation of the author of Zechariah 9. In describing YHWH's activity in explicit military language, this text draws on a Divine Warrior motif that is already evident in the oldest Hebrew poetry (e. g., Exodus 15; Deuteronomy 32; Judges 5), and before that, ancient Canaanite and Mesopotamian conflict myth traditions (e. g., the Baal Cycle, Enuma Elish). In light of this observation, Paul D. Hanson describes Zechariah 9 as a Divine Warrior Hymn that intentionally revives an ancient textual tradition in order to envision the future restoration of Yehud (1973:40). Drawing on Hanson's work, Carol L. and Eric M. Meyers likewise contend that the presence of Divine Warrior imagery in Zechariah 9 "should be viewed as part of Second Zechariah's general tendency to echo the language of [older] authoritative literature" (1993:150).

Many commentators follow Hanson and the Meyerses on these points. Namely, they conclude that: (1) the Divine Warrior is the primary conceptual domain targeted, as it were, by the archer metaphor in Zechariah 9:13–14; and (2) this imagery alludes to the Divine Warrior by means of inter-textual references to early Israelite victory hymns or thirteenth century Ugaritic myths. While these conclusions are valuable in their own right, questions remain. For instance, outside of the Divine Warrior do other conceptual domains inform the Yhwh-as-archer metaphor? Does Late Bronze Age "authoritative literature" provide the only, or even the most relevant, comparative data for understanding the background of figurative language in this Persian period biblical text?

The purpose of this chapter is to explore how the study of a prominent motif in Persian period iconography – the royal archer – can help provide a fuller picture of the background and significance of the imagery in Zechariah 9:13–14. Rather than ruling out the possibility that Zechariah 9 depends on ancient texts about the Divine Warrior, the iconographic data presented below provides additional comparative evidence for interpretive analysis. This procedure not only recognizes the value of studying biblical metaphors in light of ancient images but it also takes seriously the ability of the minor arts (e. g., coins and seals) to function as a communicative medium in the ancient world.

2. Iconographic Evidence: The Persian King as Archer

Images associated with archers – bows, arrows, quivers, and scenes featuring bow-wielding heroes in combat or on the hunt – are widely attested throughout the history of ancient Near Eastern iconography. Yet during the reign of the Persian king Darius I (522–486 BCE), archery imagery first emerged as a distinct and pervasive feature of the visual vocabulary of the Achaemenid Empire. During this time, archer imagery appeared in all three major forms of Achaemenid iconography (monumental reliefs, seals, and coins) and, as will be shown below, was often associated with a royal figure, if not the king himself.

Since space prohibits a full review of the iconographic material (cf. Root 1979; Nimchuk 2002; Garrison 2000; 2010), I will narrow my inquiry in two ways. First, I primarily focus on archer iconography from the late-sixth through fifth centuries BCE, a time period that roughly corresponds to the date Second Zechariah was written. Second, since Zechariah 9:13 depicts Yhwh with bent bow and loaded arrow, I concentrate on iconographic scenes of active combat – that is, where the bow is drawn back into a ready-to-shoot position or is held with an outstretched hand while the other hand grasps arrows or an additional weapon (a spear or sword). Within these parameters, the most prominent depictions of archers are found on a series of coins instituted by Darius I and a collection of seal impressions on administrative tablets from Persepolis.

2.1. Coins: The Archer Series

Within the first decade of his reign, Darius introduced a new series of coins, minted in gold and silver. Four major iconographic designs are evident, each of which depicts a crowned figure, dressed in a pleated and full-sleeved robe, bearing an archer's bow. The presence of the crown and court-style robe suggests that the archer is a royal figure, probably Darius himself. In fact, it is likely that these coins represent the first example of a royal portrait being applied to coinage (Root 1991:17).

Although the coins clearly had economic value in their own right, they are equally important from an art historical perspective (Root 1989). For instance, Cindy Nimchuk argues that:

> Darius took advantage of a readily available form [coinage], in which economic and ideological values were already mingled, and adapted it to his communicative purpose. His concern was to use these small pieces of precious metal to emphasize his view of the world and his role as Great King in that world. (2002:71)

Fig. 12.1. Type I archer coin in line drawing, late 6th or early 5th c. BCE. Source: Garrison 2010:338 fig. 32.1

In this sense, an archer series coin would have functioned as a type of "mobile media" as well as a form of currency.

The iconography of the Type I coin (**fig. 12.1**) likely reflects the earliest design in the archer series. These coins, which were minted only in silver, depict a crowned archer in half-length view, facing right in profile, wearing the full-sleeved court robe. The left hand, which is slightly elevated and extended, grasps a bow. Although the bow remains undrawn, it is oriented in a ready-to-use direction (i.e., with the shaft bending away from the figure).[1] In addition, the presence of arrows in the king's other hand suggests that the archer is poised for combat.

A notable characteristic of the Type I coin design is the fact that the archer appears only from the torso up. This cropped frame of reference can be interpreted in one of two ways. This design may recall ninth-century Neo-Assyrian images of Ashur rendered in half-length, emerging from a winged disk and shooting an arrow (**fig. 12.2**).

This correspondence might suggest either that the Neo-Assyrian divine images were actually a prototype for the Type I coins or that the figure on the coin is not the Persian king but rather the Persian god Ahura Mazda. However, even though Achaemenid monumental art often depicts Ahura Mazda, much like Ashur, emerging out of a winged disk, the Persian god never bears a drawn bow. Thus, it seems better to conclude that the Type I archer depicts Darius with divine visual connotations. The Persian archer king is presented in a compositional design (i.e., half-length view,

---

1   Persian monumental art occasionally pictures the king with an un-drawn bow as in the Type I coins. However, in these cases the bow is oriented backward (i.e., with the shaft curving toward the king) and down by the king's side. Since the king is otherwise unarmed, combat does not seem immanent. These images are excluded from this study.

where the circular shape of the coin approximates a disk) that recalls the bow-bearing Assyrian deity emerging from a winged disk.

The cropped frame of reference in the Type I coins might also mimic what the king would look like while riding in a chariot, perhaps in battle or on a hunt. In these contexts, only the upper portion of the body would be visible to a spectator. The 5th or 4th century BCE Seal of Darius (**fig. 12.3**) provides a potential example of this type of scene.

Fig. 12.2. Neo-Assyrian relief, 9th c. BCE, Ashur-as-archer emerging from a winged-disk. Source: *SBW*:217 fig. 296

Fig. 12.3. Seal of Darius from Thebes, Egypt, 5th or 4th c. BCE. Source: Collon 1988: Fig. 558

This seal depicts a crowned figure in half-length view, riding in a chariot and aiming a drawn bow at a rearing lion. On the left, an Old Persian inscription reads "Darius, the great king." Ahura Mazda emerges out of a winged disk near the center of the image. While the presence of the drawn bow in the Seal of Darius is more suggestive of the design of the Type II coins (see below), the appearance of the king in half-length view recalls the compositional design of the Type I coins.

In contrast, the other three major coin designs (Types II–IV) all picture the archer king in full-length view (**figs. 12.4–6**). In each case, the king faces right in profile with his bent leg suggesting a kneeling or running position.

Fig. 12.4. Type II archer coin in line drawing, late 6th or early 5th c. BCE. Source: Stronach 1989: Fig. 1 [2]

Fig. 12.5. Type III archer coin in line drawing, early 5th c. BCE. Source: Stronach 1989: Fig. 1 [3]

Fig. 12.6. Type IV archer coin in line drawing, early 5th c. BCE. Source: Stronach 1989: Fig. 1 [7]

In the Type II design, the archer king is depicted in what appears to be a more aggressive fashion. Not only is the bow drawn and loaded with an arrow, but the sleeves of the robe are pushed back and the lower hem of the garment is pulled up. The figure wears a quiver with additional arrows on his back. The king seems poised for combat in this ready-to-shoot position.

While typologically related to the Type II coins, the Type III and IV coins are often treated separately since they are dated to just after Darius's reign. These coins blend elements of the two designs already discussed. The king appears in a kneeling/running position as in the Type II coins, but the presence of an outward facing, undrawn bow held with a slightly extended hand recalls the Type I coins. The aggressive posture of the Type III and IV coins is suggested by the pushed back sleeves and pulled up garment as well as the presence of an additional weapon (a spear in Type III; a dagger in Type IV).

2.2. Seals: Archer Scenes in the Persepolis Fortification Archive

A vast collection of seal impressions dating from 509–494 BCE have been found on administrative documents from the Persepolis Fortification (PF) archive. This collection of seal impressions includes almost 1200 different iconographic designs, some of which have recently been published for the first time (Garrison and Root 2001).[2] Among the 367 seal impressions featuring human or human activity, the most prominent motif involves archer-related imagery. Archers appear in all the major carving styles and are depicted in a variety of settings, including what Garrison and Root refer to as "heroic combat" scenes. In many cases, the archer is depicted as a hybrid creature. Though the details differ from seal to seal, the composite creature always has the head, arms, and upper torso of a human but the lower torso of an animal (**figs. 12.7–9**).

Fig. 12.7. PFS 0078 in Court Style, late 6th or early 5th c. BCE. Source: Garrison 2000:139 fig. 14

---

2   Only the first of three volumes of the seals have been published thus far. For an introduction to the archive as a whole, including a discussion of its history, sealing practices, scope of iconographic design, etc., see Garrison and Root 1998.

Fig. 12.8. PFS 0118 in Fortification Style, late 6th or early
5th c. BCE. Source: Garrison 2000:140 fig. 16

Fig. 12.9. PFS 0715 in Fortification Style, late 6th or early
5th c. BCE. Source: Garrison 2010:344 fig. 32.5c

These composite creatures may recall the Type I coins since only the upper torso
of a human archer is visible. That is, while the lower body of the archer is cropped
out of the Type I coins, in the seals the lower body of the archer is replaced with that
of a winged animal.

In contrast to the coins, it is less clear that the archers on the seals are explicitly royal figures. However, art historian Mark B. Garrison has concluded that these
seals develop concurrently with the royal archer motifs in both the coins and various
monumental reliefs (Root 1991). In addition, the carving style of a number of seals
shares a strong similarity with the archer series coins. A representative example is
found in Persepolis Fortification Seal (PFS) 0261* (**fig. 12.10**).[3] This seal pictures an
archer figure emerging out of, or perhaps riding upon, a bull-headed creature with
wings and scorpion tail.

Fig. 12.10. PFS 0261* in Court Style, late 6th or early 5th
c. BCE. Source: Garrison 2000:140 fig. 17

---

3   All seal impressions from the Persepolis Fortification are labeled "PFS" followed by a four digit
    number. An asterisks is included on seals that bear an inscription.

As in the Type II coins, the bow is drawn and loaded with an arrow. The archer takes aim at a rearing lion. As in the Type I coins, the archer in this seal wears the pleated, full-sleeved court robe and appears only in half-length view. While this archer does not wear a crown, PFS 0261* is rendered in Court Style, which in this archive is characteristic of seals associated with the king or royal officials.

Much like the Type II–IV coins, a large portion (44%) of archer scenes in the Persepolis Fortification archive depict the bow-bearing figure in a kneeling or running position. These archers are often pictured taking aim at an isolated animal as in PFS 0286 (**fig. 12.11**) or protecting an animal from a predator as in PFS 0182 (**fig. 12.12**).

Fig. 12.11. PFS 0286 in Fortification Style, late 6th or early 5th c. BCE. Source: Garrison 2010:348 fig. 32.9c

Fig. 12.12. PFS 0182 in Court Style, late 6th or early 5th c. BCE. Source: Garrison 2010:346 fig. 32.7e

The former depicts a hunting scene in which a kneeling archer with bent bow shoots at a caprid with large antlers. The caprid is hunched over on collapsed fore-legs and a spear- or arrow-like object protrudes from its neck. In contrast, PFS 0182 presents a scene in which a winged lion rears its front legs at a nearby stag. Turning away from the attacking creature, the stag looks back toward a kneeling archer. The archer's bent bow appears to be aimed at the winged lion, thus suggesting a protection scene as opposed to a hunting scene.

It should be noted, however, that the archers in PFS 0286 and PFS 0182 are not clearly royal figures. In fact, the type of kneeling archer scene discussed above rarely occurs in the Court Style. An intriguing exception is found in PFS 0071* (**fig. 12.13**).

Fig. 12.13. PFS 0071* in Court Style, late 6th or early 5th
c. BCE. Source: Garrison 2010:348 fig. 32.9b

The presence of the pleated robe, paneled inscription, and star and crescent are
all characteristic of the Court Style. The kneeling archer takes aim at a rearing lion,
which already has been impaled with several arrows. Another lion lies prone at the
archer's feet. According to Garrison, PFS 0071* "offers one of the closest parallels, in
pose and iconography, to the kneeling archer of type II coinage" (2010:354).

In sum, this brief survey of iconographic evidence demonstrates that archer imagery was a distinctive feature of the visual vocabulary of the Achaemenid Empire. Especially in the form of coinage, archer imagery became explicitly associated with the
Persian king. This is evident in Greek circles, where Herodotus refers to the coins as
"darics" (*Hist.* 7.28) and Aeschylus calls Darius *toxarchos* or "chief archer" (*Pers.* 556).
While the connection between the archer and the royal figure is less strong among the
seals from the Persepolis Fortification archive, the design and style of this material
suggest a strong representative correspondence with the archer series coins.

3. Royal Ideology in Pictorial Form

The analysis above demonstrates that archer imagery was a prominent way of representing the Persian king (or royal figure) in Achaemenid iconography. What specific messages did such imagery communicate? How do these coins and seals convey
Achaemenid royal ideology?

The half-length armed archer scene, which is found in the Type I coins, the Seal of
Darius, and seals with archers in the form of hybrid creatures, seems to call to mind
how the king would have appeared to a spectator when seated upon his throne or
riding upon his chariot. Both physically and metaphorically, this posture suggests the
upliftedness of the king as a victorious and powerful ruler. Similar themes are found
elsewhere in Achaemenid art, especially in monumental reliefs where the king is pictured as being high and lifted up, often upon the voluntary support of his subjects.[4]
In her study of the "uplifted king" motif in Achaemenid monumental art, Margaret
Cool Root concludes that this iconographic design conveys a sense of order, stability, and peace that is associated with the ascension of a new ruler (1979:131–61). By
merging iconographic representations of Darius as uplifted king and armed archer,

---

4   See, for instance, the tomb façade at Naqsh-i Rustam and the east doorjambs of the Central Build-
    ing of Darius.

the Type I coins present in miniature what is writ-large in Achaemenid monuments: as the "chief archer" the Persian king establishes a reign of peace and stability.

As noted above, the depiction of a half-length archer king may also recall the bow-bearing deity emerging from a winged disk. The divine visual connotations implied by this composition may reinforce the notion that the king is a legitimate and divinely authorized ruler. Under the auspices of Ahura Mazda, the king brings prosperity to the land, and with it, the obligation of loyalty from the people. Coins are a fitting vehicle for this message. In most cases, the archer series coins were given as gifts by the king in order to confer favor, status, and wealth to the recipient. The coins were tangible proof of the prosperity of Darius's reign. At the same time, by bearing a depiction of the king as an armed archer, anyone who received the coin would have been reminded that prosperity was a function of the king's military power. If the king's largess was not met with loyalty and submission, the archer's bow would be aimed, as it were, at the recipient of the coin. Thus, the archer series coins were both gift and threat.

The kneeling archer scene, which is found in Type II coins as well as seals with hunting or protection scenes, communicates a slightly different message. If this imagery bears royal connotations, then the king is portrayed as both a protector of those in need and an aggressor against those who threaten his "flock" (Nimchuk 2002:66). This symbolism coheres with the events surrounding Darius's rise to power in the closing decades of the sixth century. Not only did Darius subdue a number of rival claimants to the throne, but he also initiated aggressive efforts to expand the empire's borders and to consolidate its influence as a world superpower. To put the matter in iconographic terms, the story of Darius's reign might be visualized as a series of "heroic combat" scenes. Thus, even if the archers in the Persepolis Fortification archive are not always clearly marked as royal figures, the imagery on these seals likely would have resonated with the popular image of the king as protector and aggressor, one who subdues enemies and who expands borders.

Taken together, the half-length armed archer and kneeling archer as hunter/protector function as a vehicle of royal ideology. Whether in the form of coins or seals, the royal archer motif affirms notions of the king as a legitimate ruler who consolidates his kingdom through power, prosperity, and peace.

4. Zechariah 9:13–14 in Light of Achaemenid Iconography

How might the analysis of Achaemenid iconography help one reassess the meaning and conceptual background of Zechariah 9:13–14? Two issues must be considered: (1) To what extent does royal archer imagery share common themes or features with the description of Yнwн as archer? and (2) To what extent is it plausible to conclude that the production or reception of Zechariah 9:13–14 was influenced by Achaemenid iconography?

4.1. Zechariah 9's Archer as Persian King

When Achaemenid royal archer imagery is compared with the figurative language of Zechariah 9:13–14, several points of congruence are evident. For instance, the description of Yhwh bending Judah as bow and loading Ephraim as its arrow in preparation for combat (v. 13) calls to mind a battle pose that is quite similar to that which is depicted in the Type II coins and the seals with kneeling archers. In both image and text, the archer bears a drawn bow in a realistic fashion. Likewise, the larger context of Zechariah 9:13–17 might be read as a type of "heroic combat" scene in ways that are analogous to that which is found in many Persepolis Fortification seals in which an archer protects an animal threatened by a predator. Specifically, Zechariah 9:15–16 describes Yhwh as protecting (Hiphil of *gnn*) and saving (Hiphil of *yš'*) from danger "the flock of his people." Just as the royal archer fells the rearing lion in **fig. 12.13**, so too does Yhwh subdue (*kbš*) Israel's enemies with a bow in Zechariah 9.

Two other points of congruence are also evident, though in less explicit ways. First, in the theophany described in 9:13, Yhwh appears overhead, shooting forth arrows like lightning and marching forth on the storm clouds (*běsaʿărôt*). If one imagines the storm clouds as Yhwh's chariot (cf. Ps 104:3; Isa 19:1), then perhaps one might see in Zechariah 9:13 a cropped frame of reference not unlike what is found on the Seal of Darius (**fig. 12.3**) or even the Type I coins (**fig. 12.1**). Whether as a rider on the clouds or as a king in his chariot (or on his coin), the archer appears in half-length view.

Second, one might detect a point of congruence between how Yhwh "arouses" (Polel of *ʿrr*) his weaponry in 9:13b and a previously unmentioned seal from the Persepolis Fortification archive. In commenting on PFS 0848* (**fig. 12.14**), Garrison suggests that the archer is not shooting at the hybrid creature but rather is shooting under its guidance or its authority (2000:136).

Fig. 12.14. PFS 0848* in Fortification Style, late 6th or early 5th c. BCE. Source: Garrison 2000:137 fig. 11

This view reflects the fact that the creature does not appear in an aggressive posture rearing on its hind legs (as in **fig. 12.13**) and a threatened animal is not present (as in **fig. 12.12**). Though Garrison's suggestion is somewhat speculative, one might understand the relationship between the creature and archer in PFS 0848* in ways that are broadly analogous to that between Yhwh and his weaponry in Zechariah 9:13b. Just as the archer in the seal shoots under the guidance of the hybrid creature, so too are the weapons in Zechariah 9 aroused into action under the guidance or authority of Yhwh. However, even if this is the case, it must be admitted that Achaemenid iconography does not shed light on Zechariah 9's description of Judah and Ephraim as a personified bow and arrow.

In addition to these points of image-text congruence, the royal archer motif might help explain aspects of Zechariah 9 that are not as clearly traceable to the Divine Warrior motif. For instance, despite its heavy use of explicit military language in reference to Yhwh, Zechariah 9 also employs royal language. In verse 9, God is described as a king who comes to his people "triumphant and victorious" and in verse 10, his royal dominion is said to "be from sea to sea, and from the River to the ends of the earth." Royal language is continued in Zechariah 10, where God is pictured as a shepherd – a common metaphor used for ancient Near Eastern kings. The presence of this royal imagery is certainly not unrelated to the Divine Warrior motif. Not only do Yhwh-as-warrior and Yhwh-as-king metaphors often overlap in biblical literature, but the theme of the Divine Warrior is often linked to the Davidic monarchy and the royal cult. Nevertheless, a more direct connection between the archer metaphor and royal language in Zechariah 9 is found in the iconographic evidence.

Furthermore, the appearance of the bow in Zech 9:13 has traditionally been understood as a reflex of the Divine Warrior motif. This may certainly be the case since biblical literature and Canaanite myths both describe the Divine Warrior in terms of a storm god marching in battle and shooting forth arrows as lightning. However, at least in the biblical tradition, the Divine Warrior is rarely described as explicitly wielding a bow. In fact, the only other time outside of Zech 9:13 that the Divine Warrior is said to bend the bow is in Lamentations 2:4. But there, Yhwh aims his bow at Zion as a form of punishment, not protection. Thus, while the bent bow is surely implied by the Divine Warrior motif, it is more specifically and frequently related to the Persian archer king, especially at the time Zechariah 9 was likely written.

4.2. Interaction and Influence

The preceding section demonstrates the presence of substantial congruence between Achaemenid royal archer imagery and the archer metaphor in Zechariah 9. However, iconographic exegesis might also explore other aspects of the image-text relationship, such as clarifying the type of interaction present between the media (i. e., image-text correlation) and delineating plausible mechanism of contact or influence (i. e., image-text contiguity).[5] While these matters cannot be dealt with extensively here, several general points can be made.

It would, of course, be very difficult to prove that the author of Zechariah 9 had ever seen either an archer series coin or a Persepolis seal with archer imagery. Nev-

---

5   For a more detailed discussion of image-text congruence, correlation, and contiguity see the introductory chapter of this textbook.

ertheless, it is possible to conclude that both the coins and seals reflect a concept of kingship that was pervasive throughout the Achaemenid Empire during the late-sixth and fifth centuries. Due to their miniature size and relative ease of production, the minor arts, including coins and seals, would have been ideally suited to disseminating ideas across vast territories and through diverse segments of the population (Uehlinger 2000). In fact, the administrative documents from the Persepolis Fortification archive attest to the fact that the officials who used the seals traveled to (or came from) extreme ends of the Achaemenid Empire. In addition, Garrison has argued that as markers of rank, social status, and identity the seals "penetrated Achaemenid society unlike any other type of artifact carrying complex visual imagery" (2000:155).

These conclusions seem to be true of archer imagery in particular. It is striking that this motif is found not only at the empire's "heartland" in the form of the Persepolis seals, but also in the empire's western-most periphery (Greece and Asia Minor) in the form of coins. Likewise, the previously discussed Seal of Darius was said to be found in a tomb at Thebes (Egypt), which is quite a distance from Persepolis. Thus, throughout the Achaemenid Empire the archer imagery had become a type of popular visual metaphor for the king himself.

A similar situation seems to obtain in the Levant during the Persian period. Christoph Uehlinger notes the presence of "persianisms" – visual motifs that reference Achaemenid iconography – in certain Palestinian seals and amulets from the Persian period (1999:172). Especially prominent are scenes of heroic combat. Though Uehlinger admits that such persianisms are more strongly felt in Asia Minor than Palestine, he still concludes that "as far as miniature media are concerned, the image of the Persian royal hero – which western provincials would easily identify either with the king or with Achaemenid kingship in general – must have been the most powerful and renowned among the visual expressions of Persian imperial ideology in Palestine" (1999:160). Furthermore in *GGG*, Uehlinger and Othmar Keel note that near the end of the sixth century – precisely when the archer series coins first went into circulation – depictions of the king as a "royal hero" (though not always as an archer) suddenly emerge in Palestine glyptic art.

One might also note that while few archer series coins have been found in the archaeological record of Palestine, reference to darics (*darkĕmôn* or *ʾădarkôn*) are found in several Persian period biblical texts (Ezra 2:69; 8:27; Neh 7:70–72). In addition, Uehlinger points to the presence of local coinage from fourth-century Samaria that show a royal figure engaged in a variety of heroic combat scenes. While not depicting Darius as archer, several of these coins show striking thematic and stylistic resonances with the earlier archer series coins.

Taken together, this evidence greatly raises the probability that, at about the time when Second Zechariah was written, the association between archer imagery and the Persian king was widely known and extensively deployed throughout the Achaemenid Empire. I contend that both the specificity and pervasiveness of this imagery makes it no longer tenable to assert that the presence of the archer metaphor in Zech 9:13–14 *solely* reflects a recapitulation of the Divine Warrior motif from ancient literary traditions. While some degree of textual dependency is certainly possible, Achaemenid royal archer imagery provides an equally relevant comparative context for understanding the meaning and background of this metaphor. Moreover, in view of the fact that literacy rates were quite low in the ancient world, it is at least plausible, if not highly likely, that the original audience of Zechariah 9 would have been more apt to interpret the Yhwh-as-archer metaphor in light of the visual culture of their day rather than centuries old textual materials.

5. The Divine Warrior in the Image of the Achaemenid King

In light of the evidence discussed above, it is possible to conclude that the figurative description of Yhwh in Zech 9:13–14 shares at least as much – and perhaps more – in common with visual depictions of the Persian king as it does with literary descriptions of the Divine Warrior. This conclusion does not invalidate the claims of Hanson, the Meyerses, or numerous other interpreters who see in Zechariah 9 literary allusions to an ancient textual tradition regarding the Divine Warrior. It might be best to say that the archer metaphor in Zechariah 9 reflects a type of blending of concepts related to both the Divine Warrior and the Persian king. In fact, recent studies in metaphor theory suggest that most metaphors are the product not of a one-to-one comparison of two entities (i. e., a source and target domain) but rather of the conceptual blending of multiple source domains that are then projected onto a target domain. In the case of Zech 9:13–14, elements of the Divine Warrior and Persian king are merged together, thus producing a complex conceptual frame for understanding the activity of Yhwh. In this view, Yhwh is *both* Divine Warrior *and* Persian king in the theological (or better yet, metaphorical) imagination of the author of Zechariah 9.

Such blending, in fact, is already implied by the iconography itself. As mentioned above, the Persian royal archer in the Type I coins are replete with divine visual connotations on the basis of certain shared compositional features with images of the bow-wielding Ashur in a winged disk. Thus, the Type I coins, much like Zechariah 9:13–14, might be understood as a polysemic symbol or metaphor in which aspects of the earthly king and divine warrior are blended together. One might say that allusions to the Divine Warrior in Zechariah 9 are (re)made in the image of the Achaemenid king.

How might this conclusion further inform an interpretation of this text? Zechariah 9 seems to adapt Achaemenid royal ideology as a framework for describing Yhwh's heroic acts in delivering his people. Like a Divine Warrior, Yhwh appears on the scene waging battle against Israel's enemies (vv. 1–7) and serving as a guard for the temple (v. 8). But like the Persian king, Yhwh is a triumphant and victorious ruler who establishes a reign of peace and maintains his dominion over a vast empire (v. 10). In the guise of an (Achaemenid) archer, Yhwh bends his bow for battle (vv. 13–14) in order to protect his people (v. 15), save his "flock" (v. 16), and restore order and fertility to the land (v. 17). Yhwh ushers in a reign of peace, stability, and prosperity on a cosmic level that the Persian king sought to establish in his earthly empire. Thus, the literary description of YHWH in Zechariah 9 mirrors many aspects of the iconographic profile of the royal archer in Achaemenid iconography.

Positing a connection between the archer metaphor and the iconography of the Persian king has important implications for how one understands the theological imagination of Zechariah 9. Like other proto-apocalyptic texts, Zechariah 9 is often thought to imagine the future restoration of God's people occurring at a cosmic level and thus apart from historical and political realities. Thus, in contrast to Second Isaiah (cf. Isaiah 42), the author of Second Zechariah no longer looked to an anointed Persian king to restore Israel to its land and temple. To be sure, this task falls to YHWH alone and occurs outside of history in Zechariah 9. However, just because hope for deliverance was no longer found *in* the Achaemenid king did not mean that the author of Second Zechariah stopped imagining deliverance *through* the imagery of Achaemenid kingship. Thus, even as Zechariah 9 looks to the eschatological future for the restoration of Yehud, the conceptual framework of its prophetic imagination remains firmly rooted in the visual culture of the Persian period.

Assignment/Exercise

1. Read the rest of Second Zechariah (chs. 10–14) and make a list of other metaphors used to describe YHWH. Analyze how these metaphors are used in the context of Second Zechariah. What message(s) do they convey? Do they, or how do they, build on the archer metaphor in Zechariah 9?
2. Choose one of these metaphors for further study. Using commentaries, lexicons, and/or a concordance, identify other places this metaphor occurs in the Hebrew Bible. Is it used in those contexts in the same way as it is used in Second Zechariah? Does this metaphor blend multiple concepts together? If so, which ones?
3. Using books that present Persian period iconography (e. g., *GGG*; Garrison and Root 2001; Root 1979), try to locate images that display some level of congruence with the metaphor you have chosen. Is there any evidence that these images were widely distributed or conveyed a certain message? How does this iconographic evidence help you gain new insight into the background and meaning of the metaphor?

Bibliography

Bonfiglio, Ryan P. 2012. "Archer Imagery in Zechariah 9:11–17 in Light of Achaemenid Iconography." *Journal of Biblical Literature* 131: 507–27.

Garrison, Mark B. 2000. "Achaemenid Iconography as Evidenced by Glyptic Art: Subject Matter, Social Function, Audience and Diffusion." In *Images as Media: Sources for the Cultural History of the Near East and the Eastern Mediterranean: 1st Millenium BCE,* edited by Christoph Uehlinger, 115–63. Orbis Biblicus et Orientalis 175. Freiburg/Göttingen: Universitätsverlag/Vandenhoeck & Ruprecht.

Nimchuk, Cindy L. 2002. "The 'Archers' of Darius: Coinage or Tokens of Royal Esteem?" *Ars Orientalis* 32: 55–79.

Root, Margaret Cool. 1989. "The Persian Archer at Persepolis: Aspects of Chronology, Style and Symbolism." *Revue des etudes anciennes* 91: 33–50.

Uehlinger, Christoph. 1999. "'Powerful Persianisms' in Glyptic Iconography of Persian Period Palestine." In *The Crisis of Israelite Religion: Transformation of Religious Tradition in Exilic and Post-Exilic Times,* edited by Bob Becking and Marjo C. A. Korpel, 134–82. Boston: Brill.

Part III: The Ketubim/Writings (and Beyond)

Chapter 13
Lion Hunting in the Psalms: Iconography and Images for God, the Self, and the Enemy

Brent A. Strawn

1. Introduction

It has been stated that lions are "so burdened … with symbolism that it's surprising they manage to stagger a few paces, let along spring at their prey" (Alexander McCall Smith, cited in Pyper 2014:60). This abundance of symbolism also obtains for the lions that appear in the Old Testament, where no less than the seven Hebrew terms for "lion" (ʾaryēh, ʾărî, kĕpîr, lābîʾ, gôr/gûr, šaḥal, layiš) occur more than 150 times (Strawn 2005a:293–326; 357–74). This is a large dataset that is made still larger by recourse to the wider semantic domain of leonine imagery – those places where the animal is somehow evoked or alluded to, yet without specific mention of one of the lion-terms proper (see § 2 below).

Burdened as it is by symbolism, and well-attested as it is in the Old Testament, the lion seems an especially good figure for iconographical analysis, especially in those places where the beast is employed figuratively. A number of studies have been devoted to leonine iconography in the Old Testament and/or ancient Israelite religion (e. g., Cornelius 1989; Strawn 2000, 2005a, 2009b; Dick 2006; Ornan et al. 2012; Eggler fc; more generally, see Schweitzer 1948; Rühlmann 1964; Watanabe 2002; Buchholz 2005). Several of these have been large-scale studies, even general overviews, and there is obviously not space for a wide-ranging analysis here. Moreover, just as Keel (1992b) has demonstrated the problems of *artistic fragmentation* (studying only one excerpt from a larger visual tableau), LeMon (2009, 2010) has documented the problem of *literary fragmentation* (studying only one literary image isolated from the iconic structure of a larger, unified text). In several publications, LeMon has confirmed the utility of focusing on *all* the imagery (and its congruent iconography) that is found within a smaller composition such as a psalm (see also Chapter 14).

The present chapter builds on previous work on the lion in the Hebrew Bible and in ancient Near Eastern iconography but without neglecting LeMon's important theoretical advances. What follows, then, is an attempt to "hunt" the lion image in one book – namely, the Psalter. To be sure, insofar as the book of Psalms is made up of a host of smaller individual compositions (the various individual psalms), the present study might be subject to the charge of literary fragmentation *à la* LeMon. It is certain, regardless, that space limitations prevent the present essay from doing justice to each of the psalms that mention or evoke lion imagery. Nevertheless, it is also the case that recent research has emphasized the composition of the Psalter *as a book* (see,

e. g., Gertz, Berlejung, Schmid, and Witte 2012:527–49; Zenger et al. 2012:428–52; Hossfeld and Zenger 2005, 2011), and so it is justifiable to trace the lion's tracks across the entire Psalter to see what light such an approach might cast on leonine imagery, especially when considered vis-à-vis ancient Near Eastern iconography.

2. On the Tracks of the Lion in the Psalter

The hunt must begin with those instances that explicitly employ one of the Hebrew terms for "lion." There are no less than fourteen mentions across ten different psalms:[1]

Ps 7:3	Lest he [my pursuer] rip my life like a lion [ʾaryēh], dragging off with no deliverer.
Ps 10:9	He [the wicked] lurks in secret like a lion [ʾaryēh] in his covert; he lurks in order to seize the poor. He seizes the poor when he drags him into his net.
Ps 17:12	His [the wicked's] likeness is like a lion [ʾaryēh] who longs to tear, and like a young lion [kĕpîr] waiting in hiding.
Ps 22:14	They [the enemies] open their mouth against me, a roaring and rending lion [ʾaryēh].
Ps 22:17	For the dogs surround me, the congregation of evildoers has encompassed me, like a lion [ʾărî] <…> my hands and my feet.[2]
Ps 22:22	Save me from the mouth of the lion [ʾaryēh] and from the horns of the wild oxen. You have delivered me!
Ps 34:11	The young lions [kĕpîrîm] are impoverished and hungry, but those who seek Yhwh will not lack any good (thing).
Ps 35:17	O Lord, how long will you watch? Deliver me from their ravages, my only life from the young lions [kĕpîrîm].
Ps 57:5	As for my soul: I lie down in the midst of lions [lĕbāʾîm] aflame for human children. Their teeth are spear(s) and arrows, their tongue is a sharp sword.
Ps 58:7	O God, rip out their teeth from their mouth, break the fangs of the young lions [kĕpîrîm], O Yhwh.
Ps 91:13	You [the righteous] will ride on the lion [šaḥal] and the snake. You will tread on the young lion [kĕpîr] and serpent.
Ps 104:21	The young lions [kĕpîrîm] are roaring for the prey, and seeking their food from God.

---

1   Translations follow Strawn 2005a:369–71.
2   This verse is a famous interpretive crux, with most scholars thinking the Hebrew text is corrupt in some way. For bibliography see Strawn 2005a:370 and n. 78. An iconographical probe is found in Strawn 2000.

Already several things are obvious: the Psalter prefers the terms 'aryēh (5x) and kĕpîr (6x). In contrast, it utilizes 'ărî, lābî' (plural),[3] and šaḥal only once, and it never employs layiš or gôr/gûr. Four of the six instances of kĕpîr, moreover, are plural, as is the one instance of lābî', whereas all other mentions of the lion are in the singular. Unfortunately, the precise distinctions between the various lion-terms used in these verses – and the others found elsewhere in the Old Testament – are not obvious. All that seems (relatively) certain is that kĕpîr designates a young(er) lion, perhaps a not-yet-fully-mature adult (Strawn 2005a:304–10; 2009a).[4] Beyond that, little more can be said about the specific differences between a lābî' and an 'aryēh, for example, or a šaḥal and an 'ărî, though presumably such terms did have different connotations for the ancients, with the varying terms somehow encoding such local knowledge.

Explicit use of one of the lion terms is not the only way leonine imagery might be present, however. The Old Testament employs a rather large semantic domain that is associated with the animal, which is comprised of various nouns, verbs, participles, adjectives, and the like that are often used – sometimes exclusively – of the lion. These domain elements can be searched elsewhere in the Old Testament to determine if their presence there is also meant to evoke or allude to leonine imagery, even if one of the seven lion-terms is not present (see Strawn 2005a:25–26, 327–56). When this is done for the Psalter, nineteen additional verses across sixteen different psalms (ten of which were not found in the prior listing) are revealed as containing lion imagery:[5]

Ps 7:6	Let the enemy pursue my life and overtake (me), let him trample my life on the ground and lay my glory in the dust. *Selah.*
Ps 7:16	He [the evildoer] digs a pit and hollows it out. He falls into the pit that he made.
Ps 9:16	The nations have sunk into the pit that they made, their foot has been caught in the net that they hid.
Ps 10:8	He [the wicked] sits in ambush in the courts and in hiding places he slays the innocent. His eyes watch for the helpless.
Ps 25:15	My eyes are always on Yhwh, for he will deliver my feet from the net.
Ps 31:5	Deliver me from the net which they hid for me, for you are my refuge.
Ps 34:21	He [Yhwh] keeps all of his [the righteous'] bones, not one of them will be broken.
Ps 35:7–8	For no reason they [the enemies] hid their net for me, for no reason they dug a pit for my life. May ruin come upon him

---

3 The masculine plural form in Ps 57:5 is somewhat odd, suggesting a base form *lebe'; see Strawn 2005a:311 and n. 121 for discussion (with bibliography).

4 The gôr/gûr is also clearly a cub (see Strawn 2005a:319–21), though this lion-term is not found in the Psalter proper.

5 Translations follow Strawn 2005a:327–56; see further there for justification of these verses as related to the lion.

Ps 50:22   unawares; and his net which he hid – may it capture him! May he fall into it for (his) ruin.

Ps 50:22   Consider this, those who forget God, lest I [Yhwh] tear you apart with no deliverer.

Ps 57:7   They [the enemies] set a net for my steps, my soul was bowed down. They dug a pit before me, they fell into its midst. *Selah*.

Ps 71:11   They [the enemies] say: "God has forsaken him. Pursue him and seize him for there is no deliverer."

Ps 74:4   Your [God's] foes have roared in the midst of your appointed place, they have set up their signs as signs (there).

Ps 76:3   His [God's] abode was in Salem, his dwelling-place was in Zion.

Ps 76:5   You [God] are glorious, more majestic than the mountains of prey.

Ps 94:13   In order to give him [the righteous] rest from days of trouble until a pit is dug for the wicked.

Ps 104:22   When the sun rises, they [the young lions] are gathered (together), and they lie down in their dens.

Ps 111:5   He [Yhwh] provides prey for those who fear him. He forever remembers his covenant.

Ps 124:6   Blessed be Yhwh who has not given us as prey to their [the enemies'] teeth.

These additional verses are not of a piece, to be sure. First, several of them come from the same psalm – and thus the immediate context – wherein an explicit word for "lion" is found (*viz.*, Psalms 7, 10, 34, 35, 57, 104). This makes these verses more secure than some of the others in this listing by semantic domain. Second, these additional texts do not all relate to the same subdomain within the larger semantic domain of lion imagery. So, for example, one relates to movement (Ps 104:22); one to vocalization (Ps 74:4); and two to habitat (Pss 10:8; 76:3). The vast majority, as would be expected when the referent is a dominant carnivore like the lion, concern hunting, though this subdomain itself is rather large and can be further subdivided with reference to: (1) breaking, harming, or trampling (Pss 7:6; 34:21); (2) ripping, tearing, or scratching, whether that is associated with God (Pss 50:22; 76:5; 111:5) or with the wicked (Ps 124:6); (3) the inability to rescue or deliver from the lion (Pss 50:22; 71:11); or (4) hunting the lion itself (Pss 7:16; 9:16; 25:15; 31:5; 35:7–8; 57:7; 94:13). Third, as the preceding remarks already make clear, when the lion is used metaphorically it does not always have the same referent. To be precise, it is found in the Psalms for the righteous, for God, and for the wicked. Finally, one might note the interrelationship(s) between the explicit lion-texts and those that are more implicit or evocative. The following interleaved list maps the lion's movement within the five constituent parts of the Psalter (**bold** = verse containing a lion-term; *italic* = verse identified by semantic domain; *underlined italic* = verse identified by semantic domain in close proximity to verse with explicit lion-term).

	Book I (Psalms 1–41)		
Psalm 7	**7:3**		_7:6; 7:16_
Psalm 9		_9:16_	
Psalm 10	**10:9**		_10:8_
Psalm 17	**17:12 (2x)**		
Psalm 22	**22:14; 22:17; 22:22**		
Psalm 25		_25:15_	
Psalm 31		_31:5_	
Psalm 34	**34:11**		_34:21_
Psalm 35	**35:17**		_35:7–8_
	Book II (Psalms 42–72)		
Psalm 50		_50:22_	
Psalm 57	**57:5**		_57:7_
Psalm 58	**58:7**		
Psalm 71		_71:11_	
	Book III (Psalms 73–89)		
Psalm 74		_74:4_	
Psalm 76		_76:3; 76:5_	
	Book IV (Psalms 90–106)		
Psalm 91	**91:13 (2x)**		
Psalm 94		_94:13_	
Psalm 104	**104:21**		_104:22_
	Book V (Psalms 107–150)		
Psalm 111		_111:5_	
Psalm 124		_124:6_	

This listing, too, is intriguing, and for several reasons. One might consider, first, patterns of distribution: Nine of the twenty psalms containing lion imagery are found in Book I of the Psalter; these account for seventeen instances – more than half of the total number of hits in the entire Psalter (thirty-three).[6] Four psalms belong to Book II and contain five hits. Book III contains only two psalms with three hits. Book IV has three psalms and five hits, with Book V having two psalms and two hits. Not all

---

6   The tabulation here and below treats Ps 35:7–8 as one hit.

of these instances are of the same type, of course. Once again, the most explicit of these verses – those that actually employ a word that means "lion" – cluster primarily in Book I (nine of fourteen). Book II has only two such hits, Book III has none, Book IV has three, and again Book V has none.

Three further observations on distribution might be offered: (1) Four of the twenty "lion psalms" contain only explicit references to the animal (Psalms 17, 22, 58, 91); six are hybrids, containing explicit mention and evocation via semantic domain (Psalms 7, 10, 34, 35, 57, 104); and the remaining ten contain only allusions to leonine imagery (Psalms 9, 25, 31, 50, 71, 74, 76, 94, 111, 124). (2) The explicit and implicit mentions are variously interleaved, as demonstrated in the listing above. It is particularly interesting that in the hybrid psalms, the explicit mention of lions does not always precede the implicit. The explicit reference typically comes first (Psalms 7, 10, 34, 57, 104), but Psalm 35 is noteworthy in reversing that sequence. Finally, (3) the genre of these lion psalms might be considered since the clear majority are individual laments.[7]

With the lion's tracks in the Psalms now laid out – at least in preliminary fashion – we can turn to a closer look at the beast within the Psalter and its psalms. As implied by the visual language, this "closer look" will be furthered by paying attention to the evidence provided by iconography.

3. Hunting the Various Lions of the Psalms

The first thing to say about the lions of the Psalter is that they are not of the same sort, but fall into two distinct categories: real lions and metaphorical lions. Use of real lion imagery is restricted to Psalm 104. Verse 21 notes the roaring of young lions, associating that vocalization with their seeking food from God. The very next verse adds further comment on these young lions' behavior: they gather when the sun rises, at which point they recline in their "dens" (v. 21).[8] The remaining thirty-one instances of lion imagery in the Psalms are all metaphorical.

As already noted, metaphorical use of leonine imagery in the Old Testament generally revolves around three primary referents: the self, the deity, and the other – typically a wicked enemy. In the Psalms proper, lion metaphors are rarely used of the self, which is often identified as or with the righteous; more frequently lion metaphors are used of YHWH (and in more than one way); and, most commonly of all, these metaphors are used with the wicked or the enemy. Each of these uses is discussed in turn before a curious admixture of the three is evaluated.

---

7   Scholars dispute the psalm genres (or types). For the lion in the individual laments, see Keel 1969; Riede 2000.

8   Lions do not live in dens in the wild, but the Hebrew noun *mĕʿōnâ* is unspecific and may mean only "place of residence" or "dwelling-place" (see Strawn 2005a:38, 349).

3.1. The Righteous Self and/as the Lion

The infrequent use of the lion metaphor for the self/righteous is in line with the same general tendency elsewhere in the Old Testament (Strawn 2005a:47–49), though its attenuation in the Psalms is especially pronounced. Three (sub)types of usage may be mentioned:

1. Psalm 111:5 is not unrelated to Psalm 104 insofar as it portrays YHWH providing "prey" (*ṭerep*), only this time it is for "those who fear him" not for "young lions" by name. The noun *ṭerep* is derived from the root *ṭrp*, which has to do with ripping or tearing and which is frequently found with lion imagery (e. g., Gen 49:9; Num 23:24; Isa 5:29; 31:4; Ezek 19:3, 6; 22:25; Amos 3:4; Nah 2:13–14; Job 4:11, 38:39; Ps 104:21; see Strawn 2005b:337–39). Although some would date Psalm 111 late,[9] and find in *ṭerep* a semantic weakening so that it means generically only "food," the prevalence of the root *ṭrp* with the lion – not to mention the proximity of Psalm 111 to Psalm 104 – suggests that the image in Ps 111:5 may be of YHWH providing for his "young lions" *à la* Ps 104:21. If so, it would mean that the God-fearers are "lionized,"[10] even as it might simultaneously portray YHWH as an adult lion providing for its cubs (see below). But, apart from this one instance in Psalm 111, itself far from transparent, there are no clear instances of the righteous self *as* a lion in the psalms, though the next two uses may recommend careful (re-)consideration on this point.

2. Psalm 91:13 employs lion iconography in conjunction with the righteous self. In this passage, the righteous individual is portrayed as riding on a lion (*šaḥal*) and treading on a young lion (*kĕpîr*). Here, then, the righteous one is not metaphorized as a lion but is symbolically portrayed as dominant over it. The position of the righteous vis-à-vis the lion in Psalm 91 implies subjugation. Placing a subject, human or animal, under the feet is a well-known index that they are the weaker party, subordinate to the dominant entity. This posture is oft-attested in both textual (2 Sam 22:39; 1 Kgs 5:17; Pss 8:6; 18:38; 47:4; Mal 3:21; cf. Rom 16:20; 1 Cor 15:25, 27; Eph 1:22; Heb 2:8) and iconographical sources (**fig. 13.1**) – the latter include images of figures dominating the lion (**fig. 13.2**). Indeed, the subjugated animal (frequently the lion) can become a kind of companion, or at least mount, on which an anthropomorphic figure rides (**fig. 13.3**). These latter figures are probably not human, but invariably gods – or, in rare cases, perhaps divinized ancestors (**fig. 13.4**; see Strawn 2005a:221). Indeed, the frequent presentation of gods riding on or treading upon the lion suggests that the righteous self in Psalm 91 may be less *lionized* so much as *divinized*. If so, it should be quickly pointed out that this divinization (of a sort) is accomplished precisely by means of the lion image and its rich tradition in ancient Near Eastern texts and iconography, both of which include frequent association

---

9   E. g., Kraus 1993:357 places the psalm in the postexilic period.
10 I use this term differently than standard English usage (where it has to do with celebrity status), meaning by it here only "to portray as a lion."

of the lion with the realm of the gods (see Strawn 2005b:58–65, 187–217, 250–73). Quite apart from the possible divinization of the righteous self in Psalm 91, it is clear that the positioning indicates that the specific lions upon which the righteous treads are symbols for defeated enemies (see Strawn 2005b:51 and further below).

3. The last (sub)use concerns those instances where the psalmist seems to be portrayed as a lion hunted by the wicked enemies. Insofar as these passages also function to lionize the enemy, if not also God, they represent a hybridized use and are treated separately below (§ 3.4).

Fig. 13.1. Painting, Abd el-Qurna (tomb of Hekaerneheh), Thutmose IV (1422–1413). Source: *SBW*: Fig. 342

Fig. 13.2. Boss of shield; Luristan, beginning of first millennium. Source: Strawn 2005a: Fig. 4.209

3.2. Yнwн and/as the Lion

As already noted above, Yнwн is associated with lions in Ps 104:21 as the one who provides them with "prey" (*ṭerep*). This imagery may also lie behind Ps 111:5, where Yнwн is said to provide "prey" (*ṭerep*) for those who worship him. Both texts, then, may figure Yнwн as an adult lion providing for its cubs, though since male lions have very little to do with the rearing of young (Schaller 1972:143), Yнwн's lion profile in these psalms, if it is that, would likely derive from the behavior of *female* lions (see Strawn 2005a:49 and n. 97; cf. Strawn 2009b; note also Nah 2:12–14).[11]

---

11 Psalm 34:11 may be similar, though antithetical in sentiment: the impoverishment of the young lions may be due to Yнwн *withholding* food (note the parallelism).

Fig. 13.3. Electron pendant; Tel Miqne-Ekron (Stratum IB); IA II. Source: Strawn 2005a: Fig. 3.84

Fig. 13.4. Reconstruction of portico; Tell Ḥalaf; 9th c. Source: Strawn 2005a: Fig. 4.303

But even if these two passages are metaphorical instances of lion imagery applied to Yhwh, they need not be read too woodenly. They may not portray Yhwh as an adult lion as much as one who *controls lions* – a concept that is common among portrayals of various deities in the ancient Near East, both female (**fig. 13.2**) and male (**fig. 13.5**; see further Strawn 2005b:187–90). As lion-master, Yhwh can protect the righteous from the lion-like enemies as in Ps 34:21, where the imagery of broken bones evokes the realm of the lion from which Yhwh protects the psalmist, as in Ps 124:6, which blesses Yhwh for not giving the psalmist to the enemies' leonine teeth, as prey (*terep*). Other texts that show how Yhwh has the power to deliver from the mouth of the lion and is thus, ultimately, in control of these beasts (real or otherwise) include Pss 22:22; 34:21; and 35:17 (cf. also Ps 58:7; Daniel 6). Perhaps Pss 25:15; 31:5; and 94:13 deserve consideration at this point as well, but are discussed further below (§ 3.4).

Finally, Yhwh is explicitly likened to a lion in Ps 50:22, which promises that those who forget God will be torn apart (*trp*) without possibility of rescue. Here Yhwh *is* a (metaphorical) lion in much the same way as Yhwh is figured as a lion in Amos 1:2. This latter text is instructive since it, too, is an implicit passage, metaphorizing Yhwh as lion primarily and particularly by means of the verb *šʾg*, "to roar," which is one of the main verbs used in the Old Testament for leonine vocalization (see Strawn 2005b:345–46). The divine lion image that is initiated in Amos 1:2 is developed as one moves throughout the rest of that book. It is even possible that these lion-references in Amos, combined with objects from controlled excavations (e. g., **fig. 13.6**), indicate that at least some of the solitary lion images on seals found in ancient Israel/Palestine, but especially in Iron Age II (e. g., **figs. 13.7–8**), are meant to depict Yhwh (see Ornan et al. 2012; Strawn fc [a]).

Fig. 13.5. Seal impression of Šaušattar; Nuzi; 15th c. Source: Strawn 2005a: Fig. 4.212

Fig. 13.6. Agate scaraboid (Aramaic) of *rpty*; Krhosabad (Palace of Sargon); second half of 8th c. Source: Strawn 2005a: Fig. 4.178

Fig. 13.7. Seal of Shema, the servant of Jeroboam; Megiddo; IA II, 8th c., but date debated, possibly IA I. Source: Strawn 2005a: Fig. 3.96

Fig. 13.8. Seal (from *lmlk* jar); Ramat Raḥel; IA II. Source: Strawn 2005a: Fig. 3.94

Be that as it may, the fact that the divine-lion passages in Amos are mostly implicit lends support to finding a similar dynamic in the two implicit passages found in Psalm 73. This psalm locates Yhwh's "abode" (*sōk*) and his "dwelling-place" (*mĕʿōnâ*) in Zion (Ps 73:3; cf. Amos 1:2) and goes on to praise Yhwh as "more majestic than the mountains of prey *[ṭerep]*" (Ps 73:6). Here again, both verses are, at best, *evoking* lion imagery – with the latter one sometimes emended – but they are at least suggestive, and the two of them together, in close proximity, coupled with texts like Ps 50:22 and others that associate Yhwh with the lion, may indicate that Psalm 73, too, figures Yhwh as a divine lion, one even more majestic than the mountain lairs where the animal resides (see Song 4:8; Strawn 2005b:338 and n. 53; *HALOT* 2:380; BDB 383). It should be recalled that the connection between the lion and the divine realm is a longstanding one in the textual and artistic record of the ancient Near East (Strawn 2005a:187–217), making a leonine profile for Yhwh neither unreasonable nor unlikely (Strawn 2005a:58–65, 250–73; 2009b).

3.3. The Enemy and/as the Lion

The vast majority of lion images in the Psalms are associated with the wicked enemy. This is true of explicit passages where the lion is a metaphor for the wicked in at least eleven, and probably thirteen (Ps 91:13 [2x]; see above) of the fourteen mentions, the only exception being Ps 104:21 (see above). It is equally true of the implicit instances, where the enemy is somehow involved in no less than thirteen of the nineteen hits. Taken altogether, then, the passages that somehow connect the lion and the enemy comprise (generously) twenty-six of thirty-three instances, more than 78 %. To be sure, "somehow connect" is rather vague, but intentionally so, since the lion is used with reference to the wicked enemy in a number of ways.

Despite this variety, there can be little doubt that leonine imagery when used of the wicked enemy draws heavily on the ferocity that is one of the animal's "associated commonplaces" (to borrow the language of Max Black 1962). So, for example, the wicked is like a lion that tears (*ṭrp*) the psalmist's life, dragging them off with no hope for rescue (Ps 7:3; see also 17:12; 22:14, which also employ *ṭrp*; cf. 35:17), or is like a lion that lurks in secret so as to seize the vulnerable (Ps 10:8–9; cf. 17:12; 71:11). Texts mentioning lionized enemies often refer to the lion's mouth (Ps 22:14, 22) or its teeth, fangs, or tongue (Pss 57:5; 58:7), focusing the threat posed by the animal on its primary weapons. The graphic nature of this literary imagery is captured visually in the iconographic evidence, which frequently highlights the predatory prowess of the lion, especially vis-à-vis prey (e.g., **fig. 13.8**). Indeed, images of lions with disarticulated body parts (**figs. 13.9–10**) – even human heads and hands (**figs. 13.11–13**) – may indicate that the MT of Ps 22:17, a long standing *crux interpretum*, may not be as corrupt as is often thought, especially if a verb has dropped out (see Strawn 2000 with literature). Be that as it may, the texts that show Yʜᴡʜ capable of delivering from the lion (§ 3.2) demonstrate, at one and the same time, that the enemies are frequently portrayed as such.

Fig. 13.9. Agate scaraboid of *ʾlḥ*; unprovenanced, 8th c. (?). Source: Strawn 2005a: Fig. 3.155

Fig. 13.10. Bulla; unprovenanced (Samaria?); IA III/Persian Period. Source: Strawn 2005a: Fig. 3.142

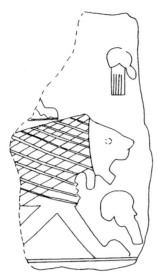

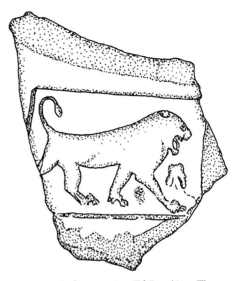

Fig. 13.11. Stamp seal; probably Nineveh; probably 7th c. Source: Strawn 2005a: Fig. 4.58

Fig. 13.12. Seal impression; Tel Dan (Area T); mixed late IA/Persian Period context, after 8th c., perhaps 7th c. Source: Strawn 2005a: Fig. 3.102

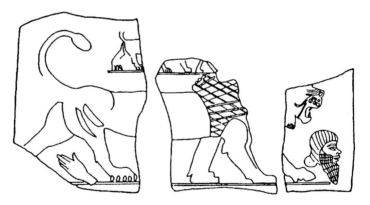

Fig. 13.13. Stamp seal; probably Nineveh; probably 7th c. Source: Strawn 2005a: Fig. 4.57

While it must be admitted that wicked enemies are portrayed in numerous ways, not just as lions, the lion image is particularly frequent – indeed, the preeminent animal metaphor by far (Strawn 2005a:274–75; Keel 1969:201). And so it is that the Psalter, as a literary work, "attests to a higher concentration of leonine enemy metaphors than comparable literature in the ancient Near East" (Strawn 2005a:274 n. 161). But why should this be the case? Even if this question of "why" is ultimately unanswerable, perhaps the question of "to what end" might be addressed – what, that is, is the function or effect of leonine imagery when applied to the enemy?

The function or effect is probably not singular at all, but several in number (see Strawn 2005a:273–76). As already noted, the ferocity of the lion is famous in both text and image, so one might begin by stating that, rhetorically, these lion metaphors present the enemy not simply as a nuisance but as a dominant, carnivorous predator capable of complete and total destruction. Beyond simply lionizing them, that is, the psalmists' use of lion metaphors for their enemies has the effect of *demonizing* them (Keel 1969:202; Strawn 2005a:274–75). These metaphors also function to highlight the *completely dire straits* of the psalmist. Presenting one's enemies as super-power-ful and one's own self as ultra-weak within the context of prayer is a rhetorical way to motivate the deity to intervene on one's behalf (see Strawn 2005a with literature).

This function or effect (or both) is furthered by the long-standing tradition of associating lions with both monarchs and gods (Strawn 2005a:54–65, 152–217, 236–73; 2009b). These entities are the most powerful in ancient Near Eastern societies and religions. So, "[w]hen the psalmists describe their personal enemies as lions … they are employing a metaphor of power and dominance often and long reserved for gods and kings" (Strawn 2005a:274). In this light, the enemy-as-lion metaphors paint the enemies not only as super-powerful animals but *supra*-powerful entities – like gods and kings – and do so precisely by means of the lion image. In this way, the lion metaphor doubly signifies the absolute power of the psalmists' enemies.[12] It is for this reason that they pray "Save me from the mouth of the lion!" (Ps 22:22; cf. 35:17; 58:7), especially because it is only Yhwh, the lion-master (§ 3.2), who is ultimately stronger than a lion (cf. Judg 14:18; Strawn 2005a:276).

3.4. A Hybrid Use

The interesting but curious fact that the lion image can be used of the righteous, the deity, and the enemy leads to a final set of texts which reflect what might be consid-ered a kind of hybrid use. In these texts the lion imagery seems movable, if not down-right malleable, as it does not remain fixed in terms of its referent. At one moment, the righteous seem to be presented as lions that are hunted; in the next moment, it is the enemies who turn out to be the hunted – and captured, if not defeated – lions; all of this takes place within the context of prayer to Yhwh who is thus in control of these lions, whether they be righteous or wicked. The texts in question are Pss 7:16; 9:16; 35:7–8; 57:7 (cf. also Pss 25:15; 31:5; 94:13) – all of which are implicit lion pas-sages (but note the explicit references to lions in Pss 7:3; 35:17; 57:5).

To be sure, the primary or fundamental image used here is that of the hunt, and the hunting imagery in question is not restricted solely to lions (see Riede 2000:150–94; *SBW*:89–95). Frequent mention of nets (*rešet*), for instance, and pits or traps (*bôr, šaḥat, šîḥâ*), implies that other animals, too, may be in mind (**figs. 13.14–15**). And yet, the fact that such terms can occur in close proximity with explicit lion imagery (as, e. g., in Ps 10:8–9) demonstrates that even non-exclusive hunting language can be

---

12 But not only the psalmists' enemies – also Yhwh's, as in Ps 74:4.

used of the lion – this terminology, too, comprises part of the lion's semantic domain (Strawn 2005a:341–42).

In these hybrid texts the wicked is portrayed as a hunter, using strategies that could also be used for lion-hunting – particularly that of the pit (see Ezek 19:4, 8; Strawn 2005a:161–74, 340–43). These passages thus implicitly present the righteous psalmist as the hunted lion. But, in a stunning reversal, the wicked hunter ends up falling into their own trap (Pss 7:16; 9:16; 35:7–8; 57:7). Insofar as the hunters are now the captured prey – which was previously the leonine righteous – the wicked are revealed as the true lions, a depiction altogether in line with the predominant use of explicit leonine metaphors in the Psalms, where the enemies are frequently called or likened to ferocious lions (§ 3.3). Furthermore, since the psalms are prayers to Yhwh, who is known to be the ultimate lion-master (§ 3.2), it comes as no surprise to find the psalmist not only describing the demise of the wicked-lion-hunter-turned-captured-lion (Pss 7:16; 9:16; 35:7–8; 57:7), but also praising Yhwh for deliverance from the net (reset; Ps 25:15) or pit (Ps 94:13) or begging Yhwh to do so (Ps 31:5; cf. 35:7–8). These hybridized instances thus metaphorize the righteous self as lions – and in more than one way – but lions that are divinely protected from their hunters. In so doing, these passages may also evoke the psalmists as Yhwh's leonine companions, along the lines of lions as divine familiars (see above).

Two final observations on the hybrid passages are in order: (1) The double use of lion imagery in these hybrid passages fits into a larger reversal motif that is found at many points in the psalms (e. g., Pss 10:2; 64:6–8; 69:23; 91:3; 124:7; 140:5–10; 141:9–10). The presence of this motif elsewhere, and also with hunting imagery, lends support to seeing the same sort of dynamic in the hybrid lion psalms. Moreover, the fact that many of these reversals take place precisely within the hybrid lion psalms indicates that the lion image is one that is well suited to facilitate the motif.

(2) That the wicked-as-hunter becomes the wicked-as-captured-lion receives support not only from the explicit use of lion imagery for the enemies in the psalms but also from a text like Ps 58:7, which demonstrates that Yhwh not only controls lions but can act in aggressive, even violent ways against them – that is, permanently removing the danger they pose by defanging them, as it were.

4. Conclusion

Despite the methodological observations in § 1, the present essay, too, could be seen as being guilty of literary fragmentation. I have not offered a full reading of any one lion psalm – let alone several – though that is certainly possible in the case of multiple-hit lion-psalms like Psalms 7, 10, 22, 34, 35, 57, 76, or 104 (cf. LeMon 2010:129–40 on Psalm 57; see also the assignment/exercise below). Even so, the present probe has demonstrated that significant benefits accrue when one focuses on a particular book – even one as disparate as the Psalter.

I conclude with two remarks – the first more general, the second more specific:

First, it can be somewhat confusing that the lion image can be used of God, the self, and the enemies and in more than one way for each. This has occasionally led interpreters to posit some sort of inherent ambiguity in lion imagery per se. But the lion image is not ambiguous so much as ambivalent or, perhaps better, polyvalent: capable of a variety of different kinds of deployments. The lion

> draws its strength and vitality as an image and as a metaphor primarily from the power and threat it represents and symbolizes, but that power and threat is differently experienced and variously portrayed depending on the perspective of the observer, the user of the image/metaphor, and the one who encounters the image or receives the metaphor. (Strawn 2005a:284)

A recent study by Pyper seconds this point:

> The lion is consistent; the difference depends on where we are standing ….
> Once allowed past the threat of the lion, one moves into its protection. The lion does not move, the spectator moves, but its symbolic force changes. What is strong and fierce enough to protect me can also threaten me, and the image of the lion uncannily ties together this duplicity of protector and threat, ruler and unruly. (2014:64)

Maybe the lion isn't as burdened with symbolism as we originally thought – or, at least, the lion's polyvalent symbolism proves not to be so burdensome after all, and no impediment to its effective predation (see § 1).

Second, the hybrid use of the lion image (§ 3.4), along with the fact that lion imagery can be used of enemies (as also for the deity) in close proximity to and not always in logical succession with other types of animal imagery, underscores the play of such figurative imagery in the poetry of the Psalms (and elsewhere). The dense and close concatenation of this type of complex imagery suggests that, ultimately, the enemy and deity are – at some level at least – beyond description. Said differently, no one image suffices to capture all that these entities symbolize and represent, even though the lion remains a central piece of the puzzle (for more on this kind of mixed imagery, see Chapter 5).

Assignment/Exercise

Take up one of the multiple-hit lion psalms (e. g., Psalms 7, 10, 22, 34, 35, 57, 76, or 104) or another book of the Bible and investigate its lion imagery along the same lines as modelled in this chapter (Strawn fc [a] does this for Amos). For example, in the prophetic corpus the following books have instances of leonine terms (fuller semantic allusions are not included in these counts): Ezekiel has sixteen hits (Ezek 1:10; 10:14; 19:2 [4x], 3 [2x], 5 [2x], 6 [2x]; 22:25; 32:2; 38:13; 41:19); Isaiah thirteen (Isa 5:29 [2x]; 11:6; 11:7; 15:9; 21:8; 30:6 [2x]; 31:4 [2x]; 35:9; 38:13; 65:25); Jeremiah twelve (Jer 2:5,

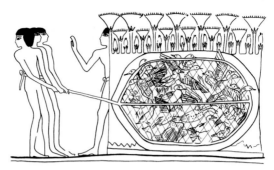

Fig. 13.14. Painting, Sheikh ʿabd el-Qurna (Tomb of
Nakht), Thutmose IV (1422–1413). Source: *SBW*: Fig. 115

Fig. 13.15. Relief, Nineveh, Palace of Assurbanipal (669–
626), BM 124827. Source: *SBW*: Fig. 119

30; 4:7; 5:6; 12:8; 25:38; 49:19; 50:17, 44; 51:38 [3x]); Nahum ten (2:12 [6x], 13 [3x],
14), Hosea five (5:14 [2x]; Hos 11:10; 13:7; 13:8); Amos five (3:4 [2x], 8, 12; 5:19); Joel
and Micah two each (Joel 1:6 [2x]; Micah 5:7 [2x]); and Zephaniah and Zechariah
one each (Zeph 3:3; Zech 11:3). The exercise would also work on a more tightly circumscribed pericope. Note, for example, the particularly dense use of lion imagery
in Ezekiel 19 and Nahum 2. The exercise could also be executed with other theriomorphic images (bird imagery, for example) or with other kinds of imagery, whether
zoological or otherwise, that are also attested in the artistic record.

Bibliography

Cornelius, Izak. 1989. "The Lion in the Art of the Ancient Near East: A Study of Selected Motifs." *Journal of Northwest Semitic Languages* 15:53–85.

Pyper, Hugh S. 2014. "The Lion King: Yahweh as Sovereign Beast in Israel's Imaginary." In *The Bible
and Posthumanism*, edited by Jennifer L. Koosed, 59–74. Semeia Studies 74. Atlanta: Society of
Biblical Literature.

Riede, Peter. 2002. *Im Spiegel der Tiere: Studien zum Verhältnis von Mensch und Tier im alten Israel.*
Orbis Biblicus et Orientalist 187. Freiburg/Göttingen: Universitätsverlag/Vandenhoeck & Ruprecht.

Strawn, Brent A. 2005a. *What is Strong than a Lion? Leonine Image and Metaphor in the Hebrew Bible
and the Ancient Near East*. Orbis Biblicus et Orientalist 212. Freiburg/Göttingen: Universitätsver-
lag/Vandenhoeck & Ruprecht.

_____. 2009b. "Whence Leonine Yahweh? Iconography and the History of Israelite Religion." In *Images and Prophecy in the Ancient Eastern Mediterranean,* edited by Martti Nissinen and Charles A. Carter, 51–85. Forschungen zur Religion und Literatur des Alten und Neuen Testaments 233. Göttingen: Vandenhoeck & Ruprecht.

_____. Forthcoming (a). "Material Culture, Iconography, and the Prophets." In *Oxford Handbook to the Prophets,* edited by Carolyn J. Sharp. Oxford: Oxford University Press.

7 (2x), 8 (2x), 9 (2x), and 10. Second person singular pronouns (you/your), always referring to God, appear even more frequently. The Hebrew pronominal suffix -$k\bar{a}$ ("you" or "your") occurs in vv. 2 (3x), 3 (2x), 4 (2x), 5 (2x), 7 (2x), 8, and 9 (2x). The repetition of these pronouns results in frequent rhyme throughout this poem, a feature sadly lost in English translation. Additionally, vv. 2, 3, 4, 5, 6, 8, 12 contain lines that begin with the letter k, which lends an alliterative quality to the entire psalm. Throughout, the consistency and repetition of sound underline the psalmist's basic message, that the relationship between God and the psalmist is marked by constancy and unswerving devotion. In addition to the frequent use of pronouns and alliteration, other repeated phonetic elements (e. g., inclusio) contribute a sense of tonal cohesion to the psalm.

Such cohesion serves to unify an otherwise convoluted literary structure. The psalm contains elements fundamental to individual psalms of lament (e. g., invocation, complaint, confession of trust, vow of praise, thanksgiving), yet the ordering of these elements is rather unorthodox (see Gerstenberger 1988:11–14) and thus potentially difficult to understand:

> Invocation and Complaint (v. 2)
> Confession of Trust and Vow of Praise (vv. 3–5)
> Thanksgiving (vv. 6–9)
> Imprecation and Requests (vv. 10–12)

In part because of this unique literary structure, the location and purpose of the psalm(ist) are difficult to grasp. The "holy place" (v. 3) seems to refer to the temple where one can behold God and experience God's presence. The two other locations mentioned in the psalm – the waterless desert (v. 2) and the residence of the worshipper (v. 7) – seem to refer to a different locale, where one would not necessarily expect to find God's presence. Yet the psalmist holds to a confidence based on his relationship to God, that God's saving, protecting, and especially nourishing presence can be felt in these locations too.

Though the psalmist's physical location must remain open to debate, one may be reasonably confident that the king is the speaker of the psalm. The third person reference to the king (vv. 11–12) parallels similar formulations elsewhere in the Psalter (e. g., Ps 61:7–8) in which the psalmist-king uses "I" and "the king" interchangeably. The king, first mentioned explicitly in v. 12, is the referent of "him" at the beginning of v. 11. Thus it seems that the psalmist-king appeals to the protection explicitly granted him by his office in the climactic conclusion of the psalm.

3.1 Characterization in the Psalm: The Psalmist/King

In the opening strains, the psalmist depicts himself as utterly desiccated in an arid land (v. 2). His soul and flesh are parched. This dry place may evoke the image of the dusty, dry land of the dead. But whether or not the desert here refers to the netherworld, the forces of chaos and death are much more visible in this place than in the arable land, which remains under the orderly administration of God and his king.

The psalmist first describes his current chaotic situation as far from the presence of God (v. 2), then he turns immediately to a description of an intimate experience of the divine presence (v. 3). The psalmist remembers a time when he had seen God's power on display. This lingering image of God's might spurs the psalmist to praise (vv. 4b–9).

The images of desiccation from v. 2 are completely reversed in v. 6. The dry mouth and cracked lips of v. 2 now ring with praise to God (v. 6) and meditate on God (v. 7) because the deity has nourished the psalmist with "fat and tallow" (ḥeleb wādešen, v. 6). This phrase has prompted several interpretations, including a cultic meal or other great feast. What is particularly striking, regardless, is the double evocation of images of fat. Some have argued that the two words refer to both solid and liquefied abundance since the verb "is satisfied" (tiśbaʿ) in v. 6 has the sense of "drink oneself full" in other contexts (Amos 4:8; Ps 104:16; see Hossfeld and Zenger 2005:123). If so, the fat could include liquefied fat from offerings, or possibly milk, especially if one were to read the MT's ḥēleb ("fat") as ḥālāb ("milk"), a very slight alteration. The image of the psalmist being filled with nourishment provides a fitting contrast to his earlier state in v. 2. The psalmist's once-thirsty soul (v. 2) is now utterly satisfied (v. 6).

The soul (nepeš) of the psalmist is a motif that recurs throughout the psalm: in v. 2 it thirsts, in v. 6 it is filled and contented, in v. 9 it clings to God, and in v. 10 it is threatened by enemies. This repetition of soul imagery, along with the numerous first-person singular independent pronouns and pronominal suffixes, underscores the sense of intimacy between God and the psalmist as well as the personal urgency of the poet. The most vivid image of the psalmist's relationship to God appears in the description of the soul as clinging (dbq) to God, with God supporting him in return (v. 9). The image calls to mind a child embraced by and embracing a parent.

Familial terms often describe the relationship between a king and his divine sponsor (see, e.g., Ps 2:7). The blessing that the psalmist utters in the last verse further amplifies the bond between God and king: "May all who swear by him boast" (v. 12). But who is the antecedent of him? God or the king? Both are possible according to Hebrew grammar and syntax. Indeed, the ambiguity may be intentional because, in the psalmist's mind, God and the king are so intimately related that to swear by one is to evoke the authority of the other. It is perhaps for this reason – if not also the notion of a familial connection between a human child and the divine parent – that the psalmist calls upon God to protect him against his enemies (vv. 10–12).

3.2. Characterization in the Psalm: The Enemy/Enemies

Explicit references to the enemy or enemies come only in the last verses of the psalm. Prior to v. 10, the psalmist describes his trouble as entirely due to his location. The early verses conjure images of chaotic forces at work in the desert. When the psalmist does turn to describe his enemies explicitly, he does so with a series of deathly images, which provide a stark contrast to the images of intimacy, comfort, and joy that pervade vv. 3–9.

The psalmist employs bitter irony to describe the enemies. The ones who sought the psalmist's destruction are bound for an untimely death (v. 10). They descend "to the lowest parts of the earth" (v. 10), a clear reference to the realm of the dead. Regarding the identity of these enemies, the psalmist portrays them initially through military images: they wield swords and threaten violence against the psalmist (v. 10). The subsequent description of the enemies being eaten by jackals (v. 11) may be yet another military allusion, referring to canines ravaging the bodies of soldiers slain on the battlefield. The last verse of the psalm indicates that the enemies who seek to destroy the psalmist are also those who testify against him. The imagery thus moves between military and juridical contexts. But, despite the diverse portrayal of the enemies, the psalmist's bitter tone remains constant.

3.3. Characterization in the Psalm: God

"Seeing God" provides a dominant theme in the psalm's opening verses (cf. Smith 1988). The psalmist "looks eagerly" (v. 2) for God, "sees" God in the holy place, and "beholds" God's strength and glory (v. 3). What form of the deity, then, does the psalmist see? Many interpreters have suggested that the psalm alludes to a tradition of divine theophany, possibly in the temple. Others argue that the trope of "seeing God" (v. 3) is merely metaphorical. Ultimately, an examination of the psalm's constellation of images for the deity is necessary to discern what the psalmist might have "seen" and in what sense he is seeing.

The psalmist highlights several characteristics of God, including God's strength, glory (v. 3), and "loyalty" (ḥesed, v. 4). Of these three characteristics, God's loyalty receives pride of place; the psalmist proclaims it to be the highest good. He expresses this sentiment through a "better than …" formula (see Gerstenberger 2001:14) that conveys the supreme goodness of God's loyalty, so much so that nothing can exceed it.

The psalmist expands the loyalty trope by employing several images of divine care and protection (vv. 8–9), thereby depicting God as the psalmist's "help" and as one who supports the psalmist with the right hand. With the psalmist "clinging" to God (v. 9) and God supporting him with his right hand – as I suggested above – one can easily imagine God and the psalmist in something of an embrace: as a child in the arms of a father or mother, for example. The image of God's wings (v. 8) confirms this sense of closeness and intimate protection.

God as judge, the divine guarantor of order, appears in the last verse of the psalm, in which the psalmist notes that the enemies who speak against him are responsible for his distress. The presence of the norms of justice and order at the end of the psalm provides a fitting conclusion to a poem that first located the psalmist in the desert, that liminal place where God's order does not rule, but rather chaos.

The psalm also suggests some connection between God and light or the sun. The use of the verb šḥr (Piel), translated "I *look eagerly* for you" (v. 2), hints that the psalmist has in mind a deity with solar aspects (cf., e. g., Ps 78:34; Hos 5:15; Isa 26:9; Prov 8:17). Though the verb may be unrelated etymologically to the noun meaning "dawn" (*šaḥar*), in the wider context of Psalm 63, the verb may be employed as a pun or "subtle 'popular etymological' play" (Hossfeld and Zenger 2005:124) to mean "look eagerly (as one would await the dawn)." This language of eager watching for God might even, in this reading, evoke an experience of a solar theophany at dawn, as a number of scholars have posited.

3.4. The Constellation of Images in Psalm 63

In sum, Psalm 63 presents a complex constellation of imagery, from images of battle and conflict to images of intimate nurture by the deity. On the one hand, the poem creates an image of God as a winged deity who serves as divine judge, meting out judgment by destroying those who falsely accuse the psalmist. On the other hand, alongside these military and juridical images, one also sees another representation of God: a winged deity with solar aspects, one who provides liquid nourishment for the psalmist. Then there are the images of the psalmist himself, whom we can identify as the king: images of a desiccated poet are set in contrast with a picture of the same individual sated by the provisions of his divine sponsor, supported by God's own right hand.

4.   Congruent Images in Ancient Near Eastern Art

With the iconic structure of Psalm 63 clearly in view, the next step in utilizing ancient Near Eastern iconography as a tool in the interpretation of the Psalms is to identify artistic images that are congruent with that iconic structure – in this case, Psalm 63's depiction of Yнwн in composite, winged form. Of the many representations of wings in ancient Near Eastern iconography, the image of the winged deity in Psalm 63 finds a particularly strong set of congruencies in the iconography of the winged sun disk and the winged *Dea Nutrix* (nursing goddess).

4.1. The Winged Sun Disk

The portrayal of God as a winged deity who is concerned with preserving justice and the orderly administration of the kingdom in Psalm 63 accords well with the iconography of ancient Near Eastern winged solar deities. Throughout the ancient Near East (and beyond), solar deities are associated with order and kingship because of the regular movement of the sun, its dominant position in the heavens, and its unique, supreme perspective on all that lies below it on earth. An example of a winged solar deity appears in a ninth-century BCE wall relief from Tell Ḥalaf (**fig. 14.2**). The constellation of images – a winged disk supported by an atlant (a hero who holds the sky aloft; cf. the Titan Atlas) and bull men – suggests that the deity represented here is the god Shamash, the Mesopotamian solar god of order, justice, and law (see Wiggermann 1993:226; Black and Green 1992:49).

Fig. 14.2. Wall relief, Tell Ḥalaf, 9th c. BCE. Source: Seidl 2001: Fig. 2

The winged sun disk in the Tell Ḥalaf relief developed from an originally Egyptian form (Ornan 2005b). In its classical Egyptian renderings, the winged sun disk comprises a central disk, to which two broad wings are affixed. Occasionally, *uraei* (hooded cobra heads; singular: *uraeus*) adorn the sides of the disk or are suspended slightly below the wings (**fig. 14.3**).

Fig. 14.3. Winged sun disk from a pectoral, Third Intermediate Period, Tanis. Source: Parayre 1990: Pl. 1.2

This winged sun disk appears frequently in funerary steles of the New Kingdom, representing the sun god Re, whose extended wings show the deity's protection and authorization. In some periods, the wings only extend over royal and divine figures, underscoring the strong connection between Re and office of king. Such is the case in the stele of Amenhotep, the high priest of Onnuris (**fig. 14.4**).

The stele contains several representations of royalty beneath the wings of the solar disk. The central cartouche contains the throne name of King Thutmose IV. At each side of the cartouche are two *uraei*, themselves symbols of kingship, one with a crown of Upper Egypt and the other of Lower Egypt. Facing the *uraei* is the cartouche containing another name for the king, his "Son of Re name." The final element directly beneath the wings are the hieroglyphs reading (*n*)*swt bjt*(*j*), "King of Upper and Lower Egypt."

The idea that the winged sun disk represents divine protection and authorization of the king is not limited to early New Kingdom Egypt. It also appears in Syro-Palestinian and Mesopotamian materials. The most evocative examples from Syria-Palestine come from the Iron-Age Judahite *lmlk* seal impressions, so called because they often contain an inscription that means "of/for the king" (e. g., **fig. 14.5**).

Fig. 14.4. Upper half of the stele of the high priest Onnuris, Amenhotep, Limestone, Eighteenth Dynasty. Source: British Museum EA 902, © The Trustees of the British Museum; Cf. Robins 2008: Fig. 164

Fig. 14.5. Bulla (inscription: *lmlk mmšt*), Judah, late 8th c. BCE. Source: Galling 1977: Abb. 78

The central image is a permutation of the originally Egyptian winged sun disk. In the *lmlk* seals, scholars have understood the image to represent the king in some fashion, or the sponsoring deity of the king. In fact, Tally Ornan has argued persuasively that the winged disk on the seals is an image of YHWH himself as "the patron god of the ruling dynasty at Jerusalem" (Ornan 2005b:213).

In Mesopotamia, winged disks often reinforce the notion of divine protection for the king through the addition of explicitly military imagery. For example, in the Neo-Assyrian Broken Obelisk two hands extend beneath the feathers that surround the disk (**fig. 14.6**). One hand holds a bow and arrow. These weapons convey that the winged deity gives protection by granting military power to the king (here likely Assur-bel-kala, 1073–1056 BCE; see Moortgat 1969:122).

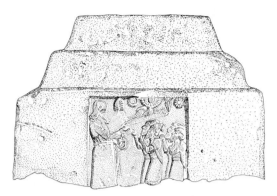

Fig. 14.6. Broken Obelisk, Nineveh, 1073–1056 BCE.
Source: Börker-Klähn and Shunnar-Misera 1982: Abb. 131

Mesopotamian artists also pictured the winged disk actually fighting on behalf of the king in several contexts. The glazed tile of Tukulti-Ninurta II (890–884 BCE) (**fig. 14.7**) provides an example in which a two-winged deity with feathers for lower-parts – or wearing a skirt made from feathers – is incorporated within a blazing sun disk. Like the Broken Obelisk, the deity in the disk bears a bow and arrow. The posture is, however, much more aggressive, for the bow is drawn. The slightly-dipped forward wing –discernible by reference to the registers of text above – and the face of the deity in profile combine to suggest that this deity is in motion, even on the attack, shooting down on his targets from the militarily superior higher position. On the basis of comparison with similar images, we can probably safely assume that the king is positioned below the sun disk, where the tile is now broken.

Fig. 14.7. Glazed tile of Tukulti Ninurta II, 888–884 BCE.
Source: *SBW*: Fig. 295

The association of the solar disk with the king and military triumph also appears in the Megiddo ivory discussed above (**fig. 14.1**). Though the winged disk does not have anthropomorphic characteristics in this ivory as in the later Assyrian examples, the winged disk hovers above the victorious prince returning from battle in his war chariot. Military images abound in the right half of the plaque. Captives from a military campaign are in front of the king, tied to his chariot; soldiers with various weapons process along with the chariot.

Returning again to the constellation of literary images in Psalm 63, we recall that God is pictured there as a winged deity meting out justice to the enemies of the psalm-ist – king (vv. 10–11). We immediately see that these literary images are congruent with the widely attested iconography of the winged sun disk as a god of order and justice, *especially* when the winged sun disk is associated with the protection of the king. This imagery is well known throughout the ancient Near East, both geographically and tem-porally. It is fully justified, therefore, to use the images as comparative data for under-standing the psalm. Moreover, the fact that the iconography is also found in Syro-Pal-estinian materials further justifies the association of the literary imagery of Psalm 63 with artistic images of the winged sun disk. The psalmist's desire to behold the (solar-ized) deity, perhaps in a morning theophany (v. 3), ties the presentation of God in the psalm quite closely to the representation of the winged sun disk in Syro-Palestinian art.

There is another aspect to consider, however. As a winged deity, God not only pro-tects the king and metes out justice, God also provides nourishment that refreshes and satisfies the psalmist (v. 6) who describes his trouble through images of desicca-tion (v. 2). These details suggest another area of congruence between the iconography of the winged sun disk and Psalm 63. In a number of representations of the winged disk, particularly Mesopotamian ones, streams of water emanate from the deity, sig-nifying rain falling from the heavens.

An excellent example of such a "water-providing god" scene is found in an unprov-enanced cylinder seal that can be dated to the Iron Age I on the basis of the Assyri-an-style garments (Klingbeil 1999:205–206) (**fig. 14.8**).

At the top center of this scene hovers a winged disk with two long straight hands extending diagonally downward from the bottom of the disk. From the open hands flow parallel streams of water, which run directly into two pots. Between the wings and under the disk is a stylized sacred tree standing upon a sacred mound or mountain. The picture presents something of an ecosystem, for the tree grows from a pot like those that receive the water from the winged sun disk. The three pots together, then, represent the earth's reception of the waters of heaven and their power of generation. The entire constellation of images represents the life-giving power that comes from the heavens, both in the form of light (sun) and water (rain). Two figures flank the central constel-lation of images: a royal figure on the right and a fish-garbed *apkallu* (see Black and Green 1992:82–83) on the left. The figures may be understood as protecting, observing, and/or worshipping this orderly system of growth and fertility. A pattern of intertwined lines and hatched triangles borders the scene, probably representing flowing water and mountains respectively. These are associated with Ea the mountain-god and water-god.

Another Mesopotamian example of the winged disk emanating water appears in a seventh-century cylinder seal from Nimrud (**fig. 14.9**). In this seal, the water flows directly from the disk and into pots (not clearly distinguishable in the line drawing) that are suspended in midair. Several of the details in this scene are difficult to discern, including the mound-like object beneath the disk, but like **fig. 14.8** a bearded figure stands with arms raised in adoration of the sun disk.

Fig. 14.8. Cylinder seal, Assyria, 1250–1000 BCE. Source: Frankfort 1965: Text-Fig. 65

Fig. 14.9. Cylinder seal, Nimrud, 7th c. BCE. Source: Klingbeil 1999: Fig. 47

One further representation of the sun disk with water deserves mention here: an unprovenanced seal with both Neo-Assyrian and Babylonian characteristics, probably dating to the seventh–sixth centuries BCE (**fig. 14.10**).

The seal depicts a winged sun disk with two streams emanating from beneath its wings. Supporting the winged disk is an atlant similar to the one pictured in the Tell Ḥalaf relief (**fig. 14.2**). In this seal, the waters surrounding the winged disk and atlant likely represent the cosmic waters, while the streams flowing from the winged sun disk symbolize rain, falling from the heavens. The adorant's open left hand receives one of the streams of water, indicating that the individual is a direct beneficiary of the water provided by the winged sun disk.

Fig. 14.10. Cylinder seal, Ashur, 9th–8th c. BCE. Source: Ward 1910: Fig. 656

To summarize to this point: The portrayal of a winged God providing nourishment to a desiccated psalmist in Psalm 63 clearly resonates with the iconography of the winged disk emanating water. In light of these images, one wonders whether indeed the psalmist imagined a winged deity with an effluence of life-giving water. Certainly, the constellation of images in the psalm bears striking resemblance to the constellations of images in these Mesopotamian cylinder seals. Caution is warranted, however, before one posits a direct relationship between the literary and artistic imagery because the water-providing winged sun disk is found *only* in Mesopotamia (an exilic context for this psalm is possible but not likely given the reference to the king). So far, we have no unambiguous examples of this image in Syro-Palestinian iconography. It must remain an open question, then, as to whether the image of the winged disk emanating water should directly inform the exegesis of Psalm 63.

4.2. The Winged Suckling Goddess

There is still one more congruent image from ancient Near Eastern iconography that can help us make sense of the constellation of literary images in Psalm 63. Representations of winged deities providing nourishment are found in the iconographic record of Syria-Palestine. One example, the so-called Syro-Phoenician *Dea Nutrix* from Ugarit (**fig. 14.11**) finds multiple points of congruence with the constellation of images from Psalm 63.

This small ivory plaque depicts a four-winged goddess suckling two lads. The long, up-curled locks of hair and the sun disk between two cow horns on her head accord with the iconography of the Egyptian cow goddess Hathor (Black and Green 1992:385–86). Yet her overall figure demonstrates a thorough mixture of Egyptian, Syrian, and Hittite styles: the sun disk between the horns is a rosette following Anatolian conventions, and the intricately patterned dress is characteristically Syrian. Her suckling of the two lads is reminiscent of the Egyptian iconography for Hathor, who is frequently represented (both in bovine and human form) suckling the king. The parallels to the iconography of Hathor suggest the two lads are princes or gods (or both). The identity of the winged goddess remains contested, however, with proposals including Asherah, Astarte, Anat, Qudshu, and, of course, Hathor herself. For the purposes of establishing congruence with Psalm 63, the precise identification of the goddess is not of critical importance. Instead, it suffices to

Fig. 14.11. Ivory relief, Ugarit, Late Bronze Age IIB (Middle Syrian). Source: Winter 1983: Abb. 409

compare the representation of the *Dea Nutrix* (nurturing goddess) with the iconic structure of the psalm.

The chief similarities between Psalm 63 and the *Dea Nutrix* image concern the descriptions of the psalmist clinging to God (v. 8), with God, in turn, supporting the psalmist with the divine right hand. A remarkably similar picture obtains in the ivory plaque. Each lad clings to a breast of the goddess, while the goddess places her hands around each lad's shoulder in a gesture of support and protection. Furthermore, like the picture of God in the psalm, the winged goddess provides life-giving (liquid) nourishment to her thirsty protégés. The sun disk on her head provides another point of connection to the portrayal of God with solar aspects in Psalm 63.

Fig. 14.12. Seal, Tell Megadim, Iron Age III (6th–5th c.BCE). Source: *GGG:* Fig. 363b

Other images of the suckling winged goddesses are found in early and late Syro-Palestinian art. The ivory from Ugarit (**fig. 14.11**) is an early example, while an Iron Age III seal from Tell Megadim provides a later expression (**fig. 14.12**). Like the Ugaritic example, the seal from Tell Megadim draws heavily from Egyptian iconography, but here the goddess Isis suckles Horus (*GGG*:378). Isis's wing is outstretched in a gesture of protection around the body of Horus, who wears the double crown, symbolizing his embodiment of kingship. As in the **fig. 14.11,** this winged, nursing deity also has a sun disk on her head, emphasizing her aspect as a solar deity.

5. The Multistable Image of the Winged God in Psalm 63 and Beyond

In this chapter, I have analyzed the iconic structure of Psalm 63 in light of the iconography of the ancient Near East, noting numerous examples where art and text present congruent constellations of images. Psalm 63 presents multiple vivid pictures of God in winged form: as a winged sun disk who protects the king, as a winged disk with an effluence of water, and as a winged suckling goddess. The winged god of order and justice protects the psalmist/king from treacherous enemies. This winged deity also provides liquid nourishment to a desiccated psalmist, upholding him in an intimate embrace.

My analysis shows that no *single* iconographic representation provides the key for understanding the portrayal of God in winged form in Psalm 63 (or elsewhere in the Psalter, for that matter). In fact, multiple iconographic tropes illuminate the image of God in winged form within Psalm 63 (and the Psalter writ large). The image of God's wings corresponds simultaneously to (1) the iconography of the winged sun disk as a god of order and justice who protects the king, especially in military contexts; (2) the winged sun disk emanating liquid nourishment from heaven; and (3) the winged goddesses suckling and protecting royal figures. The psalmic portrayal of God with wings is thus congruent with several distinct iconographic tropes, all within one poem.

But how are all those images operative – or able to operate – within one artistic piece (poem or otherwise)? One answer is found in the phenomenon of multistability in certain types of visual imagery. Multistability occurs where an image conveys two different, but equally valid, "interpretations" simultaneously (Mitchell 1994:43). Two classic examples of this phenomenon are the rabbit-duck (**fig. 14.13**) and the faces-goblet (**fig. 14.14**). In each of these images, two equally valid interpretations toggle back and forth in the perception of the observer. Even if the brain or eye can only focus on one at a time, both can be perceived or seen and thus remain possible "readings" or interpretations of the image.

Fig. 14.13. Rabbit or Duck?   **Fig. 14.14.** Faces or Goblet?

The winged God in Psalm 63 is a *literary* image that exhibits similar multistability. Indeed, it is the multistability of winged Yhwh that makes this image so compelling. God's wings can convey divine protection in different and yet equally striking ways, *simultaneously.*

Describing the allure of visual images that exhibit multistability, W. J. T. Mitchell writes:

> the ambiguity of their referentiality produces a kind of secondary effect of auto-reference to the drawing as drawing, an invitation to the spectator to return with fascination to the mysterious object whose identity seems so mutable and yet so absolutely singular and definite. (1994:43)

One can apply these comments to the literary image at work in Psalm 63. For the ancient psalmist, evoking God's winged form with its "ambiguity of referentiality" may have produced a "secondary effect of auto-reference" to the divine image because, as the opening lines of the psalm attest, the visual dimension of an experience of God is one of the primary ideas of the composition. The psalmist looks eagerly for God, with a sense of expectation equated with profound thirst in a land of drought (v. 2). The psalmist "sees" and "beholds" God, and observing God this way creates renewed energy and satisfaction in the psalmist (v. 3). The experience of apprehending God's form has such transformative power that the psalmist remembers it and meditates upon it (v. 7). In sum, the psalm's employment of the multistable image of God's winged form reinforces the psalmist's fascination with God's powerful, transforming, and transformative image.

At the start of this essay I noted that Psalm 63 is just one of several psalms in the Psalter where God appears in winged form (see § 1). Beyond the book of Psalms, there are additional instances of God figured as a winged deity (see Exod 19:4; Deut 32:10–12; Ruth 2:12; Mal 3:20; Matt 23:37; Luke 13:34). To determine the explanatory value of the ancient Near Eastern iconography of wings for each of these literary contexts, one must map the iconic structure of each of these texts. Since each pericope (psalmic or otherwise) presents a unique constellation of literary images, the portrayals of God therein have their own distinct contours, so much so that no text presents *exactly* the same image of God, even though all portray the deity with wings. The following exercise prompts one to explore some of these constellations of literary imagery in light of the world of images from which the texts emerged.

Assignment/Exercise

Choose one of the texts cited above that describes God in winged form (Exod 19:4; Deut 32:10–12; Ruth 2:12; Pss 17:8; 36:9; 57:3; 61:6; 63:9; 91:4; Mal 3:20; Matt 23:37; Luke 13:34).

1. Map the iconic structure of the literary pericope. Describe the characteristics of the main actors in the texts, paying particular attention to the ways that God is pictured, as well as the protagonists and antagonists (e. g., the psalmists and enemies in a psalm). Treat the text as if its literary images were the elements of a painting, a constellation of images that comes together and through which the text makes its meaning.
2. Next, when you have established this composite literary scene, turn to iconographic representations of wings. You can start with the images included in this essay, but you may want to find other examples in anthologies of ancient Near Eastern iconography, such as *ANEP*, or other books that contain a large amount of ancient Near Eastern imagery (e. g., *GGG, SBW*). A study devoted exclusively to wing iconography and the Psalms is LeMon 2010.
3. As a final step, see if you can find constellations of pictorial imagery that appear to be congruent with the literary imagery in your selected text. In what ways are these congruent pictorial representations consistent or inconsistent with the study of Psalm 63 offered above? To what extent do the pictorial representations share a common geographic or temporal proximity with the text you are analyzing (this will involve having some sense of the text's provenance)? How do differences in proximity affect the potential explanatory value for the literary imagery?

Bibliography

Brown, William P. 2002. *Seeing the Psalms: A Theology of Metaphor.* Louisville: Westminster John Knox.

Keel, Othmar. 1997b. *The Symbolism of the Biblical World: Ancient Near Eastern Iconography and the Book of Psalms.* Translated by Timothy J. Hallett. Repr. ed. Winona Lake, IN: Eisenbrauns.

Klingbeil, Martin. 1999. *Yahweh Fighting from Heaven: God as Warrior and as God of Heaven in the Hebrew Psalter and Ancient Near Eastern Iconography.* Orbis Biblicus et Orientalis 169. Fribourg/Göttingen: Academic Press/Vandenhoeck & Ruprecht.

LeMon, Joel M. 2009. "Iconographic Approaches: The Iconic Structure of Psalm 17." In *Method Matters: Essays on the Interpretation of the Hebrew Bible in Honor of David L. Petersen,* edited by Joel M. LeMon and Kent H. Richards, 143–68. Society of Biblical Literature Resources for Biblical Study 56. Atlanta: Society of Biblical Literature.

_____. 2010. *Yahweh's Winged Form in the Psalms: Exploring Congruent Iconography and Texts.* Orbis Biblicus et Orientalis 242. Fribourg/Göttingen: Academic Press/Vandenhoeck & Ruprecht.

Chapter 15
Masking the Blow: Psalm 81 and the Iconography of Divine Violence

Joel M. LeMon

1. Identifying a Vexing Text

As amply attested elsewhere in the present volume, ancient Near Eastern iconography provides a rich resource for understanding the background and meaning of metaphors and imagistic language in the Hebrew Bible. But exploring ancient Near Eastern iconography also helps unlock complex problems relating to the Hebrew text and its interpretation.

For readers who cannot consult the original Hebrew, many of these problems lie hidden in relatively clear and smooth modern translations of the Bible. But translation is an extremely difficult task, especially when translators are far removed from the context of the original text, the exact case that obtains with the Hebrew Bible. All readers of the Hebrew Bible should be aware that each translation relies on hundreds, even thousands, of interpretive decisions regarding the best ways to render individual words and how most appropriately to understand the syntax.

A useful place to begin developing this awareness is by comparing multiple translations of the same text. An excellent example – one of many – is found in Ps 81:15. The NRSV translates as follows:

> Then I would quickly subdue their enemies,
> and turn my hand against their foes.

The NJPSV (Tanakh), however, offers a different translation:

> Then would I subdue their enemies at once,
> strike their foes again and again.

So what exactly is YHWH (the "I" in this verse) doing to the enemies in v. 15? Subduing or quickly subduing? Turning his hand against the enemies or repeatedly striking them? The immediate context makes it quite clear that God is dominating the enemies, but the exact nature of God's activity is uncertain. This difficult text, and the various options for translating it, prompt additional (and larger) interpretive questions: What does this text say about the nature of divine violence? How does God's violence in this psalm relate to the violent activities attributed to other gods in the ancient Near East? In short, what kind of theology is reflected through such depictions of divine violence?

2. Steps for Addressing Textual Problems

In order to address the particular questions arising from Ps 81:15, one should begin with an exploration of the form, structure, and content of the psalm as a whole. Following a call to praise God in its opening verses (vv. 2–6b), Psalm 81 contains a divine oracle in which God recounts Israel's salvation from bondage in Egypt and the testing in the wilderness (vv. 6c–17). The oracle culminates in a double promise: if Israel would listen and be obedient (v. 14), God would act decisively against its enemies (vv. 15–16) and provide sustenance (v. 17). Again, while the general sense of the psalm is clear enough, the nature of God's promised action against Israel's enemies is decidedly less clear, especially as v. 15b describes it (in a wooden translation): "And against their foes I will turn my hand" (wĕʿal ṣārēhem ʾāšîb yādî).

Many translations offer something similar, "I will then turn my hand against their foes," or the like (see, e. g., KJV, NIV, NASB, NRSV). The interpretation of the specific verb used here (ʾāšîb) is critical in these and other understandings of the verse. The verb comes from the root šwb, which in the Qal stem conveys the sense "to turn" or "to return." But the form in Psalm 81 is in the Hiphil stem, which usually carries a causative sense – in this case, then, it would mean something like "to cause [someone or something] to turn (or return)." Despite the Hiphil form, many translations and interpreters presume that šwb in Psalm 81 conveys a simple act of turning, with no distinction between the Hiphil and the Qal meaning in this particular case.

There is, of course, more than one way or reason to turn one's hand. We might wonder, then, what the poet had in mind in this verse. Is the hand turning *away* from the Israelites, *toward* the enemies? If so, does the turning indicate a *negative* outcome for the latter? Most interpreters believe so. Hands often serve as the object of the verb šwb in the Hiphil stem (see, e. g., Gen 38:29, 1 Kgs 13:4; Josh 8:26; Lam 2:3, 8; Ps 74:11; Ezek 18:8, 17; 20:22). But in the majority of these cases, the verb suggests a drawing back of the hand as a means of ceasing activity or stopping aggressive actions. In Josh 8:26, for example, Joshua does not "draw back" his hand until all of the enemies have fallen. In this context, the act of "drawing back" (Hiphil šwb) the hand is the opposite of "stretching it out" (the verb nṭh). Likewise, in Ps 74:11, the psalmist questions why God would draw back his hand, which in this case means to cease action against the psalmist's enemies. These texts complicate the idea that Hiphil šwb in Ps 81:14 designates aggressive action because, in these other contexts, the verbal form, when used with the object "hand," indicates a *cessation* of activity or a *pulling back* of an outstretched hand.

Complicating matters further, some translations, as the NJPSV cited above, provide an alternative understanding of Ps 81:15, which takes the phrase wĕʿal ṣārēhem ʾāšîb yādî as signaling a repeated activity of some kind: "strike their foes *again and again.*" This translation reflects a closely-similar phrase in Jer 6:9:

> Thus says the LORD of hosts:
>> Let them glean thoroughly as a vine the remnant of Israel;
>> Bringing your hand back again (*hāšēb yādĕkā*) like a grape-
>> gatherer over ('*al*) its branches.

In this text, the notion of bringing back one's hand over the branches and/or passing one's hand through the branches repeatedly is found; this is essentially the standard causative use of the Hiphil stem with an additional iterative (repeated) sense.

The parallelism between the poetic lines (cola; singular: colon) of Jer 6:9 informs its translation. Since the thorough gleaning described in the first colon can only be accomplished through the repeated hand movements of a grape-gatherer, the second colon likely indicates just that. But without such contextual clues, it would be difficult if not impossible to establish the precise nature of Yʜwʜ's hand movement in Jer 6:9. Furthermore, while the NJPSV has imported the repetitive sense of the phrase in Jer 6:9 into Ps 81:14 ("strike their foes *again and again*"), other translations have not based their understanding of the psalm on this text from Jeremiah 6, choosing instead to render the verse in accordance with similar expressions in Isa 1:25; Ezek 38:12; Amos 1:8; and Zech 13:7. Hebrew lexica suggest translating the phrase in these latter instances as "to turn or direct one's hand against someone" (see, e. g., HALOT 2:1443). And so many translations have adopted this adversarial sense for Ps 81:15 as well (e. g., NRSV, NIV, NJPSV, KJV).

The differing translations of Hiphil *šwb* + the direct object "hand" + the preposition '*al* (which I will refer to as the "syntagma" [a particular syntactical construction] under investigation in the rest of this essay) lead one to question if it ever achieved a firm and consistent meaning such as "to turn one's hand *against* someone." Jeremiah 6:9 clearly argues against that possibility. Thus the syntagma in Ps 81:15 warrants further (re)analysis. After exploring Psalm 81 in light of ancient Near Eastern iconography, I will return to the other instances of the syntagma in Isa 1:25; Ezek 38:12; Amos 1:8; and Zech 13:7 to suggest what it might mean in those passages beyond the rather nondescript translation, "to turn one's hand against someone."

3.   The Threat of Yʜwʜ's Blow

Set within a larger divine oracle, Ps 81:12 begins with a statement that God's people are not listening or submitting to God, but are instead walking according to their own counsels. After announcing the problem, the oracle then moves to a conditional statement (vv. 14–15). Its protasis (the "if" part of the conditional formula), recalls the themes of v. 12 and suggests that listening to Yʜwʜ and walking according to his way provide the conditions for Yʜwʜ's actions against enemies on Israel's behalf.

> If only my people would listen to me,
> If Israel would walk in my ways, (v. 14)

The second part of the conditional statement (the apodosis or "then" part) comes in v. 15 and presents a picture of God's divine acts, beginning with God's defeat of Israel's enemies.

> Then I would quickly subdue (*'aknîaʿ*) their enemies. (v. 15a)

The verb used here, *knʿ* (in the Hiphil stem), appears several times in the Hebrew Bible. In most cases, the object of the verb is a person or people (see Deut 9:3; Judg 4:23; 2 Sam 8:1; 1 Chr 17:10; 18:1; 2 Chr 28:19; Neh 9:24; Job 40:12).[1] These instances of the verb suggest a condition in which the enemies are defeated but not necessarily killed, or, at least, not yet killed. In fact, these texts reflect a pattern or process of violence in which incapacitation and humiliation (Hiphil *knʿ*) precede the actual killing of the enemies. An example is Judg 4:23–24, which describes God subduing King Jabin (v. 23) before the Israelites destroy him. Nehemiah 9:24 provides another example, describing God's subjugation of the Canaanites so that the Israelites could then "do with them as they pleased."

In both of these cases, it is important to note that *God* is the one who subdues the enemies. Indeed, God is the agent in virtually every case where Hiphil *knʿ* appears; David's subduing of the Philistines in 2 Sam 8:1 (= 1 Chr 18:1) is the only exception. The act of subduing enemies thus seems to be a *distinctly divine* and/or *royal activity* in the Hebrew Bible. So as the picture of Yhwh begins to emerge in the first half of v. 15, we see God exercising uniquely royal/divine power to subdue the enemies, an action that signals that the complete destruction of the enemies is foregone if not imminent.

The next colon (v. 15b) describes the actions of God's hand. As noted above, several verses showcase the hand as the object of Hiphil *šwb* (*viz.*, Gen 38:29; 1 Kgs 13:4; Josh 8:26; Lam 2:3; Ps 74:11; Lam 2:8; Ezek 18:8, 17; 20:22). Those instances uniformly warrant translating the verbal form with causative sense: to *bring* or *draw* back. As such, the syntagma typically indicates a cessation of action or aggression. The context of Ps 81:15, however, suggests that God's violent action – *not* cessation of such – is at issue. Indeed, the use of Hiphil *knʿ* indicates that destruction is imminent.

What, then, of Hiphil *šwb* in this context? At this point, ancient Near Eastern iconography proves helpful. In its light, a causative sense of Hiphil *šwb* that conveys an aggressive action of Yhwh's hand is easily seen, producing the translation: "I will *rear back* my hand above their foes (in preparation to strike)." Such an understanding resonates with the image of the Egyptian god-king rearing back his hand in preparation for striking a blow against a subdued enemy.

This image, typically called "the smiting posture," originated in Egyptian art in the Predynastic period as a way to represent the ruler's lordship over enemies and the chaos they embody. The famous Narmer palette from Hierakonpolis (**fig. 15.1**)

---

1   In two passages, the object is not the person specifically, but metonymically: the heart (Ps 107:12) and noise, i.e., the mouth (Isa 25:5).

provides one of the earliest representations of this scene, dating from the late fourth to early-third millennium BCE.

Fig. 15.1. Narmer palette, Hierakonpolis, Naqada III period, ca. 3100–2920 BCE. Source: *SBW*: Fig. 397

In this palette, the ruler stands above and strides toward the kneeling enemy. The ruler's left hand holds the enemy's hair and the right hand draws back the mace ready to strike the deathblow. These essential elements constitute one of the most common ways of representing the power of the king against his enemies from the Predynastic period through the Roman period. Some of the clearest examples come from New Kingdom art, both monumental and miniature. A good example is a relief on a column from the forecourt of the temple of Ramesses III at Medinet Habu (**fig. 15.2**).

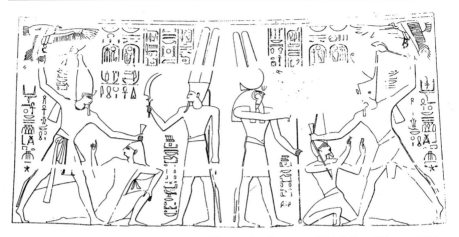

Fig. 15.2. Column relief from the forecourt of the temple of Ramesses III, Medinet Habu, ca. 1186–1155 BCE. Source: Keel 1974: Abb. 47

Here Ramesses III appears twice, wearing the red and white crowns, poised to slay subjugated enemies. The king is the same size as the gods who authorize and observe his action, suggesting that the king is equal to the gods and indeed can be construed as a god himself. Another example from this same temple complex shows Ramesses III holding multiple enemies visible in profile, all of whom have their hands raised in entreaty and humiliation (*SBW:* Pl. xxi). The same imagery is found in miniature art on an ostracon from the same period (**fig. 15.3**). Like Ps 81:15, the ruler in the ostracon is depicted with not just one, but many subjugated enemies at the precise moment before the deathblow is struck.

Fig. 15.3. Ostracon, Egypt, ca. 1186–1155
BCE. Source: *SBW:* Fig. 399

The image of the smiting king appears outside of Egypt as well, especially in Late Bronze Age Syria-Palestine, where Egyptian power and influence were palpable. Testifying to its prevalence in the Levant, the motif of the king rearing back his hand to strike the enemy can be found in scarab seals from Beth-Shean (1345–1200 BCE), Tell Beit Mirsim (1301–1234 BCE), and Tell el-Far'a South (1345–1200 BCE) for example (**fig. 15.4a–c,** respectively).

Figs. 15.4a–c. Scarab seals from Beth Shean (1345–1200 BCE), Tell Beit Mirsim (1301–1234 BCE), and Tell el-Far'a South (1345–1200 BCE). Source: *SBW*: Fig. 400

Though the minor art is more rudimentary than the large, detailed images in **figs. 15.1–3** from Egypt, the seals nevertheless show the king with hand reared back, ready to strike the enemy with the blow of a sickle sword. In each case, the enemy is subdued and humiliated in a completely submissive posture. In **fig. 15.4a–b,** the enemies kneel before the king, who grasps their hair. In **fig. 15.4c,** the arms are bound behind the back, rendering the captive unable to plead and/or resist the impending blow.

This image of domination and subjugation remains remarkably stable through generations of Egyptian and Egyptianizing art (cf. Hall 1986). Levantine examples from the Iron Age include scarabs from Tell Masos (1050–900 BCE, **fig. 15.5a**) and Tell el-Far'a South (1190–1075 BCE, **fig. 15.5b**), and an ivory carving from Samaria from the early-ninth century BCE, which reflects the thoroughly Egyptianizing elements of Phoenician workmanship (**fig. 15.6**). Later Phoenician seals from the sixth-fifth centuries BCE also render the same artistic constellation: a ruler with a reared-back hand and a subdued enemy (**figs. 15.7a–b**).

Figs. 15.5a–b. Scarab seals from Tell Masos (1050–900 BCE) and Tell el-Far'a (1190–1075 BCE). Source: Keel, Shuval, and Uehlinger 1999: Figs. 17–18

Fig. 15.6. Ivory carving from Samaria-Sebaste, 9th c. BCE. Source: *SBW*: Fig. 401

Figs. 15.7a–b. Phoenician seals, Ibiza, 6th–5th c. BCE. Source: Cornelius 1994: Figs. 31, 36b

The smiting posture occurs in various forms throughout Mesopotamia, Syria-Palestine, and Anatolia as early as the nineteenth – eighteenth centuries BCE. Indeed, several non-Egyptian deities, including Baal (**fig. 15.8**), Resheph, Adad, and Teshub, have the smiting posture within their iconographic profiles, testifying to the visual power and wide distribution of this originally Egyptian image (cf. Eggler 2007). As the posture migrated through different cultures, the weapons, headgear, and dress varied, but the essential element, the reared-back hand, remained constant. It is significant that, outside of Egyptian and explicitly Egyptianizing art, the subdued enemies generally do *not* appear before the smiting figures. The non-Egyptian(iz-ing) images, therefore, do not exhibit the same levels of congruency (see LeMon 2009; 2010:24, 73) with the imagery in Psalm 81 as do the Egyptian(izing) examples. Both types of the smiting posture support an interpretation of Hiphil *šwb* as "to rear back" or "bring back" one's hand to strike a blow, but it is the Egyptian iconography with its combination of images of domination *and* subjugation that reflects the literary imagery of Psalm 81 most closely. The smiting posture, it would seem, cinches the correct interpretation of Hiphil *šwb* when used with the direct object "hand."

Fig. 15.8. Bronze statuette of Baal, Minet el-Beida, Late Bronze Age (ca. 1200 BCE). Source: Cornelius 1994: Fig. 27a

But what, then, of the prepositional phrase *wĕʿal ṣārēhem* in Ps 81:15b? The preposition *ʿal* has a wide range of meanings. Among them is a spatial sense, which is primarily locational, meaning "upon, on, over," or "at, beside, by" (see Waltke and O'Connor 1990:216 [§ 11.2.13]). But there are also metaphorical uses of the preposition, among which "against" (a marker of disadvantage) is an acceptable, though less frequent, rendering (cf. 2 Kgs 17:3). So while the typical translation of Ps 81:15, "I will turn my hand *against* their foes," is entirely possible, it is just as likely that such an expression would employ the preposition *bĕ-* rather than *ʿal*. Indeed, *bĕ-* frequently means "against" in the context of someone using one's hand violently against a foe (see, e. g., Deut 2:15). In light of this prepositional usage and the iconography of the reared-back hand, the more common spatial-locational rendering of *ʿal* seems the most likely one. Thus: "I will rear back my hand *above* (or *over*) their enemies." Even so, it remains possible that the preposition *ʿal* may have something of a double sense here, denoting both spatial-location and metaphorical-disadvantage, such that both "over/above" and "against" may be evoked.

In the figures discussed above, the king towers above his enemies as the largest figure in the scene. These images reflect the Egyptian (and wider ancient Near Eastern) iconographic principle of hierarchy of scale, whereby size and, particularly, height encode importance (Robins 2008:21). The upraised hand in these images is the highest point, further emphasizing the king's position in relation to his enemies. Understanding *wĕʿal ṣārēhem* in Ps 81:15 as "above/over their enemies," therefore, provides a literary correlate to the hierarchy of scale in the iconography of the blow. Understood in this way, Psalm 81 portrays YHWH as utterly dominant.

Moving forward in the psalm to v. 16, one finds further evidence of the congruency between the literary and visual imagery (again see LeMon 2009; 2010:24, 73). This verse provides a fuller description of the fate of those whom YHWH has subdued and whom he is preparing to strike.

> Those who hate YHWH will shrink before him
> And their submission will last forever.

This verse has its own fair share of translational difficulties that cannot be addressed here. It must suffice to say that the expression of the diminution in size of the sub-

jugated enemies ("*shrink* before him," v. 16a) also accords well with the artistic principle of hierarchy of scale. In brief, then, verse 16 pictures the enemies in a state of
perpetual *smallness* (cowering and subjugation) vis-à-vis Yhwh who is over/above
them ('*al*) by comparison.

Returning to the art, it is clear that the Egyptian smiting posture was a powerful visual
trope, received into and reemployed in various regions and cultures in the ancient Near
East. At least part of the power of the image is due to how it captures a moment preg-
nant with expectation. In this smiting tableau, the *potential* energy of the reared-back
hand is represented, not the *kinetic* energy of the *actual* blow crushing the enemy's skull.
The iconography of the blow has the ability to hold the viewer's gaze in anticipation of
the event that is about to be realized (see Davis 1992). And yet, by its very potentiality
rather than kinesis, the same iconography admits, however subtly, the unsettling reality
that the enemies are not yet vanquished. The enemy is still *alive* in these representations.

The smiting of the enemy thus acknowledges the persistence of danger and enmity,
even while simultaneously (and primarily) emphasizing that the king (or god) holds
these chaotic forces in check. He will obliterate them *momentarily*. Picturing the
moment *prior* to that final blow captures both the hope of those who would seek salvation from the enemy, and the dread and despair of those about to be slain – enemies, whether real or would be. In the process, this image creates, somewhat para-
doxically, a timeless moment in the drama of domination, suggesting a violence that
is never quite realized and a victory never quite won.

Psalm 81:15–16, when seen in the light of the iconography of the blow, relays the
same sense of expectation. Here, too, Yhwh has subdued the enemies but has yet to
completely vanquish them. Israel waits for Yhwh to strike the deathblow and forever
conquer evil (vv. 15–16). At the same time, Yhwh waits, staying his poised hand until
Israel would listen and follow in the paths he has directed (v. 14).

The larger poetic structure of Psalm 81 also confirms vv. 15–16 as a literary instantiation of the iconography of the blow. As noted above, the image of the king drawing
back his hand over the enemies in preparation for the deathblow is a distinctly Egyptian one. Psalm 81, notably, situates itself in the context of Yhwh's dominance over
the Egyptians. The call to praise Yhwh in vv. 2–6b explicitly recalls the exodus from
Egypt, and locates the decreed festival as deriving from the same period (vv. 5–6). The
divine oracle beginning in v. 7c also recalls the events of the exodus, from the cries of
the people in slavery to their salvation, and ultimately to their testing in the wilderness. Verse 11 contains another explicit reference to the exodus with the self-identi-
fication of Yhwh as the God "who brought you up out of the land of Egypt."

The confluence of references and allusions to the exodus along with a literary image
ultimately derived from Egyptian iconography (vv. 15–16), suggests that the picture of
Yhwh acting against the foes of Israel in Psalm 81 reflects both a borrowing from and a
bold reappropriation of Egyptian royal imagery.[2] Rather than the pharaoh as god-king

---

2   Indeed, such a reappropriation of Egyptian imagery is not unique in the Hebrew Bible. See Strawn
     2009c:163–211.

poised to smite the subjugated foreigners, the psalm flips the imagery of domination on its head. Yнwн now stands above the subjugated enemies of Israel with his arm reared back. The psalm pictures the enemies frozen in the position of humiliation as Yнwн's deathblow looms above them. They await the deadly violence of God while the Israelites await sustaining and nourishing acts of God, who promises to fill their open mouths (v. 11), satisfying Israel with the finest wheat and honey from the rock (v. 17).

4. Yнwн's Reared-Back Hand Elsewhere in the Hebrew Bible

The preceding argument has largely operated with the assumption that the immediate literary context of difficult phrases in the Hebrew Bible should be the primary tool we employ in making sense of them. But sometimes, as is the case with Psalm 81, the immediate literary context is not helpful or only helpful to an extent. In cases like this, where the literary context is unclear or somehow not determinative, we can and must look beyond it, and, as the preceding argument also shows, ancient Near Eastern iconography is often extraordinarily helpful. But, to come full circle back to the problems so often faced in the biblical text, the insights afforded by the iconography must fit the literary context. The better the fit, the more helpful the iconography proves to be, and the better the interpretation that results.

Reading Psalm 81 in the light of Egyptian(izing) imagery confirms that the syntagma Hiphil *šwb* + "hand" + preposition ʿ*al* in v. 15 should be understood to mean "to rear back one's hand over (an enemy)" in a menacing gesture. But what of the other occurrences of this syntagma in the Hebrew Bible? Is the usage in Ps 81:15 simply an exception to an otherwise well-established meaning of this syntactical construction that should be understood also in other contexts as "to turn one hand against (someone or something)"? Surely not, for already we have seen that in Jer 6:9 the context demands that the syntagma has a causative-iterative sense of drawing the hand back and forth over something, over and over again. Further, in the other occurrences of the syntagma, the immediate literary context suggests that understanding the phrase to mean "to rear back one's hand over (someone or something)" is, at the very least, a viable option, and, still further, often one that should be preferred over other interpretations.

We might note, first, that the syntagma often occurs with divine threats and descriptions of God's violent judging action: against Israel (Isa 1:25; Zech 13:7), and the Philistines (Amos 1:8). Isaiah 1:25 could certainly be translated "I will rear back my hand above you," given the immediate context of vengeance (v. 24) and acts of purification (v. 25b). Since the context contains numerous threats of violence, a portrayal of God in a threatening posture would make good sense, as it does in Ps 81:15.

Zechariah 13:7 contains another divine threat:

> Awake, O sword, against my shepherd, against the man who is my associate,
>> says the LORD of hosts.

> Strike the shepherd, that the sheep may be scattered;
> I will *rear back my hand against* (wahăšībôtî yādî ʿal) the little
> ones.

Many translators understand the syntagma here to designate a "turning of the hand." But a threatening gesture – Yhwh's hand reared back to strike "the little ones" – may be in view here, especially since v. 7 begins with a reference to the sword. If so, the verse would be about God wielding a sword against the shepherd, with a hand poised to strike "the little ones."

In Amos 1:8, the syntagma appears with reference to God's judgment against the Philistines:

> I will cut off the inhabitants from Ashdod
> And the one who holds the mace from Ashkelon.
> I will *rear back my hand above* (wahăšībôtî yādî ʿal) Ekron,
> And the remnant of the Philistines will perish
> says the Lord God.
> (author's translation)

The prophet pictures Yhwh moving through Philistia, destroying city after city. The ruler of Ashkelon is "the one who holds the mace" and thus equipped for violence and domination. He is no match for Yhwh, however. The poetry invites one to imagine Yhwh seizing the mace of the ruler of one Philistine city (Ashkelon) in order to rear it back against yet another (Ekron). The ultimate result of all of this divine violence is the complete destruction of the Philistines.

Ezekiel 38:12 is the last passage where our syntagma is found, though the context there does not describe God's hand in judgment. Instead, in Ezekiel 38, Gog is considering an evil scheme to attack the newly resettled Judeans. Among the actions Gog considers, is:

> to *rear back my*[3] *hand above* (lĕhāšîb yādĕkā ʿal) the repopulated waste-
> lands and against the people who were gathered from the nations, who
> acquired cattle and belongings, who dwelled at the center of the land.
> (author's translation)

In this context, the syntagma clearly indicates aggressive action. And yet, translations vary widely. NJPSV opts for the sense of "turning one's hand against," while the NRSV provides a more figurative reading: "to assail the waste places that are now inhabited." While many commentators take the syntagma as referring to a "turning of the hand," some translate the verse as Psalm 81 and the iconography of the blow would suggest: as a "raising" or "lifting" of one's hand over or against the land.

---

3   Reading with LXX; though the MT is more difficult and perhaps, for that reason, to be prefered.

To summarize this section: It seems clear that Isa 1:25; Zech 13:7; Amos 1:8; Jer 6:9; and Ezek 38:12 should not be privileged unduly in the interpretation of the syntagma in Ps 81:15; if anything, the interpretation I offered of Ps 81:15 in light of the iconography of the blow casts crucial light on the meaning of the syntagma in these other passages (with the exception of Jer 6:9). While none of the latter align as well as Psalm 81 does with the iconographical trope of the smiting king over his subjugated enemies, understanding the syntagma as signifying "to rear back one's hand above (or against) someone/something" makes good sense in Isa 1:25; Zech 13:7; Amos 1:8; and Ezek 38:12. In the contexts where weapons are mentioned (Amos 1:8; Zech 13:7), the likelihood is even stronger that the syntagma depicts or evokes an armed Yнwн about to strike.

If these other texts, like Psalm 81, also reflect the iconography of the blow by means of the syntagma Hiphil *šwb* + "hand" + *ʿal*, the imagery may ultimately stem from images of ancient Near Eastern deities in smiting poses (e. g., Baal in **fig. 15.9**) rather than the particular image of the Egyptian king standing above his enemies. If so, these texts might take their place with others, like Ps 10:12, in which scholars have noted a correspondence between Yнwн as divine warrior with uplifted hand and similar iconographic portrayals of ancient Near Eastern deities (see Keel 1974; Brown 2002:175–78; Klingbeil 1999).

5. Conclusion

This chapter has demonstrated how ancient Near Eastern iconography can help one untangle difficult text in the Hebrew Bible. For students without recourse to the Hebrew text, many of these issues will only become apparent when one compares different modern translations and finds significant variation. But, whether one has access to the Bible in Hebrew or not, ancient Near Eastern iconography often casts crucial light on the meaning(s) of a text, as well as the ways that the text structured its message for subsequent audiences.

In the specific case of Psalm 81, we have seen how vv. 15–16 are a literary instantiation of the iconography of the blow in which the Egyptian king lifts his hand menacingly above his subjugated enemies. As for the particular rhetorical function of these verses, the iconography (and textuality) of the blow reminds the audience of the stark threat posed by their enemies even as it radically inverts the standard Egyptian iconographic trope of domination and subjugation. In the psalmist's vision, Yнwн has supplanted the pharaoh in his position of dominance and now stands ready to vanquish any other foe who might oppose Israel (cf. Strawn 2009c). Psalm 81 has recast an ancient image in a new form, and in the process, has vividly pictured hope for the people: that Yнwн will again act – decisively, even violently – as he once did for their ancestors.

Assignment/Exercise

Identify another text in the Psalms (or elsewhere) that describes God's violent action against enemies. How does the picture of Yhwh in Psalm 81 compare to your text? Does your text explicitly depict Yhwh engaged in graphic acts of violence? Or, like Ps 81:15, does it only hint at the potential for divine violence? Alternately, does your text point to the *results* of divine violence (e. g., injuries, corpses) without describing the particular activities that caused the death or injury of the enemies? How do these various possibilities, especially when considered in light of ancient Near Eastern iconography like that found in this chapter or elsewhere in this book, communicate the idea of God's sovereign power?

Bibliography

Cornelius, Izak. 1994. *The Iconography of the Canaanite Gods Reshef and Ba'al: Late Bronze and Iron Age I Periods* (c 1500–1000 BCE. Orbis Biblicus et Orientalis 140. Fribourg/Göttingen: University Press/Vandenhoeck & Ruprecht.

Davis, Whitney. 1992. *Masking the Blow: The Scene of Representation in Late Prehistoric Egyptian Art.* California Studies in the History of Art 30. Berkeley: University of California Press.

Hall, Emma Swan. 1986. *The Pharaoh Smites His Enemies: A Comparative Study.* Münchner Ägyptologische Studien 44. Munich: Deutscher Kunstverlag.

Keel, Othmar. 1974. *Wirkmächtig Siegeszeichen im Alten Testament: Ikonographische Studien zu Jos 8,18.26; Ex 17,8–13; 2 Kön 13,14–19 und 1 Kön 22,11.* Orbis Biblicus et Orientalis 5. Freiburg/Göttingen: Universitätsverlag/Vandenhoeck & Ruprecht.

———. 1999. "Powerful Symbols of Victory: The Parts Stay the Same, the Actors Change." *Journal of Northwest Semitic Languages* 25: 205–40.

Klingbeil, Martin. 1999. *Yahweh Fighting from Heaven: God as Warrior and as God of Heaven in the Hebrew Psalter and Ancient Near Eastern Iconography.* Orbis Biblicus et Orientalis 169. Fribourg/Göttingen: University Press/Vandenhoeck & Ruprecht.

LeMon, Joel M. 2013. "Yahweh's Hand and the Iconography of the Blow in Psalm 81:14–16." *Journal of Biblical Literature* 132: 865–882.

Strawn, Brent. 2009c. "Yahweh's Outstretched Arm Revisited Iconographically." In *Iconography and Biblical Studies: Proceedings of the Iconography Sessions at the Joint EABS/SBL Conference, 22–26 July 2007, Vienna, Austria,* edited by Izaak J. de Hulster and Rüdiger Schmitt, 163–211. Alter Orient und Altes Testament 361. Münster: Ugarit-Verlag.

Chapter 16
"The Fear of the Lord" in Two (or Three) Dimensions: Iconography and *Yir'at Yhwh*

Brent A. Strawn

1.   Introduction

It is clear from other chapters in this book that iconography has been profitably used in the study of figurative language, particularly in the case of biblical metaphors. Metaphorical language is often imagistic in some way, employing an image from the world (or from mental representations thereof). As a result, it is not difficult to look for representations of the same or similar images in artistic depictions and compare the two – an endeavor not entirely unlike the metaphoric process itself. Study of biblical metaphors is certainly not the only way iconography has proven helpful for biblical exegesis, though it remains a large and significant area (see de Hulster 2009a:105–18; cf. Strawn 2005b; LeMon 2010). But what of *less*-imagistic or even *non*-imagistic language in the Bible? Can iconography help with its understanding and analysis? If so, how? As but one example among many, language concerning emotions is a case in point. Can and does iconography help with assessing this kind of language?[1]

The present chapter looks at a particular Hebrew root, *yr'* ("to fear"),[2] especially when it is conjoined with Yнwн – as it often is in the Hebrew Bible, whether in verbal phrases (e. g., *yr'* + *yhwh*, "to fear Yнwн") or in nominal constructions (e. g., *yir'at yhwh*, "the fear of Yнwн") – in order to investigate how iconography can shed light on what it means to "fear God." This is an important topic because several texts indicate that "the fear of the Lord is the beginning of knowledge/wisdom" – or something similarly significant (see Prov 1:7; 9:10; cf. Prov 15:33; 31:30; Job 28:28). Still further, *yr'* is one of the most frequently employed roots to describe worship of or service to the deity. A better understanding of *yir'at yhwh*, then, may contribute to a better understanding of ancient Israelite religion, not to mention the theology of the Old Testament. An iconographical approach to "fearing Yнwн" allows one to actually *see* fear in two- or, as the case may be, three-dimensions. This investigation can contribute to the exegesis of numerous texts throughout the Hebrew Bible – even if the Wisdom literature remains a special locus for this concept – particularly because philological study of *yr'* has reached something of an impasse. The present essay begins with the

---

1   For some of the problems besetting the study of emotions in the artistic record, see Zwickel 2012:2–3.

2   In what follows, I often refer to the root and to its verbal and/or nominal derivatives as simply *yr'*. I also use the term "word-group" with the same sense.

scholarly study of *yr'* in text-only modes (§ 2) before turning to the iconography of fear proper (§ 3). The chapter concludes by considering some ramifications for the study of *yr'* and for iconographical theory more broadly (§ 4).

2. The Problem of "Fear" and "Fearing Yнwн" in Text-Only Perspective

No less than any other word in the Old Testament, the root *yr'* has been vigorously investigated (see bibliography in Strawn 2014). Its pattern of use in the Old Testament and its study by scholars reveal four problems.

2.1. Four Problems

The first problem concerns *the use of yr'* – or, to be more precise, what might be called its "dual use." On the one hand, the root *yr'* is used for real, even visceral terror (see, e. g., Exod 14:10; Deut 2:4, 25; 7:19; 1 Sam 7:7; Jer 41:18; Jonah 1:10; cf. Jer 42:1; Ezek 11:8), and, on the other hand, for religious fear or religious devotion – "the fear of the Lord" proper. The word-group is thus equally appropriate for "real" fear *and* for correct behavior towards, and the proper response to, the deity. Are these two uses related somehow? Is the latter a subcategory of the former such that the fear of the Lord begins and ends with terror? If so, it is worth noting that many modern readers stumble at precisely this point. Many contemporary people think that "fearing the Lord" as pure dread must either (a) be wrongly understood/interpreted, or (b) remain a hopelessly arcane holdover from a primitive and defunct religiosity, if not both (cf. Gruber 1990:411; Egger-Wenzel 2005:211–12, 226; Castelo 2008).

The second problem concerns *the scholarly study of yr'*. Two tendencies might be noted. The first is how scholars have investigated the question of whether or not the meaning of *yr'* develops diachronically through the course of time by means of semantic drift. To be even more specific, the question is whether the drift in question is in fact a *devolution* of sorts – a shift from a "strong" sense of *yr'* (real fear) to a "weakened" sense, where it means little more than "reverence" or "respect," even "piety" or "religion" (see Pfeiffer 1955:41; Strawn 2014:92 n. 2). The second tendency is for scholars to fillet the various biblical occurrences of *yr'* chronologically, sometimes on the basis of determinations regarding the (purported) semantic development of the word, but also for a host of other reasons pertaining to source-, redaction-, and composition-critical approaches. So, not only does *yr'* mean different things in different texts, it may also mean different things in different time periods – and vice versa. This subjunctive "may mean different things" would shift to a confident "does mean different things" if the texts could be securely dated, which would enable a clear typology.

This leads directly to the third problem, which concerns *how these two scholarly tendencies interact*, or perhaps better, how they *fail* to interact. Unfortunately, most biblical texts cannot be dated – to the despair of many scholars – and so determinations about date and, correlatively, semantic drift are consistently frustrated and revealed as no less interpretive (and thus subjective) as any other aspect of the hermeneutical project. So, for example, many scholars posit a devolution of *yr'* through the course of time, but Elias Bickerman memorably asserted that the fear of God in Ecclesiastes (a very late book) meant nothing less than "to be on guard against *Elohim*" (1967:149), which is hardly a "weak" notion of piety, reverence, or respect! If Bickerman is right, it puts the lie to all theories of semantic devolution for *yr'*, at least when it comes to fearing the deity. In point of fact, the Dead Sea Scrolls continue to attest to the dual use of *yr'* as a term suitable for "real" as well as "religious" fear, and this supports the continued existence of the strong sense of the word-group *à la* Bickerman, even in very late contexts subsequent to Ecclesiastes (see Strawn 2013:266; 2014:93, 96, 127).

The fourth and final problem has to do with *the meaning(s) of yr'*, and of course this issue is profoundly interconnected with the preceding problems. Most scholarly assessments of the fear of God motif fall into three groupings:

1. *Developmental assessments* attempt to delineate various uses of the *yr'* word-group and assign them to different chronological periods so as to trace diachronic change or semantic drift, as noted above (see, e. g., Fuhs 1990:296–305; Stähli 1997). The major problems besetting developmental assessments is that the redaction-critical filleting of texts is largely hypothetical, and the subsequent placement of these pieces in definite chronological order is thus far from certain (cf. Fuhs 1990:298; Clines 2003:62–64). These problems commend great caution in accepting any arguments about any development or devolution in the meaning(s) of *yr'*.

2. *Thematic assessments* care more about literary and theological categories than chronological ones. These categories may be several, but largely boil down to two: positive and negative varieties. In the former, the fear of YHWH is "a virtue" leading to right behavior; in the latter, such fear is mostly terror through which God "frighten[s] people into submission" (Longman 2008:201–204). If developmental assessments are overly precise, thematic ones seem too generalizing if not simplistic (cf. Van Pelt and Kaiser 1997:527–33; Clines 2003:60; Eichrodt 1967:270). The dichotomous perspective also splits what the ancients seem to have thought of as a unified notion, one characterized by a single lexeme: *yr'*.

3. Finally, there are *mediating assessments* that place the fear of God somewhere in between outright "terror" and mild "respect" (cf. Longman 2008:201). This kind of approach is sometimes complimented by attention to positional aspects of the fear of YHWH – namely, that people who fear God "know their rightful place in the universe" (Longman 2008:201). In some ways, mediating options can effectively counter or avoid the pitfalls of the other two approaches. If the truth of the matter is "in between," then there need not be a direct development from "strong" to "weak" understandings of *yr'* in contrast to how developmental assessments would have it. *Contra* thematic assessments, the notion of positioning vis-à-vis

the deity is a different and more helpful way than simply deeming an instance of *yr'* "positive" or "negative," perhaps because the position in question is somehow foundational to both interpretive poles.[3]

2.2. The Persisting Problem

While mediating assessments of the fear of YHWH motif may reflect a distinct advance over the other types, the problem that persists is that – whichever approach is adopted – the word remains *yr'*, which has to do with *fear*, a point confirmed by the word-group's frequent congeners.[4] But, once again, why "fear" per se? And why this consistent employment of *yr'* despite its different uses (at least two) and the many other terms that were available to connote things like "reverence" or "respect" if that was, in fact, the point?[5] Most previous studies of *yr'* seem to stumble at this juncture, perhaps because they have been almost exclusively *textual* in orientation.[6] Given this impasse, it makes good sense to move beyond the texts to consider *non-textual realia* so as to see if these might offer a way beyond the text-only impasse by affording greater insight into the meaning(s) and interpretation(s) of the fear of the LORD in the Old Testament. In fact, the iconographical data may allow us to *actually see fear*. This would be very helpful if the mediating assessments are right that the fear of the LORD is fundamentally a positional phenomenon (cf. Gruber 1975:77) insofar as the artistic data contain information on matters of space and position as well as about gesture and affect (cf. Zwickel 2012:10, 17, 23).

3. The Iconography of Fear

Before turning to the art, one might note that ancient Near Eastern texts from Egypt and Mesopotamia also know of the dual use of the fear motif as something appropriate for the gods and for a powerful entity like the king (see Hornung 1996:197; Gruber 1990; Strawn 2014:98–99). Just as in the Old Testament, "fear" as such was an appropriate attitude toward the divine realm and the realm of the superior, before whom lesser subjects are rightly afraid. This philological point is well known; less well known or at least less often cited, is the fact that ancient Near Eastern iconography also reflects this "fear-full" posture before both gods and kings. The positions and gestures of people at worship or bringing tribute is often exactly the same as that of prisoners or enemies who are about to be conquered.

---

3   See Zwickel 2012:3–4 on various emotional polarities, alongside "neutral" emotions.
4   These include *ḥtt, pḥd, ḥrd, ḥwl,* and *bhl.* See Van Pelt and Kaiser 1997:529; Fuhs 1990:293–95; Clines 2004:67–69; Eichrodt 1967:269; Stähli 1997:573.
5   For example: *'bd, šm', šmr, kbd,* and *'hb,* among others.
6   For exceptions, see *SBW*:307–23; Langdon 1919; Strawn 2014.

3.1. Egypt

The Narmer palette (**fig. 16.1**) provides a very early example. The smiting posture present here becomes iconic for centuries of pharaonic art (see Hall 1986; Davis 1992; LeMon 2013), but equally enduring are iconographical aspects of the subjugated enemy that are found here. The leg positioning is particularly noteworthy with the right leg at 60° and the left at 45°. In **fig. 16.2** the same leg positioning is seen in postures of adoration. This image may reflect a progression from standing in worship, to kneeling, to the full bow (*proskynesis;* cf. *SBW*:310). Whatever the case, the leg positioning of the middle figure is identical to that of the enemy in the Narmer palette: the right leg back at a 60° angle, the left leg forward at 45°. The outstretched arms with palms faced outward toward the venerated object are also a standard element (*SBW*:312–13; Langdon 1919:548–49), characteristic of the Egyptian attitude of prayer (**fig. 16.3**).

Fig. 16.1. Narmer Slate palette of Narmer, found at Hierakonpolis (Kom el-Ahmar), Nagada 3/Early Dynastic I (ca. 3000 BCE). Source: Strawn 2014:99 fig. 1

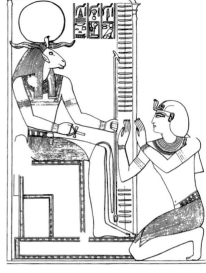

Fig. 16.2. Limestone sketch, New Kingdom (ca. 1550–1069 BCE). Source: *SBW*: Fig. 412

Fig. 16.3. Relief, Abydos, Mortuary temple of Seti I, 1294–1279 BCE. Source: *SBW*: Fig. 422

Highly similar, if not identical, iconography is also found in smiting scenes. In **fig. 16.4,** from Ramesses III, the king is seen smiting his enemy. The enemy on the right combines the leg positioning encountered in **figs. 16.1–2** with the hand positioning of **figs. 16.2–3.** The parallel presentation suggests that the enemy's posture on the left (with slightly different leg positioning and a hand with uplifted finger) corresponds to the one on the right: in both cases, the enemy is attempting to stay the final blow somehow. Indeed, both hand gestures can be made by the very same figure, as evidenced in **fig. 16.5.**

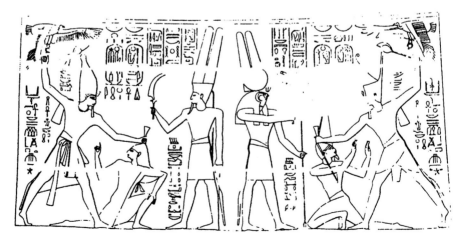

Fig. 16.4. Sandstone relief, West Thebes, Medinet Habu, Ramesses III, 1184–1153 BCE. Source: Strawn 2014:101 fig. 5

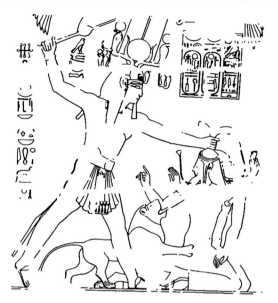

Fig. 16.5. Sandstone relief, West Thebes, Medinet Habu, Ramesess III, 1184–1153 BCE. Source: Strawn 2014:102 fig. 6

Other images could be shown but these would be mostly small variations on the theme. The gestures, hand and arm extensions, leg positioning, and the like would be entirely similar, closely comparable, and oftentimes precisely identical between those adoring a god or monarch and the enemies who are about to be struck down. Keel summarizes the point nicely:

> The gesture of raised arms with palms forward is as appropriate to aversion as to veneration. In the final analysis, it expresses the attempt to restrain a superior, numinous opposite by means of conjuring, thus rendering it serviceable or averting it. (*SBW*:313)

And so, he continues:

> In the presence of the king or a high official, one assumed the same posture as one did before the deity; and especially in the cultus, the deity was generally understood by analogy to the king. (*SBW*:322–23).

One last image from Egypt is instructive in capturing these points: a pectoral from Amenhemhet III (**fig. 16.6**). Once again the pharaoh and his enemy are doubly presented, with the latter portrayed in the now familiar leg- and arm-positions, though here the outstretched arms extend what seem to be weapons to the king "in a gesture of complete submission" (Hall 1986:15). But, insofar as the gesture evokes the giving of offerings to a god (see, e. g., *SBW*:331–32 figs. 442–443; cf. Bär 1996), the posture is not solely one of subjugation but also and simultaneously veneration. In this same vein, it is worth noting how the vulture goddess Nekhbet oversees the action depicted on the pectoral. Her talons extend *ankh*-signs to the king, but these are connected to *djed*-signs, and it is these latter that make direct contact with the pharaoh's smiting arm. The message is that the deity supports and enlivens the pharaoh's action and participates in his victory. Correlatively, the enemy's posture and gesture are equally applicable to both god and king. That posture and gesture are, in the end, one thing that connotes the same deference: worship to the god, fear of the dominant king – and vice versa.

Fig. 16.6. Pectoral from Amenemhet III, Dashur, Middle Kingdom, 1843–1798 BCE. Source: Hall 1986: Fig. 26

3.2. Mesopotamia

Mesopotamian iconography is also replete with gestures before the victorious opponent and before the god that are identical or nearly so. An example is the obeisance posture known as *appa labānu* or *labān appi* in the textual sources.[7] The pose is known in three variants: "holding the hand close to the nose, touching the nose and rubbing the nose" (Ornan 2005b:119). The gesture is used in textual sources of people approaching the gods and is also used to describe the behavior of defeated foes before kings (see Gruber 1975; 1980:61–62). The connection between these two recipients of the posture is made explicit in a text that states "may the kings whom I defeated humble themselves before me as (they do before) Šamaš."[8] The textual sources also refer to another gesture of deference known as *ubāna tarāṣu*, "to point the finger."[9]

Both postures are found in the visual remains where, once again, they are used before kings (**figs. 16.7–8**) as well as gods (**figs. 16.9–10**). Not unrelated are images where subjects are portrayed in postures of supplication before a king (**figs. 16.11–12**) and, in many cases, before divine figures or symbols (**figs. 16.13–14**). Keel believes the extended finger gesture "may have a significance similar to the Egyptian gesture of the raised hands" (*SBW*:313) because it is used in contexts of veneration (e. g., **figs. 16.9–10**) and ones where it apparently wards off evil (**fig. 16.15**). Another instructive example in three-dimensional art is a statue from Larsa, dedicated to the god Amurru, which describes the person as a "suppliant" (**fig. 16.16**). Here, the fear (or worship) of the god(s) is depicted in the round, not solely in two-dimensional art.

Fig. 16.7. Black Obelisk of Shalmaneser III, 858–824 BCE.
Source: Strawn 2014:106 fig. 11

---

7   "To rub the nose," but with the sense of "to beg humbly, to exhibit utmost humility (in gestures), to pray contritely" (*CAD* L, 11).

8   Angim IV 7 (*CAD* L, 10).

9   *CAD* T, 211. For discussion, see Ornan 2005b:37 and Gruber 1975:78.

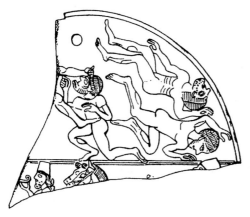

Fig. 16.8. Pyxis lid, Ashur, time of Tukulti Ninurta I, 1243–1207 BCE. Source: Ornan 2005b: Fig. 52

Fig. 16.9. Pedestal of Tukulti Ninurta I, Gypsum, Ishtar temple at Ashur, 1243–1207 BCE. Source: Strawn 2014:107 fig. 12

Fig. 16.10. Impression C, attributed to Tukulti Ninurta I (1243–1207 BCE), but used on the Vassal Treaties of Esarhaddon (680–669 BCE). Source: Strawn 2014:108 fig. 14

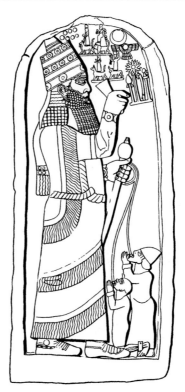

Fig. 16.11. Til Barsip, Esarhaddon, 680–669 BCE. Source: Strawn 2014:109 fig. 17

Fig. 16.12. Zinjirli, Esarhaddon, 680–669 BCE. Source: Strawn 2014:109 fig. 18

Fig. 16.13. Cylinder seal, 7th–6th c. BCE. Source: Strawn 2014:110 fig. 19

Fig. 16.14. Aramaic seal, 7th–6th c. BCE (?). Source: Strawn 2014:110 fig. 20

Fig. 16.15. Cylinder seal, jasper, Assyria. Source: Strawn
2014:111 fig. 22

Fig. 16.16. Bronze statue, probably   Fig. 16.17. Stela, Baluʿah, 12th–11th
Larsa, 1792–1750 BCE. Source: c. BCE. Source: Strawn 2014:118
Strawn 2014:111 fig. 23   fig. 37.

It must be stated that these images are not entirely coterminous in terms of either
presentation or function (cf. Langdon 1919; Cifarelli 1998; Porter 1995, 2003:59–79,
2004). Even so, they demonstrate that a set of highly similar, and at times identical,
postures can be used in: (1) contexts of deity worship and ruler veneration; and (2)
contexts of combat, subjugation, and imminent death. The fact that the same/similar
postures can be used in these distinct settings suggest that there is something comparable about these settings. The most obvious common element would be that both
involve the real fear – even terror – that is felt by the weaker party due to the unequal
power dynamics (cf. Zwickel 2012:9). So, in context (2), that of combat and subjugation, the weaker party is terrified in the face of the blow that is about to be struck or
the punishment that is about to take place. Context (1), in turn, would seem to derive
at least some of its meaning from context (2) insofar as, even in non-combat situa-

tions, the gods and monarchs are dominant entities that exercise power over worshipers, adorants, and so forth – power that could be wielded in beneficent (blessing) or malevolent (punitive) ways. This helps to explain why one "assumes the position" before both the deity and the king, namely, because both wield the power of life and death (cf. Prov 24:21).

3.3. Israel/Palestine

Artistic remains recovered from Israel/Palestine also attest to the iconography of fear in the land and in the periods within which the biblical texts were composed and transmitted. We might note, first, instances of adoration postures that are similar to the Egyptian and Mesopotamian pieces discussed above (**figs. 16.17–18**). Indeed, even without the object of veneration present, the posture suffices to communicate its symbolic meaning in *ipse* (**fig. 16.19**). Adoring postures can also be found in contexts where the defeated enemy is in view, even if in the background (**fig. 16.20**). The finger-pointing gesture is also attested (**fig. 16.21**).

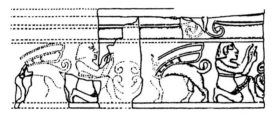

Fig. 16.18. Ivory casket, Hazor, Str. V A, Iron Age IIB (ca. 925–700 BCE). Source: Strawn 2014:119 fig. 38

Fig. 16.19. Seal, Hazor, Str. VI, Iron Age IIB (ca. 830–700 BCE). Source: Strawn 2014:119 fig. 39

Fig. 16.20. Seal, Tel Far'ah South (tomb 762), probably MB IIB (ca. 1650–1500 BCE). Source: Strawn 2014:120 fig. 41

Fig. 16.21. Seal, front and back, Megiddo, Iron Age IIC (ca. 700–600 BCE). Source: Strawn 2014:120 fig. 42

The most important objects are those that combine the various poses of domination and power, on the one hand, and those of subjugation and fear, on the other (cf. **fig. 16.20**). Late Bronze Age and Iron Age seals do exactly that in presentations that are obviously dependent on Egyptian exemplars (**figs. 16.22–23**). In **fig. 16.23**, from Tel Masos, one figure venerates the smiting pharaoh while another begs of mercy, vividly emphasizing the parallel nature of the gestures of praise and fear, even as it suggests the power dynamic that underlies both. An ivory inlay from Samaria (**fig. 16.24**) shows that the fear-motif is attested across various media.

Fig. 16.22. Seal, Beth Shean, Str. VI   **Fig. 16.23.** Seal, Tell Masos, Iron Age I
Late Bronze Age III or Iron Age IA   (ca. 1250–1000 BCE). Source: Strawn
(ca. 1190–1150 BCE). Source: Strawn   2014:123 fig. 49
2014:122 fig. 47

Fig. 16.24. Ivory with inlay, Samaria,
Iron Age IIB (ca. 900–850 BCE).
Source: Strawn 2014:123 fig. 51

While more images could be included (see Strawn 2014:117–23), these suffice to demonstrate that: (1) just as in Egypt and Mesopotamia, the postures of fear and worship were similarly if not identically portrayed in ancient Israel/Palestine; (2) their particular combination in the smiting scene (but not only there) is well attested from the Late Bronze Age through the Iron Age; and (3) the objects that attest to these two points have been recovered from northern and southern sites in both the Transjordan and Cisjordan. Taken together, then, it is safe to conclude that the iconography of fear was widely known and available in the land before and during the periods in which the biblical materials were taking shape.

4.   Conclusion

The preceding discussion of the iconography of fear is directly pertinent for understanding *yr'* in the Hebrew Bible and especially for the specific notion of *yir'at yhwh*, the fear of the LORD. The two datasets – the artistic remains and the use of the *yr'* word-group in the Old Testament, especially with God – are quite comparable on the conceptual level and seem closely interrelated. The fact that the biblical authors continued to use *yr'* for true terror *and* for the worship of YHWH begins to make more sense when fear is seen by means of the iconographical evidence. Indeed, when the fear of God is visualized in this way, one "sees" that it, too, is predicated on God's power and the potential threat God's power poses to worshippers who might disobey (Clines 2003:64; Hazony 2012:250; Eichrodt 1967:270). Texts like 2 Sam 6:9, where David fears after Uzzah is struck down, or Deut 5:5, where the Israelites fear when they see what happens at Horeb, capture the sentiment nicely.

And yet the other half of the dual use of *yr'* must not be forgotten. It is not just punitive power that God, or some other powerful figure like a king, wields. Super-powerful entities can also bring blessing, which means they are worthy of praise and adoration. And so it is that worshipers, adorants, and tribute-bearers assume postures before their lords that are entirely similar to enemy combatants. In this sense, *yr'* can be (and is!) used as a term connoting worship of God or proper respect of the monarch (Prov 24:21). This other half of the dual use helps to explain why "*nôrā'* as a characterization of the 'frightful' deeds of God" in the Old Testament "usually refers to occurrences that *benefit* Israel" (Stähli 1997:572; emphasis added). Or, to return to the Dead Sea Scrolls, it explains why God is "fear-full" not just because God is "frightful [*nôrā'*] for the deliberation of his anger," but equally because God is "renowned for his patience" (4Q301 3a-b, 4–5; Strawn 2013:266).

I offer three comments in conclusion:

First, despite the preceding remarks, it is not entirely accurate to speak of a "dual use" of *yr'* – not, at least, when it comes to religious usage. One must resist any intimation that there are two entirely discrete meanings of "fear" – one "positive," the other "negative."[10] Instead, the iconography underscores that there is something fundamentally similar, if not identical, between the fear-response in, for example, combat, and the correct posture of veneration before a superior being. Indeed, both can be represented on the very same object (**fig. 16.23**). The iconography further suggests that real fear plays an important role in both reflexes. When *yr'* is viewed in this way, it suggests that the terror-filled aspects of the word-group are never fully lost.[11] Instead, we should probably acknowledge that one position (or disposition), one posture, or

---

10   Note that some studies have shown that it is possible to feel different emotions simultaneously and that non-Western cultures often witness a higher tolerance for emotional complexity than Western ones (see Goetz, Spencer-Rodgers, and Peng 2008; Schimmack, Oishi, and Diener 2002:715; Williams and Aaker 2002).

11   See note 4 above.

one gesture can be admitted into and deployed in a number of different contexts to different effect. This is not to say that the word *yr'* never developed over the course of time; it may well have (see § 2.1). But it is to say that, even if the semantics of *yr'* developed, the lexeme did not. If, that is, this one (dis)position, posture, or gesture came to mean different things later, it is significant that it was not described by the several other words that were available and that might have more clearly conveyed different, even "weakened," nuances.[12] Instead, *yr'*, "to fear," remained stubbornly in place. The iconography helps to explain why.

Second, as already intimated above, the iconography lends support to those scholars who have suspected that the fear of YHWH is ultimately about proper human position or disposition before the deity (§ 2.1). Such a (dis)position is generally understood as an interior affect state, but the iconographical data shows that it could also be understood as physically manifested in gesture, body posture in space, and so on. Indeed, when the textual data is combined with the artistic, the fear of the LORD is seen to involve *both:* both interior and exterior, both the affective and the physical (see *SBW*:308; cf. Zwickel 2012). This would indicate that the fear of the LORD demands a proper perspective but also a proper posture before the deity. That posture and perspective is one marked by subordination, even subjugation, before the all-powerful God who (again) is capable of great wrath but also great mercy. The iconography of fear is thus a perfect complement to the iconography of divine power wherein deities are often presented in integrated but bi-polar fashion: life-giving and benevolent but also death-wielding and punitive (see Strawn 2005b:636–38). The former lead humans to praise whereas the latter cause them to fear – but both poles belong to the same deity and both responses belong to the same human worshiper.

Third, readers of this book will have probably noticed that the present chapter has paid less attention to the historical details of the images in question than some other chapters. That is partly due to the fact that the biblical texts referring to the fear of God are widely dispersed in the Old Testament, and that, despite numerous diachronic studies, we remain uncertain about the dating of many of those texts and traditions (see § 2.1). Without a specific period to focus on, this chapter has ranged widely and has not worried as much about diachronic aspects of the iconographical data. Once again, it is not impossible that *yr'* developed through the course of time and it is possible that composition-critical studies will eventually attain better certainty about such matters; perhaps the artistic data will prove helpful in that endeavor. But the present chapter has demonstrated that iconographic exegesis need not wait for diachronic or compositional certainty. Instead, the artistic evidence discussed here has been highlighted as a way to access ancient *visual thinking* – the way meaning is made in non-textual ways – and how that might impinge on meaning-making in textual ways.[13]

---

12   See the list of terms in note 5 above.

13   For visual culture studies, see, *inter alia*, Arnheim 1966, 1969, 1986, 2004; Davis 2011; Elkins 2003; McDannell 1995; Mirzoef 1999; Mitchell 1986, 1994, 2005; Morgan 1998, 2005, 2010; Pasztory

Ideally, one might hope for wide attestation of a motif across the ancient world and in ancient Israel/Palestine, in the right time frame, and with full confirmation from both image and text in clearly datable strata (literary and archaeological). Unfortunately, such a situation is almost never encountered (cf. Taylor 2008). While historical propinquity and geographical proximity remain hallmarks of comparative methodology (Talmon 1991:386), a major methodological point of this chapter is that iconographic exegesis need not always be obsessed solely nor even excessively with them. Instead, it can traffic primarily – and just as validly – in *cognitive* matters. Images cast precious and irreplaceable light on cognitive functioning and meaning-making in antiquity precisely by granting us access to the ancients' visual culture and their visual thinking (low literacy rates must always be kept in mind). The interface between visual studies and cognitive theory is thus a promising horizon for future research in iconography.[14]

Assignment/Exercise

Building off the work done in this chapter, see if you can analyze another emotion – for example, joy, love, or grief (see Zwickel 2012; Strawn 2014:113–17 and figs. 26–34) – with similar results. How is this emotion manifested in biblical texts? Can the emotion be traced in the visual record of the ancient Near East as well? What are the hallmarks of the emotion in both datasets and are there important points of connection (or lack thereof)? Finally, correlate the two: how does the art cast light on the interpretation of the texts and vice versa?

Bibliography

Clines, David J. A. 2003. "'The Fear of the Lord is Wisdom' (Job 28:28): A Semantic and Contextual Study." In *Job 28: Cognition in Context,* edited by Ellen van Wolde, 57–92. Biblical Interpretation Series 64. Brill: Leiden.

Gruber, Mayer I. 1990. "Fear, Anxiety and Reverence in Akkadian, Biblical Hebrew and Other North-West Semitic Languages." *Vetus Testamentum* 40:411–22 = Gruber 1992:193–208.

Keel, Othmar. 1997b. *The Symbolism of the Biblical World. Ancient Near Eastern Iconography and the Book of Psalms.* Winona Lake, IN: Eisenbrauns.

Langdon, Stephen. 1919. "Gesture in Sumerian and Babylonian Prayer: A Study in Babylonian and Assyrian Archaeology." *Journal of the Royal Asiatic Society* 51:531–56.

Strawn, Brent A. 2014. "The Iconography of Fear: *Yir'at Yhwh* (יראת יהוה) in Artistic Perspective." In *Image, Text, Exegesis: Iconographic Interpretation and the Hebrew Bible,* edited by Izaak J. de Hulster and Joel M. LeMon, 91–134. Library of Hebrew Bible/Old Testament Studies 588. London: Bloomsbury.

Zwickel, Wolfgang. 2012. "The Iconography of Emotions in the Ancient Near East and in Ancient Egypt." *Deuterocanonical and Cognate Literature Yearbook 2011: Emotions from Ben Sira to Paul,* edited by Jeremy Corley and Renate Egger-Wenzel, 1–26. Berlin: de Gruyter.

2005; Ramachandran 2004:24–59; Rose 2007; cf. Strawn 2008. For a sophisticated application of these works and many others to biblical iconography, see Bonfiglio 2014.

14 For studies that bring the scientific study of emotion to bear on the fear of God, see Gruber 1990; Arnold 2011; Yoder 2005.

Chapter 17
Iconography, Love Poetry, and Bible Translation: A Test Case with Song of Songs 7:2-6

Izaak J. de Hulster

1. Introduction

One of the first steps of any exegetical project is to establish a working translation of the text under consideration. This may involve a careful comparison of a variety of translations in one's own language, or, for those with knowledge of Greek, Hebrew, and Aramaic, a close analysis of the text in its original language. In either case, this working translation must subsequently be refined through further interpretive work that seeks, among other things, to clarify the meaning of the text's language and imagery in a way that is comprehensible to the modern reader. An exegetically informed translation is contingent on decisions about the reconstruction of the text, the connotations of certain words in their original cultural context, the meaning of syntactical arrangements, and the purposes of the translation. Among the numerous analytical tools that can help guide some of these decisions is the study of ancient iconography. The purpose of this chapter is to explore the intersection of Bible translation and iconographic exegesis. Before turning to a specific test case (Songs of Songs 7:2–6 [Eng. 1–5]), this chapter surveys various challenges of translation, including how certain translation styles (or philosophies) approach these issues.

2. Challenges in Translation

In its most basic definition, translation is the process by which the meaning of a word or text in one language (the source language) is made comprehensible in another language (the target language). This process is fraught with difficulty at almost every turn. The source and target languages are informed by distinct cultural contexts such that even some of the most basic elements of grammar vary between languages, including whether nouns reflect grammatical gender or how various elements of a sentence are ordered. These sorts of challenges are exemplified in the following examples:

1. In the Papua New Guinea language Dani there are only two words that indicate color: *mili* ("dark-cold") and *mola* ("light-warm"). This peculiarity would raise obvious challenges when it comes to translating into Dani the description of the blue, purple, and crimson yarns used to make the curtains of the wilderness tabernacle (Exod 26:31).

2. The Amazon Pirahã language lacks exact numerals, even "one." How might a translator represent in Pirahã the age of Moses at his death (120 years) or the delineation of days in the priestly creation account (Gen 1:1–2:4a)?
3. In some languages, such as English, the singular and plural forms of second person pronouns are identical ("you" in both cases) while in Hebrew these forms are distinct ('*āttâ* = second person masculine singular; '*āttem* = second person masculine plural). Because of this, English translations often fail to clarify whether Hebrew second person pronouns refer to an individual or to a community – an issue that sometimes has important interpretive implications.

Knowing how to translate certain words or phrases raises its own set of challenges, especially when the target language does not have an equivalent term. In these cases one can choose to use a generic term, a loanword, or an approximate substitute term. Another strategy is evident in the Septuagint. When the translators could not find an appropriate Greek equivalent for a Hebrew term, they transliterated the Hebrew word using the corresponding Greek letters. This strategy does little to aid in the comprehensibility of the text.

Even in less ambiguous cases, it is rarely (if ever) possible to find an exact "match" in the target language for a word in the source language. Given this situation, making decisions about how to translate specific words or phrases involves numerous factors, including: the range of possible meanings (or semantic field) of a word; the function of a word in a given context; its frequency of use; the genre of the text in which a word is found; the presence of alliteration; and the potential for anachronisms in the target language.

These and other challenges of translation require extensive background information about the target language's literary genres, idioms, euphemisms, figurative expressions (especially metaphors), and certain stylistic features (e. g., use of parallelism, indirect speech, etc.). In addition, translators face the challenge of knowing what to do when the target language deviates from its own principles of grammar and syntax. Doing so entails deciding if such variations are used for some communicative purpose, such as when Hebrew inverts its normal verb-subject word order in order to indicate emphasis. In other cases, translators have to consider if or how they should render ambiguities and/or irregularities in the source language (such as spelling errors or grammar mistakes). For instance, when working with Song 4:3, a translator would face the challenge of translating the term *midbār*, which typically means desert or wilderness but here is used to describe what appears to be the instrument of speech (NRSV: "mouth").

In all of these situations, a translation should aim for accuracy (regarding meaning), accessibility (with respect to the intended audience), and naturalness (in the target language). These criteria are negotiated in different ways by different philosophies, or styles, of translation (cf. Wilt 2002; Hill 2006).

3. Styles and Strategies of Translation

Most translations can be mapped onto a continuum of styles based on how they nego-
tiate issues regarding the form and meaning of the source and target languages (cf.
Fee and Strauss 2007; Floor 2007):

1. Closest to the source text in terms of form is an interlinear Bible. This style of
    translation reproduces the text in its source (original) language and inserts imme-
    diately beneath each line a word-for-word translation without regard for proper
    syntax in the target language. While this strategy preserves the word order and
    other syntactical features of the source language, the resulting translation is often
    difficult to read or understand. As a result, many interlinear Bibles often include
    another full translation, typically in a parallel column, that reflects a different
    translation style (see below).
2. Another major style of translation within this continuum is called *verbal* or *for-
    mal equivalence* (also known as idiolect, concordant, or idiosyncratic). The goal
    of this type of translation is to reproduce as closely as possible the form (vocabu-
    lary and syntax) of the source language while still obeying the grammatical rules
    of the target language. Among other things, this style typically attempts to ren-
    der a given Hebrew word consistently throughout the whole translation. Popular
    English translations such as the King James Version (KJV) and the New Ameri-
    can Standard Bible (NASB) reflect this translation philosophy.[1]
3. The translation style known as *dynamic* or *functional equivalence* (also called "idi-
    omatic") was pioneered by Nida and Taber (1969) and is motivated by a concern
    for cultural differences between the source and target languages. At the level of
    meaning rather than form, it attempts to provide natural equivalents in the tar-
    get language in a way that is sensitive to issues of comprehensibility and the prag-
    matic aspects of communication. Although nowadays criticized for its rather loose
    concept of equivalency (often to the neglect of key formal differences between
    various literary genres or important historical and cultural connotations found
    in the source language), this style influenced many Bible translations in the past
    several decades, including the Good News Translation (GNT) and the Contem-
    porary English Version (CEV).
a. It should be noted that many Bible translations, such as the New International
    Version (NIV) and the New Revised Standard Version (NRSV), fall somewhere
    between formal (2) and functional (3) equivalence on the continuum. These "medi-
    ating translations" opt for a more natural language in the target text (especially
    for the translation of collocations, dead metaphors, and idioms) while at the same
    time showing concern for maintaining certain formal features of the source lan-
    guage. As such, these translations maintain a tension between comprehensibility

---

1   One example of a formal equivalent translation in German is the so-called *Verdeutschung* by Buber
     and Rosenzweig.

in the target language and accuracy with respect to the form and meaning of the source language.

4. One might also speak of a translation style known as the "paraphrase." This style, which is found in the Living Bible, the Amplified Bible, the Message, and the Voice, employs very free and often informal translations of the source language.

Regardless of its style, no single translation can capture all aspects of the source language. The inclusion of multiple translations, as in a parallel Bible or a polyglot, testifies to the fact that different translations shed light on different aspects of the source language. As such, when establishing a working translation as a basis for exegesis, the interpreter would do well to consult Bible versions that reflect different translation styles, being mindful of the potential advantages and disadvantages of each.

In addition to being aware of different translation styles, one must also attend to the nature of the translation process as a model of communication. Communication within a single language is often schematically represented as follows:

sender → message → audience

Translation, however, is a more complex communicative process, and thus is better represented in terms of:

sender → message → translator → translated message → second audience

With respect to this latter model, one of the primary questions facing any translation is how much the translator can be part of both the language community of the sender and the language community of the second audience (i. e., those receiving the translation). Even when a translator is a part of both communities (e. g., through bilingual education), translation requires interpretive choices that go beyond those related to translation style. The strategies that lie behind these choices can be understood with respect to a term used often in translation studies: *skopos* (Greek for "scope, purpose, aim").

Skopos theory attends to the social function or intended purpose of a translation, including how it meets expectations of the target audience. Such considerations bring into focus the intention of the text, the context of the target audience, the cultural distance between the sender and the target audience, and the medium (audio, internet, hard copy) of the resulting translation. Any translation is a product of the strategies a translator uses to navigate these various issues. As such, a translation can be evaluated not only on the basis of its style but also on the accuracy, communicative effectiveness, and naturalness of its language, all in relation to its skopos (cf. Nord 1991 and 1997).

One final issue to consider when dealing with Bible translations in particular has to do with the presence of "meta-textual" data – that is, content or formatting choices in modern translations that are not reflected in the most ancient manuscripts of the Hebrew Bible or Greek New Testament. These include verse numbering, chapter divisions, section headings, study notes, cross-references, maps, introductory essays, and so forth. Outside of verse and chapter divisions, much of this meta-textual data can vary greatly not only between different translations but also between different editions of the *same* translation (e. g., between the *NIV Teen Study Bible,* the *NIV Life Application Study Bible,* and the *NIV Women's Devotional Bible*). In either case, one should be mindful of the ways in which this data (including the title of the edition) can influence – whether implicitly or explicitly – how interpreters understand the biblical text itself.

4. Translation of Biblical Poetry and Metaphors

Although biblical translation in general surfaces numerous challenges, several features of Hebrew poetry in particular deserve special attention.

4.1. Features of Hebrew Poetry

Poetry is an important literary feature of the Hebrew Bible, with most modern editions (e. g., *BHS*) presenting certain texts in a poetic layout. However, this style of formatting is not attested in ancient manuscripts. In fact, there is much debate over the hallmarks of Hebrew poetry and some have wondered whether maintaining a sharp distinction between prose and poetry in the Hebrew Bible is warranted. Nevertheless, there are several features that commonly occur in Hebrew "poetry" that require special attention when translating.

The most characteristic feature of Hebrew poetry is a phenomenon called parallelism. First studied extensively by Robert Lowth (1753), parallelism refers to the "correspondence" between two (subsequent) elements in a text, often appearing in paired lines or poetic cola. Classically speaking, this correspondence often involves a restatement of a concept (synonymous parallelism), though it is also possible that the second statement contrasts with the first (antithetical parallelism) or heightens/extends its meaning (synthetic parallelism).

Other features of Hebrew poetry include rhythm, anadiplosis (starting a new line with the last word of the previous line), and alphabetical acrostics. As formal characteristics of the source language, translators must consider how to translate these features of Hebrew poetry into the target language in a way that is both comprehensible to the receiving audience and comparable in form and meaning to what was intended by the sender.

4.2. Metaphors in the Hebrew Bible

Broadly construed, a metaphor is a figurative expression that pictures one thing in terms of another and then uses this association to evoke meaning. Metaphorical meaning emerges from an interplay between two (or more) related things (see chapter 5).

For instance, the phrase "your eyes are doves" (*'ênayik yônîm*) in Song 4:1 implies an association of the eyes with a certain variety of messenger birds. As is evident in ancient iconography, these birds were themselves associated with the love goddess (**figs. 17.1a–b**), thus further expanding the range of possible meanings.

Fig. 17.1a. Syrian cylinder seal depicting the goddess (right) stripping and sending doves to the seated god (center) as a sexual provocation, ca. 1750 BCE. Source: Keel 1994:70 fig. 25

Fig. 17.1b. Syrian cylinder seal depicting a half-dressed goddess offering a drink to her partner, the weather-god, and sending a dove to signal her readiness for love, ca. 1750 BCE. Source: Keel 1994:72 fig. 26

How might an English translation render the complex, multi-layered associations implicit in the phrase *'ênayik yônîm?* When translating this particular Hebrew metaphor one could potentially pursue the following options:

1. *Use of a simile (with explication):* "your eyes are like doves, telling me how much you love me." This translation employs a simile in order to imply that the eyes, much like doves, convey a message of love from the beloved. This option maintains the figurative nature of the expression but restricts the metaphor to one explicit ground of comparison (i. e., between eyes and doves).
2. *De-metaphorization:* "with your eyes you show how much you love me." In this option feelings of love are directly inferred from the outward appearance of the eyes. Alonso Schökel suggests that while this procedure helps make obscure Hebrew metaphors comprehensible to non-Hebrew readers, the result is often less expressive and does away with an explicitly metaphorical aspect of the phrase (1988:100).
3. *Transculturation of the metaphor:* "your glances[2] are messengers of love" (Keel 1994:71). This option utilizes a comparable figurative expression in the target language to express a metaphor in the source language. When making a choice for a metaphor specific to the target audience, one runs the risk of a certain degree of anachronism, as would be the case in the phrase "your eyes are a Valentine's Day card."

---

2   Note that Hebrew words for body parts often communicate more than just anatomy or biology. For instance, the word *'āp* means both nose and anger while *nepeš* can denote breath, life, soul, and person (Schroer and Staubli 2001).

These observations mainly apply to words or phrases in a single verse. However, in the case of conceptual metaphors, which are more pervasive and not restricted to one or two verses (e. g., "YHWH is king" metaphors in the Hebrew Bible), it is sometimes more effective for the translator to "de-metaphorize" the phrase (as in option 2 above). This might be an especially helpful strategy in cases where the kingship metaphor would no longer be immediately relevant to a receiving audience. However, one also has to be aware of the canonical interconnections that may be lost when the kingship metaphor is minimized or removed from the translation. For instance, if a translator completely reworks language in the Hebrew Bible that describes YHWH as king, then Jesus' references to the "kingdom of God/heaven" may be dislodged from their cultural and theological background.

These considerations are especially important when it comes to translating poetic texts, which are densely layered with metaphors, other figurative expressions, and intertextuality. The translation of poetry involves not only a consideration of individual verses but also the entirety of the composition, including its "iconic structure" (see chapter 14), rhythm, alliteration, assonance, and aesthetics. Finally, for metaphors using place names, one is faced with questions about the familiarity of the terms and their associations. Do the references make sense for the target audience? If not, the translation might provide some adjectives for the place names as well, as is demonstrated below (e. g., Song 7:6).

4.3. Present Procedure: A Pleonastic Approach to Translation

Hebrew poetry is characterized by brevity of expression. It is very hard to keep this feature in an English translation, especially when metaphors in Hebrew call for some form of additional explanation. In these situations, metaphors should not simply be translated into similes, which effectively reduce the meaning of metaphors to one ground of comparison. Rather, metaphors should be translated in such a way that respects their multiplicity of associations and open-endedness of meaning and, at the same time, brings forth clarity of communication in the target language.

Reflecting a skopos that values both clarity and accuracy, I suggest a "pleonastic" approach to translating biblical metaphors, especially those in poetic texts. Pleonasm refers to a redundancy of expression, often as a rhetorical strategy to add emphasis or clarity. In reference to translation, a pleonastic approach aims at comprehensibility while preserving the culturally specific connotations of the source language. This can be accomplished by means of descriptive adjectives and/or by retaining the metaphorical associations of the source language. In other words, the pleonastic approach retains formal features of Hebrew poetry (although not brevity) even as it also makes accessible for contemporary readers the "mental furnishings" that undergird the imagistic quality of much poetic language. In this approach, readers of the translation do not need to scan footnotes or commentary boxes in order to grasp the meaning of the text; rather, they find all the relevant information reflected in the translation of the text itself.

Picking up on the example discussed above of "your eyes are doves," the pleonastic approach might produce the translation "your sparkling eyes are love-delivering doves."[3] Though the word "sparking" is not present in the Hebrew, this translation reflects the fact that the eyes, like other body parts, play a role in the ideal of beauty in the ancient Near East. At the same time, this translation also preserves both the association between eyes and messenger birds (i.e., doves) and messenger birds and (the goddess of) love.

5. Song of Songs 7:2–6

Thus far this chapter has surveyed some of the challenges involved in translation, including those specifically related to metaphors and/in poetic texts. In response to these challenges, various translation styles and strategies can be identified, one of which is the "pleonastic" approach described in § 4.3. Having sketched out these preliminary matters, it is now time to turn to questions surrounding the translation of a particularly interesting (and vexing) sample text – namely, Song 7:2–6. Before doing so, it will be helpful to first assess more general features of this biblical text, including matters related to the text's unity, meaning, and theology. Though interpretively significant in their own right, such matters can only be touched upon briefly in the present chapter.

5.1. Setting in Life of the Song of Songs

The original setting in life of poetry is an important issue in translation. However it is not always easy to establish, and neither is it determinative for issues related to interpretation or translation. Various life settings have been suggested for the Song of Songs in particular: a human wedding song; a song used in an annual ritual wedding of two deities; a play; an erotic dream; a parody on prophetic speech; a protest song; or even a female counterpart to Proverbs 1–9. These proposals reflect the fact that Song of Songs contains language related to wisdom, folklore, and possibly also the cult.

However, the most common proposal is that Song of Songs represents a type of love poetry. While often minimized or allegorized in certain theological readings of this text, themes surrounding physical or erotic desire are prominent. Walsh (2000:45) describes the Song of Songs as a book of yearning in which erotic metaphors function to prompt "the audience's imagination and desires along with its arousal."

---

3   In a pleonastic approach, one might choose to put added words, such as descriptive adjectives, in italics: "your *sparkling* eyes are *love-delivering* doves."

5.2. Hermeneutical Key to the Song of Songs

Theological readings notwithstanding, approaching Song of Songs as love poetry offers the most appropriate starting point for translation and interpretation. Studies by Urs Winter (1983) and Othmar Keel (1994) have shown that an apt hermeneutical key for viewing the woman in the Song of Songs (especially in the description songs) is to see her in both "military-aggressive" and "erotic-attractive" terms. In this sense, the woman could be perceived as a warrior (e. g., the goddesses Anat or Ishtar) and at same time as a beautiful and desirable figure. For instance, study of ivory sculpture shows that ancient Near Eastern physical ideals include large eyes, fair skin, and a slender but curvy youthful body (**fig. 17.2** combines this ideal with lions as powerful "lady of the animals" characteristics).

Song of Songs 7:2–6 is the third of the "description songs" (along with 4:1–7 and 5:9–16). This genre, like the ancient Arabic love poetry known as the *wasf,* describes the bodies of lovers, both female and male. Some exegetes have taken a literal approach to the descriptions, understanding these as descriptions of Egyptian plastic arts employed as a metaphor for human bodies. Others have emphasized the evocative nature of these descriptions, claiming that the metaphors "titillate the senses, not the capacity to reason" (Soulen 1967:190). Another approach is to read the descriptions as riddles about purity, attraction, and sensuality.

Whatever hermeneutical approach one takes to these descriptions, they must be translated in a way that honors their evocative nature and is attentive to their aesthetic quality. For instance, a generic translation such as "you are so beautiful" does not do justice to the source text insofar as it subdues the power of the metaphors used. Yet at the same time, translators should recognize that the Song of Songs "renders our looking less voyeuristic, and our pleasure more aesthetic than erotic by clothing the lovers' bodies with metaphors, which never quite give access to the body described" (Exum 2005:24).

5.3. Exegetical Remarks

As demonstrated in numerous other chapters in this volume, iconographic exegesis is employed to gain insight into biblical metaphors. A good deal of the iconographic material used for illuminating the Song of Songs is much older than the text. This material is employed not only because of the presence of congruent themes but also because the "sentiments" expressed in the images were received by the subsequent culture in which the text was composed and (initially) read. While one need not include iconographical material along with the translation itself, studying pictorial themes and motifs can further inform how certain literary expressions are translated. In that vein, the following comments surface important considerations for the translation and exegesis of each verse in Song 7:2–6. Emphasis will be placed on Song 7:3 as an extended test case of how the study of ancient iconography intersects with and informs questions about biblical translation.[4]

---

4   For a more detailed study of the iconographic background of the Song of Songs, see Keel 1994.

Fig. 17.2. Horse frontlet with a nude goddess holding lotus flowers and lions, Nimrud, 9th–8th c. BCE, ivory, h. 16.21 cm. The Metropolitan Museum of Art, Rogers Fund, 1961 (61.197.5). Source: Black and white representation adapted from Gansell 2014:53 fig. 4

7:2. Within the context of this description song, *pěʿāmayēk* is often translated "your feet" (the Septuagint has "steps"). They are described with the verb *yph* ("to be beautiful").

One of the many *hapax legomena* (words appearing only once in the Hebrew Bible) in the Song of Songs is *ʾāmmān*. It is sometimes translated as "skillful artist." This translation already contains an adjective that elucidates its meaning. According to Hess, this word indirectly alludes to God's role as Creator (2005:213). If understood this way, one could draw out this allusion in translation by rendering the Hebrew *maʿ(ă)śê* as "creation" instead of "work." However, beside its theological association this wording can also simply point to creativity and aesthetics.

7:3. The word *šorrēk* is typically translated "your navel" but some argue that the word means "your vagina" or "your vulva" because of the present context (Pope 1977:40; Wilkinson 1991:209–10; Brenner 1997:40). Keel (1994) argues that the navel and vulva are interchangeable in iconographic sources based on figurines in which either the navel or vulva appear in or just above the pubic triangle and are encircled with a ring (**fig. 17.3**).

The text employs the term *šor* in a context of drinking and iconography reveals this as a context associated with sexual intercourse (**figs. 17.4a–b**). This context would support "vagina" as the implied meaning but is not decisive for the lexical meaning of the word *šor*, which, if referring to the navel, could be used as a metonymic euphemism. The meaning of navel gains added support from the use of *šor* in Prov 3:8, where it refers to a male body part.

One way of preserving the lexical meaning of navel while still picking up on an implied contextual reference to vagina is to place the translation navel in quotes. One could object against such a translation on the basis that the quotation marks do not reflect good style, or that – even considering the remarks below on the other parts of the phrase – the reference to intercourse can be brought across only with a more explicit translation. For the English context one could opt for "most intimate body parts" (or "private parts"), but this might sound generic, flat, and a bit prosaic. Of course, other translators might feel differently, or, the target audience of a particular translation might dictate a different sort of approach.

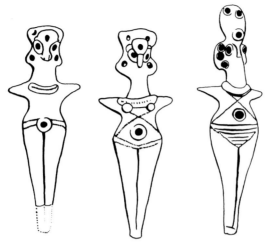

Fig. 17.3. Syrian female (goddess) figurines emphasizing interchangeably the navel and the vulva. Source: Keel 1994:232 fig. 127

Fig. 17.4a. Old-Babylonian terracotta relief showing a woman drinking (beer) and a man approaching her, ca. 1750 BCE. Source: Keel 1994:179 fig. 111

Fig. 17.4b. Small soapstone chest from Syria depicting a couple drinking (upper section) and a man holding a woman's breast (lower section), 8th c. BCE. Source: Keel 1994:232 fig. 128

Even if one opts to translate Hebrew *šor* as navel without quotes or additional adjectives, other elements in the translation of the sentence could potentially make the implied association stronger. One should be reminded that the poem is a song of desire and does not describe intercourse as such. This is another reason to prefer the body part (navel, or alternatively, vagina even if understood as metonymy) over a more explicit translation focused on fertility and erotic arousal. This implication is strengthened by rendering "not lacking mixed wine." The phrase "not lacking" is a litotes (negation of the contrary) for abundance, expressed with "spilling over." If one interprets mixed wine as a kind of aphrodisiac then one might use "arousing" in place of "mixed" to communicate sensual stimulation. For poetic reasons, the translation below has dropped the litotes.

Together with wine, "wheat" expresses something of the riches of the land, being a main ingredient of the ancient Israelite diet. Wheat could be encircled with flowers at a harvest festival. Also, when food was served it could be embellished with flowers (**fig. 17.5**), stressing its appetizing character and its delicious nature. Thus, what is beautiful and enjoyable is presented as even more desirable. The lotus symbolizes life-renewing strength and could be related to birth.

Taking these considerations together, I have chosen to convey some of these implications by translating "womb" instead of stomach, implying the life-giving fertility of the woman and her capacity for recreation. In addition, the word "womb" could be associated with security, thus making a link to the following verse. Nevertheless, "womb" should not be regarded as an interruption of the bottom-up structure of the poem/song (starting from the feet and proceeding to the head and hairdo). It is to be noted here that the floral embellishment does not serve any kind of protection and therefore the "unprotected" rendering of "womb" might imply similar accessibility for this festive occasion. The adjective "voluptuous" underscores the idea of observed beauty. The alliteration "lush lotus" strengthens the poetic character of the English translation and fits the pleonastic approach advocated for here.

This verse can further illustrate the possibilities of § 4.2. Turning the verse into a simile and explicating its meaning, one could translate as follows:

> Your vulva is desirable, like a round bowl full of mixed wine.
> Your stomach is gorgeous, like wheat surrounded by flowers!

If one de-metaphorizes this verse, it is possible to translate the implied desire more directly:

> Your stomach is gorgeous,
> I want to enjoy your navel!

A more abstract translation, which is also more personal (introducing the speaker with a first person reference) than the original, could be:

> Your navel is an aphrodisiac,
> your stomach is my favorite food!

Rendered with more concrete modern imagery, one might suggest the following translation:

> Your navel is a goblet spilling over with fine wine,
> your stomach is a chocolate fountain, garnished with strawberries!

As pointed out above, iconography informed the nuances of the use of *šor* in this verse. It also confirmed the association between drinking and sexual intercourse in an explicit way. Furthermore, it showed how flowers could heighten "appetite" in a context of food, a metaphorical donor field (see chapter 5) for erotic enjoyment. While it is possible that these associations could have been possibly detected through other methods, such as literary comparisons, iconographic exegesis makes these keys to interpretation more explicit – and indeed, more visible.

7:4. Gazelles live in the steppe. As a prey animal they are endangered by both chaos and death. Young gazelles are especially shy and playful. Reference to twin gazelles is combined with breasts, which are symbols of warmth, security, food, intimacy, blessing, and life.

7:5. The neck is associated with pride (Keel 1994:147). The ivory tower could be associated with precious, exclusive, royal buildings for recreation, thus combining senses of pleasure and beauty, but also due to its nature as a tower, and with it, source of security and impregnability.

Transjordan Heshbon had water reservoirs that could have been royal ponds or public spaces. The connection with the gate implies that desert travelers could satisfy their thirst there. The phrase *bat-rabbîm* literally means "daughter of many." The Septuagint translates in this manner, apparently not knowing of any town with this name (i.e., Bath-rabbin).

Lebanon, in association with Solomon's manor, could represent an idyllic place. In association with the strong enemy of Damascus, this word evokes a military image, like the tower in Song 4:4. Women could be represented as well-defended cities, especially with crowns and necklaces (**figs. 17.6–7**).

Fig. 17.5. Bowl with lotus garlands, Israel, 8th–7th c. BCE. Source: Keel 1994:233 fig. 130

Fig. 17.6. Part of a limestone stele depicting the wife of Ashurbanipal with a crenellated crown, 7th c. BCE. Source: Keel 1994:145 fig. 83

7:6. Reference to Carmel might evoke an image of pride, or if understood as *kerem-ʾēl* ("vineyard of God") it could also evoke a sense of fascination, enchantment, joy, and lust.

The word *ʾargāmān* is not the color purple itself, but refers to the expensive purple dyed cloth, which in Antiquity was produced from mollusks in Tyre.

The phrase *dallat rōʾšēk* has several possible meanings. *Dallat* maybe be related to the Hebrew root *dlh*, which in Isaiah 38:12 means "loom-threads." In this case, it is possible to interpret *dallat rōʾšēk* as a metaphor ("the threads of your head"). But if the root meaning of this word instead comes from *dll*, meaning "to hang," another metaphorical interpretation comes into view. In this sense, "the hanging of your head" would more likely refer to hair. Hair was associated with power and possibly wildness. Hair would also be an element of attraction. (**fig. 17.8;** cf. Schroer and Staubli 2001:96–102).

The reference to a king forms a ring composition with "daughter of a prince," in between which are placed images from nature, agriculture, and military. In sum, this song depicts a woman celebrating her loveliness, beauty, attractiveness, and strength. In this mix of impregnability and intimacy the song expresses yearning.

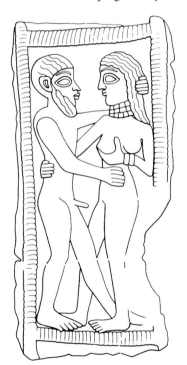

Fig. 17.7. Old-Babylonian terracotta relief showing a woman with jewelry and a man on a bed. Source: Keel 1994:90 fig. 44

Fig. 17.8. Painting on limestone showing an acrobatic dancer with long hair (a wig?), Deir el-Medina, 13th c. BCE. Source: Keel 1994:140 fig. 78

5.4. Translation of Song of Songs 7:2–6

The following translation emerges from the brief reflections offered above:

> [2] I admire your courageous feet in your elegant sandals,
> charming princess.
> The curves of your thighs are like precious jewels,
> created by the hands of a skillful craftsman.
> [3] Your "navel" is a moon-shaped chalice,
> with arousing wine spilling over.
> Your voluptuous womb is a mound of wheat,
> encircled with lush lotus flowers.
> [4] Both your breasts are like frolicking fawns,
> tender twins of a gazelle.
> [5] Your jeweled neck is like a tall ivory tower,
> your sparkling eyes are like the cool pools of Heshbon in the desert
> quenching the thirsty at the travelers' gate.
> O, Lebanon-tower-like is your noble nose,
> boldly facing Damascus.
> [6] Your head is like majestic Mount Carmel,
> while your unbound hair flows like deep dark royal purple.
> Keep your king captive in your captivating locks!

6. Conclusion

Bible translation provides us with a particular set of challenges that have to do with how the form and meaning of a source language can be effectively – and, hopefully, beautifully – conveyed in a target language. As such, translation decisions not only require knowledge of grammar, vocabulary, and syntax but also sensitivity to the cultural distance between the sender and the receiving audience, strategies about how to bridge this distance, and the purposes of the translation (*skopos*). A variety of styles and strategies of translation are employed as a way of negotiating these issues. I have advocated for a "pleonastic approach" to translation, which aims at comprehensibility in the target language while preserving the culturally-specific connotations of the source language.

As a test case, I have taken up the challenge of providing a translation of one of the description songs from the Song of Songs, trying to render more of the implied, associated meanings in these verses than a literal, word-for-word translation would give. This goal required reflection on aspects of Hebrew poetry, the translation of metaphors, and the literary context of Song 7:2–6.

In addition, this chapter has attempted to show how the study of ancient iconography can help guide important translation decisions, especially those that relate to densely descriptive language. Thus, the purpose of this chapter was to demonstrate how iconographic exegesis entails the use of images not only in the interpretation of biblical texts but also in their translation, especially through a pleonastic approach. Iconography sheds light on the ancient communication of the text and makes the translator aware of what (s)he needs to express for the audience of the translation.

Assignment/Exercise

1. If you know Hebrew, establish a working translation of Song 4:1–7 (the first description song). Formulate a *skopos,* and, based on that particular *skopos,* choose one of the styles of translation mentioned above and revise your first translation to fit this approach.
2. If you do not know Hebrew, compare various translations of Song 4:1–7 that reflect different translation strategies (including the ones mentioned above). Identify significant differences between the translations, explaining how they might influence your interpretation of the text.
3. Having completed exercises 1 and/or 2, study some of the images included in this chapter or those found in Keel 1994. Does your study of ancient iconography influence any of your translation decisions? If so, how?

Bibliography

Fee, Gordon D. and Mark L. Strauss. 2007. *How to Choose a Translation for All Its Worth: A Guide to Understanding and Using Bible Versions.* Grand Rapids, MI: Zondervan.

Hill, Harriet S. 2006. *The Bible at Cultural Crossroads: From Translation to Communication.* Manchester: St. Jerome.

Hulster, Izaak J. de. Forthcoming (b). "The Challenge of Hebrew Bible Love Poetry: A Pleonastic Approach to the Translation of Metaphor."

Keel, Othmar. 1994. *Song of Songs: A Continental Commentary.* Translated by Frederick J. Gaiser. Minneapolis: Fortress.

Nida, Eugene A. and Charles R. Taber. 1969. *The Theory and Practice of Translation.* Leiden: Brill.

Schroer, Silvia and Thomas Staubli. 2001. *Body Symbolism in the Bible.* Collegeville, MN: Liturgical Press.

Wilt, Timothy, ed. 2002. *Bible Translation: Frames of Reference.* Manchester: St. Jerome.

Chapter 18
Judith's Victory Celebration and the Iconography of Twigs in Judith 15:12-13

Thomas Staubli

Dedicated to Tal Ilan

1. Introduction

As is evident in other chapters in this volume, iconographic exegesis offers a powerful tool for interpreting biblical metaphors in poetic texts, especially the Psalms. However, the study of ancient art can also aid in the interpretation of various other types of biblical texts, including prophetic visions and accounts of rituals, festivals, and celebrations. Texts in this latter category offer a potentially fruitful topic of study since they often provide vivid descriptions of visual objects (cult vessels, cult stands, special garments, etc.) and/or visual practices (dance, processions, etc.). Deciphering the symbolic meaning of these objects and activities calls not only for a careful analysis of the text at hand but also an assessment of iconographic sources that display similar themes. In this chapter, I use this procedure to help explain the significance of twigs/branches (Greek: *thyrsos;* Hebrew: *lûlāb* [pronounced "lulav"]) in Judith's victory celebration (Jud 15:12–13). My iconographic exegesis begins with a brief textual analysis of the book of Judith and then proceeds to a fuller evaluation of the background, development, and ongoing significance of twig imagery in the visual arts of the Levant.

2. Judith 15:12-13 and its Background

The book of Judith was probably written during the first century BCE (Ilan 1999:136) during the reign and under the protection of Salome (Shelamzion) Alexandra (76–67 BCE), the wife and successor of Alexander Jannaeus (Rocca 2005). It is uncertain whether the book was originally written in Hebrew (Hanhart 1979:9) or Greek (Schmitz 2006). In either case, no ancient Hebrew manuscript survives and the oldest extant version is from the Septuagint.

Not unlike Esther and Susanna, Judith features a female protagonist and is missing from the anti-Hasmonean library of the Qumran sect. For this reason, Ilan suggests that Judith was composed as "propaganda for Hasmonean queenship" (1999:141). According to Ilan, the historical background of Judith is the crisis at the end of Alexander Jannaeus's life in a situation of civil war. Specifically, Ilan contends:

When Shelamzion eventually ascended the throne, she completely reversed the policies of her husband, and for a while curbed the crisis. If this policy change was anticipated by the author of Judith, his/her writing in the service of the prospective queen is better understood. (1999:151)

The character Judith features prominently in the second half of the book (chs. 8–16). Distinguished by both her piety and courage, Judith devises a plan to save the Israelites. In the climactic moment of the story, Judith beheads the tyrant Holofernes (13:1–10), thus inspiring her people to victory over their enemies. The book concludes with a series of celebrations, including that which is found in 15:12–13.

> [12] Then all the women of Israel ran together to see her [Judith], and blessed her, and made a dance among them for her. She took twigs (*thyrsous*) in her hand, and gave also to the women that were with her. [13] And they crowned themselves with olive wreaths (*tên elaian*), she and those (women; Karrer and Kraus 2011:1314) who were with her. She went before all the people in the dance, leading all the women; and all the men of Israel followed in their armor and wearing garlands (*stephanōn*), and with songs on their lips. (author's translation)

Twigs play a key role in this short but important scene in the story. In v. 12, Judith distributes twigs to the women who accompanied her in the celebration. It is also likely that twigs were used in the making of the olive wreaths and garlands mentioned in v. 13. What do these twigs symbolize and how might one understand their role in Judith's victory celebration? Understanding their symbolic meaning involves more than just properly translating the underlying Greek (or Hebrew) term. Rather, it is necessary to explore the various associations twig imagery would have activated for ancient listeners or readers of this text. In order to do so, we have to study not only relevant texts from the time period in which the Judith novel written but also relevant pictorial sources from the same period. This procedure brings us squarely into the realm of iconographic exegesis.

3. *Thyrsos* and *Lûlāb* as Symbols of a Dionysos-YHWH Linkage

The Greek term *thyrsos* typically refers to a staff of giant fennel covered with ivy vines and leaves, topped with a pinecone. This bouquet-like object was often utilized as a cultic instrument and most commonly was associated with Dionysos, the Greek god of wine. Cult images of Dionysos show him holding a *thyrsos,* which according to Greek mythology, was mockingly given to him by the Titans in place of his scepter. Several other motifs from Greek vases point to the prominent connection between twigs and the cult of Dionysos.

Yet, what does the cult of Dionysos have to do with Judith's victory celebration? While the use of the word *thyrsos* in the context of the book of Judith does not explicitly point to a feast of Dionysos, it would have suggested to a Hellenistic reader a special, artificial bouquet for a cultic context. This is evident because the cult of Yнwн and the cult of Dionysos shared several common features during the period in which Judith was written. First, Greek pottery art shows Dionysos's female followers, known as maenads, dancing around the deity with torches, twigs, and tambourines (**fig. 18.1**). In a similar fashion, women playing the tambourine are a familiar element of Yнwн's cult (cf. Ps 68:26 [Eng. 25]; Paz 2007; Staubli 2007:13–17). Second, in Greece Dionysos was often associated with the Levantine region. Not only was he known as the Cadmean, "the one from the Levant" (Euripides, *Phoen.* 638–52), but on an Attic krater (a large vessel used to mix wine and water) from the fifth century BCE we find Dionysos and a maenad, each of them with a twig in the hand, attending an acrobatic dance performed by a person in what appears to be Near Eastern costume (**fig. 18.2**). Third, Dionysos was often associated with Heracles, as is the case on an Attic psykter (a type of Greek pot with a narrow base and wide body) from the fifth century BCE that pictures Heracles side-by-side with Dionysos, who is holding a large Greek cup in his right hand and a twig in his left (**fig. 18.3**). This observation is potentially revealing because Heracles came to be identified with the Phoencian god Melqart, who in turn was occasionally perceived as a variant of Yнwн. The Dionysos-Heracles-Melqart-Yнwн linkage might further suggest parallels between Dionysiac and Yahwistic cults.

Fig. 18.1. Greek vase, ca. 420 BCE, Museo Nazionale, Napoli H2419. Source: *LIMC* III, Dionysos Nr. 33

Several other lines of evidence point to the possibility of this cultic connection. For instance, extensive trade networks in the eastern Mediterranean during the Hellenistic period likely facilitated cultural (and by extension, cultic) contact between Greece and the Levant (Ridgway 1992; Abulafia 2012:89–94). In addition, according to 3 Macc 2:29 Ptolemy IV Philopator gave orders to mark all visitors of the temple of Jerusalem with an ivy-leaf, the symbol of Dionysos. Tacitus (*Hist.* V, 5) reports that some identified the Jewish cult with the cult of Father Liber (also known as Bacchus, the Roman name for Dionysos). Tacitus here is probably referring to Plutarch, who reports that the Jews, some days after the Feast of Sukkot, celebrate "a feast amongst

Fig. 18.2. Greek vase, 5th century BCE, Aleppo Museum.
Source: *LIMC* III, Dionysos Nr. 841

Fig. 18.3. Greek vase, beginning of the 5th century BCE,
Musée de Vivenel 1068. Source: *LIMC* III, Dionysos Nr. 839

them called Kradephoria, from carrying palm-trees, and Thyrsophoria, when they enter into the temple carrying thyrsi (*Quaest. conv.* 4.6.2.)." On a Roman coin a conquered Judean, kneeling beside his camel, is called Bacchius Iudaeus, "Judean worshiper of Bacchus" in the inscription (Grueber 1910:490). Finally, on some of their first coins the Judeans themselves seem to have adapted Dionysos imagery for Yнwн (Keel 2007:978 with **fig. 604**).[1]

Yet, perhaps the most "Dionysian" element in the Jewish cult was the Feast of Sukkot, which developed from the festival of the vine/grape harvest (Exod 23:16). According to the book of Jubilees (16:30), during Sukkot people not only dwelt in booths, but also set wreaths upon their heads, and took leafy boughs and willows from the brook and daily surrounded the altar with the branches seven times. In addition,

---

1   The coin is usually interpreted as the adaption of a Zeus-imagery for Yнwн, but the satyr-mask, opposite to the figure on the wheel, fits the realm of Dionysos much better.

similar rites involving twigs are described in texts about the re-inauguration of the temple by Simon, including 2 Macc 10:7 (using the word *thyrsoi*) and 1 Macc 13:51. Grintz (1957:172–174) lists further evidence from the Talmudic literature of the popularity of twigs in Jewish circles, especially for their use in wreaths. When used in Jewish texts, *thyrsos* typically translates Hebrew *lûlāv* and refers to the closed frond of the date palm tree that is used during Sukkot.

Summarizing the above-mentioned data, one might tentatively conclude that YHWH and Dionysos were linked, and perhaps even identified, with one another (Schneider 2003:156 n. 26). This association was made possible by the intensive exchange in the eastern Mediterranean in commerce and cult during the Hellenistic period. It was also suggested that a *thyrsos,* a bouquet-like object consisting of twigs and ending in an arrangement of plants, played a role in the cult of Dionysos and the cult of YHWH. The *lûlāv* in the Jewish Sukkot Festival (and probably also the *thyrsos* of the Dionysiac festivals) has its roots in an old Levantine or eastern Mediterranean tradition that is attested over millennia in the pictorial art of the region. Viewed in this historical perspective, the episode in Judith featuring twigs exists within a very long tradition within Levantine culture. Understanding the symbolic meaning of the twig motif can be reconstructed from a survey of the iconographic history of this motif throughout the ages.

4. Twigs and the Iconography of the Southern Levant[2]

Beyond its connection to Dionyos in Greek art, twig imagery played a prominent role in the iconography of the Southern Levant. To understand the significance of this imagery, one must consider the geography of the region. Located between the Mediterranean and the desert area surrounding the Dead Sea, the southern Levant can be topographically divided into several longitudinal zones. These areas vary greatly in terms of their climate, vegetation, and water sources. Furthermore, rainfall amounts fluctuate in this region from the rainy winter season to the dry summer months. It is in this context that twig imagery became a symbol of the yearly regeneration of the earth that would accompany the coming of the winter rains. In this sense, twig imagery served as an enduring symbol of fertility and regeneration.

4.1. Twig Imagery as Symbol of the Blessing of the Goddess

Due to its association with fertility and regeneration, twig imagery is often combined with goddess imagery. For instance, on a Late Neolithic bone object from HaGosherim (Northern Galilee; **fig. 18.4**), a figurative decoration shows a caprid feeding on a twig that comes out of the vulva of an anthropomorphized earth goddess. In the Early Chalcolithic period, the twig-caprid combination appears on one of the

---

2   This chapter is based on Staubli 2005 but includes alternative images and offers some further aspects of the main subject

most famous bronze scepters from Naḥal Mishmar (**fig. 18.5**). In the initial phase of the Early Bronze Age, the motif of dancing or mourning women with twigs in their hands is first attested in the Southern Levant (**fig. 18.6**).

Fig. 18.6. Clay pot, Late Bronze Age, Bab edh-Dhra. Source: *IPIAO* 1: Nr. 100

Fig. 18.4. Bone object, late Neolithic, Ha-Gosherim. Source: Getzov 2008:1760

Fig. 18.5. Scepter, Chalcolithic, Nahal Mischmar. Source: *IPIAO* 1: Nr. 60

In Canaanite art of Middle Bronze Age II, twigs are nearly omnipresent. They are frequently combined with a naked woman, sometimes flanking her or being held by her. In some cases they sprout out from her vulva or from her navel (**fig. 18.7**). The divine character of the frontally depicted female figure is emphasized by a neb-sign (master/mistress) under her feet. Sometimes she has big ears, which suggests her receptivity to human prayers. She occasionally wears signs of divinity on her head, such as horns or crowns, or she appears with uplifted arms. She can be represented by a so-called Hathor fetish (a cult stand topped by the head of the goddess Hathor) combined with a twig (**fig. 18.8**). She can also be venerated by women in one of her forms: as an anthropomorphic goddess, as a fetish, or as a twig (**fig. 18.9**). Sometimes the women are doing a cartwheel (as part of a dancing performance) and are flanked by twigs (**fig. 18.10**).

Fig. 18.7.   Fig. 18.8.   Fig. 18.9.   Fig. 18.10.

Figs. 18.7–10. Stamp seal amulets, MB IIB: **Fig. 18.7.** Gezer. Source: Schroer 1989: Nr. 6. **Fig. 18.8.** Southern Levant. Source: Schroer 1989: Nr. 0101. **Fig. 18.9.** Tell el-Ajjūl. Source: *CSAPI* 1: Nr. 955. **Fig. 18.10.** Southern Levant. Source: Schroer 1989: Nr. 53

Silvia Schroer (1987) refers to the motif of this type of female figure as the "twig-goddess" during the Middle Bronze Age IIB. She is the Levantine variant of the ancient Near Eastern goddess of the earth, representing the earth's regenerating powers as it is fertilized by the winter rain. It is noteworthy in this context to remember that God does not directly create the plants, according to the language of Genesis 1. Rather, God says, "Let the earth put forth vegetation: plants yielding seed, and fruit trees of every kind on earth that bear fruit with the seed in it" (v. 11). One possible interpretation of Gen 1:11 is that God makes use of the regenerating power of the earth to bring forth vegetation (Keel and Schroer 2002:52 abb. 18).

Various animals can also appear within the twig-goddess constellation. They represent conceptual aspects of the goddess, such as regeneration, refreshment, fertility, power, and defense of life. While the caprid is most commonly found in these constellations (**figs. 18.4–5**), a goat, an ibex, and a gazelle (**fig. 18.11**) are also attested. Other animals that commonly accompany the goddess in iconographic representations are the lion, the vulture, different kinds of serpents (**fig. 18.12**), the crocodile, the hippopotamus, the vervet monkey, and the fish.

4.2. Twig Imagery Combined with Cultic Elements

Twigs also appear in combination with the falcon-headed god, a Levantine variant of the weather god, inspired by the Egyptian Horus (**fig. 18.13**). He often holds twigs as a kind of scepter. In a local Levantine variant, the veneration of the Egyptian creation-god Ptah is also combined with a twig (**fig. 18.14**). From here it is a small step to the combination of twigs with representations of royal authority and power. For instance, twigs often appear combined with symbols of the pharaoh. They also accompany the very typical Canaanite motifs of the city-ruler in his robe with the broad hem (**fig. 18.15**) and the prince on the donkey. Twigs are also held by the worshipers of the weather god (**fig. 18.16**).

Fig. 18.11.   Fig. 18.12.   Fig. 18.13.   Fig. 18.14.

Figs. 18.11–14. Stamp seal amulets, MB IIB: **Fig. 18.11.** Bet Mirsim.
Source: *CSAPI* 2: Nr. 54. **Fig. 18.12.** Tell Far'ah (South). Source: *CSAPI*
3: Nr. 6. **Fig. 18.13.** Tell Far'ah (South). Source: *CSAPI* 3: Nr. 26.
Fig. 18.14. En Samije. Source: *CSAPI* 2: Nr. 7

In addition to being attributes of the earth goddess and certain gods, twigs also
are symbols of the cosmos-regenerating powers of vegetation. We may deduce this
from constellations where the twig forms the center of a composition, sometimes in a
series (**fig. 18.17**), sometimes in isolation (**fig. 18.18**). In such a position the iconeme
of the twig converges syntactically with the holy or stylized tree.

Fig. 18.15.   Fig. 18.16.   Fig. 18.17.   Fig. 18.18.   Fig. 18.19.

Figs. 18.15–19. Stamp seal amulets, MB IIB: **Fig. 18.15.** Amman. Source: *CSAJ*: Nr. 27. **Fig. 18.16.**
Emmaus. Source: *CSAPI* 2: Nr. 1. **Fig. 18.17.** Tell el-Ajjul. Source: *CSAPI* 1: Nr. 1122. **Fig. 18.18.** Tell
Far'ah (South). Source: *CSAPI* 3: Nr. 273. **Fig. 18.19.** Dor. Source: *CSAPI* 2: Nr. 14

In the Late Bronze Age the twig is also combined with the name of Amun (**fig. 18.19**).
The full text in this image reads *jmn-r' jmn* ("Amun-re is hidden") or *jmn-re nb m3't*
("Amun-Re is the master of truth"). The twig is an ornament in the middle of a composition and may at the same time function as the character *j* if a cryptographic reading is taken into account. This example shows how even the abstract and sophisticated
Amun iconograpy could have been combined with the popular local twig iconography, which is otherwise absent in Egypt.

In the Late Bronze Age the twig motif is rarely found in the Levantine iconography.
During the Iron Age the (stylized) tree is more common. But the lines separating twig
and tree are fluid as may be seen from the fragments of a painted jar, where the twig
or tree has the explicit legend *elat*, "goddess" and is flanked by caprids (**fig. 18.20**; cf.

figs. **18.4–5; 11**). On a Late Bronze cylinder seal from Tell Der Alla (**fig. 18.21**) two human figures are holding batons that are very similar to the later Greek thyrsos (cf. **fig. 18.2**).

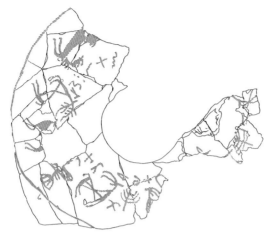

Fig. **18.20**. Ewer fragment, Lachish, Late Bronze Age. Source: *IPIAO* 3, Nr. 852

Fig. **18.21**. Cylinder seal, scaraboid, Tell Deir Alla, Late Bronze Age. Source: CSAJ: Nr. 42

During the Iron Age the twig motif is still present, but sometimes in new constellations. A singular stamp seal from Akko gives us insight into a cult scene, most probably during a new moon rite (**fig. 18.22**). We see a praying man between a twig and a cult stand with a twig motif. Indeed, twig motifs on cult stands are not rare, as may be seen, for instance, from the recently published Yavneh stands (Kletter, Ziffer, and Zwickel 2010). Also associated with the twig is an anthropomorphic goddess from Lachish (**fig. 18.23**), this time presenting her breasts – a gesture rooted in the Near East and not in Egypt (cf. **fig. 18.7**). The combination of the name of the seal owner with a twig first appears in the Late Iron Age and is frequently attested (**fig. 18. 24**). The moon was venerated as a regeneration symbol in combination with symbols from the realm of animals and vegetation (**fig. 18.25**).

Fig. 18.22.   Fig. 18.23.   Fig. 18.24.   Fig. 18.25.

Figs. 18.22–25. Iron Age stamp seals: **Fig. 18.22.** Akko. Source: *CSAPI* 1: Nr. 17. **Fig. 18.23.** Lachish. Source: *GGG:* Fig. 323. **Fig. 18.24.** Jerusalem. Source: *GGG:* Fig. 355. **Fig. 18.25.** Judah. Source: *GGG:* Fig. 317c

4.3. Twig Imagery on Coins

During the Persian period twigs are prominent on coins, the new mass media. Just as twigs once flanked the naked goddess, twigs now flank the owl of Athena (**fig. 18.26**). Instead of adapting the typical Athenian iconography of the olive twig, the Levantine designers integrated the owl in their own traditional concept of the flanking twigs. At the end of the Persian period, Hellenistic art forms became more and more visible in the Levant. But very often the motifs are not new for the Levant, as is the case of a worshiper with a twig on a Samarian bullae (**fig. 18.27**).

Fig. 18.26.   Fig. 18.27.   Fig. 18.28.   Fig. 18.29.   Fig. 18.30.

Fig. 18.26. Coin, Samaria. Source: Meshorer/Qedar 1999: Fig. 206. **Fig. 18.27.** Seal impression, Wadi ed-Daliyeh. Source: *CSAPI* 2: Nr. 4. **Fig. 18.28.** Coin of Alexander Jannaeus. Source: Madden 1864:66, 3 Obv. **Fig. 18.29.** Coin of Herod Antipas. Source: Madden 1864:97, 2 Obv. **Fig. 18.30.** Coin of Simon bar Gamaliel. Source: Madden 1864:178, 1 Obv.

From Hellenistic times onwards plants are by far the most important iconemes on local Judean coins. Apart from laurel and olive wreaths, palm trees, ears of wheat, reeds, pomegranates, grapes, and grape leaves, it is a simple twig (sometimes a palm twig) that appears most often. On a coin of Alexander Jannaeus (**fig. 18.28**) the inscription "Jonathan, the king" is written to the left and to the right side of a twig and may be an allusion to Zech 4:1–4 (cf. also Sirach 50:10) where the prince and the high priest are represented by two olive trees flanking the menorah, representing God. In the same line stands a coin of Herod Antipas (**fig. 18.29**) in which his title, "Herod the Tetrarch," is surrounded by a twig. A further variant is the coin of Shimon bar Gamaliel with the inscription "Shimon (prince) of Israel" (**fig. 18.30**).

Still closer to the vision of Zechariah is a coin of Herod the Great on which a star flanked by twigs appears over a plumed helmet (**fig. 18.31**). In this case, the star replaces the menorah of Zechariah's vision. But it is also possible that Herod saw himself as the messianic star (Num 24:17; Küchler 1989). In a variant of Herod's coins the twigs flank a tripod, maybe pointing to libations poured during the Sukkot festival (**fig. 18.32**). Even on local coins of Roman Caesars we find twigs, as an example of Claudius shows (**fig. 18.33**). On the coins of the first and the second Jewish revolt the twig is sometimes combined with a vessel (**fig. 18.34**). The setting probably refers to a rite of Sukkot in which water is spattered by a twig in order to prompt God to send rain.

Fig. 18.31.   Fig. 18.32.   Fig. 18.33.   Fig. 18.34.

Fig. 18.31. Coin of Herod the Great. Source: Madden 1864:83, 2 Obv. **Fig. 18.32.** Coin of Herod the Great. Source: Madden 1864:88, 6 Obv. **Fig. 18.33.** Coin of Claudius. Source: Madden 1864:152, 2 Obv. **Fig. 18.34.** Coin of Simon bar Giora. Source: Madden 1864:167, 2 Rev.

Especially noteworthy for the ongoing symbolic importance of the twig are the coins of Eleazar and Simon bar Giora, minted during the first revolt (**fig. 18.35**). They show a *lûlāv* (sprout of a tree) and an *'etrôg* (a citrus fruit) together with the writing "Year xy of the liberation of Israel." In accordance with their interpretations of Lev 23:40, the rabbis viewed the *lûlāv* as an elaborate bouquet of a palm branch, a myrtle twig, and a willow twig. This bouquet is swung during ceremonies associated with Sukkot. The *lûlāv* is evidently the rabbinic version of the age-old Levantine tradition of symbolizing divine blessings by a twig. The twigs are even present on Hadrianic coins, minted in Rome and celebrating the victory over the second Jewish revolt (**fig. 18.36**). They show the children of Judah paying homage to the Caesar with twigs in their hands. What is probably the first Islamic coin of Jerusalem, minted by caliph Abd al-Malik, pursues the old tradition in a more abstract form by displaying a menorah with five arms, which could also be interpreted as a stylized tree or twig (**fig. 18.37**).

Fig. 18.35.   Fig. 18.36.   Fig. 18.37.   Fig. 18.38.

Fig. 18.35. Coin of Eleasar. Source: Madden 1864:164, 4 Rev. **Fig. 18.36.** Coin of Hadrian. Source: Madden 1864:212, note 5 Rev. **Fig. 18.37.** Coin of Abd el-Malik. Source: Madden 1864:231 Rev. **Fig. 18.38.** Coin from Ashkelon. Source: line drawing by author after Meshorer 1985: Fig. 49 Rev.

Fig. 18.39. Terracotta figure from Petra. Source: Parlasca 1990: Plate IV, Nr. 12

Fig. 18.40. Detail of Samarian stone coffin, École Biblique, Jerusalem. Source: Photograph by author, courtesy of the École Biblique

Meanwhile, the Canaanite twig tradition also continues in the coinage of other areas in the southern Levant. This is seen, for instance, in coinage from Ashkelon depicting iconography of the deity Phanebal ("the face of Baal;" **fig. 18.38**). A coin from the late second century CE shows a juvenile god holding a weapon in his right hand and a twig in his left. This image is an iconic condensation of the fight of Baal (symbolized in the weapon in the right hand) against Mot and Yamm, the result of which causes the earth to once again sprout forth twigs (symbolized by the twig in the left hand).

An example of how the local twig tradition continues in the hand of a goddess is found in a terracotta figure from Petra. As a variant of Isis, this goddess appears in the role of a sitting mourner: her right hand is on her cheek and her left hand holds a twig pointing to the earth (**fig. 18.39**). This goddess was very important in Petra. For example, a rock sculpture of Isis from Wadi Abu Olleqa recalls the prominent combination of twigs and mourning women that appear already in the local Transjordan art of the Early Bronze Age (cf. Isa 66:14; **figs. 18.6; 47**). Twigs also appear on local byzantine coffins of the Byzantine period (**fig. 18.40**). The iconographic evidence of the coins demonstrates that the old local symbol of the twig in Hellenistic and Roman times was still very popular. It was a favorite symbol for rulers to express the prosperity of their leadership and rule and it was a perfect symbol to connect the political with the cultic realm, as it also does in the story of Judith.

5. Judith 15 Through the Eyes of Art

Having surveyed the various associations of twig imagery with the cults of Dionysos and YHWH (§ 3) and with the symbols of fertility and regeneration (§ 4), it is now possible to return to Judith 15:12–13 in order to reevaluate the role and symbolic meaning of twigs in the heroine's victory celebration.

The iconographic evidence discussed above suggests that references to twigs during the festival of Judith's triumph turn out to be symbols of a very deep and long lasting tradition. By distributing twigs, Judith acts like a goddess towards her venerators. By crowning themselves with olive wreaths, the women participate in a messianic symbolism reserved for victors, liberators, and redeemers. And by joining the dance of the women adorned in such a way, the armed men, wearing garlands, acknowledge the women's success. In using the term *thyrsos* for the twigs of Judith the author/translator alludes to the *lûlāv* of Sukkot, the main festival of the year with its symbolism of the regeneration of life. The mention of the twigs also emphasizes the superlative character of the event with messianic overtones coming out of women's age old opposition to death, still present in the palm branches of the servants of God from Israel and all nations (Rev 7:9).

The importance of twig imagery does not end with the book of Judith. Indeed, a symbol so deeply rooted in the iconographic and environmental context of the Southern Levant has quite a long and vibrant afterlife in Palestinian folk art traditions, the state emblems of Israel, and various aspects of Abrahamic religions. Although not always included in iconographic exegesis, an examination of the ongoing significance of ANE imagery in post-biblical periods can serve as a way of shedding light on the culture that produced both the visual and textual expressions of this motif.

5.1. Palestinian Folk Art Traditions

On Arab amulets only abstract signs (typically accompanying texts) are to be found. In Palestine, however, the twig is the exception to this rule (**fig. 18.41**). Even today, the olive branch is sometimes combined with the Bismillah on amulets (**fig. 18.42**). On certain amulets a twig may connote prosperity, wealth, and life. When found on storage containers, the iconography of twigs implies blessing in the form of barley or wheat grains (**fig. 18.43**), or, alternatively, oil or water (**fig. 18.44**). The twigs in this context sometimes tend to look like an ear of wheat or a palm tree.

5.2. The Israeli State Emblem

Fig. 18.48. State emblem of Israel.
Source: Israeli 1999:15

In addition to its survival in Palestinian folk art traditions, twig-imagery is also prominent in the iconography of the modern, secular State of Israel (**fig. 18.48**). While Lebanon honored the old Canaanite respect for the holiness of plants by putting the cedar in the middle of their flag, the Israeli state honored the Canaanite tradition by flanking the menorah with olive twigs on their official seal. The olive branches are often interpreted as symbols of the democratic and secular state, while the menorah is thought to be a sign of the religious tradition. When these elements are taken together, the constellation can be understood as a quotation of Zechariah's vision (4:1–14) in which two figures, perhaps representing the royal and the priestly authorities, flank a lampstand. Further, Zechariah's vision itself might represent a variation on the old constellation of twigs flanking a main symbol of the goddess. As we have seen, by the prophet's time the blessing of the goddess was especially depicted through the constellation of twigs flanking the new moon (cf. **figs. 18.22; 25**).

5.3. The Jewish Tradition of Sukkot

As we have already seen from the coins of the Second Temple period (**figs. 18.28–35**) – and as we can still see from synagogue mosaics of later periods – the twig is a main component of Sukkot as it also was for other feasts (cf. Ps 118:27; 2 Macc 10:6–7; 1 Macc 13:51). However, Nehemiah 8 seems to restrict the use of branches to the building of the hut: "Go out to the hills and bring branches of olive, wild olive, myrtle, palm, and other leafy trees to make booths, as it is written" (v. 15). This latter phrase ("as it is written") probably refers to Lev 23:40, but there we read: "On the first day you shall take the fruit of majestic trees, branches of palm trees, boughs of leafy trees, and willows of the brook; and you shall rejoice before the Yʜwʜ your God for seven days." Nehemiah's effort to limit the use of branches is perhaps due to his awareness of their pagan background.

The eventual connection of Sukkot to the time when Israel was living in huts before the conquest of Canaan did not override the festival's original connection to the hope for regeneration with the coming rainy season. For instance, during the Second Temple period there existed a custom that involved pouring out water with the festive bouquet. These libations, evidently a magic rite to bring forth rain, were accompanied by acrobatic dances and formed the climax of the Sukkot festival. The rabbis not only defended this folk tradition against the Sadducee's attempts to stop

Bibliography

Abitz, Friedrich. 1995. *Pharao als Gott in den Unterweltsbüchern des Neuen Reiches.* OBO 146. Freiburg/Göttingen: Universitätsverlag/Vandenhoeck & Ruprecht.

Abū ʿAssāf, A. 1990. *Der Tempel von ʿAin Dārā.* Damaszener Forschungen 3. Mainz: P. von Zabern.

Abulafia, David. 2011. *The Great Sea: A Human History of the Mediterranean.* New York/London: Oxford University Press.

Adkins, Lesley and Roy Adkins. 1989. *Archaeological Illustration.* Cambridge: Cambridge University Press.

Aldred, Cyril. 1988. *Akhenaten: King of Egypt.* New York: Thames and Hudson.

Alter, Robert. 2011. *The Art of Biblical Poetry.* New York: Basic Books.

Andrae, Walter. 1913. *Die Stelenreihen in Assur.* Ausgrabungen der Deutschen Orient-Gesellschaft in Assur, A: Baudenkmäler aus Assyrischer Zeit III. Leipzig: Hinrichs.

Anthes-Frey, Henrike. 2007. *Unheilsmächte und Schutzgenien, Antiwesen und Grenzgänger: Vorstellungen von "Dämonen" im alten Israel.* OBO 227. Fribourg/Göttingen: Academic Press/Vandenhoeck & Ruprecht.

Arnheim, Rudolf. 1966. *Toward a Psychology of Art: Collected Essays.* Berkley: University of California Press.

_____. 1969. *Visual Thinking.* Berkeley: University of California Press.

_____. 1986. *New Essays on the Psychology of Art.* Berkeley: University of California Press.

_____. 2004. *Art and Visual Perception: A Psychology of the Creative Eye.* Berkeley: University of California Press.

Arnold, Bill T. 2011. "The Love-Fear Antinomy in Deuteronomy 5–11." *VT* 61: 551–69.

Assmann, Jan. 1977. "Die Verborgenheit des Mythos in Ägypten." *Göttinger Miszellen* 25: 7–43.

_____. 1982. "Die Zeugung des Sohnes, Bild, Spiel, Erzählung und das Problem des ägyptischen Mythos." In *Funktionen und Leistungen des Mythos: Drei altorientalische Beispiele,* edited by Assmann et al., 13–61. OBO 48. Freiburg/Göttingen: Universitätsverlag/Vandenhoeck & Ruprecht.

Aston, Emma. 2011. *Mixanthrôpoi: Animal-human Hybrid Deities in Greek Religion.* Liège: Center International d'Étude de la Religion Greque Antique.

Auffret, Pierre. 1981. *Hymnes d'Égypte et d'Israël: Etudes de structures littéraires.* OBO 34. Fribourg/Göttingen: Éditions universitaires/Vandenhoeck & Ruprecht.

Augustinovic, Agostino. 1971. *"El-Khader" e il Profeta Elia.* Pubblicazioni dello Studium Biblicum Franciscanum: Collectio minor 12. Jerusalem: Franciscan Printing Press.

Avner, Uzi. 2001. "Sacred Stones in the Desert." *BAR* 27.3: 30–41

Avrahami, Yael. 2012. *The Senses of Scripture: Sensory Perception in the Hebrew Bible.* LHBOTS 545. New York: T&T Clark.

Baetschmann, Oskar. 2003. "Anleitung zur Interpretation: Kunstgeschichtliche Hermeneutik." In *Kunstgeschichte: eine Einführung,* edited by Hans Belting et al., 199–228. Berlin: Reimer.

_____. 2009. *Einführung in die kunstgeschichtliche Hermeneutik: die Auslegung von Bildern.* 6th ed. Darmstadt: Wissenschaftliche Buchgesellschaft.

Bahrani, Zainab. *The Graven Image: Representation in Babylonia and Assyria.* Archaeology, Culture, and Society. Philadelphia: University of Pennsylvania Press, 2003.

Bär, Jürgen. 1996. *Der assyrische Tribut und seine Darstellung: Eine Untersuchung zur imperialen Ideologie im neuassyrischen Reich.* AOAT 243. Neukirchen-Vluyn: Neukirchener Verlag.

Barag, Dan. 1993. "Bagoas and the Coinage of Judea." In *Actes du XIe Congrès International de numismatique, organisé à l'occasion du 150e anniversaire de la Société Royale de Numismatique de Belgique Bruxelles, 8–13 Septembre 1991*, edited by Tony Hackens and Ghislaine Moucharte, 261–65. Louvain-La-Neuve: Association Professeur Marcel Hoc pour l'encouragement des recherches numismatiques.

Bauks, Michaela, 2007. "Bilderverbot (AT)." In *Das wissenschaftliche Bibellexikon im Internet/AT*, edited by Michaela Bauks and Klaus Koenen. Stuttgart: Deutsche Bibelgesellschaft. Cited 13 May 2015. Online: http://www.bibelwissenschaft.de/stichwort/15357/.

Beal, Timothy K. 2001. *Religion and Its Monsters.* New York: Routledge.

Becking, Bob. 1999. "Shem." in *Dictionary of Deities and Demons in the Bible*, edited by Karel van der Toorn, Bob Becking, and Peter Willem van der Horst, 763–64. Leiden: Brill.

Bernett, Monika and Othmar Keel. 1998. *Mond, Stier und Kult am Stadttor: Die Stele von Betsaida (et-Tell).* OBO 161. Freiburg/Göttingen: Universitätsverlag/Vandenhoeck & Ruprecht.

Berges, Ulrich. 2012. *The Book of Isaiah. Its Composition and Final Form.* Sheffield: Phoenix.

Berman, Louis A. 1997. *The Akedah: The Binding of Isaac.* Northvale, NJ: J. Aronson.

Beuken, Willem A. M. 2004. "The Manifestation of Yahweh and the Commission of Isaiah: Isaiah 6 Read Against the Background of Isaiah 1." *Calvin Theological Journal* 39: 72–87.

Beuttler, Ulrich. 2010. *Gott und Raum – Theologie der Weltgegenwart Gottes.* Forschungen zur systematischen und ökumenischen Theologie 127. Göttingen: Vandenhoeck & Ruprecht.

Beyer, Dominique. 2001. *Emar IV – Les sceaux: Mission archéologique de Meskéné-Emar Recherches au pays d'Aštata.* OBO.SA 20. Fribourg/Göttingen: Academic Press/Vandenhoeck & Ruprecht.

Beyerlin, Walter, ed. 1978 [German orig.: 1975]. *Near Eastern Religious Texts Relating to the Old Testament.* Translated by J. Bowden. OTL. Philadelphia: Westminster.

Bickerman, Elias. 1967. *Four Strange Books of the Bible: Jonah, Daniel, Koheleth, Esther.* New York: Schocken.

Biran, Avraham. 1994. *Biblical Dan.* Jerusalem: Israel Exploration Society.

Black, Jeremy and Anthony Green. 1992. *Gods, Demons and Symbols of Ancient Mesopotamia: An Illustrated Dictionary.* Austin: University of Texas Press.

Black, Max. 1962. *Models and Metaphors: Studies in Language and Philosophy.* Ithaca: Cornell University Press.

Blair, Judith M. 2009. *De-demonizing the Old Testament: An Investigation of Azazel, Lilith, Deber, Qeteb and Reshef in the Hebrew Bible.* FAT II/37. Tübingen: Mohr-Siebeck.

Blenkinsopp, Joseph. 2000. *Isaiah 1–39. A New Translation with Introduction and Commentary.* AB 19. New York: Doubleday.

Blocher, Felix. 1992. *Siegelabrollungen auf frühaltbabylonischen Tontafeln im Britisch Museum: ein Katalog.* Münchener Universitätsschriften, Philosophische Fakultät; 12 Münchener vorderasiatische Studien 10. München/Wien: Profil.

Bloch-Smith, Elizabeth. 2005. "Maṣṣēbôt in the Israelite Cult: An Argument for Rendering Implicit Cultic Criteria Explicit." In *Temple and Worship in Biblical Israel*, edited by John Day, 28–39. LHBOTS 422. New York/London: T&T Clark.

Boehm, Omri. 2004. "Child Sacrifice, Ethical Responsibility and the Existence of the People of Israel." *VT* 54: 145–156.

_____. 2007. *The Binding of Isaac: A Religious Model of Disobedience.* LHBOTS 468. New York/London: T&T Clark.

Bonatz, Dominik. 2000. *Das syro-hethitische Grabdenkmal. Untersuchungen zur Entstehung einer neuen Bildgattung in der Eisenzeit im nordsyrisch-südostanatolischen Raum.* Mainz: P. von Zabern.

Bonfiglio, Ryan P. 2012. "Archer Imagery in Zechariah 9:11–17 in Light of Achaemenid Iconography." *JBL* 131: 507–27.

_____. 2014. "Reading Images, Seeing Texts: Towards a Visual Hermeneutics for Biblical Studies." Ph.D. diss. Emory University.

Börker-Klähn, Jutta and Adelheid Shunnar-Misera. 1982. *Altvorderasiatische Bildstelen und vergleichbare Felsreliefs.* Baghdader Forschungen 4. Mainz: P. von Zabern.

Brassey, Paul. 2001. *Metaphor and the Incomparable God in Isaiah 40–55.* Bibal Dissertation Series 9. North Richland Hills, TX: Bibal.

Brenner, Athalya. 1997. *The Intercourse of Knowledge: On Gendering Desire and "Sexuality" in the Hebrew Bible.* Biblical Interpretation Series 26. Leiden/New York: Brill.

Brettler, Marc Zvi. 1998. "Incompatible Metaphors for Yhwh in Isaiah 40–66." *JSOT* 78: 97–120.

Briggs, Richard S. 2010. "Humans in the Image of God and Other Things Genesis Does Not Make Clear." *JTI* 4: 111–26.

Brown, Brian and Marian H. Feldman, eds. 2014. *Critical Approaches to Ancient Near Eastern Art.* Boston: de Gruyter.

Brown, William P. 1999. *The Ethos of the Cosmos: The Genesis of Moral Imagination in the Bible.* Grand Rapids, MI: Eerdmans.

_____. 2000. *Seeing the Psalms: A Theology of Metaphor.* Louisville: Westminster John Knox.

Buchholz, Hans-Günter. 2005. "Beobachtungen zur nahöstlichen, zyprischen und frühgriechischen Löwenikonographie." *UF* 37: 27–216.

Bunnens, Guy. 1995. "The So-called Stele of the God El from Ugarit." In *Actes du IIIème Congrès International des Études Phéniciennes et Puniques, Tunis, 11–16 novembre 1991,* 1: 214–21. Tunis: Institut National du Patrimoine.

Cahill, J. M. 2000. "Rosette-Stamp Handles." In *Excavations at the City of David 1978–1985 Directed by Yigal Shiloh: Volume VI: Inscriptions,* edited by D. T. Ariel, 85–108. Qedem 41. Jerusalem: Hebrew University.

Castelo, Daniel. 2008. "The Fear of the Lord as Theological Method." *JTI* 2: 147–60.

Chan, Michael J. 2013. "The City on a Hill: A Tradition-Historical Study of the Wealth of Nations Tradition." Ph.D. diss. Emory University.

Chapman, Stephen B. 2013. "Martial Memory, Peaceable Vision: Divine War in the Old Testament." In *Holy War in the Bible: Christian Morality and an Old Testament Problem,* edited by Heath Thomas, Jeremy Evans, and Paul Copan, 47–67. Downers Grove, IL: IVP Academic.

Cifarelli, Megan. 1998. "Gesture and Alterity in the Art of Ashurnasirpal II of Assyria." *The Art Bulletin* 80: 210–28.

Claassens, L. Julianna M. 2004, *The God Who Provides: Biblical Images of Divine Nourishment,* Nashville: Abingdon.

Clements, Ronald E. 1997. "'Arise, Shine; For Your Light Has Come': A Basic Theme of the Isaianic Tradition." In *Writing and Reading the Scroll of Isaiah: Studies of an Interpretive Tradition,* edited by Craig C. Broyles and Craig A. Evans, 1:441–54. 2 vols. VTSup 70. Leiden: Brill.

Clines, David J. A. 2003. "'The Fear of the Lord is Wisdom' (Job 28:28): A Semantic and Contextual Study." In *Job 28: Cognition in Context,* edited by Ellen van Wolde, 57–92. Biblical Interpretation Series 64. Leiden: Brill.

Collon, Dominique. 1975. *The Seal Impressions from Tell Atchana/Alalakh.* AOAT 27. Kevelaer: Butzon und Bercker.

_____. 1988. *First Impressions: Cylinder Seals in the Ancient Near East.* Chicago: University of Chicago Press.

_____. 1995. *Ancient Near Eastern Art.* Berkeley: University of California.

Collon, Dominique, Margaret Sax, and Christopher Bromhead Fleming Walker. 1986. *Catalogue of the Western Asiatic Seals in the British Museum: Cylinder Seals III: Isin/Larsa and Old Babylonion Periods.* London: The British Museum.

Cornelius, Izak. 1989. "The Lion in the Art of the Ancient Near East: A Study of Selected Motifs." *JNSL* 15: 53–85.

_____. 1994a. *The Iconography of the Canaanite Gods Reshef and Ba'al: Late Bronze and Iron Age I Periods (c 1500–1000 BCE).* OBO 140. Fribourg/Göttingen: University Press/Vandenhoeck & Ruprecht.

_____. 1994b. "The Visual Representation of the World in the Ancient Near East and the Bible." *JNSL* 20: 193–218.

Croft, William, and D. Alan Cruse. 2004. *Cognitive Linguistics*. Cambridge Textbooks in Linguistics. Cambridge: Cambridge University Press.

Cross, Frank Moore. 1973. *Canaanite Myth and Hebrew Epic: Essays in the History of the Religion of Israel*. Cambridge: Harvard University Press.

D'Albert de Luynes, H. T. P. J. 1846. *Supplément à l'essai sur la numismatique des satrapies et de la Phénicie sous les rois Achaeménides*. Paris: Firmin-Didot.

Dalman, Gustaf. 1908. *Petra und seine Felsheiligtümer*. Palästinische Forschungen zur Archäologie und Topographie 1. Leipzig: Hinrichs.

Darby, Erin. 2014. *Interpreting Judean Pillar Figurines: Gender and Empire in Judean Apotropaic Ritual*. FAT II/69. Tübingen: Mohr Siebeck.

Darby, Erin and Izaak J. de Hulster. Forthcoming. *Iron Age Terracotta Figurines in the Southern Levant*. CHANE. Leiden: Brill.

Davies, Nina M. and Alan H. Gardiner. 1926. *The Tomb of Huy, Viceroy of Nubia in the Reign of Tutʿankhamūn (No 40)*. Theban Tomb Series 4. London: Egypt Exploration Society.

Davies, Norman de Garis. 1900. *The Mastaba of Ptahhetep and Akhethetep at Saqqareh: Part 1, The Chapel of Ptahhetep and the Hieroglyphs*. Archaeological Survey of Egypt 8. London: Egypt Exploration Fund.

_____. 1903. *The Rock Tombs of El Amarna, Part 1: The Thomb of Meryra*. London: London Egypt Exploration Foundation.

Davis, Ellen F. 2008. *Scripture, Culture, and Agriculture: An Agrarian Reading of the Bible*. Cambridge: Cambridge University Press.

Davis, Whitney. 1992. *Masking the Blow: The Scene of Representation in Late Prehistoric Egyptian Art*. California Studies in the History of Art 30. Berkeley: University of California Press.

_____. 2011. *A General Theory of Visual Culture*. Princeton: Princeton University Press.

Day, John. 1989. *Molech. A God of Sacrifice in the Old Testament*. University of Cambridge Oriental Publications 41. Cambridge/New York: Cambridge University Press.

Deist, Ferdinand. 1987. "Genesis 1:1–2:3: World View and World Picture." *Scriptura* 22: 1–17.

Delaporte, Louis. 1923. *Catalogue des cylindres, cachets et pierres gravées de style oriental – Musée du Louvre 2: Acquisitions*. Paris: Hachette.

Deutsch, Robert. 1999. *Messages from the Past: Hebrew Bullae from the Time of Isaiah through the Destruction of the First Temple*. Tel Aviv: Archaeological Center Publications.

Dick, Michael B. 2006. "The Neo-Assyrian Royal Lion Hunt and Yahweh's Answer to Job." *JBL* 125: 243–70.

Dion, Paul E. 1991. "YHWH as Storm-God and Sun-God: The Double Legacy of Egypt and Canaan as Reflected in Psalm 104." *ZAW* 103: 43–71.

Dorrell, Peter G. 1994. *Photography in Archaeology and Conservation*. Cambridge Manuals in Archaeology. Cambridge University Press.

Ebach, Jürgen. 2004. "Die Einheit von Sehen und Hören: Beobachtungen und Überlegungen zu Bilderverbot und Sprachbildern im Alten Testament." In *Im Zwischenreich der Bilder*, edited by Rainer M. Jacobi, Bernhard Marx, and Gerlinde Strohmaier-Wiederanders, 77–104. Erkenntnis und Glaube: Schriften der Evangelischen Forschungsakademie 35. Leipzig: Evangelische Verlagsanstalt.

Egger-Wenzel, Renate. 2005. "'Faith in God' Rather Than 'Fear of God' in Ben Sira and Job: A Necessary Adjustment in Terminology and Understanding." In *Intertextual Studies in Ben Sira and Tobit: Essay sin Honor of Alexander A. Di Lella*, edited by Jeremy Corley and Vincent T. M. Skemp, 211–26. The Catholic Biblical Quarterly Monograph Series 38. Washington: Catholic Biblical Association.

Eggler, Jürg. 2005. "Baal." In *Iconography of Deities and Demons in the Ancient Near East: An Iconographic Dictionary with Special Emphasis on First-Millennium BCE Palestine/Israel*. Cited 26 July 2011. Online: http://www.religionswissenschaft.unizh.ch/idd/prepublications/e_idd_baal.pdf (text); http://www.religionswissenschaft.unizh.ch/idd/prepublications/e_idd_illustrations_baal.pdf (images).

_____. Forthcoming. "Iconography of Animals (Mammals)." In *Encyclopedia of Material Culture in the Biblical World*, edited by Angelika Berlejung et al. Tübingen: Mohr Siebeck.

Eggler, Jürg and Othmar Keel. 2006. *Corpus der Siegel-Amulette aus Jordanien: vom Neolithikum bis zur Perserzeit.* OBO.SA. 25. Fribourg/Göttingen: Academic Press/Vandenhoeck & Ruprecht.

Eichler, Raanan. 2011. "כרקבי תפקיד הארון." *Tarbiz* 79/2: 165–85.

Eichrodt, Walther. 1967. *Theology of the Old Testament.* OTL. Vol. 2. Translated by J. A. Baker. Philadelphia: Westminster.

Eilberg-Schwartz, Howard. 1990. *The Savage in Judaism: An Anthropology of Israelite Religion and Ancient Judaism.* Bloomington: Indiana University Press.

Elayi, J. and A. G. Elayi. 2009. *The Coinage of the Phoenician City of Tyre in the Persian Period (5th–4th Cent. BCE).* OLA 188. Studia Phoenicia 20. Leuven: Peeters.

Elbow, Peter. 1998. *Writing Without Teachers.* New York: Oxford University Press.

Elkins James. 2003. *Visual Studies: A Skeptical Introduction.* London: Routledge.

El-Safadi, Hicham. 1974. "Die Entstehung der syrischen Glyptik und ihre Entwicklung in der Zeit von Zimrilim bis Ammitaqumma [1]." *UF* 6: 313–52.

Enns, Peter. 2012. *The Evolution of Adam: What the Bible Does and Doesn't Say about Human Origins.* Grand Rapids, MI: Brazos.

Eravşar, Osman. 2008. "Miniature Paintings of Prophet Elija (Ilyas) and al Khodor (Hidir) in the Ottomon Period." Aram 20: 137–62.

Exum, J. Cheryl. 2005. *The Song of Songs: A Commentary.* OTL. Louisville: Westminster John Knox.

Exum, J. Cheryl and Ela Nutu, eds. 2007. *Between the Text and the Canvas: The Bible and Art in Dialogue.* The Bible in the Modern World 13. Sheffield: Sheffield Phoenix.

Fauconnier, Gilles and Mark Turner. 2002. *The Way We Think: Conceptual Blending and the Mind's Hidden Complexities.* New York: Basic Books.

Fee, Gordon D. and Mark L. Strauss. 2007. *How to Choose a Translation for All Its Worth: A Guide to Understanding and Using Bible Versions.* Grand Rapids, MI: Zondervan.

Feldmeier, Reinhard and Hermann Spieckermann. 2011. *God of the Living: A Biblical Theology.* Translated by Mark E. Biddle. Waco: Baylor University Press.

Finkel, Irving. 2014. *The Ark before Noah: Decoding the Story of the Flood.* London: Hodder & Stoughton.

Finkelstein, Israel. 2000. "Omride Architecture." *ZDPV* 116: 114–38.

Floor, Sebastian J. 2007. "Four Bible Translation Types and Some Criteria to Distinguish Them." *Journal of Translation* 3/2: 1–22.

Flückiger-Hawker, Esther. 1999. *Urnamma of Ur in Sumerian Literary Tradition.* OBO 166. Fribourg/Göttingen: University Press/Vandenhoeck & Ruprecht.

Forceville, Charles. 1996. *Pictorial Metaphor in Advertising.* New York: Routledge.

Franke, Patrick. 2000. *Begegnung mit Khidr: Quellenstudien zum Imaginären im traditionellen Islam.* Beiruter Texte und Studien 79. Beirut: Franz Steiner.

Frankfort, Henri. 1965. *Cylinder Seals: A Documentary Essay on the Art and Religion of the Ancient Near East.* London: Gregg.

_____. *The Art and Architecture of the Ancient Orient.* 1996. 5th ed. Yale University Press Pelican History of Art. New Haven: Yale University Press.

Frei, Peter and Klaus Koch. 1996. *Reichsidee und Reichsorganisation im Perserreich.* 2d ed. OBO 55. Freiburg/Göttingen: Universitätsverlag/Vandenhoeck & Ruprecht.

Fretheim, Terence E. 1984. *The Suffering of God: An Old Testament Perspective.* Philadelphia: Fortress.

Friebel, Kelvin. 1999. *Jeremiah's and Ezekiel's Sign-Acts: Rhetorical Nonverbal Communication.* JSOT-Sup 283. Sheffield: Sheffield Academic.

Fuhs, H. F. 1990. "yārēʾ, yirʾâ, môrāʾ." In *Theological Dictionary of the Old Testament,* edited by G. Johannes Botterweck and Helmer Ringgren, translated by David E. Green, 4:290–315. Grand Rapids: Eerdmans.

Gaifman, Milette. 2012. *Aniconism in Greek Antiquity.* Oxford Studies in Ancient Culture and Representation. Oxford: Oxford University Press.

Galling, Kurt, ed. 1977. *Biblisches Reallexikon.* 2d ed. Handbuch zum Alten Testament 1/1. Tübingen: Mohr.

Gansell, Amy. 2014. "The Iconography of Ideal Feminine Beauty Represented in the Hebrew Bible and

Iron Age Levantine Ivory Sculpture." In *Image, Text, Exegesis: Iconographic Interpretation and the Hebrew Bible,* edited by Izaak J. de Hulster and Joel M. LeMon, 46–70. LHBOTS 588. London: Bloomsbury.

Garbini, Giovanni. 2012. *I Filistei: Gli antagonisti di Israele.* Studi biblici 170. Brescia: Paideia.

Garr, W. Randall. 2003. *In His Own Image and Likeness: Humanity, Divinity, and Monotheism.* CHANE 15. Leiden: Brill.

Garrison, Mark B. 2000. "Achaemenid Iconography as Evidenced by Glyptic Art: Subject Matter, Social Function, Audience and Diffusion." In *Images as Media: Sources for the Cultural History of the Near East and the Eastern Mediterranean: 1st Millenium BCE,* edited by Christoph Uehlinger, 115–63. OBO 175. Freiburg/Göttingen: Universitätsverlag/Vandenhoeck & Ruprecht.

_____. 2010. "Archers at Persepolis: The Emergence of Royal Ideology at the Heart of the Empire." In *The World of Achaemenid Persia: History, Art and Society in Iran and the Ancient Near East,* edited by John Curtis and St. John Simpson, 337–68. New York: I. B. Tauris.

Garrison, Mark B. and Margaret Cool Root. 1998. *Persepolis Seal Studies: An Introduction with Provisional Concordances of Seal Numbers and Associated Documents on Fortification Tablets 1–2087.* Achaemenid History 9. Leiden: Nederlands Instituut Voor Het Nabije Oosten.

_____. 2001. *Seal Impressions on the Persepolis Fortification Tablets, Volume 1: Images of Heroic Encounter.* OIP 117. Chicago: The Oriental Institute.

Gellman, Jerome I. 1994. *The Fear, the Trembling, and the Fire. Kierkegaard and the Hasidic Masters on the Binding of Isaac.* Lanham, MD: University Press of America.

Gerstenberger, Erhard S. 1988. *Psalms, Part 1 with an Introduction to Cultic Poetry.* FOTL 14. Grand Rapids, MI: Eerdmans.

_____. 2001. *Psalms, Part 2, and Lamentations.* FOTL 15. Grand Rapids, MI: Eerdmans.

Gertz, Jan Christian, Angelika Berlejung, Konrad Schmid, and Markus Witte, eds. 2012. *T&T Clark Handbook of the Old Testament: An Introduction to the Literature, Religion and History of the Old Testament.* New York/London: T&T Clark.

Getzov, Nimrod. 2008. "Ha-Gosherim." In *NEAEHL* 5: 1759–61.

Gibson, McGuire and Augusta McMahon. 1995. "Investigation of the Early Dynastic-Akkadian Transition: Report of the 18th and 19th Seasons of Excavation in Area WF, Nippur." *Iraq* 57: 1–39.

Goetz, J. L., J. Spencer-Rodgers, and K. Peng. 2008. "Dialectical Emotions: How Cultural Epistemologies Influence the Regulation of Emotional Complexity." In *Handbook of Motivation and Cognition across Cultures,* edited by Richard M. Sorrentino and Susumu Yamaguchi, 17–39. San Diego: Academic Press.

Good, Robert M. 1983. *The Sheep of His Pasture: A Study of the Hebrew Noun ʿam(m) and its Semitic Cognates.* HSM 29. Chico: Scholars Press.

Gopher, Avi and Vered Eshed. 2012. "Burials and Human Skeletal Remains from Naḥal Zehora II in PN Perspective." In *Village Communities of the Pottery Neolithic Period in the Menashe Hills, Israel: Archaeological Investigations at the Sites of Naḥal Zehora,* edited by Avi Gopher, 3:1389–1412. 3 vols. Tel Aviv: Emery and Claire Yass Publications in Archaeology.

Görg, Manfred. 1986. "Der starke Arm Pharaos: Beobachtungen zum Belegspektrum einer Metapher in Palästina und Ägypten." In *Hommages à François Daumas,* edited by H. Altenmüller, 1:323–30. 2 vols. Montpellier: Université de Montpellier.

Gould, Stephen Jay. 1999. *Rocks of Ages: Science and Religion in the Fullness of Life.* New York: Ballentine.

Graesser, Carl F. 1972. "Standing Stones in Ancient Palestine." *BA* 35: 34–63.

Grayson, A. Kirk. 1991. *Assyrian Rulers of the Early First Millennium BC (1114–859 BC).* RIMA 2. Toronto: University of Toronto Press.

Green. Anthony. 1993–1997. "Mischwesen B." In *Reallexikon der Assyriologie und vorderasiatischen Archäologie,* vol. 8, edited by D.O. Edzard, 246–64. Berlin: de Gruyter.

Gressmann, Hugo. 1927 [1909]. *Altorientalische Bilder zum Alten Testament.* 2d ed. Berlin: de Gruyter.

Grintz, Yehoshua M. 1957. *Sefer Yehudith: A Reconstruction of the Original Hebrew Text with Introduction, Commentary, Appendices and Indices.* Jerusalem: Bialik Institute.

Groenewegen-Frankfort, H. A. 1951. *Arrest and Movement: An Essay on Space and Time in the Representational Art of the Ancient Near East.* Chicago: University of Chicago Press.

Gruber, Mayer I. 1975. "Akkadian labān appi in the Light of Art and Literature." Journal of Ancient Near Eastern Studies 7: 73–83.

_____. 1980. *Aspects of Nonverbal Communication in the Ancient Near East.* 2 vols. Studia Pohl 12/I-II. Rome: Biblical Institute Press.

_____. 1990. "Fear, Anxiety and Reverence in Akkadian, Biblical Hebrew and Other North-West Semitic Languages." VT 40: 411–22. = Gruber 1992:193–208.

_____. 1992. *The Motherhood of God and Other Studies.* South Florida Studies in the History of Judaism 57. Atlanta: Scholars Press.

_____. 2007. "Love Conquers Anger: The Aqedah in the Rabbinic Liturgy." In *Unbinding the Binding of Isaac,* edited by Mishael Caspi and John T. Greene, 1–8. Lanham, MD: University Press of America.

Grueber, Herbert A. 1910. *The Coins of the Roman Republique in the British Museum.* 3 vols. London: Trustees of the British Museum.

Grün, Anselm. 2000 [German orig. 1999]. *Everybody Has an Angel.* 2d ed. New York: Crossroad.

Gutmann, Joseph. 2001. "The Sacrifice of Abraham in Timurid Art." *The Journal of Walter's Art Museum* 59: 131–35.

Gutt, Ernst-August. 2000. *Translation and Relevance: Cognition and Context.* Manchester: St. Jerome.

Hall, Emma Swan. 1986. *The Pharaoh Smites His Enemies: A Comparative Study.* Münchner Ägyptologische Studien 44. Munich: Deutscher Kunstverlag.

Hallo, William W. 1980. "Biblical History in Its Near Eastern Setting: The Contextual Approach." In *Scripture in Context Essays on the Comparative Method,* edited by Carl D. Evans, William W. Hallo, and John B. White, 1–26. PTMS 34. Pittsburgh: Pickwick.

_____. 1990. "Compare and Contrast: The Contextual Approach to Biblical Literature." In *The Bible in the Light of Cuneiform Literature: Scripture in Context III,* edited by William W. Hallo, Bruce William Jones, and Gerald L. Mattingly, 1–30. ANETS 8. Lewiston, NY: Mellen.

Hanhart, Robert. 1979. *Text und Textgeschichte des Buches Judith.* Mitteilungen des Septuaginta-Unternehmens 14. Göttingen: Vandenhoeck & Ruprecht.

_____. 1990. *Dodekapropheton: Sacharja 1–8.* Biblischer Kommentar, Altes Testament 14/7. Neukirchen-Vluyn: Neukirchener Verlag.

Hanson, Paul D. 1973. "Zechariah 9 and the Recapitulation of an Ancient Ritual Pattern." *JBL* 92: 37–59.

Hartenstein, Friedhelm. 2005. "Ikonographie." In *Proseminar I: Altes Testament: Ein Arbeitsbuch,* edited by Siegfried Kreuzer, 173–86. Stuttgart: Kohlhammer.

_____. 2008. "Weltbild und Bilderverbot. Kosmologische Implikationen des biblischen Monotheismus." In *Die Welt als Bild. Interdisziplinäre Beiträge zur Visualität von Weltbildern,* edited by Christoph Markschies and Johannes Zachhuber, 15–37. Arbeiten zur Kirchengeschichte 107. Berlin: de Gruyter.

Harvey, John. 2013. *The Bible as Visual Culture: When Text Becomes Image.* The Bible in the Modern World 57. Sheffield: Sheffield Phoenix.

Hazony, Yoram. 2012. *The Philosophy of Hebrew Scripture.* Cambridge: Cambridge University Press.

Henle, Paul. 1965. "Metaphor." In *Language, Thought, Culture,* edited by Paul Henle, 173–95. Ann Arbor: University of Michigan Press.

Hess, Richard. 2005. *Song of Songs.* Baker Commentary on the Old Testament Wisdom and Psalms. Grand Rapids, MI: Baker Academic.

Herrmann, Christian. 1994. *Ägyptische Amulette aus Palästina/Israel: mit einem Ausblick auf ihre Rezeption durch das Alte Testament.* Vol. 1. OBO 138. Freiburg/Göttingen: Universitätsverlag/ Vandenhoeck & Ruprecht.

_____. 2002. *Ägyptische Amulette aus Palästina/Israel.* Vol. 2. OBO 184. Freiburg/Göttingen: Universitätsverlag/Vandenhoeck & Ruprecht.

_____. 2006. *Ägyptische Amulette aus Palästina/Israel.* Vol. 3. OBO.SA 24. Fribourg/Göttingen: Academic Press/Vandenhoeck & Ruprecht.

Herrmann, Christian and Thomas Staubli. 2010. *1001 Amulett. Altägyptischer Zauber, monotheisierte Talismane, säkulare Magie.* Freiburg/Stuttgart: BIBEL+ORIENT Museum/Katholisches Bibelwerk.

Hiebert, Theodore. 1992. "Theophany in the OT." In *Anchor Bible Dictionary,* edited by David Noel Freedman, 6:505–11. 6 vols. New York: Doubleday.

Hilbrands, Walter. 2006. "Das Verhältnis der Engel zu Jahwe im Alten Testament, insbesondere im Buch Exodus." In *The Interpretation of Exodus: Studies in Honor of Cornelis Houtman,* edited by Riemer Roukema, 81–96. CBET 44. Leuven: Peeters.

Hill, Harriet S. 2006. *The Bible at Cultural Crossroads: From Translation to Communication.* Manchester: St. Jerome.

Hoffmeier, James K. 1986. "The Arm of God Versus the Arm of Pharaoh in the Exodus Narratives." *Biblica* 67: 378–87.

Holladay, William L. 1986. *Jeremiah 1: A Commentary on the Book of the Prophet Jeremiah Chapters 1–25.* Hermeneia. Philadelphia: Fortress.

Hornung, Erik. 1977. "Himmelsvorstellungen." In *Lexikon der Ägyptologie,* edited by Wolfgang Helck, Eberhard Otto, and Wolfhart Westendorf, 2.1215–18. 7 vols. Wiesbaden: Harrassowitz.

_____. 1982. *Conceptions of God in Ancient Egypt: The One and the Many.* Translated by John Baines. Ithaca: Cornell University Press.

_____. 1999. *Akhenaten and the Religion of Light.* Translated by David Lorton. Ithaca: Cornell University Press.

Horowitz, Wayne. 2011. *Mesopotamian Cosmic Geography.* Mesopotamian Civilizations 8. Winona Lake, IN: Eisenbrauns.

Hossfeld, Frank-Lothar and Erich Zenger. 2005. *Psalms 2: A Commentary on Psalms 50–100.* Edited by Klaus Balzer. Translated by Linda M. Maloney. Hermeneia. Minneapolis: Fortress.

_____. 2011. *Psalms 3: A Commentary on Psalms 101–150.* Edited by Klaus Balzer. Translated by Linda M. Maloney. Hermeneia. Minneapolis: Fortress, 2011.

Houtman, Cornelis. 1993. *Der Himmel im Alten Testament: Israels Weltbild und Weltanschauung.* OTS 30. Leiden: Brill.

_____. 1993–2002. *Exodus.* Historical Commentary on the Old Testament. 4 vols. Kampen/Leuven: Kok/Peeters.

Hrobon, Bohdan. 2010. *Ethical Dimension of Cult in the Book of Isaiah.* BZAW 418. Berlin: de Gruyter.

Hübner, Ulrich. 2009. "Der Mondtempel auf Ruğm al-Kursī in der Ammonitis." In *Israel zwischen den Mächten: Festschrift für Stefan Timm zum 65. Geburtstag,* edited by Michael Pietsch and Friedhelm Hartenstein, 145–53. AOAT 364. Münster: Ugarit-Verlag.

Hulster, Izaak J. de. 2009a. *Iconographic Exegesis and Third Isaiah.* FAT II/36. Tübingen: Mohr Siebeck.

_____. 2009b. "Illuminating Images: A Historical Position and Method for Iconographic Exegesis." In *Iconography and Biblical Studies. Proceedings of the Iconography Sessions at the J EABS/SBL Conference: 22–26 July 2007, Vienna, Austria,* edited by Izaak J. de Hulster and Rüdiger Schmitt, 139–62. AOAT 361. Münster: Ugarit-Verlag.

_____. 2012a. "God en de kosmos in Genesis 1." *Amsterdamse Cahier voor Exegese van de Bijbel en zijn Tradities* 27: 35–49.

_____. 2012b. Review of John H. Walton, *Genesis 1 as Ancient Cosmology. Journal of the Hebrew Scriptures* 12. Cited 9 June 2015. Online: http://www.jhsonline.org/reviews/reviews_new/review589.htm.

_____. 2013. "(Ohn)Macht der Bilder? (Ohn)Macht der Menschen? TC242.5 in ihrem Entstehungs- und in ihrem Forschungskontext." In *Macht des Geldes–Macht der Bilder,* edited by A. Lykke, 45–68. Abhandlungen des Deutschen Palästina-Vereins 42. Wiesbaden: Harrassowitz.

_____. Forthcoming (a). "Religion, Pictoriality, and Materiality: A Hebrew Bible Perspective." *Religion and Material Culture: Studying Religion, Religious Elements and Cultural Memory on the Basis of Objects, Architecture and Space: Proceedings of an International Conference Held at the Center for Bible and Cultural Memory (BiCuM), University of Copenhagen and the National Museum of Denmark, Copenhagen, May 6–8, 2011,* edited by Lisbeth Bredholt Christensen and Jesper Tae Jensen. Turnhout: Brepols.

_____. Forthcoming (b). "The Challenge of Hebrew Bible Love Poetry: A Pleonastic Approach to the Translation of Metaphor."

Hundley, Michael B. 2011. *Keeping Heaven on Earth: Safeguarding the Divine Presence in the Priestly Tabernacle.* FAT II/50. Tübingen: Mohr Siebeck.

Ilan, Tal. 1999. *Integrating Women into Second Temple History.* Text and Studies in Ancient Judaism 76. Tübingen: Mohr Siebeck.

Imhoof-Blumer, Friedrich. 1871. *Choix de monnaies grecques du cabinet de F. Imhoof-Blumer.* Winterthur: s.n.

Israeli, Y., ed. 1999. *In the Light of the Menorah: Story of a Symbol.* Jerusalem: Israel Museum.

Jacob, Benno. 2000. *Das Buch Genesis.* Repr. ed. Stuttgart: Calwer.

_____. 2007. *The First Book of the Bible.* Abridged, edited, and translated by Ernst Jacob and Walter Jacob. Jersey City: Ktav.

Janowski, Bernd. 1990. "Tempel und Schöpfung: Schöpfungstheologische Aspekte der priesterschriftlichen Heiligtumskonzeption." *Jahrbuch für Biblische Theologie* 5: 37–69.

_____. 2001. "Das biblische Weltbild. Eine methodische Skizze." In *Das biblische Weltbild und seine altorientalischen Kontexte,* edited by Bernd Janowski, Beate Ego, and Annette Kruger, 3–26. FAT 32. Tübingen: Mohr Siebeck.

Japhet, Sara. "יד ושם (Isa 56:5) – A Different Proposal." *Maarav* 8: 69–80.

Jeremias, Jörg. 1977. *Theophanie: Die Geschichte einer alttestamentlichen Gattung.* 2d ed. Neukirchen-Vluyn: Neukirchener Verlag.

Johnston, Philip. 2002. *Shades of Sheol: Death and Afterlife in the Old Testament.* Downers Grove, IL: IVP.

Jones, David A. 2011. *Angels: A Very Short Introduction.* Oxford: Oxford University Press.

Jónsson, Gunnlaugur A. 1988. *The Image of God: Genesis 1:26–28 in a Century of Old Testament Research.* ConBOT 26. Lund: Almqvist & Wiksell.

Kantorowicz, Ernst H. 1957. *The King's Two Bodies: A Study in Medieval Political Theology.* Princeton: Princeton University Press.

Karrer, Martin and Wolfgang Kraus, eds. 2011. *Septuaginta Deutsch: Erläuterung und Kommentar.* 2 vols. Stuttgart: Deutsche Bibelgesellschaft.

Katz, Dina. 2003. *The Image of the Netherworld in the Sumerian Sources.* Bethesda, MD: CDL.

Keel, Othmar. 1969. *Feinde und Gottesleugner: Studien zum Image der Widersacher in den Individualpsalmen.* Stuttgarter biblische Monographien 7. Stuttgart: Verlag Katholisches Bibelwerk.

_____. 1972. *Die Welt der altorientalischen Bildsymbolik und das Alte Testament: Am Beispiel der Psalmen.* Zürich/Benziger/Einsiedeln: Neukirchener Verlag.

_____. 1974. *Wirkmächtig Siegeszeichen im Alten Testament: Ikonographische Studien zu Jos 8,18.26; Ex 17,8–13; 2 Kön 13,14–19 und 1 Kön 22,11.* OBO 5. Freiburg/Göttingen: Universitätsverlag/Vandenhoeck & Ruprecht.

_____. 1977. *Jahwe-Visionen und Siegelkunst: eine neue Deutung der Majestätsschilderungen in Jes 6, Ez 1 und 10 und Sach 4.* Stuttgart Bibelstudien 84/85. Stuttgart:Verlag Katholisches Bibelwerk.

_____. 1982. "Der Pharao als 'Vollkommene Sonne': Ein neuer ägypto-palästinischer Skarabäentyp." In *Egyptological Studies,* edited by Sarah Israelit-Groll, 406–529. Scripta Hierosolymitana 28. Jerusalem: Magnes.

_____. 1985. "Das sogenannte altorientalische Weltbild." *Bibel und Kirche* 40: 157–61.

_____. 1989a. "Die Ω-Gruppe: mittelbronzezeitlicher Stempelsiegel-Typ mit erhabenem Relief aus Anatolien-Nordsyrien und Palästina." In *Studien zu den Stempelsiegeln aus Palästina/Israel II,* edited by Othmar Keel and Hildi Keel-Leu, 39–87. OBO 88. Freiburg/Göttingen: Universitätsverlag/Vandenhoeck & Ruprecht.

_____. 1989b. "Jahwe in der Rolle der Muttergottheit." *Orientierung* 53: 89–92.

_____. 1990. "Der Bogen als Herrschaftssymbol: Einige unveröffentlichte Skarabäen aus Ägypten und Israel zum Thema 'Jagd und Krieg.'" In *Studien zu den Stempelsiegeln aus Palästina/Israel III: Die Frühe Eisenzeit: Ein Workshop,* edited by Othmar Keel, Menakhem Shuval, and Christoph Uehlinger, 27–65. OBO 100. Freiburg/Göttingen: Universitätsverlag/Vandenhoeck & Ruprecht.

_____. 1992a. *Das Recht der Bilder gesehen zu werden: Drei Fallstudien zur Methode der Interpretation altorientalischer Bilder.* OBO 122. Freiburg/Göttingen: Universitätsverlag/Vandenhoeck & Ruprecht.

_____. 1992b. "Iconography and the Bible." In *Anchor Bible Dictionary,* edited by David Noel Freedman, 3:358–74. 6 vols. New York: Doubleday.

_____. 1992c. "'Mit Cherubim und Serafim.' Ein Exegetenstreit und seine theologischen Hintergründe." *Bibel heute* 28: 171–74.

_____. 1993. "Fern von Jerusalem: Frühe Jerusalemer Kulttraditionen und ihre Träger und Trägerinnen." In *Zion, Ort der Begegnung: Festschrift für Laurentius Klein zur Vollendung des 65. Lebensjahres,* edited by F. Hahn et al., 439–50. BBB 90. Bodenheim: Athenäum–Hain–Hanstein.

_____. 1994 [German orig.: 1986, 1992²]. *Song of Songs: A Continental Commentary.* Translated by Frederick J. Gaiser. Minneapolis: Fortress.

_____. 1995. *Corpus der Stempelsiegel-Amulette aus Palästina/Israel. Von den Anfängen bis zur Perserzeit. Einleitung.* OBO.SA 10. Freiburg/Göttingen: Universitätsverlag/Vandenhoeck & Ruprecht.

_____, 1997a. *Corpus der Stempelsiegel-Amulette aus Palästina/Israel: von den Anfängen bis zur Perserzeit: Katalog Band I: Von Tell Abu Faraǧ bis ʿAtlit.* OBO.SA 13. Freiburg: Universitätsverlag; Göttingen: Vandenhoeck & Ruprecht.

_____. 1997b [German orig.: 1972, 1996⁵]. *The Symbolism of the Biblical World. Ancient Near Eastern Iconography and the Book of Psalms.* Translated by Timothy J. Hallett. Winona Lake, IN: Eisenbrauns.

_____. 1998. *Goddesses and Trees, New Moon and Yahweh: Two Natural Phenomena in Ancient Near Eastern Art and in the Hebrew Bible.* JSOTSup 261. Sheffield: Sheffield Academic.

_____. 2007. *Die Geschichte Jerusalems und die Entstehung des Monotheismus.* 2 vols. Orte und Landschaften der Bibel 4/1. Göttingen: Vandenhoeck & Ruprecht.

_____. 2010. "Antike Vorläufer der Engel – Von den heidnischen Ahnen einiger jüdisch-christlicher Engel-Vorstellungen." In *Engel: Mittler zwischen Himmel und Erde,* edited by Klaus Peter Franzl, 226–49. Berlin: Frölich und Kaufmann.

_____. 2010a. *Corpus der Stempelsiegel-Amulette aus Palastina/Israel. Von den Anfangen bis zur Perserzeit. Katalog Band II: Von Bahan bis Tel Eton.* OBO.SA 29. Fribourg/Göttingen: Academic Press/Vandenhoeck & Ruprecht.

_____. 2010b. *Corpus der Stempelsiegel-Amulette aus Palastina/Israel. Von den Anfangen bis zur Perserzeit. Katalog Band III: Von Tell el-Farʿa bis Tel el-Fir.* OBO.SA 31. Fribourg/Göttingen: Academic Press/Vandenhoeck & Ruprecht.

_____. 2013. *Corpus der Stempelsiegel-Amulette aus Palästina/Israel. Von den Anfängen bis zur Perserzeit. Katalog Band IV: Von Tel Gamma bis Chirbet Husche.* OBO.SA 33. Fribourg/Göttingen: Academic Press/Vandenhoeck & Ruprecht.

Keel, Othmar and Silvia Schroer. 2002. *Schöpfung. Biblische Theologien im Kontext altorientalischer Religionen.* Freiburg/Göttingen: Universitätsverlag/Vandenhoeck & Ruprecht.

Keel, Othmar, Menakhem Shuval, and Christoph Uehlinger. 1999. *Studien zu den Stempelsiegeln aus Palästina/Israel, Band III.* OBO 100. Freiburg/Göttingen: Universitätsverlag/Vandenhoeck & Ruprecht.

Keel, Othmar and Christoph Uehlinger. 1998 [German orig.: 1992, 2012⁷]. *Gods, Goddesses, and Images of God in Ancient Israel.* Translated by T. H. Trapp. Minneapolis: Fortress.

Keel-Leu, Hildi, and Beatrice Teissier. 2004. *The Ancient Near Eastern Cylinder Seals of the Collections "Bible+Orient" of the University of Fribourg.* OBO 200. Fribourg/Göttingen: Academic Press/Vandenhoeck & Ruprecht.

Kemp, Barry J. 1989. *Ancient Egypt: Anatomy of a Civilization.* London/New York: Routledge.

Kempinski, Aharon and Ronny Reich. 1992. *The Architecture of Ancient Israel: From the Prehistoric to the Persian Periods.* Jerusalem: Israel Exploration Society.

Kent, Roland G. 1953. *Old Persian: Grammar, Texts, Lexicon.* 2d ed. AOS 33. New Haven: American Oriental Society.

King, L. W. 1912. *Babylonian Boundary-Stones and Memorial-Tablets in the British Museum.* London: Trustees of the British Museum.

Kletter, Raz, Irit Ziffer, and Wolfgang Zwickel. 2010. *Yavneh I: The Excavation of the "Temple-hill" Repository Pit and Cult Stands.* OBO.SA 30. Fribourg/Göttingen: Academic Press/Vandenhoeck & Reuprecht.

Klingbeil, Martin. 1999. *Yahweh Fighting from Heaven: God as Warrior and as God of Heaven in the Hebrew Psalter and Ancient Near Eastern Iconography.* OBO 169. Fribourg/Göttingen: University Press/Vandenhoeck & Ruprecht.

Knight, Douglas A. 2006. *Rediscovering the Traditions of Israel.* 3d ed. Atlanta: Society of Biblical Literature.

Köckert, Matthias. 2008. "Suffering from Formlessness: The Ban on Images in Exilic Times." In *Exile and Suffering: A Selection of Papers Read at the 50th Anniversary Meeting of the Old Testament Society of South Africa OTWSA/OTSSA, Pretoria, August 2007,* edited by Bob Becking and Dirk Human, 33–49. Oudtestamentische Studiën 50. Leiden: Brill.

Korpel, Marjo C. A. 1990. *A Rift in the Clouds. Ugaritic and Hebrew descriptions of the Divine.* UBL 8. Münster: Ugarit Verlag.

Kövecses, Zoltan. 2010. *Metaphor: A Practical Introduction.* 2d ed. Oxford: Oxford University Press.

Kraus, Hans-Joachim. 1993. *Psalms 60–150: A Continental Commentary.* Minneapolis: Fortress.

Krebernik, Manfred. 1993–1997. "Mondgott A. I. in Mesopotamien." In *Reallexikon der Assyriologie und Vorderasiastischen Archäologie,* edited by Erich Ebeling, Bruno Meissner, and Dietz O. Edzard, 8:360–69. 16 vols. Berlin: de Gruyter.

Kriss, Rudolf and Hubert Kriss-Heinrich. 1960. *Volksglaube im Bereich des Islam. Bd. I: Wallfahrtswesen und Heiligenverehrung.* Wiesbaden: O. Harrassowitz.

Kroneman, Dick. 2004. "The Lord is My Shepherd: An Exploration into the Theory and Practice of Translating Biblical Metaphor." Ph.D. diss. Free University [Vrije Universiteit], Amsterdam.

Küchler, Max. 1989. "'Wir haben seinen Stern gesehen …' (Mt 2,2)." *Bibel und Kirche* 44: 179–86.

Kurht, Amélie. 2007. *The Persian Empire: A Corpus of Sources from the Achaemenid Period.* London: Routledge.

Labuschagne, C. J. 1966. *The Incomparability of Yahweh in the Old Testament.* Leiden: Brill.

Lakoff, George. 1993. "The Contemporary Theory of Metaphor." In *Metaphor and Thought,* edited by Anthony Ortony, 202–51. Cambridge: Cambridge University Press.

Lakoff, George and Mark Johnson. 2003 [1980]. *Metaphors We Live By.* Chicago: University of Chicago Press.

Landsberger, Benno. 1976 [German orig: 1926]. *The Conceptual Autonomy of the Babylonian World.* Translated by Thorkild Jacobsen, Benjamin Foster, and Heinrich von Siebenthal. Monographs on the Ancient Near East 1/4. Malibu: Undena.

Langdon, Stephen. 1919. "Gesture in Sumerian and Babylonian Prayer: A Study in Babylonian and Assyrian Archaeology." *Journal of the Royal Asiatic Society* 51: 531–56.

Layard, Austen Henry. 1852. *A Popular Account of Discoveries at Nineveh.* New York: Harper.

Leclant, Jean. 1956, "La 'Mascarade' des bœufs gras et le triomphe de l'Egypte." *Mitteilungen des Deutschen Archäologischen Instituts Abteilung Kairo* 14: 128–45.

Lecoq, Pierre. 1984. "Un problème de religion achéménide: Ahura Mazda ou Xvarnah?" In *Orientalia J. Duchesne-Guillemin Emerito Oblata,* 301–26. Acta Iranica 23. Leiden: Brill.

Lefebvre, Gustave. 1923. *Le Tombeau de Petosiris.* 3 vols. Le Caire: Institut Français d'Archéologie Orientale.

LeMon, Joel M. 2009. "Iconographic Approaches: The Iconic Structure of Psalm 17." In *Method Matters: Essays on the Interpretation of the Hebrew Bible in Honor of David L. Petersen,* edited by Joel M. LeMon and Kent H. Richards, 143–68. SBLRBS 56. Atlanta: Society of Biblical Literature.

———. 2010. *Yahweh's Winged Form in the Psalms: Exploring Congruent Iconography and Texts.* OBO 242. Fribourg/Göttingen: Academic Press/Vandenhoeck & Ruprecht.

———. 2013. "Yahweh's Hand and the Iconography of the Blow in Psalm 81:14–16." *JBL* 132: 865–882.

LeMon, Joel M. and Brent A. Strawn. 2015. "Once More, Yhwh and Company at Kuntillet 'Ajrud." *Maarav.*

Lescow, Theodor. 1993. "Sacharja 1–8: Verkündigung und Komposition." *Biblische Notizen* 68: 75–99.

Levenson, Jon D. 1984. "The Temple and the World." *JR* 64/3: 275–98.

———. 1994. *Creation and the Persistence of Evil: The Jewish Drama of Divine Omnipotence.* Rev. ed. Princeton: Princeton University Press.

Lewis, Theodore J. 1992. "Dead, Abode of the." In *The Anchor Bible Dictionary*, edited by David Noel Freedman, 2:101–105. 6 vols. New York: Doubleday.

Lippman, Bodoff. 2005. *The Binding of Isaac, Religious Murders and Kabbalah: Seeds of Jewish Extremism and Alienation?* Jerusalem/New York: Devora.

Longman, Tremper III. 2008. "Fear of the Lord." In D*ictionary of the Old Testament: Wisdom, Poetry & Writings,* edited by Tremper Longman III and Peter Enns, 201–205. Downers Grove, IL: IVP Academic.

Loretz, Oswald and Ingo Kottsieper. 1987. *Colometry in Ugaritic and Biblical Poetry: Introduction, Illustrations and Topical Bibliography.* Altenberge: CIS-Verlag.

Loud, Gordon. 1939. *The Megiddo Ivories.* OIP 52. Chicago: The Oriental Institute.

Lowth, Robert. 1971 [Latin orig.: 1753]. *Lectures on the Sacred Poetry of the Hebrews.* New York: Garland.

Lurker, Manfred. 1984. *An Illustrated Dictionary of the Gods and Symbols of Ancient Egypt.* Revised edition. London; Thames and Hudson.

Macalister, Robert Alexander Stewart. 1903. "Second Quarterly Report on the Excavation of Gezer." *Palestine Exploration Fund Quarterly Statement* 35: 7–50.

MacDonald, Nathan. 2007. "Aniconism in the Old Testament." In *The God of Israel,* edited by Robert P. Gordon, 20–34. University of Cambridge Oriental Publications 64. Cambridge: Cambridge University Press.

_____. 2013. "A Text in Search of Context: The *Imago Dei* in the First Chapters of Genesis." In *Leshon Limmudim: Essays in the Language and Literature of the Hebrew Bible in Honour of A. A. Macintosh,* edited by David A. Baer and Robert P. Gordon, 3–16. LHBOTS 593. London: Bloomsbury.

Mach, Michael. 1992. *Entwicklungsstadien des jüdischen Engelglaubens in vorrabbinischer Zeit.* Texte und Studien zum antiken Judentum 34. Tübingen: Mohr Siebeck.

Madden, Frederic W. 1864. *History of Jewish Coinage and of Money in the Old and New Testament.* London: Bernard Quaritch.

Magen, Ursula. 1986. *Assyrische Königsdarstellungen – Aspekte der Herrschaft: eine Typologie. Baghdader Forschungen* 9. Mainz: P. von Zabern.

Martens, Karen. 2001. "'With a Strong Hand and an Outstretched Arm': The Meaning of the Expression ביד חזקה ובזרוע נטויה." *SJOT* 15: 123–41.

Matthiae, Paolo. 1987. "Una stele paleosiriana arcaica da Ebla e la cultura figurativa della Airia attorno al 1800 A. C." Scienze dell'Antichità 1: 447–95.

Matthiae, Paolo, Frances Pinnock, and Gabriella Scandone, eds. 1995. *Ebla: Alle origini della civiltà urbana: Trent'anni die scavi in Siria dell'Università di Roma "La Sapienza."* Milano: Electa.

McCarty, Matthew M. 2011. "Representations and the 'Meaning' of Ritual Change: The Case of Hadrumetum." In *Ritual Dynamics in the Ancient Mediterranean: Agency, Emotion, Gender, Representation,* edited by Angelos Chaniotis, 197–228. Heidelberger Althistorische Beiträge und Epigraphische Studien 49. Stuttgart: Steiner.

McCormick, Clifford Mark. 2002. *Palace and Temple: A Study of Architectural and Verbal Icons.* BZAW 313. Berlin: de Gruyter.

McDannell, Colleen. 1995. *Material Christianity: Religion and Popular Culture in America.* New Haven: Yale University Press.

Meshorer, Yakov and Shraga Qedar. 1999. *Samarian Coinage in the Fourth Century BCE.* Numismatic Studies and Researches 9. Jerusalem: Numismatic Fine Arts International.

Mettinger, Tryggve N. D. 1995. *No Graven Image? Israelite Aniconism in its Ancient Near Eastern Context.* ConBOT 42. Stockholm: Almquist & Wiksell.

Metzger, Martin. 1971. "Himmlische und irdische Wohnstatt Jahwes." UF 2: 139–158, 433–35.

_____. 1985. *Königsthron und Gottesthron: Thronformen und Throndarstellungen in Ägypten und im Vorderen Orietn im dritten und zweiten Jahrtausend vor Christus und deren Bedeutung für das Verständnis von Aussagen über den Thron im Alten Testament.* 2 Vols. Alter Orient und Altes Testament 15.1–2. Kevelaer: Butzon & Bercker.

Meyers, Carol L. and Eric M. Meyers. 1993. *Zechariah 9–14: A New Translation with Introduction and Commentary.* AB 25C. New York: Doubleday.

Middleton, J. Richard. 2005. *The Liberating Image: The* Imago Dei *in Genesis 1.* Grand Rapids, MI: Brazos.

Mildenberg, Leo. 1998. "Yehud: A Preliminary Study of the Provincial Coinage of Judea." In *Vestigia Leonis: Studien zur antiken Numismatik Israels, Palästinas und der östlichen Mittelmeerwelt,* edited by Ulrich Hübner and Ernst A. Knauf, 67–76. NTOA 36. Freiburg: Universitätsverlag.

Milgrom, Josephine. 1988. *The Binding of Isaac (the Akedah): A Primary Symbol in Jewish Thought and Art.* Berkeley: Bibal.

Miller, Patrick D. 1973. *The Divine Warrior in Early Israel.* HSM 5. Cambridge: Harvard University Press.

Milstein, Rachel. 2005. *La Bible dans l'art islamique.* Paris: PUF.

Mirzoeff, Nicholas. 1999. *An Introduction to Visual Culture.* London: Routledge.

Mitchell, W. J. T. 1986. *Iconology: Image, Text, Ideology.* Chicago: University of Chicago Press.

———. 1994. *Picture Theory: Essays on Verbal and Visual Representation.* Chicago: University of Chicago Press.

———. 2005. *What Do Pictures Want? The Lives and Loves of Images.* Chicago: University of Chicago Press.

Morgan, David. 1998. *Visual Piety: A History and Theory of Popular Religious Images.* Berkeley: University of California Press.

———. 2005. *The Sacred Gaze: Religious Visual Culture in Theory and Practice.* Berkeley: University of California Press.

———, ed. 2010. *Religion and Material Culture: The Matter of Belief.* London and New York: Routledge.

Moor, Johannes C. de. 1997. *The Rise of Yahwism: The Roots of Israelite Monotheism.* BETL 91. London: Routledge.

Moortgat, Anton. 1969. *The Art of Ancient Mesopotamia: The Classical Art of the Near East.* London: Phaidon.

Morales, L. Michael. 2012. *The Tabernacle Pre-figured: Cosmic Mountain Ideology in Genesis and Exodus.* Biblical Tools and Studies 15. Leuven: Peeters.

Morrow, Jeff. 2009. "Creation as Temple-Building and Work as Liturgy in Genesis 1–3." *Journal of the Orthodox Center for the Advancement of Biblical Studies* 2/1: 1–13.

Moscati, Sabatino, ed. 1988. *The Phoenicians.* New York: Abbeville.

———. 1991. *Gli adoratori di Moloch. Indagine su un célèbre rito cartaginese.* Arte, Storia, Archeologia. Milano: Jaca.

Müller, Frederich Max. 1893. *Introduction to the Science of Religion: Four Lectures Delivered at the Royal Institution in February and May, 1870.* New ed. London: Longmans, Green.

Murnane, William J. 1995. *Texts from the Amarna Period in Egypt.* SBLWAW 5. Atlanta: Scholars Press.

Nida, Eugene A. and Charles R. Taber. 1969. *The Theory and Practice of Translation.* Leiden: Brill.

Niehr, Herbert. 2006. "Der Sarkophag des Königs Aḥirom von Byblos." In *Tekmeria: Archäologische Zeugnisse in ihrer kulturhistorischen und politischen Dimension. Beiträge für Werner Gauer,* edited by Werner Gauer, Natascha Kreutz, and Beat Schweitzer, 231–43. Münster: Scriptorium.

———, ed. 2014. *The Aramaeans in Ancient Syria.* Handbook of Oriental Studies: Section 1; Near and Middle East 106. Leiden: Brill.

Nimchuk, Cindy L. 2002. "The 'Archers' of Darius: Coinage or Tokens of Royal Esteem?" *Ars Orientalis* 32: 55–79.

Nord, Christiane. 1991. *Text Analysis in Translation: Theory, Methodology, and Didactic Application of a Model for Translation-Oriented Text Analysis.* Amsterdamer Publikationen zur Sprache und Literatur 94. Amsterdam: Rodopi.

———. 1997. *Translating as a Purposeful Activity: Functionalist Approaches Explained.* Manchester: St. Jerome.

Noth, Martin. 1981 [German orig: 1943]. *A History of Pentateuchal Traditions.* Edited and translated by Bernhard W. Anderson. Chico: Scholars Press.

Nougayrol, Jean. 1939. *Cylindres-sceaux et empreintes de cylinders trouvés en Palestine.* Paris: Geuthner.

O'Connor, David B., and David P. Silverman, eds. 1995. *Ancient Egyptian Kingship.* Probleme der Ägyptologie 9. Leiden: Brill.

Oeming, Manfred. 2006 [German orig.: 1998, 2013⁴]. *Contemporary Biblical Hermeneutics: An Intro-duction.* Translated by Joachim Vette. Aldershot: Ashgate.

Oorschot, Jürgen van. 1999. "Die Macht der Bilder und die Ohnmacht des Wortes." *Zeitschrift für Theo-logie und Kirche* 96: 299–319.

Ornan, Tallay. 2005a. "A Complex System of Religious Symbols: The Case of the Winged Disk in Near Eastern Imagery of the First Millenium BCE." In *Crafts and Images in Contact: Studies on Eastern Mediterranean Art of the First Millenium BCE,* edited by Claudia E. Suter and Christoph Uehlinger, 204–41. OBO 210. Fribourg/Göttingen: University Press/Vandenhoeck & Ruprecht.

_____. 2005b. *The Triumph of the Symbol: Pictorial Representation of Deities in Mesopotamia and the Biblical Image Ban.* OBO 213. Fribourg/Göttingen: University Press/Vandenhoeck & Ruprecht.

Ornan, Tally et al. 2012. "The LORD Will Roar from Zion" (Amos 1:2): The Lion as a Divine Attribute on a Jerusalem Seal and Other Hebrew Glyptic Finds from the Western Wall Plaza Excavations." *'Atiqot* 72: 1–13.

Orrelle, Estelle. 2008. "Infant Jar Burials: A Ritual Associated with Early Agriculture." In *Babies Reborn: Infant/Child Burials in Pre- and Protohistory,* edited by Krum Buchvarov, 71–78. British Archaeo-logical Reports International Series 1832. Oxford: Archaeopress.

Otto, Rudolf. 1950. *The Idea of the Holy: An Inquiry into the Non-Rational Factor in the Idea of the Di-vine and Its Relation to the Rational.* 2d ed. London: Oxford University Press.

Pals, Daniel L. 2006. *Eight Theories of Religion.* 2d ed. New York: Oxford University Press.

Panofsky, Erwin. 1972 [1939]. *Studies in Iconology: Humanistic Themes in the Art of the Renaissance.* Boulder, CO: Westview.

Papazian, Elie. 1986. "Al-Khidr and Elija. Mythological background of the analogy." Palestinskii Sbornik 28: 89–97.

Parayre, Dominique. 1990. "Les Cachets Ouest-Sémitiques à Travers l'Image du Disque Solaire Ailé (Perspective Iconographique)." *Syria* 67: 269–314.

Parlasca, Ingemarie. 1990. "Terrakotten aus Petra: Ein neues Kapitel nabatäischer Archäologie." In *Petra and the Caravan Cities,* edited by F. Zayadine, 87–105. Amman: Department of Antiquities.

Pasztory, Esther. 2005. *Thinking with Things: Toward a New Vision of Art.* Austin: University of Texas.

Paz, Sarit. 2007. *Drums, Women, and Goddesses: Drumming and Gender in Iron Age II Israel.* OBO 232. Fribourg/Göttingen: Academic Press/Vandenhoeck & Ruprecht.

Pfeiffer, Robert H. 1955. "The Fear of God." *IEJ* 5: 41–48.

Pfleiderer, Otto. 1907. *Religion & Historic Faiths.* Translated by Daniel Adolph Huebsch. New York: B. W. Huebsch.

Pilcher, Edward J. 1908. "A Coin of Gaza, and the Vision of Ezekiel." *Proceedings of the Society of Bib-lical Archaeology* 30: 45–52.

Poo, Muzhou. 1995. *Wine and Wine Offering in the Religion of Ancient Egypt.* Studies in Egyptology. London/New York: Kegan Paul International.

Pope, Marvin H. 1977. *Song of Songs: A New Translation with Introduction and Commentary.* AB 7C. New York: Doubleday.

Porada, Edith, ed. 1948. *Corpus of Ancient Near Eastern Seals in North American Collections.* 2 vols. Bolligen series 14. New York: Pantheon.

Porter, Barbara N. 1995. Language, Audience and Impact in Imperial Assyria. In *Language and Cul-ture in the Near East,* edited by Schlomo Izre'el and Rina Drory, 51–72. Israel Oriental Studies 15. Leiden: Brill.

_____. 2003. *Trees, Kings, and Politics: Studies in Assyrian Iconography.* OBO 197. Fribourg/Göttingen: Academic Press/Vandenhoeck & Ruprecht.

_____. 2004. "Ritual and Politics in Assyria: Neo-Assyrian Kanephoric Stelai for Babylonia." In *CARIS: Essays in Honor of Sara A. Immerwahr,* edited by A. P. Chapin, 259–74. Hesperia Supplements 33. Princeton: American School of Classical Studies at Athens.

Pritchard, James B. 1969 [1954]. *The Ancient Near East in Pictures Relating to the Old Testament.* 2d ed. with suppl. Princeton: Princeton University Press.

Pyper, Hugh S. 2014. "The Lion King: Yahweh as Sovereign Beast in Israel's Imaginary." In *The Bible and Posthumanism,* edited by Jennifer L. Koosed, 59–74. SemeiaSt 74. Atlanta: Society of Biblical Literature.

Qleibo, Ali, 2012. "Rajab, Qamar el Zaman, and the Moon: Longing for Ramadan." *This week in Palestine* 171:8–12.

Rapoport, Amos. 1990. *The Meaning of the Built Environment: A Nonverbal Communication Approach.* 2d ed. Beverly Hills, CA: Sage.

Ramachandran, V. S. 2004. *A Brief Tour of Human Consciousness: From Imposter Poodles to Purple Numbers.* New York: Pi Press.

Rees, Valery. 2013. *From Gabriel to Lucifer: A Cultural History of Angels.* London: Tauris.

Reeves, Nicholas. 2001. *Akhenaten: Egypt's False Prophet.* London: Thames and Hudson.

Ridgway, David. 1992. *The First Western Greeks.* Cambridge/New York: Cambridge University Press.

Riede, Peter. 2002. *Im Spiegel der Tiere: Studien zum Verhältnis von Mensch und Tier im alten Israel.* OBO 187. Freiburg/Göttingen: Universitätsverlag/Vandenhoeck & Ruprecht.

Roberts, J. J. M. 1971. "The Hand of Yahweh." *VT* 21: 244–51.

Robins, Gay. 2008. *The Art of Ancient Egypt.* Rev. ed. Cambridge: Harvard University Press.

Rocca, Samuel. 1995. "The Book of Judith, Queen Sholomzion and King Tigranes of Armenia: A Sadducee Appraisal." Materia giudaica 10: 85–98.

Root, Margaret Cool. 1979. *The King and Kingship in Achaemenid Art: Essays on the Creation of an Iconography of Empire.* Acta Iranica IX. Leiden: Brill.

_____. 1985. "The Parthenon Frieze and the Apadana Reliefs at Persepolis: Reassessing a Programmatic Relationship." *AJA* 89: 103–20.

_____. 1989. "The Persian Archer at Persepolis: Aspects of Chronology, Style and Symbolism." *REA* 91: 33–50.

_____. 1991. "From the Heart: Powerful Persianisms in the Art of the Western Empire." In *Asia Minor and Egypt: Old Cultures in a New Empire,* edited by H. Sancisi-Weerdenburg and Amelie Khurt, 1–29. Achaemenid History 6. Leiden: Nederlands Instituut voor het Nebije oosten.

_____. 1992. "Art and Architecture (Persian Art)." In *The Anchor Bible Dictionary,* edited by David Noel Freedman, 1:440–47. 6 vols. New York: Doubleday.

Rose, Gillian. 2007. *Visual Methodologies: An Introduction to the Interpretation of Visual Materials.* 2d ed. Los Angeles: Sage.

Rouillard, Hedwige. 1999. "Rephaim." In *Dictionary of Deities and Demons in the Bible,* edited by Karel Van der Toorn et al., 692–700. 2d ed. Leiden: Brill.

Rühlmann, Gerhard. 1964. "Der Löwe im altägyptischen Triumphalbild." *Wissenschaftliche Zeitschrift der Martin-Luther-Universität Halle/Wittenberg* 13.9, no. 10: 651–58.

Russell, John Malcolm. 1991. *Sennacherib's Palace without Rival at Nineveh.* Chicago: University of Chicago Press.

Sandmel, Samuel. 1962. "Parallelomania." *JBL* 81: 1–13.

Savignac, Jean de. 1972. "Les 'seraphim.'" *VT* 22: 320–25.

Schaller, George B. 1972. *The Serengeti Lion: A Study of Predator-Prey Relations.* Chicago: University of Chicago Press.

Schimmack, U., S. Oishi, and E. Diener. 2002. "Cultural Influences on the Relations between Pleasant and Unpleasant Emotions: Asian Dialectic Philosophies or Individualism-Collectivism?" *Cognition and Emotion* 16: 705–19.

Schlieper, Andreas. 2006. *Himmlische Heerscharen: Eine Geschichte der Engel.* Berlin: Wolf Jobst Siedler.

Schmid, Konrad. 2012. "Schöpfung im Alten Testament." In *Schöpfung,* edited by Konrad Schmid, 71–120. Themen der Theologie 4. Tübingen: Mohr Siebeck.

Schmidt, Brian B. 1996. *Israel's Beneficent Dead: Ancestor Cult and Necromany in Ancient Israelite Religion and Tradition.* Winona Lake, IN: Eisenbrauns.

Schmidt, Erich F. 1953. *Persepolis I: Structures, Reliefs, Inscriptions.* OIP 68. Chicago: University of Chicago Press.

Schmitt, Rüdiger. 2001. *Bildhafte Herrschaftsrepräsentation im eisenzeitlichen Israel.* Alter Orient und Altes Testament 283. Münster: Ugarit-Verlag.

_____. 2004. "'Er ströme herab wie Regen auf die Felder' – Psalm 72 und die Vegationssymbolik in der Herrschaftsikonographie Israels und Judas im 1. Jt. v. Chr." In *Ikonographie und Ikonologie*, edited by Wolfgang Hübner and Klaus Stähler, 35–49. Eikon 8. Münster: Ugarit-Verlag.

_____. 2009. "The Iconography of Power: Israelite and Judean Royal Architecture as Icons of Power." In *Iconography and Biblical Studies: Proceedings of the Iconography Sessions at the Joint EABS/SBL Conference, 22–26 July 2007, Vienna, Austria*, edited by Izaak J. de Hulster and Rüdiger Schmitt, 75–96. AOAT 361. Münster: Ugarit-Verlag.

Schmitz, Barbara. 2006. Art. "Judit/Juditbuch." Cited 13 January 2013. Online: http://www.wibilex.de/nc/wibilex/das-bibellexikon/details/quelle/WIBI/referenz/10395/cache/ddad36d42f0be95b6e8bc32908fd517b/.

Schneider, Thomas. 2003. "Foreign Egypt: Egyptology and the Concept of Cultural Appropriation." Ägypten und Levante 13: 155–61.

Schökel, Luis Alonso. 1988. *A Manuel of Hebrew Poetics*. Subsidia Biblica 11. Rome: Pontificio Istituto Biblico.

Schreckenberg, Heinz. 1996. *Die Juden in der Kunst Europas: Ein historischer Bildatlas*. Freiburg/Göttingen: Herder/Vandenhoeck & Ruprecht.

Schroer, Silvia. 1987. *In Israel gab es Bilder: Nachrichten von darstellender Kunst im Alten Testament*. OBO 74. Freiburg/Göttingen: Universitätsverlag/Vandenhoeck & Ruprecht.

_____. 1989. "Die Göttin auf den Stempelsiegeln aus Palästina/Israel." In *Studien zu den Stempelsiegeln aus Palästina/Israel II*, edited by Othmar Keel, Hildi Keel-Leu, and Silvia Schroer, 89–207. OBO 88. Freiburg/Göttingen: Universitätsverlag/Vandenhoeck & Ruprecht.

_____. 2008. *Die Ikonographie Palästinas/Israels und der Alte Orient. Eine Religionsgeschichte in Bildern. Band 2: Die Mittelbronzezeit*. Fribourg: Academic Press.

_____. 2011. *Die Ikonographie Palästinas/Israels und der Alte Orient. Eine Religionsgeschichte in Bildern. Band 3: Die Spätbronzezeit*. Fribourg: Academic Press.

_____. Forthcoming. *Die Ikonographie Palästinas/Israels und der Alte Orient. Eine Religionsgeschichte in Bildern. Band 4: Die Eisenzeit bis zum Ende der persischen Herrschaft*. 2 vols. Fribourg: Academic Press.

Schroer, Silvia and Othmar Keel. 2005. *Die Ikonographie Palästinas/Israels und der Alte Orient. Eine Religionsgeschichte in Bildern. Band 1: Vom ausgehenden Mesolithikum bis zum Frühbronzezeit*. Fribourg: Academic Press.

Schroer, Silvia and Thomas Staubli. 2001. *Body Symbolism in the Bible*. Collegeville, MN: Liturgical Press.

Schubert, Kurt. 1991. "Die jüdische Wurzel der frühchristlichen Kunst." Kairos 33: 1–8.

Schubert, Ursula. 1977. "Strukturelemente der frühchristlichen Bildkunst." Kairos 19: 187–202.

Schwartz J. H. et al. 2010. "Skeletal Remains from Punic Carthage Do Not Support Systematic Sacrifice of Infants." PLoS ONE 5(2): e9177. doi:10.1371/journal.pone.0009177. Cited 1 September 2013. Online: http://journals.plos.org/plosone/article?id=10.1371/journal.pone.0009177

Schweitzer, Ursula. 1948. *Löwe und Sphinx im Alten Ägypten*. Ägyptologische Forschungen 15. Glückstadt: J. J. Augustin.

Seidl, Ursula. 2001. "Das Ringen um das richtige Bild des Samas von Zippar." *Zeitschrift für Assyriologie* 91: 120–32.

Shafer, Bryan E., ed. 1991. *Religion in Ancient Egypt: Gods, Myths, and Personal Practic*. Ithaca: Cornell University Press.

Shipp, R. Mark. 2002. *Of Dead Kings and Dirges: Myth and Meaning in Isaiah 14:4b–21*. Academia Biblica 11. Atlanta: Society of Biblical Literature.

Simonetti, Adele. 1983. "Tharros 9: Sacrifici umani e uccisioni rituali nel mondo fenicio-punico: Il contributo delle fonti letterarie classiche." Rivista di studi fenici 11: 91–111.

Smith, George. 1876. *The Chaldean Account of Genesis*. New York: Scribner, Armstrong.

Smith, Jonathan Z. 1990. *Drudgery Divine: On the Comparison of Early Christianities and the Religions of Late Antiquity*. JLCRS 14. Chicago: University of Chicago Press.

_____. 2000. "The 'End' of Comparison: Redescription and Rectification." In *A Magic Still Dwells:*

Comparative Religion in the Postmodern Age, edited by Kimberley C. Patton and Benjamin C. Ray, 237–41. Berkeley: University of California Press.

Smith, Mark S. 1988. "'Seeing God' in the Psalms: The Background to the Beatific Vision in the Hebrew Scriptures." *CBQ* 50: 171–83.

———. 2010. *The Priestly Vision of Genesis 1.* Minneapolis: Fortress.

Smyth-Florentin, Françoise. 1992. "L'Espace d'un chandelier: Zacharie 1,8–6,15." In *Le livre de traverse: De l'exégèse biblique à l'anthropologie,* edited by Oliver Abel, 281–89. Paris: Patrimoines.

Soulen, Richard N. 1967. "The Waṣfs of the Song of Songs and Hermeneutics." *JBL* 86: 183–90.

Spieckermann, Hermann. 2007. "Gott und die Nacht: Beobachtungen im Alten Testament." *Internationale katholische Zeitschrift Communio* 36/5: 434–43.

Stähli, Hans-Peter. 1985. *Solare Elemente im Jahweglauben des Alten Testaments.* OBO 66. Freiburg/Göttingen: Universitätsverlag/Vandenhoeck & Ruprecht.

———. 1997. "yr' to fear." In *Theological Lexicon of the Old Testament,* edited by Ernst Jenni and Claus Westermann, translated by Mark E. Biddle, 2:568–78. 3 vols. Peabody: Hendrickson.

Staubli, Thomas. 1991. *Das Image der Nomaden im Alten Israel und in der Ikonographie seiner sesshaften Nachbarn.* OBO 107. Freiburg/Göttingen: Universitätsverlag/Vandenhoeck & Ruprecht.

———. 2003. "Sin von Harran und seine Verbreitung im Westen." In *Werbung für die Götter: Heilsbringer aus 4000 Jahren,* edited by Thomas Staubli, 65–90. Freiburg/Göttingen: Universitätsverlag/Vandenhoeck & Ruprecht.

———. 2005. "Land der sprießenden Zweige." *Bibel und Kirche* 60: 16–21.

———, ed. 2007. *Musik in biblischer Zeit und orientalisches Musikerbe.* Welt und Umwelt der Bibel. Stuttgart: Katholisches Bibelwerk.

———. 2009. "'Den Namen setzen.' Namens- und Göttinnenstandarten in der Südlevante während der 18. ägyptischen Dynastie." In *Iconography and Biblical Studies,* edited by Izaak J. de Hulster and Rüdiger Schmitt, 93–112. AOAT 361. Münster: Ugarit-Verlag.

———. 2010. "Alttestamentliche Konstellationen der Rechtfertigung des Menschen vor Gott." In *Biblische Anthropologie: neue Einsichten aus dem Alten Testament,* edited by Christian Frevel, 88–133. Quaestiones disputatae 237. Freiburg: Herder.

———. 2012. "Cherubim: I. Ancient Near East and Hebrew Bible/Old Testament." *EBR* 5: 55–58.

———. 2014. *Begleiter durch das Erste Testament.* 5th ed. Patmos: Ostfildern.

Steck, Odil Hannes. 1986. "Der Grundtext in Jesaja 60 und sein Aufbau." *ZTK* 83: 261–96.

———. 1991. *Studien zu Tritojesaja.* BZAW 203. Berlin: Walter de Gruyter.

Stein, Diana. 1993. *Das Archiv des Šilwa-Teššup: H. 9. The Seal Impressions.* Wiesbaden: Harrassowitz.

Steiner, Mélanie and Lindsay Allason-Jones. 2005. *Approaches to Archaeological Illustration: A Handbook.* Practical Handbooks in Archaeology 18. York: Council for British Archaeology.

Stern, Ephraim, ed. 1993-2008. *The New Encyclopedia of Archaeological Excavations in the Holy Land* [= *NEAEHL*] 5 vols. Jerusalem: Israel Exploration Society.

Strawn, Brent A. 2000. "Psalm 22:17b: More Guessing." *JBL* 119: 439–51.

———. 2003. "Pharaoh." In *Dictionary of the Old Testament: Pentateuch,* edited by T. Desmond Alexander and David W. Baker, 631–36. Downers Grove, IL: InterVarsity.

———. 2005a. *What is Strong than a Lion? Leonine Image and Metaphor in the Hebrew Bible and the Ancient Near East.* OBO 212. Fribourg/Göttingen: Academic Press/Vandenhoeck & Ruprecht.

———. 2005b. "Who's Listening to Whom?" A Syntactical Note on the Melqart Inscription. *UF* 37: 621–41.

———. 2007. "'A World Under Control': Isaiah 60 and the Apadana Reliefs from Persepolis." In *Approaching Yehud: New Approaches to the Study of the Persian Period,* edited by Jon L. Berquist, 85–116. SemeiaSt 50. Atlanta: Society of Biblical Literature.

———. 2008a. "Imagery." In *Dictionary of the Old Testament: Wisdom, Poetry and Writing,* edited by Tremper Longman III and Peter Enns, 306–14. Downers Grove, IL: IVP Academic.

———. 2008b. "'Israel, My Child': The Ethics of a Biblical Metaphor." In *The Child in the Bible,* edited by Marcia Bunge, Terence E. Fretheim, and Beverly R. Gaventa, 103–40. Grand Rapids, MI: Eerdmans.

———. 2009a. "Comparative Approaches: History, Theory, and the Image of God." In *Method Matters:*

Essays on the Interpretation of the Hebrew Bible in Honor of David L. Petersen, edited by Joel LeMon and Kent H. Richards, 114–42. SBLRBS 56. Atlanta: Society of Biblical Literature.

_____. 2009b. "Whence Leonine Yahweh? Iconography and the History of Israelite Religion." In *Images and Prophecy in the Ancient Eastern Mediterranean,* edited by Martti Nissinen and Charles A. Carter, 51–85. FRLANT 233. Göttingen: Vandenhoeck & Ruprecht.

_____. 2009c. "Yahweh's Outstretched Arm Revisited Iconographically." In *Iconography and Biblical Studies: Proceedings of the Iconography Sessions at the Joint EABS/SBL Conference, 22–26 July 2007, Vienna, Austria,* edited by Izaak J. de Hulster and Rüdiger Schmitt, 163–211. AOAT 361. Münster: Ugarit-Verlag.

_____. 2013. "jāreʾ, jirʾāh, môrāʾ." In *Theologisches Wörterbuch zu den Qumrantexten,* edited by Heniz-Josef Fabry and Ulrich Dahmen, Band II, cols. 257–66. Stuttgart: Kohlhammer.

_____. 2014. "The Iconography of Fear: *Yirʾat Yhwh* (יראת יהוה) in Artistic Perspective." In *Image, Text, Exegesis: Iconographic Interpretation and the Hebrew Bible,* edited by Izaak J. de Hulster and Joel M. LeMon, 91–134. LHBOTS 588. London: Bloomsbury.

_____. Forthcoming (a). "Material Culture, Iconography, and the Prophets." In *Oxford Handbook to the Prophets,* edited by Carolyn J. Sharp. Oxford: Oxford University Press.

_____. Forthcoming (b). "'Mischmetaphors': Complex Divine Images, Conceptual Blending, and Ancient Near Eastern *Mischwesen.*"

Strawn, Brent A. and Joel M. LeMon. 2007. "'Everything That Has Breath': Animal Praise in Psalm 150:6 in the Light of Ancient Near Eastern Iconography." In *Bilder als Quellen/Images as Sources: Studies on Ancient Near Eastern Artefacts and the Bible Inspired by the Work of Othmar Keel,* edited by Susanne Bickel, 451–85. OBO.S 6. Fribourg/Göttingen: Academic Press/Vandenhoeck & Ruprecht.

Stronach, David. 1989. "Early Achaemenid Coinage: Perspectives from the Homeland." *Iranica Antiqua* 24: 255–83.

Strong, John T. 2008. "Shattering the Image of God: A Response to Theodore Hiebert's Interpretation of the Story of the Tower of Babel." *JBL* 127: 625–34.

Strunk, William, Jr. and E. B. White 2000. *The Elements of Style.* 4th ed. Needham Heights, MA: Allyn and Bacon.

Sui, Claude W. 2008. "Die Pilgerfahrt zu den heiligen Stätten des Islam und die frühe Photographie." In *Ins Heilige Land: Pilgerstätten von Mekka und Medina bis Jerusalem; Photographien aus dem 19. Jahrhundert aus den Sammlungen der Reiss-Engelhorn Museen Mannheim,* edited by Alfried Wieczorek and Claude W. Sui, 40–63. Publikationen der Reiss-Engelhorn-Museen 18. Heidelberg: Braus.

Sweeney, Marvin A. 1996. *Isaiah 1–39: With an Introduction to Prophetic Literature.* FOTL 16. Grand Rapids, MI: Eerdmans.

Talmon, Shemaryahu. 1991. "The 'Comparative Method' in Biblical Interpretation – Principles and Problems." In *Essential Papers on Israel and the Ancient Near East,* edited by Frederick E. Greenspahn, 381–419. New York: New York University Press.

Taylor, J. Glen. 1993. *Yahweh and the Sun: Biblical and Archaeological Evidence for Sun Worship in Ancient Israel.* JSOTSup 111. Sheffield: JSOT Press.

Taylor, Paul, ed. 2008. *Iconography without Texts.* London: The Warburg Institute.

Teissier, Beatrice. 1984. *Ancient Near Eastern Cylinder Seals from the Marcopoli Collection.* Berkeley: University of California Press.

Terrien, Samuel L. 1996. *The Iconography of Job through the Centuries: Artists as Biblical Interpreters.* University Park: Pennsylvania State University Press.

Theuer, Gabriele. 2000. *Der Mondgott in den Religionen Syrien-Palästinas: Unter besonderer Berücksichtigung von KTU 1.24.* OBO 173. Freiburg/Göttingen: Universitätsverlag/Vandenhoeck & Ruprecht.

Tiradritti, Francesco and Araldo De Luca. 2000. *Kunstschatten uit Egypte.* Leuven: Davidsfonds.

Toorn, Karel van der. 1996. *Family Religion in Babylonia, Syria, and Israel: Continuity and Change in the Forms of Religious Life.* SHCANE 7. Leiden: Brill.

_____. 1997. "The Iconic Book: Analogies Between the Babylonian Cult of Images and the Veneration of the Torah." In *The Image and the Book: Iconic Cults, Aniconism, and the Rise of the Book*

Religion in Israel and the Ancient Near East, edited by Karel van der Toorn, 229–48. ConBOT 21. Leuven: Peeters.

_____. 2009. "The Books of the Hebrew Bible as Material Artifacts." In *Exploring the Longue Durée: Essays in Honor of Lawrence E. Stager,* edited by J. David Schloen, 465–72. Winona Lake, IN: Eisenbrauns.

Tuell, Steven S. 1996. "Ezekiel 40–42 as Verbal Icon." *CBQ* 58: 649–64.

Tropper, Josef. 2012. *Ugaritische Grammatik. Zweite, stark überarbeitete und erweiterte Auflage.* AOAT 273. Münster: Ugarit-Verlag.

Turner, Mark and Gilles Fauconnier. 1999. "A Mechanism of Creativity." *Poetics Today* 20: 397–418.

Uehlinger, Christoph. 1987. "'Zeichne eine Stadt … und belagere sie!' Bild und Wort in einer Zeichenhandlung Ezechiels gegen Jerusalem." In *Jerusalem: Texte – Bilder – Steine,* edited by Christoph Uehlinger and Max Küchler, 111–200. NTOA 6. Freiburg/Göttingen: Universitätsverlag/Vandenhoeck & Ruprecht.

_____. 1991. "Götterbild." In *Neues Bibel-Lexikon,* edited by Manfred Görg and Bernhard Lang, 1:871–92. 3 vols. Zürich: Benziger.

_____. 1994. "Die Frau im Efa (Sach 5,5–11). Eine Programmvision von der Abschiebung der Göttin." *BK* 49: 93–103.

_____. 1999. "'Powerful Persianisms' in Glyptic Iconography of Persian Period Palestine." In *The Crisis of Israelite Religion: Transformation of Religious Tradition in Exilic and Post-Exilic Times,* edited by Bob Becking and Marjo C. A. Korpel, 134–82. OTS 42. Boston: Brill.

_____, ed. 2000. *Images as Media: Sources for the Cultural History of the Near East and the Eastern Mediterranean: 1st Millenium BCE.* OBO 175. Freiburg/Göttingen: Universitätsverlag/Vandenhoeck & Ruprecht.

Van Pelt, Miles V., and Walter C. Kaiser, Jr. 1997. "yr'." In *NIDOTTE,* edited by Willem A. VanGemeren, 2:527–33. 5 vols. Grand Rapids, MI: Zondervan.

Vriezen, Karel J. H. 1998. "Archeologische sporen van cultus in Oud-Israël." In *Één God alleen: Over monotheïsme in Oud-Israël en de verering van de godin Asjera,* edited by Bob Becking and Meindert Dijkstra, 31–58. Kampen: Kok.

Vriezen, Theodorus C. 1950. "'ehje'ašer'ehje." *Festschrift Alfred Bertholet zum 80. Geburtstag: gewidmet von Kollegen und Freunden,* edited by Walter Baumgartner, 498–512. Tübingen: Mohr.

Wagner, Andreas. 2005. "Alttestamentlicher Monotheismus und seine Bindung an das Wort." In *Gott im Wort – Gott im Bild: Bilderlosigkeit als Bedingung des Monotheismus?,* edited by Andreas Wagner, 1–22. Neukirchen-Vluyn: Neukirchener Verlag.

Walsh, Carey Ellen. 2000. *Exquisite Desire: Religion, the Erotic, and the Song of Songs.* Minneapolis: Fortress.

Waltke, Bruce K. and M. O'Connor. 1990. *An Introduction to Biblical Hebrew Syntax.* Winona Lake, IN: Eisenbrauns.

Walton, John H. 2011. *Genesis 1 as Ancient Cosmology.* Winona Lake, IN: Eisenbrauns.

Ward, William Hayes. 1909. *Cylinders and Other Ancient Oriental Seals in the Library of J. P. Morgan.* New York: privately printed; copyright by Frederic Fairchild Sherman.

_____. 1910. *The Seal Cylinders of Western Asia.* Carnegie Institution of Washington Publication 100. Washington: Carnegie Institution of Washington.

Watanabe, Chikako E. 2002. *Animal Symbolism in Mesopotamia: A Contextual Approach.* Wiener Offene Orientalistik 1. Vienna: Institut für Orientalistik der Universität Wien.

Weinfeld, Moshe. 1981. "Sabbath, Temple and the Enthronement of the Lord: The Problem of the Sitz im Leben of Genesis 1:1–2:3." In *Mélanges bibliques et orientaux en l'honneur de M. Henrie Cazelles,* edited by M. Delcor, Henri Cazelles, and André Caquot, 501–12. AOAT 212. Kevelaer/Neukirchen-Vluyn: Butzon & Bercker/Neukirchener Verlag.

_____. 1991. *Deuteronomy 1–11: A New Translation with Introduction and Commentary.* AB 5. New York: Doubleday.

Weissenrieder, Annette and Friederike Wendt. 2005. "Images as Communication: The Methods of Iconography." In *Picturing the New Testament: Studies in Ancient Visual Images,* edited by Annette Weissenrieder, Friederike Went, and Petra von Gemünden, 1–59. WUNT 193. Tübingen: Mohr Siebeck.

Wenning, Robert. 2001. "The Betyls of Petra." BASOR 324: 79–95.

Westermann, Claus. 1969. *Isaiah 40-66: A Commentary.* OTL. Philadelphia: Westminster.

_____. 1978. *Gottes Engel brauchen keine Flügel.* Berlin: Kreuz.

_____. 1994. *Genesis 1–11: A Continental Commentary.* Translated by John J. Scullion. Minneapolis: Fortress.

White, Lynn, Jr. 1967. "The Historical Roots of Our Ecologic Crisis." *Science* 155/3767: 1203–1207.

Wiggermann. Frans A. M. 1993–1997. "Mischwesen." In *Reallexikon der Assyriologie und vorderasiatischen Archäologie,* vol. 8, edited by Dietz Otto Edzard, 222–46. Berlin: de Gruyter.

_____. 2007. "The Four Winds and the Origins of Pazuzu." In *Das geistige Erfassen der Welt im Alten Orient: Sprache, Religion, Kultur, und Gesellschaft,* edited by Claus Wilcke and Joost Hazenbos, 125–65. Wiesbaden: Harrassowitz.

Wilkinson, John. 1991. "The body in the Old Testament." *Evangelical Quarterly* 63: 195–210.

Wilkinson, Richard H. 1992. *Reading Egyptian Art.* London: Thames and Hudson.

_____. 2003. *The Complete Gods and Goddess of Ancient Egypt.* London: Thames and Hudson.

Williams, P. and J. L. Aaker. 2002. "Can Mixed Emotions Peacefully Coexist? *Journal of Consumer Research* 28: 636–49.

Willi-Plein, Ina. 2007. *Haggai, Sacharja, Maleachi.* ZBK 24.4. Zürich: Theologischer Verlag Zürich.

Wilt, Timothy, ed. 2002. *Bible Translation: Frames of Reference.* Manchester: St. Jerome.

Winter, Urs. 1983. *Frau und Göttin: Exegetische und ikonographische Studien zum weiblichen Gottesbild im Alten Israel und in dessen Umwelt.* OBO 53. Freiburg/Göttingen: Universitätsverlag/Vandenhoeck & Ruprecht.

Wood, James. 2008. How Fiction Works. New York: Farrar, Straus and Giroux.

Woods, Christopher E. 2004. "The Sun-God Tablet of Nabû-apla-iddina." *Journal of Cuneiform Studies* 56: 23–103.

Yalouris, Nikolaos, ed. 1981-1997. *Lexicon Iconographicum Mythologiae Classicae [=LIMC].* 8 vols. Zürich: Artemis-Verlag.

Yellin, Joseph and Jane M. Cahill. 2004. "Rosette-stamped Handles: Instrumental Neutron Activation Analysis." *IEJ* 54: 191–213.

Yoder, Christine R. 2005. "The Objects of Our Affections: Emotions and the Moral Life in Proverbs 1–9." In *Shaking Heaven and Earth: Essays in Honor of Walter Brueggemann and Charles B. Cousar,* edited by Christine R. Yoder et al., 73–88. Louisville: Westminster John Knox.

Young, T. Cuyler, Jr. 1992. "Persepolis." In *Anchor Bible Dictionary,* edited by David Noel Freedman, 5:236. 6 vols. New York: Doubleday.

Zenger, Erich et al. 2012. *Einleitung in das Alte Testament.* 8th ed. Edited by Christian Frevel. Stuttgart: Kohlhammer.

Zhang, Xianrong and Xingliang Gao. 2009. "An Analysis of Conceptual Metaphor in Western Commercial Advertisements." *Asian Social Science* 5: 97–103.

Zonhoven, Louis. 1997. "Was het oude Egypte een luilekkerland?" *Phoenix* 43: 63–74.

Zwickel, Wolfgang. 2012. "The Iconography of Emotions in the Ancient Near East and in Ancient Egypt." *Deuterocanonical and Cognate Literature Yearbook 2011: Emotions from Ben Sira to Paul,* edited by Jeremy Corley and Renate Egger-Wenzel, 1–26. Berlin: de Gruyter.

Contributors

Ryan P. Bonfiglio
Columbia Theological Seminary and the John H. Stembler, Jr. Scholar in Residence at the First Presbyterian Church (Atlanta, Georgia, United States)

Izaak J. de Hulster
University of Helsinki (Finland) and Georg-August-Universität Göttingen (Germany)

Joel M. LeMon
Emory University (Atlanta, Georgia, United States) and the University of Stellenbosch (South Africa)

Regine Hunziker-Rodewald
Université de Strasbourg (France)

Rüdiger Schmitt
Westfälische Wilhelms-Universität Münster (Germany)

Thomas Staubli
Université de Fribourg/Universität Freiburg and Bibel+Orient Museum (Switzerland)

Brent A. Strawn
Emory University (Atlanta, Georgia, United States)

Index

Author Index

Scripture Citation Index